Intrepid Explorer

FRONTISPIECE. The author on his first visit to the Los Calatos prospect in southern Peru , with his chartered Peruvian Army helicopter in the background, 1992.

INTREPID EXPLORER

The Autobiography of the World's Best Mine Finder

J. DAVID LOWELL

Foreword by Joaquin Ruiz

Introduction by John M. Guilbert

SENTINEL
PEAK

TUCSON

SENTINEL PEAK
An imprint of The University of Arizona Press
www.uapress.arizona.edu

Printed in the United States of America

ISBN 978-1-941451-00-7 (cloth)
ISBN 978-1-941451-03-8 (paper)

Cover design by Leigh McDonald
Front cover photo by Ross Humphreys, back cover photo courtesy of the author

Library of Congress Cataloging-in-Publication Data
Lowell, J. David, 1928–
  Intrepid explorer : the autobiography of the world's best mine finder / J.
David Lowell ; foreword by Joaquin Ruiz ; Introduction by John M. Guilbert.
    pages cm
  Includes index.
  Summary: "Intrepid Explorer is the story of the legendary career of the engi-
neer, geologist, explorer, and international businessman J. David Lowell, whose
life is recounted in his own words"— Provided by publisher.
  ISBN 978-1-941451-00-7 (cloth : alk. paper)
  1. Lowell, J. David, 1928– 2. Mining engineers—United States—Biography.
3. Mines and mineral resources—History. I. Title.
  TN140.L73A3 2014
  622.092–dc23   2014014614

♾ This paper meets the requirements of ANSI/NISO Z39.48-1992
(Permanence of Paper).

Contents

BOOK II, 1961–1972

*Consulting work with considerable freedom to plan
exploration, three discoveries, and one partial discovery.*

BOOK III, 1973–1991

*Launching new enterprises with more freedom to plan
exploration and significant finder's fees, seven discoveries.*

CONTENTS

BOOK IV, 1992–2014

Total freedom to plan exploration, more innovation and risk taking with ownership, six discoveries and large financial return.

CONTENTS

A selection of photographs follows page 174.

Foreword

You will like this book. The plot features a central character with an improbable story of success. He is a sleuth who decodes riddles hidden in the earth, travels to faraway places where he battles the elements and bureaucracy, convinces the powers that be that he is about to find a treasure and he should be funded. He *is* funded, and in the end he finds the treasure. Sounds a bit like *Raiders of the Lost Ark*, doesn't it? But this book is not fiction. This book tells the real story of an amazing man.

The improbable character is David Lowell. He is tireless, fearless. He is a sophisticated scientist and a financial wizard. He has traveled the continents and has found clues in the rocks that many others missed. These clues have taken him straight to the treasures in the form of ore deposits, and some of his finds are now among the largest copper deposits in the world.

What makes David Lowell extraordinary is that he starts with classic techniques for exploration, which include basic geological mapping and sophisticated geophysical and geochemical methods. But his genius is seeing in the data what others have missed. He is never constrained by the prevailing dogma. His imagination in geology is extraordinary. This, however, is not sufficient to discover new mineral deposits. Successful mineral exploration campaigns are very expensive and logistically complex. Amazingly, David is also a master of creating the financial structures to get the job done. And David has the managerial abilities to organize these logistically complex exploration campaigns. I do not know anyone who does all this with such ease. You can't learn all this. You have to be a natural. Perhaps that is why David Lowell is unique and fascinating.

Joaquin Ruiz
Vice President of Innovation and Strategy
Dean, College of Science
Director, Biosphere 2
University of Arizona

Introduction

You are in for a treat. David Lowell's autobiography will reveal to you both the colorful life of an Arizona legend in his own time and the life of an uncommonly productive businessman, geologist, and explorer.

Not only has Lowell personally discovered more copper than any man in history; not only has he discovered multibillion-dollar gold and copper districts that have changed the economies of nations; not only has he participated in "rewriting the book" on several ore-deposit geologic types; but also, he has done it his way, innovatively, purposefully, and essentially single-handedly or with a cadre of carefully selected colleagues. He has been the architect of his own life and success, and has appropriately become a major figure in the world of minerals, mining, and economic geology in the twentieth and twenty-first centuries.

My first contact with Dave Lowell came in September 1965. I had arrived from Butte, Montana, to Tucson in August of that year to assume a coveted position as Assistant Professor of Economic Geology in the Geology Department at the University of Arizona. My graduate schooling and my post with the Anaconda Company at Butte had inflamed my interest in the then-ill-defined deposit type called "porphyry coppers," and immediately upon arrival in Tucson I was asked to speak to the Arizona Geological Society on the controversial concept that the Butte district itself is a "porphyry copper." Indeed the porphyry-identity-crisis controversy also swirled in Arizona, as it should. In my talk, I described research progress at the Butte Geologic Research Laboratory of Anaconda Copper that not only had devolved new symmetries and processes for the ore deposits of the Butte Camp, but also had projected important ideas concerning porphyry systems overall. After my talk— to a daunting audience of three hundred or so of Arizona's most capable economic geologists—a slight, somewhat diffident man approached the podium. He said, "I enjoyed your talk, and I'm drilling a prospect over on the other side of the Santa Catalina Mountains that might have some similarities to what you described at Butte. Would you care to look at a few thin sections from it?" I was eager to get inserted into the Tucson ore deposits corporate scene, so I gladly accepted his invitation. The next day the sections arrived at the university, and after a cursory microscope examination I reported excitedly by phone that I could say nothing quantitative about his prospect but that the rocks in these sections were qualitatively so similar to those at Butte and to what I knew of other "porphyry coppers" in Chile, British Columbia, and elsewhere that it looked to me as though he had hit one "spot on." The man, of course, was J. David Lowell, and the prospect was Kalamazoo, the just-discovered "other half" of San Manuel, and Dave's first major geologic discovery triumph.

There began a long and productive friendship. I quickly discovered in Dave an uncommon mix of the geologist, the practitioner, and the businessman—it is tempting to use the term "corporate explorationist," but he was too independent for the application of that label. He consulted for and with companies in a corporate mode but always as his own man, the engineer of his own train. He believed then, as he does now, that the best vehicle of exploration is the freelancer, the small outfit whose leader can think freely, act swiftly, back away and move on when necessary, and pursue inklings of success surely and intensely when appropriate. But he was far more than a prospector, because he actively and imaginatively consulted other geologists, lawyers, and explorationists, asked questions, marshaled facts, and created knowledge as a scientist does when he needs to solve problems. For example, as we chewed things over in his office early in our friendship, he noted that Butte and Kalamazoo shared geometries, chemistries, and zonal characteristics, some on scales of miles, that appeared to define a reasonable porphyry copper deposit model for which other geologists and companies were groping. Dave already had developed his own porphyry model, and we decided to try to test that model by tabulating relevant data from other major ore bodies considered to be porphyries. His experience with scores of deposits and prospects and the analytical thought processes that led him to design the Kalamazoo Project in the early 1960s, combined with my more academic-process-oriented approach, fulminated an exciting time while we fitted pieces of the "porphyry puzzle" together in the late sixties. Almost no one had heard of either of us when the first Geological Society of America Penrose Conference was being formatted in Tucson in 1968. In fact, we had to cajole our way onto the program. But the tabulation of porphyry characteristics that we distributed there and our description of the typical porphyry copper deposit were among the skyrockets of the symposium. We learned much later that in subsequent years, after we published our synthesis in 1970, four famous geologists were spotted at different times in various parts of South America: namely, David Lowell, John Guilbert, Lowell Guilbert, and Guilbert Lowell.

Lowell's porphyry calling was toward field endeavor leading to discovery. As you will learn in the book, his steps were sure. He could at many junctures have linked up with companies in various capacities (and did so more than once), but the closer he came to that involvement the less content he was. He had many strict personal, ethical, and tactical policies and requirements of his colleagues, and many of the people with whom he worked from time to time found them chafing. His was the path of the individual, the individualist, the visionary who was always trying to figure things out. We collaborated many times during the next decades, consistent with his continued reaching out for new ideas and strategies. He was the practitioner who had no patience with office politics, the one who was focused almost totally on trying to read geologic field alteration-rock-mineral detail into usable context for finding ore. It is worth noting here that most field geologists spend their early years in the field, generally away from family, but as the years go by they get "promoted" into offices and greater corporate responsibility and gradually grow away from contact with fieldwork and outcrops. David Lowell perennially spent many months away from home, but managed either to take his family with him (as to an apartment in Santiago) or to get home frequently enough. Whatever it took, he has been able to live up to his own boot-leather-and-rock-hammer credo that "you only make ore-deposit discoveries in the field" even into his post-normal-retirement years. His modus operandi was to take his ideas on exploration strategies—he was one of the great interpolationists—to companies, to consortia, and to individuals for funding. He would then assemble an exploration team, often forming his own company, to pursue them. Throughout his career, he has shown himself to be a remarkable manager of ideas, men, and materiel, a paragon of discipline, self-discipline, and perseverance, and a man of great vision. The amazing magnitude of his success is obvious from his discoveries list and his autobiography that follows.

As you absorb his success story, you will see unfold an almost Horatio Alger–like story of growth from inauspicious but salutary beginnings through a series of formative periods of professional development, good education well received, applied learning on several job sites in the southwestern United States and Mexico, formulation of exploration strategies, and the launching of his own enterprises and exploration companies. What you will see is the enormity of his professional success as the discoverer of at least a dozen or so new porphyry deposits, two of which vie for the largest-in-the-world title, one of which (La Escondida) is a mainstay of Chile's copper profile. And he has controlled at various times at least two score of important copper prospects, some of which (like Santa Cruz and Los Calatos) may yet prove commercial. His breadth is proven by his also having discovered two major gold mines, one of them (Pierina) having produced a stock market surge that made him and Arequipa Resources the darlings of mining investors and created hundreds of millions of dollars of wealth. Pierina also resulted in one of the lowest cost–highest profit major gold mines in the world for its ultimate owner. His scientific drive is manifest in his having doggedly pursued the significance of a leached capping texture problem at what would be known as La Escondida; his correct discernment of what would be called hypersaline super leaching textures fueled his conviction to continue the project to its amazing fruition. That drive is also attested by the fact that although he dislikes writing, avoids public appearances, and dreads giving talks, he owns a long and distinguished list of technical-scientific papers, is a sought-after instructor-lecturer, and has spoken to large and enthusiastic audiences at symposia and conferences for thirty years. You should also be amazed at his ability to attract and manage scores of legal, "land-man," scientific, and business associates to press his projects forward.

I hope you will perceive from his writing the enormous respect that his longtime friends have for him, and the fact that his worldly success has affected his personal friendships not at all. His friendliness and generosity of spirit are widely recognized. His eye still twinkles merrily, and he seldom fails to stay in touch with old exploration, ranching, and business chums. He is in strong demand as a speaker, writer, and short-course instructor. And through all his success, he has remained his own man. His friends relish the story of the talk he was asked to give a few years ago to a gathering in Tucson celebrating the retirement of the chief geologist of a major multinational company. Regional chief geologists, district geologists, office managers, and scores of field staff had been assembled. Dave's topic was "The Design of a Successful Exploration Team." The assembled hierarchy expected their own vast, far-flung, and highly structured groups to get a pat on the back—but Dave proceeded to point out that the small lone-wolf, freelance exploration group had been demonstrably the most successful exploration mode in the last fifty years!

As Lowell heads into his retirement years, he is spending more time at his beloved Atascosa Ranch near Tucson with Edith, seeing more of his sons, his daughter, and a growing list of grandkids, and pursuing old hobbies and new philanthropies. His devotion to exploring and advancing are attested to by his recent perception, discovery, and development of world-class deposits of titanium in Paraguay, and his continuing hunt for porphyry coppers in Chile and elsewhere. For most men, gazing at his trophy wall (his Jackling Award, Haddon King Award, Penrose Gold Medal, honorary degrees, and plaques) might suffice. For most men, financial comfort might be a reason to relax. For most men, having discovered Kalamazoo, Casa Grande West, La Escondida, and Pierina (among others) would be enough. But Dave's head is slightly turned, his eyes on the horizon . . . his energies and enthusiasms will not subside . . . and he still travels to Mexico, Peru, and Chile . . . still plotting, still contemplating, still eager, still reaching out to find the next orebody. . . .

John M. Guilbert
Professor Emeritus of Economic Geology
Department of Geosciences
University of Arizona, Tucson
Phoenix, Arizona
September 2013

Intrepid Explorer

BOOK I, 1935–1961

**Early life, education, and work, with no freedom
to plan exploration, and no discoveries**

CHAPTER ONE

First Exposure to Mineral Exploration, 1935–1949

In 1935 my father was operating the small Silver Hill Mine northeast of Arivaca, Arizona. The mine was at the end of a two-rut desert road. The road was the only work of man visible from our camp, which consisted of a pyramid canvas tent mounted on a 2x4 lumber frame with a plywood floor, with a door made of plywood and window screen, with hinges and a latch that locked from the outside. We had two army canvas cots and two chairs, and a cabinet and a table made up the kitchen. There was no electricity, and in the evening the tent was lighted by a Coleman gasoline lantern. The tent had a barrel of water in front and an outhouse a hundred feet behind. I was seven years old and I loved everything.

About fifty yards away, the second tent for our two miners was located in the "patio," the work area near the shaft collar. The mine opening was a vertical shaft about one hundred feet deep, with a ladder built in twelve-foot sections for "us miners" along one wall and a windlass for hoisting the ore. The ladders were sixteen inches wide, made of vertical 2x4s with 1x4s nailed in fourteen inches apart as steps. The ladders were nailed to horizontal "stulls" (posts fitted into hitches, or cavities) cut into two opposite walls of the six-foot-wide shaft and secured by wooden wedges driven between the ends of the stulls and the rock in the hitch.

David at age 7 and David's dad, Arthur, at Silver Hill Mine near Arivaca.

The ore was hoisted by a one-inch manila rope or a three-eighths-inch steel cable, which wrapped around the barrel of our windlass by turning the crank. The windlass was made of an eight-foot piece of an old telephone pole with a one-inch steel bar driven into a hole on one end as an axle and a one-inch steel crank driven into the other end. The bucket was about twenty-five gallons in size, made with heavy walls and a heavy hasp. Full of rock it weighed about five hundred pounds. With a larger bucket or a deeper shaft, windlasses would be used with a crank on each end for a two-man operation.

Going down the shaft required stepping onto the ladder, behind which was the open shaft with a hundred-foot drop. My father let me do it (with a firm hold on the collar of my shirt), making sure that my hands and feet were in the correct locations. We got to the bottom of the ladder into the "drift," a horizontal tunnel, which was being driven centered on the three-foot-thick, vertical-tabular vein made up of galena, a shiny, heavy black lead sulfide mineral that also contains silver (hence the "Silver Hill" name), and pyrite, a shiny yellow iron sulfide, and some chalcopyrite, a finer grained, copper iron sulfide with a slightly different shade of yellow.

On my first trip down into the Silver Hill shaft our two Mexican miners were drilling a "round" of blast holes using "hand steel." These holes were drilled by holding in one hand a three-quarter-inch steel rod that terminated with a chisel bit, and in the other a four-pound "single-jack" hammer. The hole was about one inch in diameter, and sometimes one man could drill only one or two holes in one eight-hour shift. My father owned and managed the mine, but he also did his part of the manual labor. The round was designed to be blasted in a series of individual blasts determined by the lengths of the fuses for the dynamite charge in each hole. Typically, there were three holes in the cone-shaped "cut" in the middle of the round, which was blasted out leaving a cavity into which successive rings of holes could blast, leaving a clean two-foot advance of the five-by-six-foot drift cross section. All the broken rock had to be transported to the base of the shaft, in a wheelbarrow if the distance was short or in a steel ore car on small rail tracks if the distance was longer.

On one occasion I was allowed to spit the fuses. The dynamite was detonated by punching a hole in the last stick of dynamite in each hole with a copper or wooden punch because an iron punch might produce a spark. The detonator or "cap" for each fuse was a copper tube one and a half inches long and three-sixteenths-inch in diameter, hollow in one end to receive the fuse, which burned one foot per minute. The cap contained fulminate of mercury, a very sensitive explosive (the dynamite itself was not sensitive and was safe to handle). The fuse was inserted in the cap and then delicately crimped with a pliers-like crimper. The fuses were measured to give the correct sequence of blasts for a successful blast of the round. All the fuses were gathered together and all spitted at almost the same time to preserve the blasting sequence. Imagine the excitement of a seven-year-old boy spitting the round with the flame of a carbide light and then shouting "fire in the hole" and scampering up a hundred feet of ladders while fuses for twelve loaded holes were going *sizzzz* below him. My father was climbing immediately below to avoid any climbing accident.

My father had a small white woolly dog named Rags who waited at the collar of the shaft. Rags somehow knew when a round had been spitted, and when the holes began going off he would bark madly after each blast. At night in our tent with the lantern burning, we often heard coyotes howling, sometimes close to our tent. Rags, all five or ten pounds of him, would bark back.

The patio contained the tent our two miners shared, a forge and anvil where the drill steel was sharpened, an unsorted ore pile and a sorted ore pile, and a waste rock pile. When a quantity of unsorted ore was collected it was sorted into ore and waste. After I had served a couple of weeks of apprenticeship, my father asked me if I would like to be the (unpaid) ore sorter. Since then, I have on two occasions served as chairman of a billion-dollar company, but the thrill of becoming the Silver Hill ore sorter gave me infinitely greater satisfaction!

It was at that time that I decided several things: first, life couldn't get any better than this; second, I would become a mining engineer; and third was a dim perception that the Silver Hill vein pinched and swelled. I saw that the ore grade was sometimes high and sometimes low, and thought maybe someone who was smart enough and educated and experienced enough could work this all out and possibly find a thick, very high grade ore "shoot," or maybe discover a whole new rich, very valuable mine. I didn't know what science was, but wisps of scientific thought were already working into my plan. This moment was the beginning of my mineral exploration career dream, which has lasted for seventy-eight years.

My second mining experience was when I was eight years old and had become, after my Silver Hill experience, a very sophisticated miner. In 1936 my father bought or staked a mineral deposit in the Las Guijas Mountains about ten miles west of Arivaca, Arizona. My father named the prospect "Tunquipata" after a Quechua Indian word in Peru that meant "cock of the walk." The Pelton wheel hydroelectric generating

The tent at
Tunquipata Mine,
1939.

plant at the Santo Domingo Mine in Peru (where my mother and father had lived for three years) was also located at a place called Tunquipata.

The Tunquipata Mine was one of the few mineral ventures that turned out very profitably for my father. It was a gold-tungsten deposit, and he operated it on a small scale for about two years, then sold it. While it was in operation, our two miners worked in the mine drilling blast holes in the vein by hand with single-jack four-pound hammers and "hand steel," which was sharpened in a forge. Housing, as at Silver Hill, consisted of two tents and an open kitchen with a small wood-stove. Transportation and ore truck were combined in the same second-hand International pickup truck.

The mine had had an unusual history in that, according to legend, it had been originally worked by the Spaniards or early Mexicans, and later, twenty or thirty years before my father acquired it, it had been reopened by Americans and had been the site of a fatal accident in a cave-in. The local Mexican Americans were firmly convinced that it was haunted, and they had some evidence to support this view. I remember lying on my cot at night and listening to Dad and the Mexican miners telling ghost stories (in Spanish) about the mine. All present, including myself, had had the experience of hearing a tapping noise in the bottom of the mine as of a long-dead Spanish miner drilling with hand steel somewhere out in the rock. Verduzco, a one-legged miner, swore that he had heard a ghost pass him in the tunnel and climb down the ladder into the mine. Reyes Palomares, my dad's longtime assistant in other mines, had many other stories about supernatural events at Tunquipata, but the most difficult happenings to explain were jointly experienced by my father and my brother Bill, who worked two summers at the mine. On two occasions radio programs were heard in the camp or on the hill above camp, but there was no radio in camp and no other people living for several miles in any direction. At this time portable radios were rare, and it is very difficult to explain the origin of the sounds of the radio program. My father thought that minerals in the vein might have converted radio waves into sound waves (as in crystal radios), but this seems very unlikely. Tunquipata was definitely a spooky place.

At the Tunquipata Mine there were many mockingbirds or "wee-ta-coches" as they were called by the Mexicans. Over time my father and the miners taught one of these birds to whistle back tunes from a tree near the tent and imitate portions of songs. There were also coyotes that howled in the distance and owls that hooted at night, and sometimes at night small foxes barked on the opposite side of the canyon. I visited the site of Tunquipata thirty-four years after I lived there as a small boy. All the distances had shrunk from what they were in 1936, and you could barely see where our tent was located, or the kitchen and the forge. I don't know whether the poor Spanish miner is still down there tapping in the rock with his single-jack hammer, but there could be worse places for him to work than Tunquipata.

Cumming and Lowell Families

My mother's family name was Cumming, a Scottish surname, and I grew up convinced that the Scots were the bravest, noblest, finest people in the world, and the Cummings were the finest Scottish clan. My faith was only slightly shaken when someone in Scotland later told me that "the Cummings were a bad lot."

My great-grandfather James B. Cumming received two hundred acres in Canada on the shores of Lake Ontario—where the town of Picton, Prince Edward County, is now located—for his service in the 84th Highland Regiment, fighting on the side of the Crown in the American Revolution.

My grandfather Douglas Wallace Cumming was born in Waupoos, Ontario, in 1834. When he was twenty-one, he took his savings and traveled to California. Not much is known of my grandfather's travels after he arrived in California. We do know that he explored the Feather River country and into British Columbia and that he was a U.S. Marshal of Idaho under President Lincoln. In British Columbia he saw an isolated cemetery in which all the bodies were on platforms in trees to keep them from being destroyed by animals. Then, while taking part in the celebration of the Union victory at the end of the Civil War, Grandfather was badly burned when a cannon that had been sabotaged by filling it full of gunpowder exploded. He spent months in the hospital. When he had recovered, he went to the mines in Carson City, Nevada, accompanied by his brother James, who later died there of smallpox.

According to Mother's account, he served as Indian agent in Idaho (to the Snake Indians) and fought Indian Wars in Idaho, Arizona, and Sonora for thirty years. Grandfather told of having to eat dried grasshoppers when he lived with the Snake Indians in Idaho, and he may have been the first white man to traverse the Snake River. He made the trip through the many rapids on a raft he had made.

Mother also told us that Grandfather crossed the Great Plains in a freight wagon and along the trail found a grave marked, "Danger! John Smith who is buried here died of Smallpox." Grandfather and his companion decided that this didn't sound true and dug up the grave, which contained a barrel of whiskey the previous owner had had to abandon. She also said that after an Indian fight in Idaho with the Snake Indians, Grandfather and a fellow soldier found two Indian babies hidden in a

David's grandfather,
Douglas Wallace Cumming.

bush. They took the babies to the soldier's mother, who with some mis-givings took them both and raised two fine citizens.

Sometime after arriving in California, Douglas Wallace Cumming married Mary Huntington and had a son, Douglas Gray, and a daughter, Louise. He lived in Watsonville for a time, but his itchy feet kept him traveling. Most of his travels took him to mining towns, and we surmise that he did some prospecting, mining, and freighting. Evidently Mary became tired of his traveling and divorced him, perhaps while he returned to Canada to visit his ailing mother. She took the children, and at her death relatives offered a home to Louise. Douglas Gray would eventually seek out and find his father in Arizona.

Grandfather later had a freight business in what is now Cochise County. When night came on these trips he would stake out his horses and leave his wagon and go to a secluded spot to sleep. One night Apaches being pursued by cavalry left their horses in a state of exhaustion, taking his in their place. Before dawn Grandfather harnessed the Apaches' horses and proceeded to Tombstone. It couldn't have been easy harnessing exhausted untrained Indian horses to a wagon!

Then, on a trip into Sonora, my grandfather was in a small town that was attacked by Yaqui Indians who surrounded and besieged the town. He climbed up on the roof with his Sharps rifle and shot the Yaqui chief, which stopped the attack and saved the town. Grandfather was also present at the Clanton Earp gunfight in Tombstone in 1881. He had just driven his freight wagon into Tombstone before the fight started. Bullets whistled up and down the street beside the corral. He and his helper dropped to the ground behind a woodpile, where they remained until the bullets stopped flying.

During the early 1880s, Douglas settled in Nogales and married my grandmother, Frances Bigsby, who was in her late teens while he was in his fifties. He was a handsome, well-read man who must have had a great deal of charm to appeal to Frances. About the same time, in 1881, great-grandfather James Cumming died in Ontario and willed "Douglas Wallace of the Salt River Territory in Arizona" a share of his estate.

Frances's mother, my great-grandmother Melissa Gregory, had lived in Missouri and married William Bigsby. In 1862, shortly after their marriage, William was killed fighting for the South in the Battle of Shiloh, one of the bloodiest battles in the Civil War. Melissa then moved to Marysville, California, where she gave birth to twins, a boy and a girl. The boy, William, lived only a few weeks. The girl, Frances, thrived, but when Frances was two months old Melissa also died. Melissa's sister and brother-in-law, Wilmoth and Thomas McFadden, raised Frances as their own child. She was educated in a Catholic convent and then moved to Nogales, Arizona, to stay with her roommate from the convent, Nancy Tanner Marsteller. There she met and married Douglas. My cousin Lee described Grandmother as "a tall red-headed woman who wore men's shoes and had a terrible temper."

Douglas Wallace Cumming and Frances Bigsby had six children: my mother, Lavina Agnes (1893), and three older brothers and two younger, my uncles: Thomas McFadden (1887), William Nelson (1891), David John (1891), James Douglas (1897), and Joseph Allen (1898). When Frances and Douglas married they lived in Nogales, where they operated a small dairy while Douglas continued mining and freighting. Pregnant with her third child, Frances contracted smallpox. In those days, the official response to smallpox was to isolate the sick in a sanatorium, a "pest house," to prevent epidemic spread. But when the authorities came to take her to die in the pest house Grandfather confronted them with a .30-30 rifle, and nursed her back to health himself. As a child that baby, John (David John), did not develop a reaction or scar when he received the smallpox vaccination. Grandfather Douglas maintained close contact with his brothers and sisters through his entire life, and after settling in Nogales, he sent for his brother John and found him a job with Wells Fargo at Magdalena, Sonora, Mexico. John had always dreamed of becoming a lawyer and studied law books in his spare time. Eventually he came back to Nogales, passed his bar exams, and practiced law. He became a very successful Superior Court judge and bought the 160-acre El Bosque Ranch. He was killed in a tragic runaway buggy accident—early death for a successful man, and a blow to the family.

After Great-Uncle John's death, my grandparents moved to the Bosque Ranch, which John had willed to Grandfather. My mother described the ranch with the Santa Cruz River on the west side leaving a nice pasture for cattle between the house and the river. My grandfather installed a big steam pump on the well, which made water easy and plentiful. Rainfall was greater then than now and good crops like corn and squash grew most years. The house was made of two-foot-thick adobe. The doors were heavy pine and the windows high with small panes, maybe because of earlier Indian raids. The roof was corrugated iron. Like most common folks of that time and place, the family bathed in a large galvanized tub in the kitchen, or in the large cement tank at the pump. But Great-Uncle John had redwood closets built in the three large bedrooms.

Life at the Bosque looked promising for the couple. But shortly after the move, in 1899, when my mother was just seven years old, diabetes claimed Grandmother Frances. After her death, with six children and a ranch to run, life must have been very difficult for Grandfather. William Nelson Cumming, the second oldest boy, went to live with

Uncle William and Aunt Prudence (whom we called Prudie). They also took Uncle Joe, who was just a baby, and raised him. In 1903 Nogales bankers absconded with the family funds. About that same time, Uncle William died, and young William Nelson was sent to relatives in Picton, Ontario, for schooling. When Mother was ten, Grandfather sent her to his favorite sister, Agnes Scott, in Santa Cruz, California. The story of her trip is told in the book *I Am Lavina Cumming*, written by Susan Lowell. In 1905 a terrific drought hit southern Arizona, further devastating Grandfather's ranch.

Some years later Douglas Gray, Grandfather's son by his first marriage, arrived at the Bosque Ranch. My cousin Ruth heard the story that the brothers (Thomas, David, and James, who were still living with their father on the ranch) were helping their father work cattle

Photo of Cumming cousins about 1936. Back, William Cumming, Doug Cumming, Peggy Lowell, Lee Cumming, Jim Cumming. Front, Ruth Cumming, Joanie Cumming, Mary Lee Cumming, Alan (Buzz) Cumming, David Lowell, Kendall Cumming, and Bill Lowell. These were the 12 first cousins, sometimes called "the dirty dozen."

at the corral when the youth arrived and introduced himself saying, "I am your son." Grandfather's eyes filled with tears as he embraced his oldest son. Douglas Gray remained at the ranch until he was grown and then moved to Marysville, California. My sister and I met both Louise and Douglas in 1936. They had had a close relationship with my mother.

Grandfather must have inspired respect in the community, as there are many stories of his courage and strength. One story tells of him tossing two men through the window of a saloon in Nogales, Sonora, and strolling off. Another tale claims he could lift a barrel of whiskey one-handed and drink from same. He was in Prescott, Arizona, near the Genung Ranch, when a group of Apaches raided and drove off a herd of cattle. Mr. Genung found my grandfather in a saloon, and they immediately set off, following the tracks of the stolen cattle, and found the Indians camped the first night. Grandfather and Mr. Genung opened fire at the Indians around the campfire, killing several and recovering the cattle.

Douglas was a complex man—a traveler, miner, freighter, dairyman, rancher, family man—all of these, and a reader of the classics. When he died, he had two lead bullets in his body which had never been removed, a groove in the top of his head from a bullet, and a bicep partially crippled by an arrow. I am sorry he died before I was born.

We heard a lot of stories about Grandfather and my uncles at the Bosque Ranch. The Cumming brothers sometimes raised pigs and on one occasion they slaughtered four large hogs and were taking them to Nogales to sell to the meat market. Driving down the road to Nogales, a wheel came off the old truck and it tilted and slid into a ditch. They laid the four hogs, which were wrapped in tarps, in a row, and Uncle John stayed with the vehicle while his brother hiked off to get help. In those days people always stopped when you were in trouble, and after a while another car came by and stopped. The driver got out and said, "Anyone hurt?" Uncle John pointed with his thumb at the wrapped up hogs and said, "Count 'em."

Four of David's five Cumming uncles: from left, Jim, Joe, John, and Tom.
Missing is Bill (who later became president of a small bank in Watsonville,
California), 1925.

On another occasion the Cumming boys had a stripped-down old
Model T Ford ranch truck that had no fenders or hood, and as Uncle
John was driving down the dirt road to the ranch he saw a very big rattlesnake in the road. He swerved to be sure he hit it and then looked back
to see if it was dead, but it had disappeared and he was puzzled. At that
moment he looked down. The snake had wrapped around the wheel,
come out on the floorboard, and was crawling toward him to get even.

Another time Uncle John had a cow in the corral that was "on the
prod" and attacked when he tried to enter the corral. He knew very
little about bullfighting and thought this might be an opportunity to
practice his own skills, but he was not aware that bulls charge with their
eyes closed and cows with their eyes open. He got a saddle blanket and
entered the corral walking like a matador; the cow charged, but she

John Cumming, about 1920.

charged Uncle John, not the blanket. She knocked him down and went after him with her horns on the ground, but fortunately hooked him out under the corral gate. Uncle John told me he spent some time composing a story to explain his cuts and bruises and contusions in a more favorable light as resulting from being thrown off a horse.

I loved Uncle John almost as much as my parents. He was a good storyteller and said funny things that were often jokes at his own expense. Once Uncle John, who had a bit of a drinking problem, got home to the ranch very late and found the front door locked. He tiptoed around the house and found a window unlocked. He very gently eased the window up and stuck his head into the opening to find the barrel of a cocked Colt .45 an inch from his forehead, held by his wife, my Aunt Inez.

Uncle John owned a horse named Tumble Bug that was able to jump over fences. He finally got tired of having the horse in the wrong pasture and sold him. In due course Tumble Bug jumped over the required number of fences to get back to his friend, John Cumming. This happened with three consecutive sales and Uncle John said this was the best money-making scheme he had ever had, but I'm sure he returned all the money.

After reading Zane Grey's *Roping Lions in the Grand Canyon*, Uncle John thought "there is no reason why I couldn't do that." There were mountain lions in the Tumacacori Mountains on his ranch, and he could use Loco Manuel, his cowboy, to help. Loco Manuel was a nice guy but a little bit strange in the head. John and Manuel, and probably some dogs, went lion hunting. There was one flaw in the scheme: neither Manuel nor either of the horses had read the Zane Grey book and didn't know what to expect. Horses are instinctively terrified of lions. They treed a lion and John roped one end and Manuel the other, all this from terrified horses, and then Manuel didn't follow instructions. John had a bad temper and loosened his rope to allow the lion to threaten Manuel and finally everything got very out of control and John shot the lion with his pistol. At this point Manuel, who was justifiably mad, got off his horse and started throwing rocks at Uncle John, who threatened to shoot him also. I'm not exactly sure what Uncle John would have done with his lion if the scheme had succeeded.

On one occasion my father, Arthur Lowell, who was very polite, and Uncle Jim and Uncle John Cumming, who were both tough cowboys, were riding together in a Model T Ford on the way to a funeral. Driving a road along a power line, they encountered a repair crew. My father stopped the truck and asked the repairman, "Are you looking for trouble?" meaning, "Are you looking for a break in the line?" Uncle Jim and Uncle John thought that for reasons unknown my father was about to get in a fistfight, so they jumped out of the car and took their fancy funeral coats off, ready for action. At that time my uncles were building up their cattle herd by catching wild cows in the Tumacacori Mountains, which was a continuous rodeo and no job for the faint of heart.

During the prohibition period Uncle John occasionally drove across the border between Nogales, Arizona, and Nogales, Sonora, and bought a pint of liquor. The pint size was favored because it would fit in a cowboy boot. He was not the only one interested in this gambit, and the Customs inspectors were in the habit of putting their foot on the run-

Reuben Lowell house, Farmington Falls, Maine, about 1800.
David's father, Arthur Lowell, was born here and lived in the
house until he left for prep school. Edith and David spent one
night in the Lowell farm which was cold and dank and had been
unoccupied for years. Edith, who is not superstitious, thought it
was haunted.

Arthur Lowell while student
at Tufts College, about 1900.

David Lowell's grandfather, Hervey William Lowell, about 1900, and grandmother Henrietta Keith Currier Lowell, 1900.

ning board and their hands on the roof of a car and rocking the car and listening for a gurgling sound. Uncle John said if you crossed your legs and let the leg with the whiskey swing free there would be no gurgle. The Cumming family members were a little rough around the edges.

Back in New England, the Lowell family was an elegant group, and the Arizona Lowells had at least a little of that polish. My father, Arthur Currier Lowell, was born in 1884 in Farmington, Maine, to Hervey William Lowell, an apple grower and apple broker, and Henrietta Keith Currier Lowell. His father was a member of the Boston Lowell family, and his mother was a member of the Currier family of Currier and Ives fame. One hundred years ago the Lowells were an important family in New England. One well-known poem of the time said, "And here's to good old Boston / The land of the bean and the cod / Where Lowells talk only to Cabots / And Cabots talk only to God," but no one in Arizona knew or cared about any of that.

The family owned a farm and a vacation camp in the woods beside a

David's step-grandmother, Florence Robison Lowell, about 1920. Hervey William Lowell died a year after marrying Florence, who many years later lived with us in Arizona for about five years before her death. She had been a music teacher and was very kind to her little step-grandson.

small lake in the region. An only child, Dad grew up hunting and fishing and camping in the woods, and he passed love of these things on to me. He had good manners and was a very quiet and considerate man. He spent one summer working on a commercial swordfishing boat. He was also a lieutenant in the National Guard. He attended Westbrook Seminary, a prep school in Portland, Maine, and then studied engineering for three years at Tufts College in Boston before dropping out, which turned out to be a mistake, since his lack of a degree prevented him from being eligible for jobs that might otherwise have been available later during the Depression. His mother, Henrietta, died when he was twenty-four years old. Hervey later married Florence Robison, who was a music teacher and a very kind person. (Florence eventually moved to Arizona. She lived with us the last five years of her life, and was loved by all her grandchildren.) A year after they were married, Hervey died, and after his father passed away Dad traveled to Arizona and northern Mexico to seek his fortune as a prospector. This wasn't necessarily a practical ambition, but I suspect that I inherited some of my treasure hunting instinct from my father.

Lavina Cumming Lowell, David's
mother, about 1935.

My mother, Lavina Cumming, came from a very different background than my father, and her personality was very different from Dad's. She spent her early years on the Bosque Ranch, which ran an open-range operation in the nearby Tumacacori and Atascosa mountain ranges.

Mother told us one story of her own mother, remembering that when she was six, a goat had chewed up her doll. She was very upset, of course. But one night while she slept her mother painstakingly repaired it, re-embroidering its face and mending its clothes. When my grandmother died, my mother became the surrogate mother of her five roughneck brothers on a hardscrabble cattle ranch. Grandfather Douglas noticed that after my grandmother's death Mother's training on the ranch was running more to how to shoot a pistol and how to brand a calf than how to dress like a lady and serve a tea party. So, in 1903, he sent her to Santa Cruz, California, to be civilized by lady relatives. At the age of ten, she traveled alone by railroad to Agnes Scott, Grandfather's sister, with a sign pinned to her dress that said "I am Lavina Cumming" and gave the address for her destination.

As an adult, she was a tough, sometimes charming, sometimes overbearing, very religious lady. She had lots of drive and was willing to attack any problem (some of that rubbed off on me). She attended Tempe Normal School (now Arizona State University), where she earned an Elementary Teaching Certificate. After graduating, she returned to Santa Cruz County and got a job teaching in the Palo Parado one-room, one-teacher school, where discipline was such that she thought it prudent to wear her six-shooter while teaching. She took over the school from another young lady, and when they went over the class enrollment it included a student named "Pancho Gomez," whom she had not met. The previous teacher said, "You have met him; he is the little dog that comes to school with José Gomez, and without him you don't have twelve students, and state regulations will not allow the school to stay open and you will not have a job."

The influence of my mother on me was both positive and negative. She was overbearing and always sure she was right. Woe betide the person who got in her way, and as a young boy I was often that unfortunate person. It created rebellion on my side, and I felt my head was bloodied but unbowed. An unexpected benefit of always being wrong as a young boy was that "being good at being wrong" would turn out to be an important factor thirty-seven years later when I began finding mines.

My father had a positive effect on my life and personality. He gave very little spoken advice, but by example caused me to try to be more reliable, resolute, kind, and hardworking. He was also a person who thought it was very important to keep your word.

My father came to southern Arizona to look at mineral prospects in Mexico; here he met my mother in 1917. When he was invited to sign a contract as mill superintendent at the Santo Domingo Mine in Peru in 1918, Arthur and Lavina decided to get married, and did so. We don't know how long Dad was in Arizona and northern Mexico before his marriage. He never discussed this with me, but trying to put the story together later, it is evident that he had taken mining jobs and odd jobs in the borderlands region, but his primary ambition seems to have been prospecting to find a rich discovery. This makes me wonder whether I may have inherited some prospecting genes from both my father and my Cumming grandfather.

Shortly after they were married, my parents traveled to Peru; my sister Peggy wrote the following about part of their trip:

"It took my parents forty-two days from Nogales, Arizona, where they were married, to Santo Domingo, Peru via train to New York, ship to Kingston, Jamaica where they met U.S. Senator Emery who owned the mine. Then they traveled through the Panama Canal and up the coast to Mollendo, Peru; thence by train and stagecoach over the Andes and finally by mule over the trail to the mine. Dad was the mining engineer, and all the supplies had to be brought in, usually by llama train. He claimed that they were 'ornery critters' who spat and refused to carry more than sixty pounds. They just sat down at sixty-one pounds. Timbers were brought in by groups of Indians. This could take time if

Mule trail between Cuzco and Santo Domingo Mine over which Lavina rode with Peggy as a baby, 1919.

they went through a village celebrating a fiesta. His Indians dropped the timbers and joined in the celebration. When they finally sobered up they picked up the timbers and went on to the mine. Once Dad had gone out to the nearest town to get some things and was walking back. He got so tired that he decided to rest and fell asleep on the trail. When he woke up he heard a strange swishing noise and turned his head. He was surrounded by various kinds and colors of snakes that were migrating down the trail and separated when they came to him and continued on either side. He said that he hardly breathed until the migration passed. Then he smelled smoke and decided that the snakes were escaping from a jungle fire which happens in the dry season when the Indians burn the area to clear for planting.

"One story stands out in my memory. Dad and Mr. Brinkman (general manager of the mine) were accused of murder. It seems that a troublemaker (we would call him a labor agitator) came to the mine and stirred up trouble, trying to get the workers to strike. Dad finally tossed him into the mine tailings pond and the fellow left very quietly, creating the impression he had died. There was only one phone line into the mine and it came through several villages. Someone at the mine heard news that a troop of soldiers were on their way down the trail to arrest Dad and Mr. Brinkman. It was decided that they should leave, hiding out by day and traveling by night until they reached Bolivia, where they registered at a hotel only to wake to gunfire the following morning. A revolution had broken out. They finally were able to contact Senator Emery who went into action and threatened to apply U.S. military pressure. Since the troublemaker was obviously still alive a reward was offered for him *alive*. He was turned in, the government apologized, and Dad returned to the mine and a very relieved wife.

"I will tell you about the Jivaro headhunter babysitter. In the early 1900s the Peruvian government received many complaints about raids having been made by the Jivaro tribe. Finally they dispatched a young captain and his troop to wipe out the tribe. The only survivor was a seven-year-old boy, and the captain decided to keep him as a slave. The troop stopped over at Santo Domingo at the small *pensión* (guest

Peggy, being held by a
nurse in Cuzco, Peru.

house) – a poker game ensued and the captain lost all his money, with
the hotel manager winning. He finally put up the boy, Toro, and lost
him too. The hotel manager felt sorry for the child and taught him
Spanish and how to work around the hotel. When Dad asked about
someone to help Mother take care of me the manager recommended
Toro. Thus my headhunter babysitter. When he reached puberty he
started chewing coca leaves and getting into trouble and Mother fired
him. He drifted back to the jungle looking for another tribe. After that
I had Pita, a Quechua woman whom I adored. When we left the jungle
Dad made a canvas chair that was carried by a relay of Indians so I left
the jungle looking back and crying my eyes out because I didn't want to
leave Pita. I had been born in the Baptist hospital in Cuzco and crossed
the Andes over Aricoma Pass at six weeks old wrapped in an eiderdown
quilt in a laundry basket. While staying overnight at a small inn with no
screen on the windows Mother awoke when a vampire bat was biting

Margaret K. Lowell

Born in Peru in 1919, my sister Peggy attended public schools in Nogales and Tucson and was a student at the University of Arizona and Arizona State University. She received a BA and an MA, and she taught elementary classes and Spanish for about twenty years. She was married to Jim Grade, an officer in the army, and they adopted a son, also named Jim Grade, who lives in Tucson. Jim and his wife Eileen have a daughter Krista. Peggy passed away in 2003.

Arthur Lowell with Peggy in Santo Domingo, Peru.

her neck. I was raised on canned milk because the bats would bite the cows behind their heads and suck their blood until they died."

Nine years after Peggy was born, and five years after Bill, I showed up. I was born at 10:00 p.m., February 28, 1928, on our little ranch north of Nogales, Arizona. The hour was important to me, because if I had been born two hours later I would have been a leap-year person. I was born at home because of a polio epidemic in progress, and Mother didn't want to risk infection in the hospitals. I escaped infection, but my brother and sister both contracted polio. (Bill recovered completely. Peggy was left with a problem with one leg, but nothing that would

26

prevent her from becoming an officer in the Waves, the women's division of the Navy, in World War II.)

Childhood in the Great Depression

The Great Depression of the 1930s hit our family very hard. My father could no longer get mining jobs because he didn't have a university degree and hadn't paid his dues by going to work for a large mining company and working his way up the ladder. For ten years he made a marginal living, buying, staking, or leasing small mines and selling hand-sorted ore to an ore buyer.

The mine names I remember from my youth are Silver Hill, Black Princess, Gold Coin, Tunquipata, and Esperanza. (Twenty-five years later Esperanza became a large, open pit copper mine.) When I was seven, Silver Hill gave me my first mining experience working with my father and our two Mexican miners, Reyes Palomares and Verduzco. They were honest, loyal, and almost members of our family, and they worked with my father for about ten years. Verduzco had a wooden leg. In 1935 the word "Mexican" denoted someone who came from Mexico and spoke Spanish. It had not much to do with U.S. or Mexican citizenship or "green cards." I don't think there were any green cards. You could drive from Nogales, Arizona, into Nogales, Sonora, and back sometimes without talking to any officials of either country.

When we had accumulated about a ton of hand-sorted ore we would load it into our old (circa 1925–1930) International four-cylinder pickup and take it to Hugo Miller, who operated an assay shop and an ore buying business in Nogales, Arizona. At that time during the Depression there were many small mines like my father's operating in southern Arizona. Hugo would buy our ore at a big discount and mix it with ore bought from other small mines and ship it to a custom smelter, which would buy it all at another big discount. I'm satisfied that Hugo Miller was an honest person and everyone profited during the Great Depression with this arrangement, when most people were poor and cash was king.

Purchase of explosives in 1935 was simple and there were no gov-

David playing with toy gun and his dog, General, at age 4, 1932, and at age 5 at Tucson home, 1933. The Lowell cats were always named "Kitty" or "Leo."

ernment permits. At that time there was a department store in downtown Tucson called Steinfeld's. It sold hardware and clothing and groceries. I can remember being in Steinfeld's with my mother and our grocery basket that contained bread, vegetables, a fifty-pound box of dynamite, a roll of fuse, and a box of caps—carefully placed in the side of the basket away from the "powder." I grew up with blasting supplies stored in the garage much of the time.

My childhood experience at the Silver Hill Mine inspired my later career. Tunquipata provided my second indelible impression of mining and by the time I was eight I had, at least in my own eyes, become a very sophisticated miner.

In addition to his mining ventures, Dad sometimes took fill-in jobs. He once leased and operated a service station on the north side of Broadway, a couple blocks east of Euclid, in downtown Tucson. I was nine or ten, and I worked as a part-time attendant, selling gas out of hand-pump gas pumps and making change and being temporary manager. I wore a Signal Oil cap made of oilcloth. Sometimes the customer would insist on pumping the gas himself because I was so small. I almost always had a part-time job by the time I was twelve years old. I didn't develop good study habits, but I certainly had good work habits.

I was fired only once in my life and that was when I was thirteen years old and working in another service station and parking lot for a friend of my father's named Mac McAlister. Part of my job was parking cars, and I made a very small dent in a fender of one and was immediately fired. I had an after-school job for two years delivering *Tucson Citizen* newspapers on my bicycle. I rode twenty miles every day and built up strong leg muscles. I had to memorize the addresses of about 125 houses, which I found very difficult and stressful. I never got an allowance, but always did family chores and sometimes contributed money to the family when I could.

All members of our family worked at part-time jobs. My mother sold real estate and raised chickens—more than just a handful of supplementary hens. We had hundreds of chickens, and as a boy I spent

David, Bill, Peggy, and General, about 1935.

one or two hours per day feeding, cleaning up, and collecting eggs, which we sold. We boarded children who had been sent to Arizona for their health. We had a fairly nice two-bedroom, contractor-built house, and two rather primitive apartments in the back, which we had

Hervey William Lowell

Bill Lowell was a person who loved life. He was big, handsome, and athletic. He was the least serious member of our family, but the one with the most friends—and girlfriends. Bill was part of the class of '44 at the University of Arizona, and played on the football team. But World War II was at hand, and in 1943, several months after signing up with the Marine Corps, he left school for training. On March 8, 1945, just two weeks after his twenty-second birthday, Bill was killed in the Battle of Iwo Jima, a battle in which most of the Marine's Fifth Division junior officers lost their lives.

Bill Lowell with Thumper at house on Ft. Lowell Road in Tucson, 1943, and in Marine officer training at Camp Lejeune, NC.

built ourselves. One was called "the lean-to." When times got especially tough we rented out one of the two apartments or sometimes rented the large house and moved into the backyard apartments. I made a consistent and determined effort to help my parents. Although our relationship was often tense when I was growing up, I became a friend and protector of my mother in her later years. My wife, Edith, also did much to help my mother.

My parents were too busy with their own problems trying to survive the Depression to pay much attention to my education. Unsupervised with regard to education, I found I could get average grades without doing homework. This didn't catch up with me until my first year in college.

In my eyes, my big brother was always the star. In my early years I was overshadowed by Bill, who was bigger, more athletic, had more friends, and was more handsome. He was a hard act to follow with blond curly hair; my own hair was straight and dark brown, almost black. He was a starter on the Tucson High football team and played on the University of Arizona football team for three years. I went to the Mansfield School when Bill was in high school, and after school, I

A group of Bill's friends at the University of Arizona. From left, Chuck Bagby, Bill, Bob Miller, and Don McCain, 1944.

Bill Lowell, third from left standing, and tent mates in officer training school. Four of these seven were killed in the Battle of Iwo Jima, 1944.

often rode my bike over to Tucson High to watch him practice football. Because he was older, we didn't do a lot together as children, but we got along well, and Bill took me hunting with him and his friends on occasion, an important activity that we all thought was great.

In 1942 Bill was the Border Conference shot put champion. He enlisted in the Marine Corps and was called up in June 1943, went through a pre-OCS university program, then into officer training at Camp Lejeune, North Carolina, and was commissioned second lieutenant. A book called *Iwo Jima* has a section on the battle in which he died, titled "How the Fifth Division Lost Its Officers." His death was a tragedy in our family that never healed. Edith and I sponsored a memorial at the University of Arizona for the members of the 1942 Football Team who were killed in WWII. The memorial has a bust of Bill.

Early in the summer of 1944 I volunteered to help my Uncle John manage his cattle ranch in Peck Canyon, Arizona, because both his sons had enlisted in the service, leaving him shorthanded. I was sixteen years old and my work at the ranch consisted of various manual chores and lots of work on horseback herding cattle. I worked without pay. On one occasion I remember Uncle John and I were trying to put a large Brahma bull through the gate and fence but when I got off the horse the bull charged me and my horse, and we had to scramble to get out of the way. Finally, on the third try, I was able to open the gate, and we got the bull through the fence.

One evening when I was working at the ranch, my aunt found a tarantula under her bed, and I volunteered to take care of it, being a heroic sixteen-year-old boy. We did not have electricity at the ranch at that time and I got a weapon and a glass kerosene lamp and put them on the cement floor next to the bed and then crawled under the bed to attack the tarantula. When I looked up at the tarantula it was staging a counterattack and was only a few inches from my nose. I retreated rapidly and tipped the lamp over and broke it and the kerosene caught on fire making a pool of flame, which upset my aunt even more than the original tarantula problem. After some frantic scrambling, we were able to put out the fire and eventually got rid of the tarantula.

At the end of July, when it appeared that the ranch would operate well enough without my help for the rest of the summer, I agreed to make a trip to Mexico with my friend Eddie. I had already been bitten by the mineral bug.

Summer Jobs

On August 1, 1944, Edwin (Eddie) King and I left Tucson by bus on a trip to the Sierra Madre Mountains in Chihuahua, Mexico, to collect rare mineral specimens, whose sale we hoped would finance part of our coming university expenses. We traveled by bus to Chihuahua City, Chihuahua, and from there by a Mexican train to Creel, Chihuahua, and from Creel to the Monterde gold mine in the high Sierra Madres. The trip from Tucson to Chihuahua was not noteworthy, but when we left Chihuahua on a backcountry railroad we found a place in the first-class (still low-cost) car, which was one of the total of six cars. It shortly after became very interesting, and a little worrisome. First, the roadbed was in very bad condition, causing the car to lurch over to the right or left frequently. Second, the roadbed restricted our speed to 5 to 15 mph, and once we thought about jumping out and walking or trotting to race with the train. Another worry was the possibility of a bandit attack a la Butch Cassidy and the Sundance Kid. Someone must have thought this was a serious possibility because we had a number of Mexican soldiers on the train to protect us. Eddie asked one soldier if he could see his rifle, and he found that there was a narrow piece of cotton inside the length of the barrel. The soldier said this was to keep the barrel clean in case they were inspected. Eddie commented that this would also cause the barrel to explode if the soldier decided to shoot at a bandit.

With us in the first-class car were two *gente decente*, sons of rich rancher "aristocrats." At that time, small cadet-sized beer bottles, about eight ounces, were popular in Mexico, and one of the ranchers' sons began buying rounds of beer for themselves, a couple of other important people, and Eddie and me. Business was brisk, because every time we all sang or told a joke (all in Spanish) or had to go to the bathroom, we would set our bottles down on the floor and the next lurch would cause them all to spill. After a while Eddie and I offered to buy a round, but the principal "aristocrat" switched languages and in a distinctly unfriendly voice said in English, "I won't drink anything bought with gringo money." This was enough to stop me and Eddie, but the number two "aristocrat" then spoke up about paying and was shouted down. After the next lurch he mentioned paying again, and at this point the number one "aristocrat" produced a pistol and aimed it at the number two along with a lot of profanity and a promise to kill him. After considering this very carefully the number two "aristocrat" changed the subject and we changed back to songs and jokes.

Some time later we arrived in Creel, near the mouth of Barranca del Cobre in the Sierra Madre of Chihuahua, Mexico. There we met Eddie's father, Clarence King, who owned and managed the Monterde Mine. Mr. King had a heavy-duty four-wheel-drive pickup (which was very rare in 1944). We then drove for two days into the mountains, mostly along one running stream, which we crossed frequently and got stuck in sixteen times by my count. Each time, we jacked the vehicle up and put rocks under the wheels, and a couple of times used a "Spanish windlass," which is a long pole cut from a tree limb. A rope is tied near the end of the pole and the other end is tied to the front bumper and then the rope is wrapped around a tree trunk, after which you walk in a circle around the tree using the long lever arm of the pole. It worked each time, but our progress was slow. Once there were several easy miles on one bank of the stream and we speeded up to 5 or 10 mph. Along the way, we passed a Tarahumara Indian who, for a stunt, ran behind the truck, keeping up for a couple of miles. The Tarahumaras are famous distance runners. At one point, after driving through a deep spot in the river, we had to drain water out of the gas line. Some gas floated on a big puddle. As we were leaving, Eddie set the "water" on fire to amaze two Indians who had come by to see what we were doing. At the end of the first day we stopped beside a cornfield and picked some ears of corn and cooked them in a campfire, and Mr. King also had something else for us to eat, and we slept on the ground in sleeping bags as we did most of the next ten days.

We arrived at the Monterde Mine the next day, and during dinner Mr. King told us a strange story. In Mexico the Spanish missions were staffed by Jesuit priests until about 1767, when the Spanish king decreed that all the Jesuit fathers be expelled from New Spain, to be replaced by members of the Franciscan order. The story was that the Jesuit fathers were operating a rich gold mine near Monterde, which they covered up before the Franciscans arrived, leaving various belongings expecting to return soon, but they never returned. Mr. King said that a couple of years earlier he had made a trip on horseback with several guides, including a local Tarahumara. Sitting around the fire after dinner, the local man said he knew the location of a cave not far away in which various things including Spanish armor and swords were hidden. Mr. King told him, "I think you are lying," hoping this might result in learning more about the lost mine. The man jumped up and walked

35

David Lowell, age 16,
1944, at Areponapuchic,
Chihuahua, on a mineral
specimen collection trip.

off in the dark. In the morning at breakfast he appeared with a book, which I have seen, that he said came from the cave. It was a church manual of some kind, which a priest had used as a notebook to record births and deaths and marriages among the Indians, with dates corresponding to the Jesuit period. My conclusion was that there is probably a hidden "cave," which is the Jesuit mine, not a rich gold mine—but nobody knows.

A little farther along the canyon, past the Monterde Mine, was a small village called Areponapuchic, not far from the place where the mineral specimens we were after occurred—doubly crystallized calcite. So we hitched a ride to Areponapuchic. At that time a railroad line was in construction from Creel to Los Mochis near the Pacific Coast. (In fact, work on this railroad had begun in the late nineteenth century, but because of lack of money, the Mexican revolution, and the difficult mountainous terrain, it wasn't completed until 1961.) The village is now along the railroad line, which is popular with tourists. From Areponapuchic we rented horses and got a guide to visit the calcite site, which is down a steep slope into Barranca del Cobre or Copper Canyon, which in some respects resembles the Grand Canyon—and in some places is as deep as the Grand Canyon. We passed caves in which Tarahumara people were living. We also passed Tarahumara living in log huts or cabins. Passing one habitation, the women and children ran into the forest, but the men stood their ground to talk to us.

Eventually we arrived at a small mine producing large, optical-grade calcite crystals up to a foot in length. During World War II, calcite from this locality was used in the manufacture of gun sights. We collected a large quantity of doubly crystallized, arrowhead-shaped mineral specimens not usable for gun sights but very rare. We camped on a ledge in the steep slope near the mine. The next morning as we were working in the mine, two of the Indian workers came up to us, but they were shy and diffident and didn't know Spanish so we couldn't communicate. Finally they went away and before long several loud explosions went off in the mine less than a hundred feet away. What they had wanted to tell us was they had spitted a round of blast holes and we had better get the hell out! However, we were not hurt, and at the end of the day we proceeded back up the canyon, arriving at Areponapuchic before dark.

Back in the village, Eddie and I inquired around for a place to stay and found that the only house that would take visitors was also having a wake for a deceased relative, but we moved in anyway. We stayed two days and we both had cases of Montezuma's Revenge, picked up when we ran out of water at the calcite mine and drank from a spring. In the house we slept on the floor and collected a large number of fleas in our sleeping bags. The next day while waiting for some kind of ride back to Creel, we found "flea boxes" for sale in the village store and bought two. When we climbed into our sleeping bags the next night and put the boxes next to our feet there was a frantic exodus of fleas crawling and hopping the whole length of the bag, leaving us in peace, but with a distinctive odor. A large flatbed truck came through town the next day and for a small fee we and about twenty other people had the pleasure of sitting on the truck bed with only a large rope to hang onto during a daylong wild ride along the canyon to Creel. We found a primitive hotel and a restaurant run by a Chinese man named José Mayo. José was married to two Mexican ladies who helped him in the restaurant, and the Chinese food was all cooked in a wok and tasted very good compared with our previous meals.

And so it was that about six o'clock in the afternoon of August 15, 1944, in the small town of Creel near the mouth of Barranca del Cobre in the Sierra Madre Mountains of Chihuahua, Mexico, we two young American pre-mining engineering students about sixteen years old and two moderately attractive young Mexican women, a little older, were walking, or skipping, or dancing, down the middle of the town's single dusty street between rows of adobe houses and small shops. The adobe buildings were old and looked partly melted where many years of rain had rounded their corners. It was pleasantly warm, and the town of Creel showed only a little evidence that it was occupied. An occasional couple was walking on the single wooden sidewalk and two shopkeepers were sitting on chairs outside their shops.

In Barranca del Cobre we had found a rare form of twinned optical calcite crystals. We were feeling, or at least I felt, an exhilaration based on the instinct some people have to look for and find hidden treasure. We also felt the exhilaration of returning from two weeks of sleeping on the ground, and walking long distances, and riding horses for hours, and catching rides on a flatbed truck, and eating bad food and getting Montezuma's Revenge.

The other exhilarating experience was that this was the first time we had had an excess of beer and the first time we had been asked to dance by "B Girls" in exchange for watered-down drinks, which seemed like a manly experience. It was as close as I had ever been to a woman and limited groping was allowed. Our two drinking and dancing companions finally asked us to buy them dinner. The bar was at the top of a hill at one end of the town and the restaurant was in the middle of the town and we launched forth, arm in arm, singing "Soy de Chihuahua" (I am from Chihuahua) and following a sinuous path down the middle of the street doing (badly) a dance step to go with the song. Eddie observed "Aplauso!" and I noticed that the townspeople were clapping at our performance.

The boxes of calcite fishtail twins that we were carrying home might net us a few hundred dollars, which to us seemed like a fortune. Neither Eddie nor I was from an affluent family. Remember that inflation over the past seventy years translates one hundred dollars then into one thousand dollars now. I remember marveling about our good fortune and imagining that instead of finding a fortune of three hundred dollars, it might, with other targets and other plans, be ten thousand dollars, or a hundred thousand dollars, or a million, or a hundred million dollars! It was beyond my imagination to think that my future ventures would actually produce treasures worth more than these amounts. The other idea, which only momentarily flitted through my mind, was that our success had a value apart from financial gain. Finding treasure might be an enormous pleasure and satisfaction more valuable than money.

Our adventure in Creel was a sort of coming-of-age event, and for me the Sierra Madre expedition was also a veiled glimpse into that compulsion to look for hidden treasure that was to control most of the rest of my career and life. It also successfully funded most of my expenses for the next school year.

In the spring of 1945 I graduated from high school and got a job, beginning June 10, working on a fire crew for the U.S. Forest Service. Our camp was near the Peña Blanca Dam near the Mexican border in southern Arizona. I was available a week before the team was organized, and my cousin Douglas Cumming was at that time working as a forest fire lookout at the Atascosa Peak lookout site. I hiked up to the site and spent one week at the lookout, and while I was there the lookout station was struck several times by lightning because it was during the monsoon rain season and it was located on top of Atascosa Peak. The cables to the lightning rod on the lookout cabin glowed with Saint Elmo's fire before the lightning strikes, which were very loud and very scary.

At the end of the week I hiked from the lookout to the Peña Blanca camp, a distance of about eight miles over very rough country with no trails, and arrived to meet the other members of the fire crew. The crew consisted of myself, Johnny O'Keefe, and Jim Hathaway. Jim later became an appellate judge and Johnny became an insurance executive. We lived in an army tent and had a woodstove and no refrigerator. For transportation we had an old Model A Ford pickup, and when there were no fires in progress we spent our time building trails for the Forest Service. We did our own cooking and drove out to Nogales to get food about once a week. Johnny O'Keefe was an orphan who lived with his grandmother in Nogales, Arizona, and I spent the night in his grandmother's house when we went to Nogales, usually arriving late Saturday. The following day, Sunday, she would insist that I attend Catholic Mass with Johnny. This certainly didn't hurt me.

The fire crew job was fairly demanding physically, but working in the field was very enjoyable. We built trails with picks and shovels and occasionally built barbed wire fences and on two occasions fought forest fires caused by lightning strikes. In one of these fires a local person who was hired to help with the fire had a heart attack and died and was taken out in the forest ranger's sedan. On another occasion the forest ranger trained us for firefighting by intentionally starting a fire that burned rapidly up a hillside, and we were expected to put it out with flappers and shovels and axes, which we did with considerable difficulty.

On one occasion Johnny O'Keefe, who was a very sociable person, arranged for several girlfriends to come out from Nogales to have a picnic with us on the weekend. At this time I was very shy and frightened by young ladies, and Jim Hathaway was even more frightened. He retreated out into the darkness when the girls arrived, but he had a large-caliber revolver which he fired several times defiantly out in the dark to indicate that while frightened away from the picnic he still had his self-respect.

That summer I had my first date with a girl. Her name was Margaret Wise. I also drank beer for the third time. At the end of the summer Johnny O'Keefe and I made a trip to California on a bus and vis-

Margaret Lowell outside her apartment in San Francisco in her lieutenant junior grade World War II Navy Wave uniform on V-J Day, August 15, 1945.

ited some of my relatives and some of his relatives in the general area of Anaheim, California, and then Santa Cruz, California. We stayed there with my Uncle Bill, who was a bank president in Watsonville, California. He had a lovely house, and his daughter Mary Lee, who was my first cousin, was an attractive young lady who I immediately fell in love with, with no benefit to myself.

From Watsonville we traveled to San Francisco where my sister Peggy was a lieutenant junior grade in the Navy Waves. We were there when V-J Day occurred at the end of the war with Japan. A humorous incident occurred while we were staying with my sister. She had a bed that folded up into the wall, and we were trying to help her manipulate the bed and inadvertently folded her inside the bed in the wall. Fortunately, we were able to extract her from the wall with no injuries. Another incident which was interesting for me was that she took me to a Navy pistol range at the Golden Gate Military Park and I qualified as "expert" with a Navy pistol. This was possible because I'd had lots of previous practice shooting pistols. I have to admit Peggy also qualified as "expert."

Earlier in the summer of 1945, my best Tucson High friend, Bob Griffin, and I had decided to enlist in the U.S. Marine Corps. We made a trip to Phoenix and passed our physicals and Bob, who was a year older than I, was able to sign his enlistment papers, but I was unable to sign mine without my parents' consent. I returned to Tucson and my parents signed the enlistment papers, reluctantly because my brother had been killed at Iwo Jima about five months earlier. The same week we had our Marine physicals, the first atom bomb was dropped on Hiroshima and this made me think the war was about to end. Then the second atom bomb was dropped and it became clear that the war was ending, so I didn't complete my enlistment. Bob Griffin went into boot camp training at Barstow, California, and was in the Marine Corps for about six months. He was discharged with quite a few perquisites, like the GI Bill, because he had enlisted while the war was still in progress. I have wondered ever since whether I would have been better off or worse off to have done the same because it would have given me financial benefits as well as more maturity when I entered the university.

On June 2, 1946, I made another mineral specimen collection trip to Mexico, this time with Dan King, older brother of Eddie, with whom I had made a collecting trip two years before. Dan and I were both students in the Arizona College of Mines. We went by bus to El Paso, Texas, then by train to Chihuahua City and by train to Creel and found that primitive bus service had been established from Creel to Areponapuchic since my visit in 1944. This provided transportation for us and for the chickens and pigs and other passengers. We traveled by foot to the specimen site where our previous shipment of fishtail double-twinned calcite crystals had been mined. We had hoped to have a second business success with more calcite crystals and were fortunate to do so.

From there our route back was by bus to Creel, then first-class rail (but still cheap) to the mainline, which continued north through Chihuahua City and on to the rail station serving Los Lamentos. Steam locomotives were used at that time in Mexico. The route from Creel by rail was to a section house and water supply station on the main north–south line at a point south of Chihuahua City. There we waited for a train that was already one and a half days late. After several hours a southbound freight train pulled in to take on water. There was a hole in the firebox of this one, with a tongue of flames reaching the ground, and there was a hole in the water tank in the rear part of the steam locomotive. The train crew had solved half of their problem by coupling a tank car full of water behind the locomotive with a hose connecting to the locomotive tank. The freight train was stopped twenty minutes and then charged out, leaving two burning ties in the middle of a large pool of water. So much for the government railroad management.

After three more hours, our northbound train arrived and we departed through Chihuahua City and north to the section house from where the road to Los Lamentos turned eastward. There were a few houses at the Railroad Section House, and we found someone with an old automobile who was willing to drive us about twenty miles to Los Lamentos. I don't remember our source of information, but I do remember that there was a sinister aura connected to Los Lamentos, which means "the sorrowful cries."

We arrived with no advance arrangements and had to find a place to live for about eight days and find a guide and helper to take us around in the mines. We assumed that the name Los Lamentos was related to the many fatal accidents that had occurred there. In 1946 during our visit there was a group of about fifteen miners with a lease agreement scavenging small amounts of high-grade mainly lead ore left after the large-scale exploitation in about 1910. There was said to have originally been a total of about fifty miles of underground mine workings. It had been operated on a large scale in the early 1900s, which was also the time of the Mexican Revolution. Mine safety was very low on the scale of importance at that time, and 2x4 crosses had been erected under-

David and underground helper at Los Lamentos, Chihuahua, 1946. His hat was rescued from the garbage to serve as an underground hard hat. When they left, their friends grabbed it and did a Mexican Hat Dance.

ground at the sites of fatal accidents. We saw about ten of these, and there must have been many more.

We made an arrangement for room and board with an old Mexican couple who lived in an adobe house with a dirt floor. Two pigs also resided in the house and the door was always open. We had two well-used, homemade canvas cots to sleep on, and the food was typical of that eaten by poor Mexicans at that time, largely frijole beans and tortillas and occasional tacos or enchiladas. The word went out the day we arrived that we needed a guide, and a cheerful twenty-year-old young man named José turned up. The next day we went underground in search of cubical wulfenite, an orange-colored lead molybdenum oxide with distinctive cube-shaped crystals, and red vanadinite, a lead vanadium mineral. Both of these were rare and valuable in the crystal forms present in Los Lamentos.

The first day was a reconnaissance day, to explore the mine for mineral specimen localities and, as a secondary consideration (remember we were eighteen and nineteen years old), we studied the safety aspect of working in the mine. We looked at alternate escape routes and "heavy ground" areas where there was evidence that the "back" (roof) might be about to come down, indicated by trickles of sand or pebble-sized rock fragments or forty-year-old partly rotten support timbers "groaning." Some old mines are deathly quiet, but Los Lamentos was a noisy, spooky mine.

It was a flat, irregular deposit, which we estimated to be about 8,000 by 2,000 feet in horizontal dimensions, with an overall thickness of about a hundred feet, but these dimensions were hard to guess because of the very bad condition of the mine. There were many places where the "back" had collapsed, and when we were in it, there was an ever-present danger of being hurt or having access cut off by a new rockfall. The average height of a Mexican miner in 1910 was probably about five feet five inches tall, but Dan was about five feet ten and I was about five feet eleven. We had slipped up and arrived without hard hats. I was wearing a felt hat, but bumped my head painfully a number of times the first day walking through mine workings designed for workers six inches shorter. The mining activity while we were there was managed by a German gentleman over six feet tall and he had an even worse problem, but had found in a war surplus store in El Paso, Texas, a tanker's helmet designed to protect soldiers operating tanks from bumping their heads. When we left the mine the first day I inquired about hats and *cascos* (hard hats), but there weren't any to buy or borrow. There was a garbage dump near the mine portal and there I found a worn-out, rather stiff straw hat which fit fairly well. I cut the brim off to a width of about two inches and turned the brim up all around and it worked surprisingly well to protect my head. When we left a week later we were on friendly terms with everyone who worked in the mine, and when I walked out the last day, they seized my hat and had an impromptu Mexican Hat Dance in front of the portal.

We decided on a mineral collecting strategy, which was to separate and work in two different locations in the mine, with José going back and forth and carrying boxes of specimens out of the mine and keeping track of both of us. This worked fine until about the fourth day.

The Mexican miners tended to be very superstitious, and the 2x4 crosses and the cave-ins and groaning timbers provided good raw material for ghost stories. Two or three of the miners at different times told me about ghosts in the mine, and about a particularly troublesome fellow who had had his head cut off in an accident and ever since had been bumbling around in the dark. When we were alone we laughed at these stories; that is, until the fourth day.

We each had a carbide light. Carbide lights are reasonably reliable, but there is a tendency for the burner to plug. Normally acetylene gas flows through the burner and produces a tongue of flame less than a quarter-inch thick and about one inch long. A sophisticated miner like me would have a wire from an old window screen fastened to the reflector of his carbide light and when it plugged and went out he would be able, even in pitch dark, to find the wire and the burner and insert the wire and unplug it. Most of the time, when it was unplugged you could easily smell the acetylene gas coming out and ignite the lamp using the flint igniter fastened to the reflector—except that this didn't always work and sometimes you had to use other measures that couldn't be done in the pitch dark with no tools. This time, my light plugged and after a few minutes trying to fix it in the dark I gave up, knowing that Dan and José would come looking for me in about two hours, at a time we agreed to meet for lunch. My only choice was to get as comfortable as possible and wait. I couldn't see my watch and didn't want to move around because I was on the steep slope of loose rock in a cave-in.

I was just fine for about five minutes. Then I started cataloging the directions toward groaning timbers (which I hadn't noticed when my light was working), and the directions to sounds of little pebbles occasionally rolling down the other side of the cave-in fifty or one hundred feet away. And other unidentifiable faint noises. After thirty minutes or an hour I was absolutely certain that the headless miner was in the same mine opening with me, and while he was moving in a somewhat random direction (after all he didn't have a head), he seemed to be getting closer and closer. This was not in any way a comfortable situation—it was a nightmare. After a very, very, long time, when I estimated he was only twenty or thirty feet away, I saw a light and was overjoyed to greet my two compadres! It took only five minutes to fix my carbide light when I could see it. Together we finished our collection for the day, but I was especially happy to return to our humble lodgings when we were done.

I have to admit that I was a little revolted living in a house with two pigs, and one day when one was near the front door, in a fit of pique and meanness, I gave him a little kick in his rear end. To my great surprise he spun around and counterattacked, and while I wasn't quite bitten, the click of his or her teeth was very loud. I immediately caved in and backed away, settling for a return to the mutual nonaggression treaty.

Our old couple had a clock which they set every day based on the time when the sun appeared, and they complained that the clock registered a different time each day. Dan wanted to give them a little astronomy lecture, but I talked him out of it. Though our "board" consisted of the simple Mexican fare, it was tasty enough. Breakfast every morning was what I thought was a mixture of frijole beans and rice. It was okay, but the rice was a little hard and crispy. A day before we left, out of curiosity, I isolated a rice grain on my spoon and looked at it carefully. It had little legs and little eyes. I turned to Dan and said, "Do you know we have been eating weevils?" He said, "Yeah I noticed that a couple of days ago, but didn't want to worry you." We survived for eight days without getting sick. We learned that a little ancient Chevrolet bus passed every several days from Los Lamentos to the railroad station house, and we timed our departure to catch it. I was sad to say good-bye to the friends I had made at Lamentos, but didn't miss the headless miner at all.

We arrived back in Tucson a week before classes began in September 1946 with time to sort and wrap mineral specimens. We felt very satisfied with the summer's work. We had a large number of double-twinned calcite crystals, vanadinite and cubical wulfenite crystal specimens, and very rare adomite specimens. More than the significant value of the specimens, I felt satisfaction in having successfully followed complicated directions in very remote locations and discovered known and new sites. Another exploration success.

In 1947 my summer job was at the Idarado Mine in Colorado. I hitchhiked to Ouray, Colorado, and then to the job site at the Idarado Mine, which was at an elevation of 11,000 feet in a forest of fir trees. It was an underground mine with ore that contained copper, gold, and silver. I showed up at the mine the morning after I arrived in Ouray and there was a line of itinerant miners applying for jobs ("the rustling line"); when it got to my turn I talked to the mine foreman and he hired me. A physical exam or proof of previous employment as a miner was not required. I may have gotten a little special consideration at times because I was a mining engineering student, but the primary qualifications were not education but strength, skill, and determination.

A couple of times they let me hold an end of the tape on a survey crew, but mostly I worked in the production part of the operation as a contract miner or a timberman in an underground mine. I lived in the bunkhouse where I was the owner of 50 percent of one bunk, which was occupied on the night shift by someone I never met, and there was a shower bath that consisted of two valves, one of which gave you ice cold melted snow water and the other live steam. We soon became expert at mixing the two to have nonlethal water temperature for our shower. We ate at the mess hall, where the food was reasonably good and abundant and sometimes I had four meals depending on what tasks I had in the mine.

The Idarado Mine was a real roughneck mine. The mine manager—I believe his name may have been Fred Wise—claimed, probably untruthfully, that he had never had a man working for him that he couldn't whip, and there were a couple of fistfights to continue this tradition. One Monday morning most of the men on my work shift were in jail in Silverton, Colorado, a nearby mining town—something about who were the toughest miners. My direct supervisor was a fellow named Bob Cockle. He was a young engineer who had just gotten out of the army. He came down with pneumonia while I was at the mine and died the next day. He probably could have been saved if the company had moved him down to Ouray or a lower elevation.

I worked on a contract mine crew where we were paid on the basis of the number of cubic feet of ore that we produced, and we earned a bonus over the day's pay rate. There were five of us on the contract and one fellow was referred to as Big Joe and another as Little Joe. Big Joe was a Hispanic fellow, a middle-aged nice guy who was about my height. Little Joe was about six feet three inches and had just gotten out of the paratroops and was bulging with muscles. We had to carry very heavy equipment up into the stope (an open space left when mineral is removed), including a percussion drill, which was the stoper. Another hydraulic drill we used was a leyner, which mounted on a column bar. The leyner had two parts, the column bar, which operated like a jack between the floor and the ceiling, and the pneumatic drill, which clamped to the column bar. Both of these parts weighed about 120 pounds. They were very hard to transport because we had to climb ladders and cross broken rock in the muck pile. One day I was carrying one of these things and Little Joe was carrying the other. I was stumbling and making slow progress, and he impatiently grabbed my piece and carried both of them up. I was relieved, as it felt like I didn't have enough arms and legs to secure myself, let alone that piece of the leyner. I was considerably stronger and huskier then than now, but that work was pretty vigorous stuff.

I was making something like two or three dollars an hour but with a bonus if we mined a lot of ore. We were not charged for room and board. It was permissible to work two shifts instead of one, and I tried to arrange to do that because I was supporting myself in college, but a suitable second shift job never opened.

The company consulting metallurgist was Frank McQuiston. Frank came to the mine and I don't remember how I met him, but somebody, maybe Bob Cockle, said to him, "This is a mining engineering student from the University of Arizona." Frank McQuiston was a famous metallurgist and also a very nice guy. He came by the university later that year; I don't think I saw him at Arizona but he talked to Dean

Thomas Chapman and told the dean that everybody at Idarado thought I was doing a very good job. Dean Chapman told me that in one of those inspirational lectures which ended with "Why don't you do better here?"

Education in the College of Mines

I entered the University of Arizona in early September 1945, a month after the end of World War II. I was admitted to the College of Mines, which was somewhat competitive, because I scored in the top decile in the university placement test. I got in okay, but I had some trouble staying in the College of Mines for the next two years. In September 1945 the university rushed to put together a football team made up mostly of men back from the war. I had not played high school football, but I tried out and was accepted for the varsity university team as a seventeen-year-old recruit. I played on the UA football team in 1945 and the spring practice of 1946. I was on the varsity team, but was on either the second or third string. I played defensive back and long snapper and played in some games. I really enjoyed football and steadily improved during the time I played. Boys from age four on enjoy bumping into other boys and the same was true for me. Arizona won every game they played in the hastily arranged schedule in the fall of 1945.

At the same time, I got some experience going out with girls, and I was on the school paper staff (delivering papers and meeting female writers) and was enrolled in ROTC. Sergeant Franklin, who was in charge of the rifle team, noticed that I was a good rifle shot and invited me to become a member of the rifle team. I remember at one point I was shooting number two on the team and our team was number two in the country, but I am not sure that was true all the time. I rode Brahma bulls and was in the wild mule riding contest in the university rodeo. All in all I had lots of fun in the first two semesters, until the chickens came home to roost and the dean of the College of Mines said it didn't look good for me to stay. He criticized me frequently for having demonstrated the capacity to be an engineer, as indicated by my placement scores, but being about to flunk out because of sloth and lack of seriousness. The competition was particularly difficult because almost all my classmates were men who had come back from the service and were more mature and more serious than I was.

While at the university I always had summer jobs and part-time jobs while taking classes. I only got one F (in differential calculus), but I got quite a few Cs and Ds. I became a good friend of Dean Thomas Chapman's because the university put out two lists every semester—a pre-delinquent list and a delinquent list. If you were on either "D list" you were obliged to have a conversation with the dean of the college, and so for this reason I became very well acquainted with Dean Chapman. However, Dean Chapman was one of the people in my life who had faith in me and went out of his way to help me in school and later. I have often thought in later years how proud he would have been if he had lived to witness my professional success.

I played spring football in 1946. At that time when you went out for football it occupied at least fourteen hours a week of your time. Most of the other players were studying agriculture or other relatively easy courses, but the engineering course required a lot more study time. After spring football I had one of my conferences with Dean Chapman and he said, "Dave, in my ten years as dean of the College of Mines, I have had one student who played football and graduated on time. I am absolutely certain that you are not going to be the second one." I thought this over and in spite of the fact that I enjoyed football more than almost anything that I had done, the awful thought of having a year added to my university sentence convinced me to give up football.

In my freshman year I had pretty much shot myself in the foot with my poor performance; this haunted me later. My work ethic improved somewhat and also my grades were better in the sophomore year. By my junior year I started to do distinctly better as a student and my senior year I completed forty-eight credit hours with fairly good grades (thirty-four hours was normal for an engineer). At the beginning of our last year we were asked to submit a plan for our senior year, and I was determined to graduate in four years.

My advisor, the professor with whom I had to discuss the program

Dean Thomas Chapman was a famous professor and metallurgist, and he held patents relating to gold recovery. He was also a very good dean and without his help and guidance David probably would not have graduated.

in which I planned to take forty-eight credit hours for my senior year, was a hard-boiled short-spoken humorless fellow. You had to present your program and get it approved, and I presented my program and he looked at it and didn't say anything. I said, "Well, what do you think about that?" and he said, "I think you're a damn fool." I was able to complete all these hours during the year, including several courses taken by examination, but at graduation time I wasn't sure I was going to graduate.

During the time I was a student at the university my parents contributed a total of less than five hundred dollars over four years and the rest of my expenses came from money I earned in summer jobs or part-time jobs. After I was married, during my senior year at the university, my family contributed a lot of eggs, butter, and turkey soup, and we lived on Edith's salary as secretary for the English Department.

It was a calculated risk to pay my fee for a cap and gown because a grade point average of a certain number was required for graduation, and mine was right on the borderline. Three years earlier I had flunked my differential calculus course and I had to take it again my last semester. It was taught by a young lady who I thought was a very nice person. When I took my final exam, this was the swing course: I knew what grades I was getting in the other courses and that if I got a B in calculus I would graduate and if I got a C in calculus I would have to come back for another semester. This was a serious problem and I went out to a florist and bought an orchid, which I presented to my teacher along with my final exam, and I explained to her what my problem was. I don't remember her name, but I will be forever grateful. She made no comment, but I got the B, which I may have deserved.

In addition to Dean Chapman, who went out of his way to find part-time and summer jobs for me, there was a mining professor, Harry Krumlough, who was helpful. I remember Professor Cunningham in metallurgy, Edwin McKee in geology, and Professor Strickler, who taught an Economics for Engineers course. Economics was a field that I seemed to have some talent for, and of the 110 students in Economics for Engineers, I got the best grade on the final exam, but that was not representative of my other courses.

My closest classmate friend in the College of Mines was Dick Moolick, who later became president of the Phelps Dodge Mining

Bill Campbell and Whoopie, hunting trip in 1947. This vehicle was purchased for $25. It was jointly owned by David and Bill Campbell, but often would not start.

Company and who led the mining industry battle against the United Mine Workers union, which was a decisive point that saved the copper industry in the United States and indirectly saved the jobs of thousands of miners. Dick had been a Navy pilot in the Pacific and was eight years older than I, but we agreed on many things. He named the two of us "the back row boys" and neither of us made an impressive academic mark at the university but we both became well known later. Other University of Arizona friends were the two students I roomed with: first, Jack Magee, who after his freshman year went to West Point and later flew jets in the Korean War and the Viet Nam War. We still exchange visits. My other roommate was Bill Campbell, an electrical engineer who had an impressive career, but passed away a few years ago. I also dated several co-eds (and married one, Edith Sykes). My football coach, Mike Casteel, taught me something about football and a lot about tough discipline. At the time, I was convinced that all football coaches had to be mean.

One of my mines courses was Underground Surveying, which was carried out in old mines in Tombstone, Arizona. It was very interesting and somewhat challenging to carry a survey line from the surface to a point a hundred feet in depth through incline shafts and through drifts to a location point on the hundred-foot level, then through incline shafts and vertical shafts back to the surface. We stayed in the Tombstone High School, which was not in session at the time of the course, and we drank beer in one of the oldest and most famous bars in Arizona.

CHAPTER TWO

Marriage to Edith, 1948

In the spring semester of my freshman year, my friend and roommate, Jack Magee, asked me to fill in on a date he couldn't keep with a co-ed named Edith Sykes. She and I had met on a skiing trip to a ski run on Mt. Lemmon, a 9,150-foot-high mountain on the northeast side of Tucson. Jack had gone out with Edith before, and all three of us were on this trip to Mt. Lemmon. I was never a very good skier, and I ended up not skiing but running the rope tow, because it was sort of a do-it-yourself arrangement and I knew something about gasoline engines.

We had a good time on our date, and kept on dating. One night, we went to a western-style dance at the old Blue Moon. As the band played "To Each His Own," we danced slowly around in a trance, both feeling a wonderful new sensation. This led to a proposal. Edith recalls that I told her that I wasn't in a position to ask her to marry me but when I was, would she then say yes? She said she would. So we were engaged in 1947. We were married on March 29, 1948.

Edith's father was Glenton Sykes, who was also a University of Arizona College of Engineering graduate and who for many years had the job of Tucson City Engineer. Her mother's name was Anna McClusky, and she had moved to Tucson from Kentucky. She also had a University of Arizona degree and taught English at Tucson High School. Edith's sister, Georgiana, is three years younger than Edith and

Edith in 1944, on
pony in 1929, and
at age 2 in 1931.

Edith with Harry Gin and
Bobbie Smail, two of her
best friends, in 1964.

Edith and David in front of the
Sykes' house, and at their wedding, 1948.

Edith and David's wedding ceremony, Grace Church, Tucson, 1948.
Bridesmaids: from left, Roberta Tulin, Alice Gibbs, Bobbie Smail, Carol Ann
Bigglestone, Georgiana Sykes. Best Man: Bill Campbell. Ushers: from left,
Kendall Cumming, Joe Cumming, and Jim Grade.

Edith's mother and father, Anna McClusky Sykes and Glenton Sykes.

later graduated from Harvard School of Medicine. There has been a tradition of scholarship in the family, and Edith was elected to Phi Beta Kappa, Phi Kappa Phi, and several other honorary societies in the university. She recalls that she was surprised when on an early date I told her I admired her grade average.

She earned a BA in anthropology with a minor in geology and in 1965 added an MA in Spanish. Edith is a person naturally liked by

Glenton and his father, Godfrey Sykes, during World War I in England. Glenton was in the British Army.

Anna and Glenton on their honeymoon in a Model T Ford, with earlier form of transportation to the rear. Photographed by Godfrey Sykes on Oracle Road.

The McClusky family in 1918: from left, Aunt Hilda, Grandmother Phoebe, Uncle Boyett, who was in the U.S. Army, Grandfather James, Mother Anna, and Aunt Hazel, in Bowling Green, Kentucky.

everybody, and is a very good diplomat. I often ask her to read a letter or report I have written to supply a "diplomacy check." I think
she is also the kindest person I have known. Her list of talents is long:
she is the best cook I have known, a very successful elementary school
and Spanish teacher, an artist, a successful part-time archaeologist who
has published archaeological studies, a Grade A Mother who has done
an exceptional job raising our three children, and lastly a pretty good
mountain lion hunter, who has been on a dozen hunts and has ridden
horses eleven hours in one day over very rough country without trails!
Her liking for people has led her to participate in auxiliaries such as the
WAAIME (mining), and the Cowbelles (ranching), and several ladies'
golf groups.

Summer Job in Aguas Calientes, Chihuahua, Mexico, with Edith

When Edith married me she was in for a wild ride. Within four months
of our marriage she was on a long mule ride in bandit country in the
Sierra Madres of Mexico, and this was just a prelude to other wild times
to come.

A summer job was arranged for me by Dean Chapman, shortly
after Edith and I were married in March 1948, working for a very small
mining company at a gold mine called Aguas Calientes near Chinipas,
Chihuahua, Mexico, in the mountains near the Chihuahua-Sonora
border. It was my first professional employment. I worked as a mining engineer and was the only professional in the operation. Part of the
summer I filled in for the mill superintendent who was on vacation. I
did some surveying and wrote some reports, but my conclusion was the
mine was more window dressing than substance, and the real objective
was selling stock.

While we were there, Edith and I lived in a one-room "apartment"
with adobe walls, a thatched roof, and a heavy canvas homemade cot
wide enough (barely) for two. Three of us occupied the room: Edith,
me, and an enormous centipede about a foot long and three-quarters of
an inch wide. It would come out occasionally then retreat back into the

Edith and David on horseback trip between Aguas Calientes Mine and town of Chinipas, July 1948.

thatch. At first we tried to kill it, but after a couple of weeks we declared a nonaggression treaty and ignored him.

We had traveled to Aguas Calientes by first taking an AeroMéxico flight to Navojoa, Sonora. The next day we flew in a very old Stinson single-engine airplane piloted by a fellow named Asunción, which means either go up like an airplane, or ascend from the grave as did Christ. In any case he made a good landing at Chinipas in a flat area primarily used for grazing goats. Someone met us with mules for the two-hour ride to the Aguas Calientes camp. The camp consisted of a number of living units in a long, narrow, one-story building. There was also an office and a mess hall; our thatched hut was a hundred feet up the hill from that complex.

In a small gold concentration plant, about 50 tons of ore were treated every twenty-four hours. The final stage of treatment used a "Wilfley table," which separated the heavy minerals out of the concentrate. In this concentrate the heavy metals included magnetite, which is a black iron oxide, and a little free gold. The plant probably only recovered 60 percent of the total gold, but it made a nice black ribbon with a few glints of free gold. I was a mining student who had taken classes and had no experience in metallurgy but was able to improve gold recovery by adjusting metallurgical reagents. The fact that I was able to do this suggests the amateur quality of the whole operation. The same low quality was evident in the mining operation, but Edith and I shrugged our shoulders and enjoyed the adventure, the landscape, and the people, and felt lucky we could communicate in Spanish better than the other staff members.

A letter Edith wrote to her sister from the mining camp gives a good picture of the setting and the social atmosphere.

Dear Georgie,   *July 8, 1948*
(no rain for 3 or 4 days)

Speaking of fiestas, I promised to write you more in detail about the wedding party we attended.

That afternoon we made the memorable raft trip down the river, and upon arrival were very damp. I had my dress in a bag which was not very wet, Dave's trousers were soaked, and he had to be spruced up before appearing at a dance. I borrowed a large flat iron full of hot coals and dried out the trousers in the hotel. This Chinipas hotel is apparently run by a woman and her son—she cooks meals, he tends bar in the cantina in front. It is built around a courtyard where there are a few vines, etc. Large rooms open off the covered arcade. We had one of these— and they are apparently all bare of furniture except for the canvas bed they trundled in and a table and chair. On the chair all bundled up was someone's embroidery—probably belonged to one of the staff—I don't think the hotel has many guests, so the rooms are not kept ready for occupancy. The ceiling of our room was very high and ornate with design—at one time those must have been handsome rooms—and we had an enormous, low window boxed over by the typical iron grill.

We had a good supper at the hotel and then Ramon engineered our invitation to the party—had the young hotel manager escort us over to the home of the bride where a reception was taking place. We talked to the Navarro girls and some others we had met including a Mr. and Mrs. Breach, at whose home we have often been dinner guests (whenever we go in with Don Santiago, who is a pariente of theirs). Mrs. Breach is lovely and very gracious. She has loaned me a sort of allegorical novel about Mexico which I must read.

Most of the guests at the reception were standing in the street as it was too crowded inside, but soon the bride and groom—a most unromantic couple—both homely and he old into the bargain—came out and began to stroll down to the "Casino" where a dance was to be held, followed by the musicians and a strolling crowd—and us. The Casino turned out to be a large room flanked on one side by a courtyard and on the other by a bar. All around the dance floor was a row of chairs for the children and married women. Most of the men stood in the door, in the courtyard, or in the bar. Some of the kids sat on the floor. The bride and groom sat at one end by the orchestra. After the dancing started, the dancers did not sit down or wander away between dances but promenaded around and around the dance floor. The music was pretty good, and Dave and I danced part of the time and spent the rest of it sitting in the nearby plaza to cool off. Also, we wandered around the dark streets a little looking at the ruined houses and high thick walls behind them. About midnight we went home (to the hotel) and went to sleep, the sounds of the dance dim in our ears. But about 3:30 or so I heard an awful uproar in the alley (or street?) outside our window, and then was roused into complete wakefulness by the opening bars of "Traigo mi Cuarenta y Cinco"! Then came a number of waltzes, including "Rosalia"—I think it must have lasted at least an hour—Dave almost went crazy at the last. Despite a decided aura of alcohol which enveloped the whole proceedings and muddled the musicians, I enjoyed it tremendously. A serenade—and outside a genuine Mexican grilled window, too! No. 1 on the hit parade around here is "La Vaca Lechera" which starts off exactly like "Dixie"! We came home the next day.

About a week ago we went in by mule back, and spent the night at the home of the old chiropractor "Doc" Reyes. He lives in solitary peace with two cats on the edge of town. We spent most of our time and ate our meals with Santiago's relatives, the Breaches. They were extremely *hospitable and kind and were also easy to talk to. It's strange how much easier some are to understand than others. All I have talked to are highly complimentary about my Spanish, so be of good cheer. Miguel, the assayer, says I speak more Spanish than Mr. Wallis! I was all puffed up over that, though Mr. W. probably could outdo me in the everyday vocabulary. But his accent—honestly Georgie, he couldn't do worse if he were making an effort to <u>caricature</u> a gringo speaking Spanish. He says "You've got to sound like a gringo"—a stupid statement if I've ever heard one. I am going to keep trying to erase <u>my</u> gringo accent. Dave is learning a lot of mining Spanish, and how to speak, too, principally from Mr. Navarro, who is a fine old man, spry, busy, and very intelligent. Though he's not had any formal geological education, he has personally evolved some very creditable explanations for natural phenomena. He <u>thinks</u> a great deal and is also a homespun philosopher with high ethical ideals. He's one of the finest people we have met this summer. He's very good to help us learn Spanish, too; speaks very clearly and makes sure we understand, corrects us, and never loses patience.*

Love to you and Mother and Daddy,
Edith

About six weeks after our arrival, the paymaster for the mine was murdered while riding his horse from Chinipas. He was a kind, pleasant, soft-spoken man about forty years old, and his murder horrified everyone. About a week later a group of about six "Rurales" rode into camp. These were the federal government's rural police, but in fact they served as judge, jury, and, on occasion, executioner. Their reputation preceded them, and we heard that there had been incidents in which Rurales investigated a rape for a few minutes and then hung the apparent perpetrator with a piece of baling wire. Our Rurales were dressed for the part. They each carried a rifle and a large revolver, and they had bandoliers of cartridges crossing their chests and wore leather suits. Most of them had large mustaches and were unshaven, with cruel, implacable, expressions. They rode up and stopped and remained silent, sitting on their horses and looking at Mr. Wallis, the mine manager, without saying anything. Then the Rurales commander told Wallis, who by now was terrified, "You will now, immediately, pay me X Mexican pesos for our expenses." I have forgotten the number, but it was exorbitant, something like four hundred U.S. dollars, which might now be several thousand dollars. Mr. Wallis ran, not walked, to get the money. Before they arrived he had said he wouldn't pay anything. The Rurales stayed for two or three days talking to people in Aguas Calientes and Chinipas, who would think very carefully what might happen if they lied. They left without executing anybody. Rumor had it that they learned that the murderer was the son of the Chinipas police chief.

One of the people we became friends with at Aguas Calientes was Mr. Navarro, the original owner of the mine. He didn't have any specific duties, but spent every day prospecting and measuring the gold content of outcrops with his *peruña*, a device for panning gold made out of a cow horn and formed by soaking the horn in hot water and shaping it into a spoon shape. Peruñas that had a black area where the gold "tail" collected were considered particularly good. I have since seen similar panning "spoons" in South America and other parts of the world. The problem with Mr. Navarro's sampling was that he never cleaned out the gold tail, but added new samples as the day progressed and the gold tail got progressively bigger and more impressive. He liked to describe the gold as "oro amarillo, amarillo"—this is not ordinary gold but is yellow, yellow gold!

While we were there, Edith and I were invited to a wedding in Chinipas (which she describes in the letter to her sister Georgie, included earlier). The mine foreman, Ramon, and I decided to build a raft to float to town on the Chinipas River. We used twenty-gallon barrels, which had contained fuel to run the gold concentration plant and the mine air compressor. The barrels were shipped by small plane to Chinipas and then hauled by mule to Aguas Calientes, and they needed to be returned to Chinipas anyway. Twenty or more empty barrels had accumulated, and we also had ropes and pieces of lumber. We optimistically set out to build a raft with zero knowledge or experience. The river was relatively fast flowing and had rapids. The first raft we built sank

Raft built from gasoline drums for trip from Aguas Calientes to Chinipas in 1948. Edith visible in lower left. The raft had multiple collisions with rocks and structural damage en route.

dangerously deep in the water and Ramon didn't know how to swim, so we added more barrels and then launched the ship and set off. There was a platform where we could in theory stay dry and where I deposited my party clothes (the fate of Edith's party clothes was described in her letter). It was immediately apparent that we would be largely unable to steer the raft with our steering pole, and it crashed into both banks and into boulders in the rapids. I periodically had to jump into the river to push it off, but by some miracle it held together. At the last curve before reaching Chinipas the river was flowing more slowly, and I climbed up on the teetering platform and took off my pants and was trying to put on the party pants. We turned the corner and there was a delegation, mostly women, waiting on the bank to greet us.

Our friend Ramon disappeared the night of the wedding party, pursued by the brother of the Navarro girls, who was seeking revenge for the seduction of one of his sisters. We never saw him again that summer.

In spite of the paymaster's murder, Edith and I continued making sightseeing trips on our mules but were apprehensive that we might also be attacked. The local opinion was that it was safer to ride a mule than a horse because the mule was more intelligent and observant than a horse, and if there was a bandit hiding in the bushes beside the trail you would know by watching the mule's ears. We did a lot of mule-ear-watching, and I was decked out like Wyatt Earp with an old Colt single-action Frontier six-shooter, which was a ranch heirloom. I had brought this with me from Arizona. At that time nobody cared, but now it would be highly illegal.

When the term of employment ended in late August, we elected not to fly out of Chinipas, but to cross one range of the Sierra Madres on muleback to the small town of San Bernardo, Mexico, where there was bus service one day a week. There was no road for automobiles to Aguas Calientes or Chinipas. We lined up an *arriero*, or mule supplier and tender, named Don Cuco. He estimated that it would take almost two days to ride to San Bernardo, and the bus usually came by early in the afternoon so we didn't have time to lose. Left to their own devices, the locals always tried to ride at a trot, and they showed very little compassion for their riding animals.

Our route to San Bernardo went through an area where there was said to be bandits, and it went by a place called Lower Gochico, which we reached about dark the first day and where Don Cuco elected to spend the night. Lower Gochico was on top of a steep ridge, and we found there were no people, but there were two or three very primitive houses and goat pens. We had blankets but no mattresses, and we slept on the ground, which was covered by goat droppings. I was sufficiently tired to go to sleep after we ate some food, but not Edith and Don Cuco. I have never been very attractive to mosquitoes, but Edith and Cuco were, and there were roughly one billion hungry mosquitoes. Sometime in the middle of the night Don Cuco woke me up (Edith had been awake all night trying to avoid being eaten by mosquitoes, as had Don Cuco). We had a small flashlight and somehow we repacked the pack mule with our one suitcase on top. Then while we were getting the animals in a line in the pitch dark the pack mule fell off the trail and rolled about forty feet down the steep hill and landed with all four feet in the air on top of the pack and our suitcase. When we went down to investigate he appeared to be totally dead, which I mentioned to Cuco, but he continued with his investigation, which included opening one of the mule's eyelids, kicking him, and twisting his tail. No sign of life. Then Don Cuco found a long pole to lever him farther down the hill. Remember this is all going on in the pitch dark on a steep rocky slope with one flashlight. Cuco got the mule rolled in a partial revolution down the hill; he landed on his feet, brayed loudly, and seemed as good as new. But not our suitcase.

We continued down the trail: first Don Cuco, then the pack mule, then Edith, and finally me. After a couple of hours it became light and on we trotted. Sometime about ten o'clock Edith confided in me, "Dave, I have appendicitis and I'm sure I am going to die, and I don't know what you can do with my body, and it will be so sad for Mother and Daddy and my sister." I said, "You do not have appendicitis; your side, like mine, hurts from trotting too much on mules. Just get off and lie down for ten minutes under the mesquite tree and you will be fine." That's how it worked out, but Edith bitterly named her mule "Limoncilla," little lemon. There were some other descriptive words I won't repeat. By this time we were also in the area said to be bandit country, and Don Cuco nervously offered to buy my six-shooter, but I refused, thinking I was probably more resolute and a better shot. I wondered a little about the mechanics of a bandit attack and tried to remember cowboy movies I had seen. About noon we arrived in San Bernardo and the bus hadn't arrived so we decided to have lunch in a little open-air restaurant. The tables had oilcloth table covers that reached almost to the dirt floor. The three of us sat down around a little table—then there was a huge explosion under the table and a family of six or eight little pigs raced out in all directions, including between our legs!

The Mexican lunch was good, the little bus on time, the sightseeing an anticlimax after our last two days. There was a miscellaneous twelve- or fifteen-passenger list including some chickens, but we couldn't claim to be part of the cleanest half of the passenger list.

When we arrived in Navojoa about three hours later we checked into the same hotel, but this time it was really hot, over 100 degrees and high humidity. There was no air-conditioning or evaporative cooling. I arranged to borrow a big washtub and bought a large block of ice weighing about one hundred pounds. We had baths, put on clean clothes, had dinner and, as I remember, the ice lowered the temperature little, but enough to be able to sleep. Then back on AeroMéxico to the Nogales airport, where my cousin Douglas Cumming picked us up and then somehow, probably by bus, we got back to Tucson. The Chinipas adventure was over.

Life in Tucson and Graduation

Before we left for Chinipas, Edith and I had rented an apartment that was a converted garage. When we came back from Mexico at the end of the summer, Chuck Bagby, a friend of mine who had been a close friend of my brother, and his wife, Faye, were moving out of a small apartment on Fifth Avenue on the south side of Tucson, which was pretty modest but much better than our garage apartment, and we were able to take it over. We paid $25 a month rent. Our landlady was a nice lady but a little bit senile, and she never figured out that we had replaced the Bagbys in the apartment or that the Bagbys were totally honest, well behaved, and kind. She told me two or three times when I was paying the rent to be careful because there were a couple of university students in one of the apartments and you never know what they will do.

Edith and I bought an old Model A Ford sedan at a very low price, which we named Limoncilla, after her mule at Chinipas. It frequently broke down. On one occasion we had driven to Cochise County in Limoncilla on a hunting trip. While returning home we had a breakdown on the highway which had a steep drop-off to one side. We attempted to push it over the cliff and hitchhike home, but the road

David Lowell and Kendall Cumming upon graduation from the University of Arizona, 1949. Kendall had spent two years in World War II in the paratroops.

was slanted in the wrong direction so I had to go back to my desperation auto mechanics talents, and I finally got it running again. Shortly after we finally sold Limoncilla it was used in a bank robbery, but it broke down during the escape.

During my senior year at the university Edith had graduated, and because of her good academic record and the friendship of faculty friends she was able to get a job as a secretary in the English Department, and that was the largest source of funding for our enterprise for nine months.

At the end of 1949, the year I graduated, we were able to buy a red World War II MB Jeep that one of the university professors had bought surplus. We paid $215 cash and owed an additional $285, which seemed like an impossible financing problem and we had to get a bank loan to do it. The banker was very dubious about our situation, but I guess because I had my university degree he thought he could risk it. When I graduated I looked around for a job and landed one with ASARCO in Mexico, but there was a delay of several months for the government permit to work in Mexico.

For a month or two I worked at a construction job in Tucson, installing a sixty-inch concrete sewer pipe in the hot sun in June, July, and August and then my guardian angel, Dean Chapman, got me a job as a low-level consultant for a fellow who had a mineral prospect near Bagdad, Arizona. He was a very nice guy named Port B. Mellinger, and he arrived in a new gold-colored Packard along with the rest of his family. He was a very flamboyant fellow, who was in the baby chick business back in the Midwest. He seemed to have quite a bit of money and was owner of this mineral prospect, which was of dubious value but required tidying up to get a clearer idea of what it was worth, if anything. So Edith and I took our red Jeep and drove to the prospect. I worked for about six weeks on this assignment, and we lived in an old shack in a sort of ghost town or mining camp with no electricity, water, or gas. The shack had a large hole in the kitchen floor through which we poured dishwater, and it had an elemental sort of woodstove that we used for cooking. No one else lived in this mining camp; in fact, there were no people within several miles, and we had a very happy time there.

We had a couple of memorable incidents. Once, I was working alone and going down old shafts to take samples to have assayed, and I put down a rope tied to a tree to help climb out of the shaft. I entered one shaft about twenty feet deep and examined the rocks and took my sample, but the shaft was in schist, which is a micaceous rock that is very slippery to hold your feet against to climb up the rope. I made several unsuccessful attempts to climb out and my feet would always slip off the walls of the shaft. I then sat down at the bottom of the shaft to examine my problem and I realized that this was one shaft out of a dozen or more scattered around the area and Edith would not know where I was so I might be looking forward to spending a day or two at the bottom of the shaft. So then I looked at the rope and daylight at the top of the shaft and said, "Dave, you're going to have to climb hand over hand twenty feet or you're not going to get out." And so I climbed twenty feet hand over hand.

Another adventure entailed a large green Mojave rattlesnake that was living close to our shack that I had to kill. Mojave rattlesnakes have a powerful venom that acts on nerves rather than muscles, and a Mojave bite can sometimes kill a horse. It is one of the most dangerous snakes in North America, with venom about twenty times more lethal than that of a Western diamondback rattlesnake.

Then word came from ASARCO that they had the papers arranged, and I wrote my report for Mr. Mellinger. We drove our Jeep to El Paso and then down to Chihuahua City and to the Santa Eulalia unit of ASARCO. I hadn't yet learned how to properly pronounce the word "Eulalia," but I had officially completed my education and become a mining engineer as I had announced I would do at age seven. I was now reporting for duty!

CHAPTER THREE

Mining Engineer, Shift Boss, and Night Foreman, Santa Eulalia Mine, Mexico, 1949

My original career plan was to work for six months or a year as a miner before seeking employment as a mining engineer. I found to my surprise that I couldn't get a job as a miner, because of the depression in the mining business at the time, but I could get a job as an engineer with ASARCO in Mexico in the Santa Eulalia Mining District. My preference in selecting my first mining engineering job was to work in an underground mine rather than an open pit mine like most of my classmates. The open pit jobs were much easier physically and much more comfortable but a somewhat less intense route to becoming a miner. One of our reasons to accept a job in Mexico was that Edith had been interested all her life in Mexico and had collections of phonograph records of Mexican ranchero music. I had also enjoyed previous visits to Mexico.

The fellow who hired me was A. A. Brown. He was vice president in charge of the Mexico division of ASARCO and his office was in El Paso, Texas. When we arrived at the Santa Eulalia Mine in October of 1949 we didn't know exactly what to expect. What we found was that the management assumed I was a competent surveyor and required no breaking in and no mentoring. They also assumed that I could communicate well in Spanish, that I already knew everything about mining, and that I was in good physical condition, ready to climb up two- or three-hundred-foot ladders in 90-degree temperatures and 90 to 100 percent humidity. When I started working in the mine, I found that I collected about one cup of sweat in each boot by the end of every day.

The temperature and humidity conditions at Santa Eulalia were marginal for a human being to work a full shift underground. Temperatures in mines like the two-mile-deep Witwatersrand mine in South Africa and the former Magma Mine in Arizona required the installation of expensive air-conditioning. A cheaper solution, which was only partly utilized at Buena Tierra (Santa Eulalia District), is mine ventilation using large fans that force surface air down one (downcast) shaft and up another (upcast) shaft on the other side of the underground workings. In some places in the mine there were incline shafts full of water, and we often walked into these with our clothes on up to chest level, which was slightly cooling. ASARCO's San Antonio mine five kilometers away was a little cooler than Buena Tierra.

I began earning $250 per month plus housing. We were assigned a small apartment, which had a small living room, bedroom, kitchen, and dining room. I received a raise to $265 a month with my promotion to shift boss and night foreman. My title in the beginning was mine engineer, and in both jobs I was expected to work about nine hours a day six days a week. I was criticized when once in two years I took a two-day weekend when my college roommate visited us at Santa Eulalia. I received a two-week vacation per year, and the rule was that if you resigned with accrued vacation time you were not paid for it. One young engineer of our acquaintance named Ham Bush—he was probably ten years older than I—was running a relatively small mine for ASARCO over near Presidio, Texas. He reported to the mine manager at Santa Eulalia. He wasn't given a great deal of appreciation or cooperation or support there, and he came in and talked to Mr. Syner, our mine manager. They talked about his problems and that he wanted a raise, and they wouldn't give him a raise, and so Ham said, "Well, I've been thinking a lot about this, and I'm afraid I'm just going to have to resign. But I do have three weeks of accrued vacation due, and I assume you'll pay me for the vacation." Ham told me that Mr. Syner laughed and laughed and just slapped his leg at the thought that somebody was going to get paid for vacation when he quit.

My job also involved working in a dangerous mine with few safety rules. In two years I was involved in three potentially fatal accidents. I began working in the engineering office for an unimpressive, not very healthy, middle-aged chief engineer named Mr. Keener, who never worked underground. My duties were to keep maps of the mine up to date using a hanging compass, which was obsolete even then, and do general surveys underground using a transit and tape. On one occasion we carried a survey from the surface to underground workings 2,500 feet below, hanging two plumb bobs on wires with the plumb bobs immersed in a bucket of oil on the bottom. This was a very complicated project done with no experience and no supervision.

Across the board, there wasn't much effort made to be diplomatic between supervisors, junior engineers, shift bosses, and people like me. Fritz Hertzel was a particularly tough, short-spoken kind of guy. His nickname with the miners was El Camarón (the shrimp). And if you thought about it and looked at him, he was a little hunched over and looked a bit like a big shrimp. There was a Mexican foreman named Macias, whose nickname was La Bestia (the beast), and this also was appropriate. I think those may have been the only two nicknames that I heard, but I assume we all had nicknames.

Our best friends were a Mexican couple—Romeo, who was a Mexican citizen with a mining engineering degree from Texas School of Mines, and Muly, his young bride living in the camp. Muly is a nickname for Emilia. Their family name was Ayub. The Ayub family had been in Mexico for a couple of generations, but was originally Syrian or some nationality from the Middle East. We went by to see Muly in about 1998; Romeo had died several years earlier. He had left ASARCO and was in business for himself. But one of their children became president of the Mining Association of Mexico, and they've done very well.

Other staff members were Hugh Clayton, a Brit who had flown Spitfires in the Battle of Britain and who became another close friend, and Al Higgins, a young American mining engineer. The management was Fritz Hertzel, mine superintendent, and Mr. Syner, mine manager. The mine foreman was first Mr. Macias then Romeo Ayub, and Severn Brown and Bill Hewitt were mine geologists at different times. Other good friends were Jack Pearson, foreman of the San Antonio Mine, and Bill Tonioli, master mechanic at the Howe Sound Mine.

The geology of both Buena Tierra and San Antonio was limestone host rock containing massive sulfide-type lead, zinc, copper, silver, and gold ore, and the limestone also contained a number of large water-filled caverns, which sometimes produced flooding in the mines. The Buena Tierra Mine contained massive sulfide ore bodies. The stoping method was open stopes, and some of the open spaces were very large. We had a stope that was 600 feet long and maybe 400 feet wide and over 200 feet high—that was all open space after the orebody was mined. That kind of mining is somewhat dangerous because you don't know when rock might be loose on the back (roof), and so it's danger-ous to walk across the floor of the stope, and most of the mining was done in the walls.

There was a Howe Sound Mining Company mine that was con-tiguous with the Buena Tierra Mine—their mine was part of the same orebody as the ASARCO one at Buena Tierra Mine. They also had a little camp that was very close by, perhaps a quarter of a mile away, that added to the parties and entertainment. The manager's name was Martin (pronounced Mar-TEEN) Nesbitt. He was born in Mexico. I think his father had been a British mining engineer. He was a very nice guy. The Howe Sound Mine had a friendlier atmosphere than Santa Eulalia.

It is now difficult to even visit a large underground mine almost anywhere in the world without getting a one- or two-hour safety lec-ture. If you work in one it is certain that you will have been put through safety training almost to the point of ridiculousness. This was not the case at Santa Eulalia, where I was never given safety instruction. In a sense the lecture was done in reverse. On one occasion two timbermen were doing some repair work on the timber lining of the 2,100-foot-deep Buena Tierra shaft. A three-by-twelve-inch plank projected out into the shaft and had to be sawed off. The man in charge thought the projecting part of the plank would make a comfortable seat and he sawed it off and then dropped over a thousand feet. In this case a safety investigation was held after the accident.

In my two years I had three narrow escapes. The first happened in this same shaft. I was coming to the surface with Romeo Ayub, who was then mine foreman. We were riding up in the "ore bucket" rather than the normal "man skip," which was more like an elevator. The bucket arrived at our level, and when we looked inside there was a splintered half plank that had been part of the shaft lining. Presumably the other half of the plank might be projecting out into the shaft and could punch into the open bucket and maybe kill one or both of us on the return trip. Control of movement of buckets and skips was done by a "bell cord," a thin steel cable that hangs loose in a corner of the shaft and is accessible on shaft stations and also inside the shaft when the bucket is moving slowly. The bell cord sends hoist signals by a coded series of tugs. Romeo, after seeing the broken plank, went to a telephone in the shaft station and called the hoist man and explained what had happened. He told the hoist man to hoist us slowly so we could stop the bucket with the bell cord if we saw the broken plank above us. The hoist man disregarded this order and hauled us to the surface full speed, which meant we could not stop the bucket with the bell cord. We had an unpleasant five minutes waiting to see what would happen but saw no sign of the other half of the plank. I didn't hear whether the hoist man was fired, but he should have been.

Another accident occurred when I was with Romeo. The mining system ASARCO used required, as a first step, driving "naked raises." These were shafts driven from the bottom up to a certain level and were "naked" because they were not lined with timber and usually were not equipped with ladders. Instead, on one side, every eight vertical feet, a twelve-by-twelve-inch stull, or horizontal beam, was installed, and instead of a ladder, a greasy rope hung in a corner of the raise. We were climbing hand over hand on the rope from stull to stull, with Romeo one stull above me. Suddenly the stull Romeo was standing on rotated because it had been improperly installed and dumped him off, and he fell on my head and I fell off my stull. It happened so fast Romeo wasn't able to speak. I think we were both able to keep one hand on the rope because we both ended up draped over stulls eight or sixteen feet lower. We were able to get our carbide lights relighted and eventually climbed to the top of the raise to see how a connection could be made. If we had not been able to stop our falls we would both have been killed or seriously injured. Later problems suggested that this incident may have compressed a vertebra in my neck.

My third accident was also related to mine development work. By this time I was a shift boss and had to look at a sublevel (a tunnel driven from the top of another untimbered raise). In this case the raise was equipped with ladders. I was by myself and climbed about eighty feet to the top of the raise and then walked a few feet into the sublevel. I noticed out of the corner of my eye that my carbide light was burning, but the flame had moved several inches away from the reflector. It took me a critical one or two seconds to understand: *Bad Air!!* I turned around and went hurriedly back to the ladder and started down. I had descended a few rungs when I felt myself passing out. I stuck my arms down through the ladder in the six-inch space between the ladder and the rock wall and I passed out and was unconscious there for an unknown period of time, held by my arms between the ladder and the wall, but eventually recovered consciousness. I had never heard of this being done by anyone else, and it was a split-second decision which probably saved my life. The carbide lamp and my hard hat had fallen to the bottom of the raise, and when I regained consciousness I had to pick my way down the ladder in pitch darkness. I was lucky enough to find the carbide light in loose rock at the bottom of the ladder and was able to get it lighted again. Had I been using an electric cap lamp, or had I spent a few more seconds in the sublevel making up my mind, it would have become a fatal accident. I still have the carbide light which saved my life.

The predominant rock type at Santa Eulalia and San Antonio was massive limestone, and there were several large, sometimes huge, underground caverns full of water. Their locations were not known, and on at least two occasions mine drifts intersected water-filled limestone caverns, which flooded large parts of mines and sometimes killed miners. ASARCO had two large mines, the Buena Tierra Mine and the San Antonio Mine, and both had been flooded.

The first flood occurred when a drift tapped high-pressure water in the San Antonio Mine, which flooded twenty-five miles of underground workings and killed six miners. ASARCO worked out a scheme to sink a winze (an underground shaft) near to the place where the water was intersected and install a pressure chamber in the bottom of the winze, which had two pressure doors. A round of blast holes were drilled from the floor of the winze into rock near the flooded drift and blasted, connecting it with the flooded drift. Deep-sea divers were then brought in to go through the pressure chamber and pour a concrete plug to seal off the water so that the mine could be pumped out and put back into production. The divers, or *buzos*, created a legend at San Antonio. They were highly paid, devil-may-care fellows who rented an old car and stocked it with cases of beer and young ladies and like-minded young men and drove at high speeds over bad mine roads. If you visit the San Antonio Mine now, seventy years later, you will still hear all the stories.

The other flood occurred in the Buena Tierra Mine during a card party in the evening. The night foreman found a stream of water squirting out of a crack and called the manager and demanded that Bill Hewitt, the mine geologist, look at the "leak." Bill left the party with bad grace and went underground and looked at the water and reported to the manager that "I could pass more water than that." During the night the crack raveled and flooded the lower levels of both the Buena Tierra and the Howe Sound mines, but in this case it was possible to pump it out.

On a later visit when I was asked to do something in the San Antonio Mine I was in the area pumped out as a result of the deep-sea divers'

work, and I passed a tiny stream of water squirting out of an impercep-
tible crack. The amazing thing was the trajectory of the stream. It shot
six feet across the drift without any drop in elevation, indicating that it
was under very high pressure, which made my back tingle.

The camp was largely an American-Canadian-British camp, but
there were Mexican engineers and professionals also. The camp society
was very structured. This was before television, and English-language
radio reception was poor. Most week-to-week recreation was dinners
followed by card parties. We had regular weekly card parties and entertainment back and forth between houses. We were at the bottom of the
ladder as far as status went, I being a recent graduate. We had a three-
room apartment, as did the Ayubs. We invited people over to dinner
and were invited to dinner. Hugh Clayton, a bachelor at that time, was
given the added job of being in charge of the hotel where he lived. He
had to go to town to shop for the coming week for the hotel. There
was a cook. Games were limited to canasta and poker. Bridge had been
outlawed, much as poison gas after World War I, because of all the
fighting it brought on, sometimes physical. The stakes were always low
and five dollars would be a very large win or loss. I always played poker
and Edith always played canasta. In the first months I consistently won
at poker, then I bought a book on poker and, after reading it, I consistently lost.

The camp was about forty kilometers of bad road from Chihuahua
City, which had a population then of about 100,000 people. We were
lucky to have our Jeep—not all the staff had cars. We drove to town
once a week to buy groceries at the La Suiza or sometimes have dinner at the Acropolis. This was an elegant restaurant where the waiters
wore black suits and carried white towels over one arm, but the prices
there were low compared to those in the United States. We were in the
Acropolis one night when one of the elegant waiters was standing in the
middle of the floor and a fat rat raced by a few feet in front of him, but
he studiously ignored it.

We got our milk from a fellow who delivered milk in cans on a
burro. The first thing you did with your milk when you got it was boil it

because you were pretty sure it wasn't very clean. This milkman, whose name I don't remember, killed people (but not, so far as I know, with the milk). He did it when he was drinking, and Mexican law, at least at that time, protected a drunken man. We heard that he had killed twelve people, and the last one occurred while we were there. He was in jail for a couple of months, and during that period, his little boy had to deliver the milk. Then they let him out. On one occasion, one of the women at our camp saw this milkman adding water to one of his cans of milk out of a garden hose at one of the houses. But no one was about to criticize him.

We found we could buy most foods we needed, and because Edith has always been an unusually good cook, we ate very well. Lots of vegetables were available, in season, and steaks were cheap and relatively good. We both spoke Spanish, which made life easier and more fun. I have always had a fairly good Spanish accent, but Edith has had a much larger vocabulary and much better command of grammar and construction. I developed a trick in speaking Spanish. I picked out two or three frequently used sentences and practiced them until I sounded like a native, but only while saying two or three things. We once went on a weekend trip with Romeo and Muly Ayub. When I spoke to someone with one of my sentences, he then insisted on speaking Spanish to me and English to Romeo—which annoyed Romeo and amused the rest of us.

Edith sometimes drove the Jeep to town alone and did fine with the exception of once bumping a large pig that said "oink" (presumably in Spanish), but didn't seem to be injured. We sometimes used Pepe, who had a taxi and was a pleasant, helpful guy. His father had been hung on a power pole by Pancho Villa, who had visited Santa Eulalia about twenty-five years earlier. The mine was in operation when word came that the revolutionary army was about to arrive. It seems the whole mine staff moved underground for two or three days and continuously played cards. We never talked to anyone who had anything good to say about Pancho Villa.

I sometimes took a lunch consisting of two sandwiches and traded

Fording the Río Conchos in the MB Jeep while on a duck hunt.

food with Chimin, my engineer's assistant. On one occasion Chimin and I were working on the surface inventorying an aerial tram earlier used to tram ore from the mine to the mill and smelter. We hiked about six kilometers and sat down somewhere in the shade. Chimin talked me into trading one of his tacos for a sandwich, telling me with a straight face that it wasn't at all "picante" (hot), while knowing this was completely untrue. I finally agreed and took one bite which nearly killed me, but Chimin laughed so hard he nearly fell down. He was my language professor in spite of having gone to school only three years. When I said something in Spanish he would say it back to me using other words, and I learned a lot of Spanish this way. The trouble was he sprinkled in quite a few profane and obscene words, which I didn't always recognize. Our camp parties were largely in Spanish and Edith would sometimes tell me, "You just used a very bad word talking to Mrs. Macias!"

I worked six days a week, and most of our recreation was on Sunday. It usually consisted of a duck hunt on the Río Conchos or a trip to Chihuahua and dinner at the Acropolis or, a few times, going to a Spanish language movie. Hunting supplied a great share of my recreation. Our first purchase in that pursuit was Spook I, a springer spaniel from Skamania County, Washington. (In 2013 Spook III, our third springer spaniel named Spook, died.) We picked him up in El Paso and returned the crate he arrived in. He was four months old, black and white. Spook was named by Bill Hewitt, because when Bill was dog-sitting Spook hid in his doghouse barrel and only his eyes and nose showed. His first notable achievement was breaking a plate and eating a whole layer cake. Spook was trained by me. In his first live-action hunt I shot a snipe, which flew away, and Spook chased it a far distance, disobeying everything he had been taught. He then came back with the bird in his mouth and so was not eligible for criticism. We hunted in the Río Conchos, which was usually less than two feet deep, and I walked in the river near one bank carrying my shotgun in my right hand and Spook, when he was young, under my left arm because he had tender feet. Hunting was good, and I usually shot mallards. If I was hunting with anyone else Spook would bring all the ducks to me. Years later I was hunting pheasants in Colorado in a large field where there were several other hunters who were strangers. I shot at three pheasants, but Spook brought me four.

We once went hunting with an elegant visiting accountant from New York and his wife. They had a picnic basket, sandwiches, and salad and a tablecloth. Edith and I built a little fire, and when it was partly burned down we threw two steaks directly on the fire and after a little while turned them over and finally brushed some of the ashes off and put them between two slices of bread. Our friends looked shocked, but didn't say anything.

Once, on a javelina hunting trip with two friends, we ran into a cloud of grasshoppers. One friend had to get out of the Jeep to take his pants off to get rid of a grasshopper, and then I had to. Then the other friend took his pants off, just in case.

On one occasion we went on a Sunday goose hunt in a Mennonite colony west of Chihuahua City called Boquilla. We had been given the name of a "Jack" Mennonite (one who didn't practice the faith religiously, so to speak, but was a member of the community) named Enrique Wibi. Wibi was a banker who loved to hunt geese. When we found him this Sunday morning he looked at our car, which was Jack

Pearson's Chevrolet sedan, and opened the trunk and said, "That trunk will hold sixty-seven geese based on my last hunt in a similar vehicle." Enrique, without any discussion or permission, took over as driver and drove us out to a stubble field in which we could see a large flock of geese some distance from the road. He drove to a point where the furrows in the stubble field intersected the road and then immediately wheeled the car and drove as fast as he could toward the geese. The geese had been watching and immediately took off, but their flying speed was slow for the first fifty or one hundred feet and the car passed under them. We all shot at flying geese through open windows, which I thought looked like a good arrangement until I saw that Enrique was also shooting through his window and not paying much attention to the car. We shot a number of geese and did this two or three times, after which I hunted alone in a slight rise where flocks of geese were flying overhead. I noticed there was an old horse standing in the pass. I walked up to him and found he was very tame and suitable to be used as a "stalking horse," so when the next flock of geese flew over I stood behind him until they were in shooting distance and then blasted away. I got one or two geese but didn't disturb my friend, who continued to graze. We didn't shoot sixty-seven geese, but we probably shot fifteen and were very pleased with the trip.

We drove our MB government-surplus Jeep on many trips, and in the backseat there was always a can of gas and a gallon bottle of oil. When we drove home on our vacation in the winter of 1950 we left the Jeep in El Paso and took a nice, comfortable, fast, warm, Greyhound bus to Tucson. It became very cold in the winter, so I built a Jeep cab in the apartment kitchen with some pieces of scrap iron, sheet metal, a drill, and some rivets. I got some pieces of rawhide and hinges for doors, and it worked very well. Later, after our daughter, Susie, was born, we drove to El Paso when she was four months old. She rode on a pillow in Edith's lap and Spook rode in the back. Shortly before we resigned from my job at the Santa Eulalia Mine we bought a two- or three-year-old Plymouth sedan and left the Jeep with my parents in Arizona. The Plymouth seemed like a Mercedes or a Rolls Royce.

At that time it was very hard for Americans to get permits to work in Mexico, but easy for Mexicans to work in the United States. We had a permit that required us to sign in and sign out of Mexico. On one trip we arrived at the Mexican Immigration Garita on the bridge between Juárez and El Paso about 7:00 p.m. to check out. The office was supposed to be open twenty-four hours, but there was no one there so we just drove into Texas. Coming back, my papers said I was still in Mexico, so I joined the stream of tourists walking into Juárez, and a little later Edith drove the Jeep to the Garita to get a tourist visa. She was obviously pregnant. A little later I wandered back and sat in the Jeep. The Immigration official figured out that something was wrong with a pregnant gringa saying she was just driving a Jeep into Mexico on a pleasure trip. Finally he said, "I saw heem do it!" and demanded to see me. I was friendly and affable, but stuck to our joint line, and he finally decided that there was no money to be made and let us go.

On the same trip, when we decided to leave our Jeep in El Paso and take the bus, we found we didn't have enough cash for the bus tickets, and we couldn't find anyone in El Paso to cash our ASARCO check. I thought I knew a bar in Juárez that might cash the check, so I left Edith at the bus station and drove back across the bridge, talked the bartender into cashing the check, and drove back through the closed Mexican Garita to the U.S. Immigration, but they remembered seeing me earlier and were intensely suspicious that I was doing something very dishonest, like smuggling drugs or diamonds or suitcases full of money. It took a little while to convince them, but I got the Jeep stashed and got to the bus terminal just in time.

On October 27, 1950, our daughter, Susan Deborah Lowell, was born at the Sanatorio Palmore hospital in Chihuahua, where mother and daughter were treated with tender care and kindness. With the exception of some temporary colic, Susie thrived and, five months later, returned with us to Tucson. We had no thought then that this beautiful little package would later become a National Merit Scholar and a Presidential Scholar, sent to Washington to meet the president.

By the time I would return to graduate school three years later, I

Susie in 1952, and with Edith in Mexico, 1951.

would have two promotions, a government GS11 rating, and be earning three times my ASARCO salary. On the other hand, I had learned a lot about underground mining production work, about being a boss, and about doing difficult work during our two years at Santa Eulalia. Most of the time I had sixty-five men reporting to me in what was a life-and-death relationship because of the safety problems.

Exploration Geologist with U.S. Atomic Energy Commission

Having learned from Ham Bush the effect of trying to collect your vacation, I resigned from my position at ASARCO just after finishing my vacation. We left Mexico in March 1951 and stayed temporarily with my parents at their cotton farm near Red Rock, Arizona. I immediately started beating the bushes for a job. In my last year at the university, I had started to tumble to the fact that I was really more interested in mineral exploration and treasure hunting than I was in mining produc-

Granddaddy Lowell and
Susie, Red Rock house, 1953.

tion work, and I started looking around for ways that I could shift into working as a geologist in mineral exploration.

In May, Edith, Susie, and our dog, Spook, and I went on a field trip to Rocky Point, Mexico, with professors Eddie McKee and John Harshbarger from the University of Arizona. This was a three-day family vacation trip in which I acted as a field assistant, digging trenches in a beach in a tidal lagoon to study sedimentary structures that demonstrated current flow directions. At that time, Professor McKee was acknowledged to be an international expert on sedimentation. What I learned on this trip was to become useful soon enough. By then, I'd been offered a job with the U.S. Atomic Energy Commission (AEC), looking for uranium in Colorado—a position that carried a GS7 rating. We discussed the job offer with John, who was a personal friend as well as the head of the Geology Department at the university. John gave his blessing to the AEC job.

During the delay between jobs, I had taken the Jeep motor out to rebuild it while we enjoyed the luxury of our nice secondhand

Plymouth sedan. In June 1951 I flew to Grand Junction, Colorado, to interview for the AEC job. I don't remember what the interview consisted of, but I learned that the work we would be doing for the Atomic Energy Commission was looking for red-bed type uranium deposits in the Morrison Formation in the Colorado Plateau. I took the job. I was assigned temporarily to an exploration camp near Blanding, Utah, where I worked about two months under Paul Malencon before being transfered to a larger project at Cove School, Arizona, on the Navajo Reservation, where I would be project manager and where Edith would join me.

I have to admit that my heart was not broken to give up a long-hour, low-pay job in a hot, deep, dangerous, mine, for a more interesting job as a field geologist for the AEC for twice the pay. I got two promotions and raises later. Back in those days, one often-heard expression describing a man with a large salary was "ten-thousand-dollar-a-year man." And so four or five hundred plus field allowances wasn't all that shabby. When I left the AEC in 1954, I had a GS11 rating, which was a middle-management government rating and salary.

A good part of my term with the Atomic Energy Commission was at the Cove School camp. It was a former Navajo day school in the Lukachukai Mountains, near the Four Corners area and near Red Rock Trading Post in New Mexico. The nearest town to us was Shiprock, New Mexico. We carried out a number of diamond drilling projects using a drill contractor who had a crew in the camp with us. Altogether, there were probably twenty house trailers.

The AEC's basic game plan wasn't necessarily a very efficient way to find uranium reserves, but they jumped right into the mineral exploration. They didn't subsidize private companies that might have done it better, but did it themselves. Their plan at Cove School was to lay out a grid of holes in each of about four mesas that contained known uranium occurrences in the Brushy Basin unit of the Morrison Formation.

The whole geological group at Cove School had been hired at almost the same time. The majority of them were recently graduated geologists from the East. Within a few months I gravitated to a job as manager of a drilling camp with five other geologists reporting to me. There was a really nice guy named Bob Rock, who was a Colorado School of Mines graduate. Nog Yeater, an ex–World War II paratrooper, was from Texas, and Louie Roberts from Columbia University. I had a non-graduate technician, Johnny Epic, who had been a Navajo Indian trader and spoke Navajo. And I had a Navajo Indian named Elwood Sosie, who had been in Merrill's Marauders in the war in the Pacific, as a code talker. Our engineer, Carl Applin, managed camp maintenance and drill contracting. Jim Clinton, Cal Fouts, and John Blagburough were also there at the time. Tom Mitchum and Bob Wright were geology supervisors in Grand Junction, Colorado, at our project headquarters, and J. O. Jones and Ernie Gordon were managers there.

Our house trailer was second-hand and somewhat banged up. It had an electrical short in its wiring. We occasionally felt a little shock stepping into the trailer and didn't think very much about it, but it was very worrisome for Spook, our springer spaniel. He got in the habit of gathering himself together several feet away from the trailer door, making a great leap onto the living room floor so as not to form a continuous contact from the damp ground and the aluminum threshold. Cove School was a very pleasant interlude for us and maybe the single most enjoyable period in my life. We were there one and a half or two years, everybody was young and healthy, and we had a lot of entertainment in the camp. Everybody was about the same age, and all felt like it was sort of an adventure living up in the mountains. There were no feuds and no drinking problems in our camp.

Exploration mapping, drill hole location, and sampling was done by my group. Mapping entailed descriptions of rock types and uranium mineralization. The drill contractor was Jones Drilling Co. and the foreman's name was Frenchie. He had a system for always having a new pickup to drive. He bought one new truck and then traded it in for another every two months without making payments. I don't know how this finally came out. The drillers had a softball team, and the geology group had a team, and once a week we had a game. I had played more than anyone else previously and was appointed pitcher, and we had a lot of fun. There were Navajos living near us and they

David and Edith's
trailer at Cove School,
summer of 1951.

used Cove School as a sort of community center and occasionally had local horse races.

Once, as camp manager, I had to listen (with the help of an interpreter) to a Navajo describing a collision with a "Vas heen dun" (a government employee, in this case an AEC geologist). The Navajo described with his left index finger his slow cautious progress along the winding project road and with his right index finger the fast, wild progress, skidding around curves, of the geologist. I was amazed by his detailed recollection of the road's geography and thought he was probably right about the geologist's driving, and I agreed to fix his pickup.

The Navajos were especially observant and seemed to remember every bush, tree, rock, and bend in the trail they had ever seen. We hired a number of them and showed them specimens of yellow carnotite uranium ore and sent them out prospecting, and they found some mineralized outcrops. They were supervised by Jack Leonard, who had also been a code talker in the Marine Corps in World War II in the Pacific.

The Atomic Energy Commission also hired several college professors as consultants to review what we were doing. There was Dr. Leo Stokes from the University of Utah (who said I was the only AEC geologist who followed his advice), Dr. Gruner from the University of Minnesota, and Edwin McKee from the University of Arizona. I was fortunate to have the opportunity to work several days with each consultant, and as a result learned a lot and also was offered a scholarship to study for a PhD in all three universities.

The AEC was organized into two divisions. One was something like a drilling division, which was a production, physical-exploration division. The other was the mapping division. Their function was to do district and regional geologic mapping to support the uranium exploration. Leo Miller was working in the mapping division, and I was working in the drilling division. We were sometimes in the same camp, but were independent of each other.

In our camp we had a small office building that housed a drafting room and a single side band shortwave radio with which we communicated every day with the Grand Junction head office. As camp manager one of my duties was a 7:00 a.m. radio call. Calls were mainly about logistical problems and supplies and visits. The AEC had a contract with Raider Flying Service, which was run by a wild, ex–World War II fighter pilot named Raider. We had an airstrip at Cove School, and supplies and mail came in and drill samples and occasional passengers were flown out.

One morning I was expecting Raider to arrive and he didn't come, so I got into my Jeep to drive to Shiprock to mail some reports. There was a long straight stretch in the graded road to Shiprock and the Jeep station wagon was pleasantly warm. I was daydreaming when suddenly a Beechcraft Bonanza appeared about five feet above my windshield making a horrible noise and creating a dust cloud. Raider landed on the road in front of the Jeep and we exchanged items and he flew off happily after his successful practical joke. On another trip with him to Grand Junction we flew near the Natural Bridges National Monument and he said, "Let's fly through a natural bridge." It looked to me to be narrow enough so that we would have to go through with our wings tilted into a vertical position. I declined, but later was sorry we hadn't done it.

On another occasion Carl Applin, the camp engineer, asked me if he could borrow my new red AEC Jeep station wagon to drive into Shiprock. I reluctantly agreed, and he left but didn't come back. The next morning I drove into Shiprock looking for him and found him sitting on a curb with lots of dried blood and bandages and a splint on his leg and walking on crutches. He told me that he had hit a horse and its head had come through the windshield and hit his chest, imbedding a lot of horse hair, and a good part of the horse went into the interior of the Jeep, spilling its entrails. The Jeep was towed to an AEC vehicle yard in Grand Junction, but was not repaired for months because of the smell. Carl was able to hobble around on crutches and continue to work, but his stock had gone down.

The next year slipped by happily at Cove School. Edith and I were expecting another child, and during the winter Edith and Susie and Spook moved to Tucson to stay with her parents. Our son Bill was born in Tucson on April 8, 1952, and I did not have enough advance notice to be present.

At Cove there was a lot of snow and cold weather. The camp was largely shut down in the winter and with the help of Johnny Eppich as a rodman I carried out a large-scale triangulation survey in the Lukachukai Mountains to locate our drill areas. We worked on snowshoes. On one occasion I was carrying the transit in a box and fell in a deep snowdrift upside down, held by my snow shoes on the surface of the snow. I was able to get out by pushing the box down to the ground and then kicking my legs out and climbing out. Every day our clothes froze stiff, and at night my wet boots froze to the floor of the house trailer. In spite of this I felt fine and enjoyed the work. However, the quality of the cooking had deteriorated greatly, and I missed my family.

One day after Edith had returned to Cove School we were driving into Farmington, New Mexico, in another Jeep when lots of black smoke suddenly came out of the engine. I stopped and raised the hood and determined that a pinhole leak had developed in the high-pressure oil hose and the oil was being sprayed on the hot manifold. I decided that I could drive the less than ten miles remaining to a garage in Farmington without damaging the engine. We started again with clouds of black smoke coming out of both sides of the Jeep, and some of the cars approaching in the opposite direction drove off the highway thinking we were about to blow up. They were also impressed in the garage, but replaced the hose and added oil in fifteen minutes.

While we were at Cove School, we went to a few Navajo "Squaw Dances," which were part of a large three-day ceremony. This part was out in the woods with a bonfire and drums, where they danced all night. We would drive up and sit on the ground with the Indians, watching the dance. We attended a total of about three Navajo Squaw Dances and also a Hopi Snake Dance. We had heard that the Squaw Dances were really healing ceremonies for a patient, whose health sometimes improved from the effect of more than a hundred people assembling for the purpose of having good thoughts about him or her. One of the three days would be at night up in the ponderosa pine Lukachukai forest, and there would be a drum beating and a Navajo singer singing in the native sing-song. Couples walked around a bonfire in the center (hence the name "Squaw Dance") and a ring of wagons and pickups completed the setting. It was a very impressive experience for us. The last day of the ceremony was in a different location and part of the ceremony was men galloping around the patient's wagon on horses shooting pistols and rifles in the air. On one occasion one fell off his horse, maybe as the result of other celebrating.

When driving across the reservation, I often stopped in trading posts to look at rugs for sale. Our Navajo rugs are mostly wearing out now. Edith's grandfather also had a collection that she inherited that is quite old, some of them more than a hundred years old.

Occasionally the geologists were called into Grand Junction for several days of meetings, and there were also some wild parties. I had heard the expression "drinking someone under the table," but I saw it happen at one of these parties. Eight or nine of us were sitting around a table and suddenly Andy Anderson disappeared when no one was looking. We found him happily sleeping under the table.

On one occasion I was driving back from Grand Junction and stopped in Moab, Utah, a uranium boom town, to buy gas, but discovered I had no money. I asked the service station owner if I could cash a $15 check. He said, "Do you live in Moab?" I said, "No, I live in Arizona." He replied, "In that case I will cash the check."

The AEC had a radio technician who did the repairs and maintenance on the dozen exploration camps' two-way radios. His name was Chuck Hay and he was pretty good at his work. He had a story he loved to tell that was probably true. On a previous job, maybe in Canada or Alaska, he rode out of an isolated camp in a two-engine DC-3 aircraft. On his return, he showed up drunk so they made him sit in the last seat in the back. The air strip was in the woods, and on takeoff an engine failed and the plane swerved to the side, hitting a tree, which severed the fuselage just in front of Chuck. His piece, including the aircraft tail, sailed off and made a safe landing, but everyone else was killed.

Early in my career I had an inkling that I might be particularly blessed in finding treasure. That began at Cove, with my scheme of adding the iron stained zone to the carnotite (uranium) zone, which made the target twice as big and maybe twice as easy to find. Six years later, at Copper Basin, adding the pyritic and quartz sericite zone would have increased the size of the disseminated chalcopyrite (copper) target zone by maybe ten times. Russell Corn, who later studied the Red Mountain porphyry copper deposit near Patagonia using the same logic said that on a map the whole area showing hydrothermal effects is one hundred times the area of the potential orebody in the center. I later, one way or another, used this increasing-the-target-size idea to find many new cop-

Moving our trailer
to White Canyon,
1953.

per orebodies, but it may have all begun with the Cove School exploration idea. Then step by step it later came into focus, including the opportunity to work with John Guilbert in a more systematic science-based analysis.

In late 1952 I was transferred from the AEC Cove School camp on the Navajo Reservation in northern Arizona to the White Canyon camp in southeastern Utah to explore in the Shinarump Formation. Here, outcrops of uranium deposits were again drilled using truck-mounted diamond-drill rigs for possible ore development. The camp, which was actually in Fry Canyon, near White Canyon, was bigger than Cove School, but more remote, located midway between Arches National Park and Lake Powell. The trip over Elk Ridge and the Bear's Ears into Blanding, the nearest small town, took three hours by Jeep over a winding road, and to Monticello the drive could be four or more hours. Nearby landmarks were the ferry at Hite on the Colorado River (about an hour's drive) and Natural Bridges National Monument. The Happy Jack Mine was also nearby.

We towed our trailer into White Canyon with an underpowered Jeep pickup. On the road there were sharp curves that required repeated passes to get around and deep dips that required use of the skids, which I had welded on the bottom of the trailer. The trailer was floated across the Colorado River on a primitive ferry powered by an old Model A Ford.

Our trip in impressed Edith, and her description, in a letter to her sister, told it well:

Lowell trailer on Hite
Ferry crossing the
Colorado River, 1953.
The ferry was powered
by a 1932 Ford Model A.

It took us two days to make the trip down from the highway running between Salt Lake and Grand Junction. All went quite well (though not very fast due to the gutless nature of jeep pickups) until we reached the brink of "North Wash," a tributary to the Colorado. There, to cheer the nervous wayfarer, stands a sign reading somewhat as follows: "Caution! Flash Flood Area. Do not enter in flood season! 60 wash crossings next 18 miles! Danger! Use Second Gear—DO NOT STOP." End of sign.

Well, we dragged our poor trailer through about 50 of those 60 wash crossings, Dave and I and even Susie threw rocks and dirt to build up the crossings and bridged things with planks and skidded on planks, etc., etc. We camped for the night there in North Wash (it not being flood season!) and the next day inched our way (average 3½ miles per hour!!!) down to the ferry at Hite. After the relatively tame crossing we dug our way through some more dips, on one occasion maneuvering our way across a creek by driving up the stream bed a distance and then backing down it directly toward a 12-foot waterfall in order to get room to turn back into the road on the other side! What a memorable trip. Finishing touches were a snow storm that blew up in the afternoon we finally rolled in to White Canyon Camp after running out of gas about 3 miles out of camp! But we made it, and miraculously enough no serious damage was done to our trailer—just a few scratches and loosened screws.

Once at the camp we were directed to park our trailer on a deep gully filled up with dirt, a parking space created for the camp.

At the new camp, the house trailers were spaced roughly in rows along the banks of Fry Canyon. They housed the AEC geologists, as well as Cat skinners and truck drivers and employees of the Jones Drilling Company. The population was mainly young, including a dozen or so little children. Wooden shacks served as the office buildings. There was a water trailer and bath and laundry house where the wife of one of the drillers kindly rented her gasoline-powered washing machine to the rest of us. When it threw off a belt that powered the agitator she would come and put it back on. There was a small dirt airstrip nearby.

I reported to Leo Miller, who was in the mapping AEC section, but my work involved looking for uranium targets that justified drill testing. In the camp, in addition to our friends Leo and Julie Miller, were Ross Seaton, the camp and logistics manager, and Jack Wickner, Paul Devergy, Darrell Spencer, and others whose names I don't now recall. Paul Devergy was the son of a professional musician who played in the Boston Pops orchestra, and Paul was a musician in his own right—and also a very good stand-up comic. On one occasion he was hauling an outhouse on a road along a bank of the Colorado River. The outhouse fell in the river and floated away forever. Paul came back and composed a report to the AEC about this incident which he shared with us. He had everyone in stitches.

Although the new location was beautiful and offered many wonders, we had a lot of challenges living in such a remote place, some of them simply getting to and from it. On one occasion Edith and I had driven to Blanding and were coming back in a snowstorm. We had gotten as far as the Bear's Ears, a couple of buttes made up of Wingate sandstone, at the highest elevation of the trip. The snow was getting deep, and I decided I had to put the chains on the tires, a job I hated. I had to slide on my back under the rear of the Jeep, which caused about one cubic foot of snow to be shoved between my back and my shirt. I finally got the chains on and drove over the Bear's Ears and on to White Canyon, but I stood accused of extreme crossness during the tire chains installation. When we arrived at camp we found our trailer key wouldn't work because of damage while bringing in the trailer. I had to enter the trailer by going headfirst through a ventilator in the roof, but halfway in I got stuck with my legs waving in the air. Edith's position was that anyone who had said the things to the wheel chains that I had said deserved no help. Finally I fell on my head into the trailer and was able to open the door.

We found ways to entertain ourselves on our days off. One day, Ross Seaton and I decided to go deer hunting. He said he was an expert at making venison jerky, the Utah deer season was open, and the limit was two deer per hunter. We had seen deer in the Bear's Ears vicinity. So we drove up one weekend to hunt in an area of scrub oak a few feet high. We got into a group of mule deer, and one jumped over a bush and I shot at it, and then another jumped and Ross shot at it. This went on for a couple of minutes, and we didn't know whether we had shot a deer or not. We walked over to where the deer had been jumping and found that I had shot three deer and he had shot two; with some difficulty we loaded five dead deer in the back of the Jeep and drove back to White Canyon. We skinned and quartered the deer and gave everybody who was interested some venison, but we had the equivalent of about two deer left to make jerky. Ross found some sagebrush-type plants that he said were excellent for smoking and jerking venison. So we packed the meat in salt and set up a couple of layers of makeshift shelves inside a vertical chimney to lay strips of meat about six by four inches long over the fire. We did this for the next two or three days. Unfortunately the meat had been too heavily salted and the flavor of the sagebrush left a lot to be desired, but we ended up with a large volume of smoked and jerked venison which was distributed to several families. Edith was reluctant to use this venison in cooking, and it very seldom made the menu. After a while I noticed that Spook had developed a habit of scratching all the time. In a diagnosis of Spook's ailment Edith admitted that she had been feeding him jerked, oversalted venison.

In the summer of 1953, our second summer there, Edith's family—her parents, sister, and her sister's beau—came to visit. It was the first time we had met Jack Boyer, who would become our brother-in-law. He arrived in Durango, Colorado, after hitchhiking from Boston. Georgie and I met him there and drove him to White Canyon. Georgie and Jack had met during their first year at Harvard Medical School, and he was going to spend the summer working in Tucson and getting to know his future in-laws. We took them to the spectacular Natural Bridges National Monument.

The family was lucky to have come when they did, because a week or so later it would not have been pleasant in our little camp, suffering from a fire and flood that started on a Thursday night. Here is Edith's account of the first onslaught, from a letter to her parents (July 20, 1953):

Dave and Darrell Spencer went out to Monticello to shop for groceries and arrived home at midnight (more about this later) and when at last Dave sat down and removed one boot preparatory to crawling wearily into bed, I said to him "What is that queer light in our mirror"—(a red glow I saw reflected in our bedroom mirror) and he, glancing out our open back door, gasped in strangled tones, "My gosh, it's a fire! The Engineering office is on fire!" And out he ran; one shoe off to leap into Leo's trailer and rouse Leo quickly with shouts of fire. Poor Leo in his deep sleep thought Dave meant the Geology office and nearly died of heart failure thinking of all his maps. Meanwhile Dave and Darrell dashed off like sprinters, Darrell's open khaki shirt flapping its tails about as he leaped around clutching fire extinguishers off posts. It soon appeared that not the Engineering office, but a small trailer behind it, was burning, so they set to work. Sue Spencer and I watched this show in the wee hours of the morning. Dave moved a line of vehicles away from the blaze, and turned off the gas and unplugged the blazing wreck from the electrical system. Leo (who had dashed past us to assist in the firefighting in his Levis, leaving behind him in midflight, limp upon the gravel, a pair of shorts adjudged far too difficult to get into when sleepy and excited) unscrewed some water hoses and started pouring water on the blaze. Darrell galloped around in high excitement, collecting more fire extinguishers and shouting like Paul Revere, but all the trailers were empty except for Harold's, and he came out rubbing his eyes like Rip Van Winkle to lend a hand at the finish. The poor trailer all but melted. It is a total loss. Rosella Biddle had smelled smoke when she went to bed but they couldn't find the source so the trailer had evidently smoldered for hours before breaking into flames in the middle of the night.

Well, that brings us up to Friday. On Friday we had a hard rain, and the canyon ran bank to bank, grinding boulders along the bottom with a boom-boom and completely eradicating Spook's pond, and all other water storage holes along the stream bed. Well into the night the flood roared past us in a boiling torrent.

Saturday morning dawned dark and thundery, though the canyon was not running by that time. Saturday afternoon the clouds really cut loose and in relatively few minutes we were ourselves surrounded by sheets of muddy water that poured down the slope above us and spilled into the canyon by our tree. It scoured out under our trailer, almost washed away lots of stuff we had stored under it, played havoc with the cesspool, and buried and cut away my garden! I caught our garbage can just as it floated by. Our erstwhile front yard was dissected into 3 gullies! This flood didn't last too long but by the time we took our eyes off our "houseboat on Fry River" the main Fry Canyon out in front of our trailer was really in flood, higher by several feet than the day before. As I watched, a sage bush on the bank's edge toppled and fell into the wild waters along with a big bite of the dirt bank. This gave me a tingling sensation along my spine although I felt sure we were in no danger from that direction. As I watched whole trunks of pine trees were borne past me on the crest of the flood, twisted juniper trees with clumps of roots in the air, sage bushes chewed off the banks, and always the grinding boom of boulders careening along the bottom. The flood waters were red as the dirt and covered with tan foam. The sand waves (or rapids?) threw dirty spray in the air several feet wherever the flood came to a boil! It was really a sight to see. I've seen flash floods before but never before have I lived six feet from the edge of one and had part of it run under my house!

Well, this, too, passed away and Sunday morning was bright and clear. We cleaned up and cleaned mud out of the trailer where we had tracked it in and Dave jacked up the right rear corner of the trailer again where the waters had carried off the big rock (or dug out beneath it, I should say) and given us a heavy list to Starboard. I plastered dirt around the naked roots of several morning glories that the waters had spared, and all in all, everything was shipshape again.

Letter to Edith's sister, August 4, 1953:

This last weekend we all went to Cove, that AEC Promised Land, beauty spot of the plateau, etc. so Dave could do some work for his thesis. All there were as helpful to Dave as could be, even working on their days off, etc.! It was fun to see everyone again.

But while we were there, flood came again to White Canyon. This time it nearly took us off our island for sure. My last squash plant is gone. The rear end of the trailer overhangs a scour down to bedrock. Between us and the Seeton trailer is a hair raising gulley about fourteen feet deep— no exaggeration—also down to bedrock. This time our garbage can went, also the top to the small washing machine (possibly insured). We have no front yard left, practically. The Millers also lost their garbage can. Our back door swings out over emptiness—a 2 or 3 foot drop to white Cedar Mesa sandstone bedrock!

Needless to say, we are moving to another location—probably down by the Spencers, to avoid being washed away.

The month after those heavy rains, I was driving a Jeep alone from our camp to Hite Ferry and had to cross Fry Canyon, which was in flood. Another pickup truck without four-wheel drive, owned by a city tourist, had tried to cross ahead of me and had stalled out in the middle of the flood and was beginning to roll over. I drove around him in the flood, got out a chain, and pulled him out to the other bank, undoubtedly saving his vehicle from being washed away. I was wearing a new pair of handmade Russell boots, the best pair of field boots I had ever owned before or since, and one washed away in the flood while I was getting the chain hitched. I pointed this out to the other driver when he was getting his truck started and he said, "Tough luck," and drove off.

By this time, I had been accepted at the University of Arizona graduate school, and I think Edith was a bit relieved to think we would be returning to Tucson in a few weeks for me to go back to school.

Then, in an unexpected turn of events, AEC offered me a promotion, with a raise. They asked me to take the job of acting district geologist for District Three in the Monument Valley, Cameron, and Holbrook area, where we would study the Chinle Formation to look for uranium mineralization. The job offer came with the promise of another promotion to district geologist. In short order I would get a GS11 rating. It was an offer I couldn't refuse. It was a tough decision, though, as I also had to contact Professor McKee at the University of Arizona Geology Department and hope they could postpone my entry for another year.

Toward the end of our stay at White Canyon we learned there had been an atom bomb test in Nevada, and we started testing the air with our Geiger counters. Very soon the radioactivity began to increase rapidly, and some readings were off the scale of our instruments. We tried to stay inside one or two days until it blew over. I remember once Spook went out and came back in very "hot." There was no official warning of this event and almost nothing in the press about it, and we wondered about the health worries, but we never learned that anyone developed any problems. We all thought the government had been very irresponsible.

When we left White Canyon, we towed the trailer with a Dodge Power Wagon, a powerful, heavy, slow-moving, awkward vehicle, and we came out on a different road. On one curve, the road was going uphill and at the same time sloping toward the cliff on the inside of the curve. I tried several times to get around the curve and each time the trailer slid toward the cliff. Finally I backed up one hundred yards, got up as much speed as possible, and turned the curve while centrifugal force kept the trailer from sliding off the road.

While still working for the AEC in Holbrook, Arizona, I was selected, along with Ernie Gordon, who was the general manager of the Grand Junction AEC office, to make a trip to the Dominican Republic.

The Dominican government had requested the services of American uranium exploration experts. I was the expert, and Ernie was the boss who had a lot of Latin American experience and who was also interested in a junket trip. We flew to Miami in a top-of-the-line Super Constellation, a Lockheed propeller-driven airplane like the one used by President Eisenhower and those involved in the Berlin airlift a few years earlier. From Miami we flew to the Dominican capital, then called Ciudad Trujillo, in honor of the dictator in power at that time, and later called Santo Domingo.

When we arrived, the Secretary of State without Portfolio met us at the airport and walked us through Immigration and Customs to a black Cadillac limousine with a military driver, a soldier with a submachine gun. We then drove to the Jaragua Hotel, which at that time was the number one hotel in Ciudad Trujillo. Nothing happened for a couple of days except that we sat under umbrellas and drank a variety of rum drinks, and had to move only when the sun moved the shadows from under the umbrella and we had to move our beach chairs.

The third day we had an audience with the Secretary of Geography (the Dominican Republic didn't have a Secretary of Mining) whose name I can't recall. He told us they thought an important uranium discovery had been made in the Dominican Republic and they wanted us to go examine it when the trip was organized. This organization required several additional days, during which we suffered the imposition of having to move our chairs when the shade from the umbrellas shifted. Then the members of the expedition arrived early one morning: the Secretary of Geography, Colonel Calderon from the Secret Police, and several heavily armed soldiers in our limousine and another similar black limousine. Also present was a small nervous-looking Italian man who we were told was the government's consulting geologist who had discovered the uranium deposit.

We drove for a couple of hours over increasingly worse roads until the low-slung Cadillac started high-centering on roads and finally came to a place where there had been a small excavation consisting of a pit about eight feet deep. The geologist said that this was the site of the discovery, but by this time he seemed even more apprehensive. I had a Geiger counter, a portable gamma-ray-detecting instrument that measures radiation, and a scintillation counter, which is more sensitive than the Geiger counter. I took readings in the pit and on the walls and around the pit and found nothing anomalously radioactive, which was reported to the Dominican officials.

Colonel Calderon, who was apparently in charge of this expedition, was carrying a Colt .45 M1911 pistol in a holster, which he then removed and said in Spanish, "I am going to pistolear this blankety blank," at which point the Italian was terrified and paralyzed and looked around for help from the other members of the group. Ernie Gordon, who spoke good Spanish and had some diplomatic talents, said to Colonel Calderon, "Calm down, Colonel, geology is not an exact science," at which point the Colonel put the pistol back in his holster and said, "We will look into this further," and he seemed to settle down. We were ready to head back to the hotel. But while we were getting organized to go back, I thought I would take advantage of my status and asked one of the heavily armed soldiers if he would mind if I tried out his submachine gun. He said "Sure," so I fired a few rounds at a palm tree with this gun which was manufactured in the Dominican Republic, and I thought it operated well.

Back at the hotel there was a period of about two days when we were again burdened by having to move our chairs to stay in the shade and had to be sure that our Planter's Punch was delivered on schedule. Then we got another communication saying that our help was going to be desired, and we again went in the two limousines with the armed soldiers and the frightened Italian geologist to the frightened geologist's home, which was quite nice and where he had an attractive young Dominican wife or girlfriend and a small child.

I was asked to check with my Geiger counter all of the rock collection in the house, and I found one specimen which was strongly radioactive, which had been previously shown to the Dominican officials. In later interrogation the geologist admitted that this specimen had been given to him by a classmate who was working at a uranium mine in Yugoslavia. We later heard that a trial had been held, and the Italian was given two years imprisonment and then banishment forever from the Dominican Republic. The Dominican government, or maybe just President Trujillo, had apparently become totally convinced that the Italian geologist (now in jail) had found a big, high-grade uranium mine in the country. It may be that this idea had in some way been translated into a nice atom bomb that would make all his Caribbean neighbors tremble in their underwear and give President Trujillo the respect he thought he deserved.

Right after our visit to the geologist's home, the officials decided that as long as I was there with my instruments I should do some regional exploration. They had a de Havilland Beaver, a Canadian-made airplane with a very loud engine, and I laid out some profiles in the jungle in the area that I thought had the highest probability of a uranium deposit and mounted the scintillation counter near the tail of the airplane away from radioactive aircraft instruments but accessible from inside the airplane. I rode with the pilots to navigate the plane on the approximate routes I had laid out and then would run back to watch the scintillation counter, but nothing ever happened. We began thinking that it might be better to give up the resort hotel and go back to Colorado. Anyway, a little while after my unsuccessful airborne radioactivity survey in the noisy de Havilland Beaver I was approached again. The Minister of Geography and Colonel Calderon (who seemed to combine the offices of secret service and national security) came to see me, not my boss. Ernie Gordon had far more status and knew a lot more about Latin American diplomacy, but the Minister and the Colonel were desperate. I could imagine that Trujillo had told them something along the lines of, "I want you to find the damn uranium mine, period." They had noticed that I was the one who had a duffel bag full of scintillation counters and Geiger counters and knew some big words relating to uranium geology, so I was summoned again. This time they had a lead on another mineral prospect out in the jungle somewhere.

Our field trip started off in the two black Cadillacs with sirens and submachine guns as far as the road would take us, then continued on mules until we arrived at the second mineral prospect. I unpacked my instruments and did another comprehensive survey of radioactivity, or lack thereof, in the mine dump, tunnels, and outcrop. The little Italian geologist was not with us pleading for his life. There also was no radio-activity. By this time it was late in the day, and our leaders decided we should spend the night in a village near where we had left the Cadillacs. When we arrived at the village, some of us moved into the mayor's house. I think he had received advance notice through a two-way radio. In the Dominican Republic at that time there was a pervasive atmosphere of hard-boiled, maybe even vicious, dictatorial power. I may have imagined it, but I thought some of the people in the village looked at me like some unfortunate Spaniard might have looked at a member of the Inquisition arriving in town.

By this time I was very dirty and soaked in sweat, and I asked where the bathing facilities were. I was shown a shower bath outside the house, enclosed by a sort of split-bamboo fence. I disrobed and got in the shower and was having a good bath when I got a funny feeling and looked carefully at the shower wall. There were several places where the bamboo strips didn't quite meet—in the gaps were vertical rows of little brown eyes, and on the outside a crowd of children trying to see what the strange gringo looked like with no clothes on. I decided I had no more modesty to lose and finished my bath.

We had dinner at a round table in the mayor's house. The dinner began with large glasses of beer filled from pitchers held by servers standing behind us. I had several swallows of beer when I noticed a fly, either on the inside surface below the beer level, or on the outside surface of the glass. I tried several casual motions intended to make the beer server notice the fly in my glass. He either didn't notice or thought it was totally unimportant. I decided the only thing I could do was drink the rest of the beer in one gulp and then see where the fly was. I did the big gulp, but before I could look for the fly the server with the pitcher darted forward and refilled the glass!

The main dish was *sancocho*, a heavily spiced, watery stew with meat and a variety of local vegetables, many of which I had never heard of. I was, and still am, a meat-and-potatoes guy, very suspicious of new vegetables and avoiding when possible large doses of spice. When my large bowl was filled with sancocho there were pieces of strange vegetables bobbing to the surface through a layer of grease. I thought this might be the final chapter for my digestive system, but I survived the meal with no ill effects. We went back to Ciudad Trujillo and then had to go back to Cameron, Arizona, where there was no swimming pool or rum drinks and no one ever told me that I was either wise or important. I look back nostalgically on my VIP tour in the Dominican Republic.

At that time I was promoted to acting manager of District Three. I was first stationed at the Cameron Trading Post, near the north side of the Grand Canyon. David Hinckley became my assistant there. He and his wife moved to Cameron also. It was a tourist site on a paved road, and it was easy for us to drive from Cameron to Flagstaff, Arizona. It was in Cameron that I became acquainted with Charles Repenning, a United States Geological Survey (USGS) paleontologist who later became one of my best friends.

In a letter to her parents Edith described Cameron:

At Cameron Trading Post our trailer was parked in the back beyond the shower house and clotheslines. There were some cottonwood trees for shade. It was an isolated motel and gas station that began as a trading post and grew with the tourist business. It was there that Bill disappeared one day while I was hanging out the washing. Susie and I ran about anxiously, even trying to get to the edge of the cliff in back in spite of sloping terrain and bushes to look over with dread! Finally we ran out to the front of the restaurant where we found Bill being held up to the pool table by a friendly Navajo man. The people there had kindly kept him safely entertained until I came looking for him. Bill was quite happy watching the game.

While we were at Cameron, a *National Geographic* photographer named Volkmar Wentzel came by. He was working on an article on the uranium industry, and a photo of David Hinckley and me staring over a cliff was published in the article.

A few months after we arrived at Cameron, I was transfered to Holbrook, Arizona, where we rented a duplex and sold our house trailer. By this time I was made permanent manager of District Three and was promoted to a government GS11 rate, which was a middle-management rate, and my salary was increased to $9,000 a year, which then was a high salary. My duties as manager of District Three consisted mainly of driving around to visit the five active projects and offer advice and instructions to the geologists. I also did some "rim flying" in a Super Cub aircraft, which is a slow-flying, short-field landing, two-passenger airplane. The plane had a very sensitive scintillation counter built into it. My pilot Don Wonder and I flew the Super Cub close to the ground along favorable formations in the side of the Grand Canyon and other places like Navajo Mountain. We found a radioactive anomaly near the top of Navajo Mountain and dropped two gallon bottles of red paint to mark the spot. Having identified an anomaly, I then organized a trip with one other geologist, renting horses from the Navajos to ride in to find that spot on the ground. We spent one day riding in and a day at the site sleeping in sleeping bags on the ground and one day returning but could never find the anomaly that had been marked. On the way in we passed a place where cavities in the top of a ledge had filled with water and the horses got a drink. By the time we returned the several gallons of water that we had carried had been drunk, and we got off the horses and went to some pools of water that had been somewhat con-taminated by the horses and had a good drink ourselves.

At this time little was known about the stratigraphy of this area of the Colorado Plateau, and at the suggestion of Charles Repenning I measured a stratigraphic section. This involved two of us, a young geologist and myself, riding horses to the bottom of this mile-long sec-tion and measuring the thickness and petrology of the different strati-graphic units, always moving uphill to the end of the one-mile-long section. We then rode our horses back and spent the night in Chinle, Arizona, which since has become a popular tourist site. Don Wonder was a very skilled Super Cub pilot and a very relaxed person. On one occasion we were flying down the river and he said, "Have you ever flown under a bridge?" I said "No," so he flew us under the bridge. Another of his tricks was to carry two short pieces of 2x4 lumber to use to "bounce" the Super Cub into the air while taking off at right angles to a paved highway. Once, we were flying from the Grand Canyon back to Holbrook and he asked, "Have you ever flown an airplane?" I said "No," and he said, "It's simple—you push the stick forward to go down and pull the stick back to climb and you push the rudders and push the stick sideways to make it turn and it's very easy and the magnetic bearing to the Holbrook Airport is such and such and I think I'll now get a little nap." So I flew for an hour and a half and woke him up when I could see the airport. That made me decide I wanted to become a pilot myself someday.

While I was working out of Holbrook we did some work on a volcanic diatreme site that had a little uranium mineralization in the Hopi Buttes District north of Holbrook. I did some mapping and sampling and later, while I was in graduate school, reproduced the diatreme structure with scale model technology. This work was later published in a short *American Journal of Science* article.

During our year with AEC in Holbrook, I changed plans for my master's degree program. Instead of going to the University of Arizona, I went to Stanford at the suggestion of University of Arizona Professor Edwin McKee, who had arranged for my admission on the basis of an entrance exam and in spite of poor undergraduate grades. I didn't have a scholarship at Stanford as I would have had at Arizona. In 1952 and '53, while I was still at White Canyon, I worked with Professor McKee determining the relationship between cross stratification in sandstones of the Brushy Basin Formation in Utah and the locations of "roll front" carnotite uranium orebodies. He was a distinguished sedimentologist.

For no specific reason, I had initiated at Cove School a study of mapping of fossil stream direction indicators: cross-bending and ripple marks and lineation. This was used as an aid in finding uranium deposits. I also noticed that the uranium deposits had iron stained halos doubling their size as drill targets. As a result I took another academic step and authored my first publication, which appeared in the *Journal of*

Economic Geology, edited by Professor McKee. These discoveries were small, and I was the only one excited, but the basic idea was part of the inspiration twelve years later for using peripheral zoning to enlarge the porphyry copper drill target. I was the only geologist in the AEC group to pursue or publish research.

I had very mixed feelings when we decided to leave the Atomic Energy Commission to enroll in Stanford graduate school. The people I worked with in the AEC were almost uniformly pleasant, well-meaning, and honest. The decision to get a geology degree was clearly a good career plan for me and made possible my later unreasonably successful professional record. It fit my increasing interest in developing independent scientific ideas. I did not feel strongly about enrolling in Stanford instead of the University of Arizona, but this decision was really made for me by Professor McKee. Edith made a loyal sacrifice because she had hoped to move back to Tucson, near her family. I attended classes at Stanford for only nine months, writing my thesis after leaving campus, but I profited from the prestige of a Stanford degree and a lot learned in a short time.

CHAPTER FOUR

MS Geology at Stanford, 1954–1955

While I was at Holbrook I built a two-wheel trailer made out of parts of a junked 1951 Ford pickup. When we left Holbrook we packed our belongings in the trailer and left for California. Somewhere in the Mojave Desert we stopped alongside the highway for a drink of water. After we had driven for thirty minutes I asked if Spook was in the car, and he was not. We turned around and drove back and had been looking carefully for about an hour when out of the corner of my eye I saw a profile that looked out of place in the desert. It was Spook on the opposite side of the highway, completely dehydrated. He panted for an hour, and we wondered if it had permanently affected his health, but probably not.

We arrived in Palo Alto in late summer 1954, about two weeks before classes started, having successfully towed that homemade trailer. We stayed in a motel for several days and had an intensive house hunt. One available house was two stories and looked very much like the Addams Family house on a popular TV program. We finally found a house in a blue-collar neighborhood in Menlo Park a little bit farther from Stanford University. Our next-door neighbor was a truck driver who had a daughter Susie's age, and when Susie told her friend that I was a student she said, "My daddy went to school when he was a boy."

We arrived at Stanford with a new Dodge automobile and thought

Bill and Susie on the Stanford campus in 1955 while David was a graduate student.

we had enough money to last three years, but everything was more expensive than we expected and, with two small children, there was no chance for Edith to get a job. And we found things around Stanford University somewhat unwelcoming. When Edith took our two kids to visit the Memorial Church, they were asked to leave because our two-year-old boy, Bill, had spoken out loud to ask a question. I tried to go swimming in a university pool and was unable to, because they had a racing pool, and a diving pool, but no swim-just-for-the-fun-of-it pool. We took Spook to a nearby park, and he got his eye on a pheasant and chased it for about a hundred yards with a bunch of locals looking very disapproving, so we didn't take Spook back to the park.

On one occasion I drove into San Francisco for a meeting with a consulting geologist. I plotted my course out on a map and got there in good shape, but on my return I turned the corner and faced four lanes of traffic coming directly at me and had to back up violently. I had misunderstood the direction of the flow of traffic.

My first event at Stanford was an orientation lecture, where a pious, self-righteous individual lectured about what a wonderful place Stanford was and assured us that we would soon get the "Stanford spirit," but sixty years later I somehow haven't gotten the Stanford spirit. One thing that was true of my classmates, most of whom had come from places like Yale and Harvard, was that they had previously taken most of my courses once before but the previous course had had a slightly different name. Needless to say, this, together with the fact that they were carefully chosen expert students, made the playing field a little bit uneven. However, overall I got reasonably good grades, and I really learned a lot of geology in nine short months, during which time I often studied fourteen hours a day.

My professors at the Stanford College of Earth Sciences were Bob Compton, who was very well known in his field; Dr. Colin Osborn Hutton from New Zealand, who was quite famous; Simon Wilhelm Mueller, who actually thought I was a good student; and Fred Park, who taught a class on ore deposits and was an effective educator. George A. Thompson, an eminent geophysicist and a young man at the time, was one of my professors as well as my advisor. He was a very kind man, and one of the most intelligent people I have known. Fred Park was the dean of the College of Earth Sciences; he was said to have been given the job because he was the only faculty member all the others would speak to.

Dr. Compton, in his homework assignments, sometimes gave us reading assignments in six languages, including Japanese. Dr. Mueller taught a course in which, at the beginning, he said, "I am going to give you some information which is correct and some info which is incorrect and it will be up to you to judge which to use." This was very disturbing to my Stanford classmates, but ignoring the dogmas was something in which I excelled, and I got an A in his class. He also offered to get me a job as a college professor at the University of Oregon. I had one article published while I was at Stanford from my work in the AEC.

Some of the other students stand out in my mind. Mario Camacho was from Mexico, and Alberto Manrique, who was from Peru, is still a close friend. Alberto and his wife, Luz, attended my Doctor Honoris Causa ceremony in Lima. Tony Payne and Jack Frost were two students who told wild tales; Don Peterson was later USGS director of the volcanology center in Hawaiʻi; and there was a girl who twice fainted when the first question was asked in her oral exam for a PhD. Also there was an attractive blonde girl with a super high IQ in my paleontology class who sat down next to me and asked me if I had a girlfriend. There was an Indonesian student who did something very dishonest, like embezzlement, who asked me to lend him $70 to save him, which I did, and then he was put in the Redwood City jail anyway, and I had to go to the jail to get my $70 back. This episode horrified several of the Stanfordians.

After three quarters at Stanford I had used up all my savings. I had qualified with languages for a PhD, but would have had lots of additional course work and the dissertation, which would take a minimum of two or three additional years, so I decided to compromise with a master's degree. George Thompson agreed that I would write a thesis on my own, which I did in the next two years, while working for Ranwick Inc. The thesis described the geology of the Menlove-Dalton uranium deposit and the geology of the mineral district in which it was located. It was not a great contribution to science, but I had jumped through all the hoops to write an acceptable thesis, and I received my master's degree in 1957.

In retrospect my career was probably more successful without the PhD, which might have pushed me into a teaching job or a big mining company job, where my maverick streak would probably have caused my career to plateau. I will never know.

Ranwick Inc., Menlove Mine, and Southwest Ventures

Prior to completing my master of science degree from Stanford, I received an offer from Tom Mitchum to become chief geologist for Ranwick Inc., which was a subsidiary of Ventures Limited, a Canadian company that operated through a large number of subsidiaries, including several important operating mining companies like Falconbridge Nickel, McIntyre Mines, Frobeshier, and Compañía La India in Nicaragua. Tom Mitchum had been one of my former bosses in the AEC and was now Ranwick's president and general manager. I was hired in 1955 with a salary of $11,000 per year, which was a very good pay rate in 1955. We moved from Stanford to Denver, Colorado, and as it happened I was alone when looking for a house in Denver. I found a house on University Boulevard, a remodeled farmhouse in the middle of a large lot. It was about an acre of land all in lawn, and a beautiful house nicely fitted out. It had one flaw: the garage opened on an alley behind the house, and it was almost impossible to drive from the alley into the garage. The car had to be backed in.

I went back to Palo Alto to get the family and drove them to Denver. I was feeling proud of this house. I thought, "Boy, you've really pulled off a coup here." Edith took one look at it and burst into tears. I think it was the garage that got her more than anything. She once knocked several palings out of the neighbors' fence trying to back in. She finally became fond of it. We had some friends in Denver, and it really was a nice house.

In this job, I was traveling most of the time. Ranwick acquired a uranium deposit, which they developed into a mine called the Menlove-Dalton Mine. It was in southeastern Utah. A year later, Tom Mitchum resigned to go to work for Kennecott Copper and I became vice president and general manager of Ranwick. By default I became manager of the uranium mine because I was the only one who knew anything about mining at that point. The mine had a short, sort of chaotic and turbulent life. The Ranwick budget was cut and most of the other geologists were fired. At one point I was in Toronto and one of the company officials gave me a Ventures Limited Company brochure, which at that time had 120 subsidiaries. Most of them were almost dormant, but a few were making money. It was a very unusual company, and the CEO was Thayer Lindsley, a legendary mine finder in Canada who wasn't very interested in the details of financing. During the mine operation we at one point ran out of funds in our bank account so I called the Ventures treasurer and asked to have some money transferred. He said, "Well, I'll look around, I think there's some money in one or another of these companies." I later read that Thayer Lindsley was severely criticized by shareholders and the Ontario Stock Commission and other people for moving money from one company to another. He wasn't doing it for any bad reasons, but just to try to keep everything going.

The Menlove-Dalton Mine was out in the flats near Dove Creek, Colorado. It was a mine that almost made it, but never quite made it, because there wasn't enough ore to support a long-term mining operation. At one point, during the spring thaw of 1956, we had two or three Jeeps, a road grader, a bulldozer, and a big haul truck. One of these got stuck in the mud, and another bigger one was sent to pull the first one out, and the second one got stuck, and so on, until every one of our whole rolling fleet were all stuck in a line in this bottomless mud pit. There were lots of problems.

We had an animal haulage ore transport system and we had, I think, three mules, including a lady mule, and they had been trained to tow ore cars that had automobile wheels so they would roll easily. They were trained to dump their cars in the ore bin. Anyway, this jenny mule backed her car and dumped a ton of ore into the ore bin, but she backed a little too far and the ore car pulled her into the ore bin, and there was great excitement. I was a nonresident manager, and I wasn't there much of the time. She was rescued and pulled out of the ore bin and dusted off and didn't have anything broken. But mules are very peculiar animals, and she decided, "That's it. No more hauling for me." And she wouldn't ever pull her car again after that. She had permanently and unequivocally resigned from the mining industry, and we had to restore her to agriculture.

While we lived in Denver we became acquainted with an attractive but very flighty young lady who had a husband named Garth. Once she called and I answered the phone and she said in a breathless voice, "Dave, I called to tell you Garth is coming up the alley!" I was frightened because it sounded like Garth might have detected a lascivious glance which I didn't remember making and decided to grab a club and come looking for me. However, the purpose of his trip was to ask me to fix the Mixmaster, because his wife thought I was a clever repairman.

Eventually the Menlove-Dalton Mine slowed down to a stop and was closed. In the meantime I had found a copper prospect for the com-

Susie, Edith, Doug, David, Spook, and Bill at the Cory Farm residence in Prescott, 1956.

pany at Copper Basin, Arizona, near Prescott. The budget had shrunk by this time, and we moved to Prescott.

On June 6, 1956, our younger son, Doug, was born in Prescott. We no longer lived in a house trailer in a remote location, as we did when Susie and Bill were toddlers. We had a nice house in the middle of a large field that was bordered by pine woods. The house was called Cory Farm, and the original occupant was an heir of the Cory Coffee Pot family.

While we lived in Prescott I visited a mine in Mexico near the town of Soyopa, Sonora, with Fred Gibbs, a mining engineer friend in Prescott. We both contracted a disease that put us in bed for two or three weeks with high fevers and drastic digestive symptoms. The disease was tentatively diagnosed as bat fever. A friend named it Soyopa Fever, and I suspect it had a permanent effect on my digestive system. Doug was a bright-eyed baby and showed an early interest in me. When I was lying on my back in bed with Soyopa Fever he climbed up on the bed and sat on my chest to try to determine why I wasn't playing with him.

I did a careful study of the Copper Basin District and eventually wrote an article on which I was joint author with Bill Johnson, who had written a dissertation on the Copper Basin District. I had done more work in the district than Bill and had also drilled several holes and developed some additional ideas regarding the breccia pipes, which were the high-grade parts of the ore deposit. The article was published in *Economic Geology*. It was then that I noticed and became fascinated by the concentric hydrothermal alteration which later became the Porphyry Copper Model. Copper Basin was the "school" that turned me into a competent porphyry copper geologist.

Toward the end of my work at Copper Basin, I was visited by Thayer Lindsley, the legendary mine finder and CEO of Ventures Limited, parent company of Southwest Ventures. I believe the two days I was in the field with Mr. Lindsley had a significant effect on the rest of my career. Mr. Lindsley was a very unusual and admirable gentleman. He was polite and kind to everyone and had a photographic memory. He was a graduate of Harvard College and a classmate of Franklin Roosevelt and J. C. Penney. He had an elegant apartment in New York and was in the habit of laying out large maps on the floor and walking over them in his stocking feet trying to decide where the orebodies were. He was called "TL" and was known by many of the prospectors in eastern Canada, and sometimes insisted on paying them more for their claims than they had asked for.

Soon after the Menlove Mine closed, Ranwick Inc. ceased to exist, but Ventures Ltd. had another subsidiary that had been active largely in Mexico, called Southwest Ventures Incorporated. They told me they were going to make me vice president of Southwest Ventures, so I just changed the letterhead and went on with pretty much the same job, but we moved from Prescott to Tucson in 1957. Edith was overjoyed because she felt very strongly about her roots in southern Arizona.

In Tucson we rented a house for a year, and then built a new home. Edith's father and mother (and Edith) had homesteaded an area in the Catalina foothills north of Tucson. They had sold some land but retained a good part of it, some of which they had given to Edith, and we had a house built on an acre lot and moved in during the spring of 1958. I built a swimming pool myself, thinking that because I knew quite a bit about making an open pit mine the swimming pool would be easy, but I ran into complications.

Brackston Whittaker, an old friend of mine who had been a friend of my brother's in Tucson, had a swimming pool company. Another friend and I both built our own swimming pools at the same time. We were both friends of Brack Whittaker, and we would go to him and ask how to do various things. We were talking to him at a party once, and he finally said, "You know what you fellows should do is get a night job and save the money and let me build your swimming pools." Which would have been very good advice to follow, but we didn't do that. Eventually, I finished our pool and the family enjoyed many cool dips in it. I have always been optimistic, or overoptimistic, about being able to do things and build things.

During my employment by Ranwick Inc., I reported to Dan Bateman, chief geologist of Ventures Limited. Dr. Bateman (as he preferred being called) was very much a member of the stiff-upper-lip, formal-English, Canadian upper-class culture. He told me once that he was twelve years old on the first occasion when he went to family dinner without wearing a necktie. He traveled a lot and prided himself in traveling with just a large briefcase containing a cardigan sweater and a spare shirt. He wore a blue serge suit and a bowler hat and a bow tie in the field and even underground in mines. When I moved to Southwest Ventures my boss was Jim Harquail who, I believe, had become chief geologist following the death of Dr. Bateman in an automobile accident. Both Bateman and Harquail were exploration geologists with complete confidence in geophysical exploration, with which I disagreed based on my own experience.

In 1956 I was asked to put in a summer field season, working directly for Ranwick's parent company, Ventures Limited, in exploration projects in northern Canada. We worked in Manitoba, Saskatchewan, and the Northwest Territories from June through September. I worked with Don MacDonald, a Canadian geologist who had some previous Canadian bush experience and was in charge of our project. Our first assignment was to fly in a floatplane, a small amphibious airplane with floats rather than wheels, to a very isolated spot called Big Assean Lake, about two hundred miles west of Fort Churchill on Hudson Bay. This site was almost completely covered with muskeg and had been located by an airborne geophysical survey. We flew in a not very new Cessna floatplane and, to bring our complete camping outfit, including tent and kitchen and geophysical equipment, the rear seat and the right front seat had to be removed and the cabin packed almost full, leaving only room for Don and me to lie flat on the load. With a certain amount of difficulty he found the lake and landed, and we set up camp. I was not convinced that the bush pilot would remember to pick us up in ten days as scheduled. There had been a snowshoe rabbit living where we pitched the tent, and he hopped up several times and looked at us (with what I thought was an accusing expression).

Our work consisted of surveying parallel lines over an area of about fifty acres and then carrying out an electromagnetic survey following the lines. One held the transmitter and the other one the receiver. We recorded a number at each station in a field book and each day filled several pages of the book. We kept a mosquito index by counting the number of squashed mosquitoes on each page and this ranged from five to twenty per page. We had a fishing pole, but no time to fish. After work one day I got it out and made three casts and caught a ten-pound pike, and we had two fish dinners.

The day before we left that site, I was suffering from my own body odor and decided to bathe in the lake, which still had a fringe of ice on the shoreline. There was a rock outcrop on the edge, and I thought if I climbed up on the rock and jumped into the lake I would at least get wet all over, but somehow I jumped and got out of the lake with part of me still dry. The plane arrived on time and we got everything loaded back in and flew back.

That summer, while we were working out of Lac La Ronge, Saskatchewan, about 150 miles north of the nearest road, which was at Prince Albert, I had a little mishap. We were a party of three on this trip: Don, the Canadian geologist; Sandy, a Cree Indian who spoke only a little English; and me. Our fieldwork was near Reindeer Lake on the Saskatchewan-Manitoba border, another two hundred miles to the northeast and near the southern border of the Northwest Territories. The terrain in this area is called the "barren lands" because the extreme winter weather stunts the evergreens, and the open areas all consist of permafrost. In the summer the upper several feet of soil thaws, creating muskeg.

When we started work each morning we headed for a patch of standing water and stepped in, sinking twelve inches or so and filling our boots up with water so we wouldn't worry the rest of the day about getting our feet wet. Along with the muskeg are thousands of little lakes from one-quarter of a mile to a mile or more in diameter. The small floatplane flew us from lake to lake, sometimes staying with us and sometimes flying back to Larange (a community of about two hundred people in the summer). Because this was a hit-and-run project mostly for the purpose of claim-staking, we had a minimum of amenities: a small nylon tent, small propane stove, canned goods and bread and ham, sleeping bags, and a five-gallon water can.

My medical problem was indirectly caused by Sandy, whose one outstanding talent was sharpening the axes we used. The way claim-staking was done was to first go to the District Mining Recorder's Office (maybe in Prince Albert) and get numbered aluminum strips to identify your new claims. In the field we located with crude surveys the corners of the claim and on the corners picked a tree five or six inches in diameter and cut the top off about head high. Using the axe we squared the top of the tree and nailed on the aluminum numbered plate. An effort was made to indicate to competitors where the claim was located with flagging and blazed lines.

I had used axes most of my life, but they were always dull or only slightly sharp. The one Sandy handed me was literally sharp enough to shave with, which I didn't remember at one point. I picked it up by the head and cut my hand badly with lots of blood. We tied it up with a rag, but it continued to bleed all day and the next night. We had a first aid kit at camp, and the hand was wrapped tightly with a bandage, but some bleeding continued. After a discussion the next morning Don got a sewing kit out of his pack and sewed the cut up with black carpet thread—not without some howling by the sew-ee! This worked fine. About a week later we flew back to Lac La Ronge, where there was a clinic operated by two young, well-educated Cree nurses. They looked at my hand and were amused, but said I was fine and removed the stitches and rebandaged the hand. They asked if they could keep the stitches and showed us their collection of do-it-yourself splints made out of pine limbs and slings and braces all improvised in the field. By the time this conversation was finished we had all agreed to meet for dinner at the Northern Lights Hotel, the best (and only) hotel in Lac La Ronge.

Once we were trying to meet someone from another company also involved in the staking rush. We saw a figure sitting on a canvas chair on the shore of Reindeer Lake in a completely isolated spot. We landed and taxied up within conversation distance and learned he was not the one we were looking for. We asked him why he was there and he said he was from Detroit and was taking a two-week vacation on the shore of the lake. He said, "I plan to sit and think the first week and just sit the second week."

Part of the summer we tied a heavy canoe under the wing of a float-plane and periodically landed and paddled, taking rock samples on the shore outcrops, prospecting for nickel. We didn't find anything of value that summer, but all our work was based on geophysics. One of our field assistants taught me how to say in the Cree language, "Sweetheart, you would look very good in a bikini bathing suit." However, I found neither anyone who fit this description nor anyone who would admit to understanding me. After about three months I was released to return to Arizona.

Following that summer in the north, my work for Southwest Ventures was largely in Mexico, Arizona, California, and New Mexico. I was mainly examining mineral prospects submitted to us and some-times making option agreements and carrying out exploration drilling projects on the prospects. On one occasion we carried out a joint exploration venture with Cominco, a large Canadian company, in the Prescott District, looking for massive sulfide deposits of the Jerome variety. We encountered some smells of mineralization but nothing that came close to a viable deposit. The representative of Cominco was a somewhat eccentric individual named Dr. Neil Campbell who was difficult to work with. He had a PhD and was a fuddy-duddy type of geologist. I examined many mineral prospects in Mexico for Southwest Ventures, but they were in the "submittal" rather than "grassroots" category and most had relatively small potential. Thirty years later I did extensive grassroots porphyry copper exploration in Sonora that produced a couple of near-miss prospects.

The political history of Mexico has a lot of bearing on the country's mineral development. Porfirio Díaz, considered a benevolent dictator, was the Mexican president from 1877 to 1910. While he was in power, there was relatively less corruption and many schools and clinics were built, and it was a golden age for mining development, although it largely preceded the later era of developing large, highly mechanized mines. A lot of the prospects we visited were found before 1910 but had been permanently shut down by the Mexican revolution, which began in 1910 and lasted more than fifteen years.

Some memorable events happened in Mexico between 1957 and 1959. Once I was asked to look at a largely promotional prospect in the state of Chiapas, in southern Mexico. I met the Canadian junior mining company president, who drove me around in a 4x4 International Scout to look at mineral showings on his property. He was a geologist, but one of many mineral explorationists who do not understand the principle that "ore is rock which can be mined at a profit," and that a few copper stains not related to a high-grade, thick, continuous, vein or a large area of pervasive, low-grade mineralization is simply a scientific curiosity. His superficial knowledge of exploration was matched by his superficial knowledge of Spanish, and after spending several hours looking at the prospect he said, "Would you like to have a cold beer?" I very seldom drink anything alcoholic during working hours, but agreed. He had hired a Mexican family as caretakers and to furnish room and board for a couple of expatriates. He drove up to the front door of the house, and when the owners came out the geologist said in Spanish in a commanding tone, "I would like to have service (*servicio*)." The problem was that in some Latin countries the restroom is called the "servicio." The two Mexicans looked at each other with dumbfounded expressions, and then one man said to me in Spanish in a low voice, "Does he want to do it right in the car?"

On one trip to Mexico a group of us from the company arrived at the place where we were supposed to meet the mules. We needed six mules but only two arrived. It sounded as though there would be a one-day delay in the trip as a result of this, and I impatiently said, "I'll go now with the guide with these two mules and you other fellows can wait until the mules arrive." (As an aside, I found that about two times out of three the mules or horses that were promised did not materialize on the first day of many visits to mineral prospects in Mexico, and this was a consistent problem.) I left with the guide, and we rode ahead to the prospect and looked around. We didn't have sleeping bags, as our sleeping bags had been due to arrive later the first day, and we slept on the ground. We didn't have anything to eat and we found a volunteer squash that had grown on a plant where the garden used to be. We divided that into two and ate it raw and had a less than comfortable night's sleep waiting for the rest of the party. In the middle of the morning the following day, the others arrived and we completed the visit the second day.

On another trip we had to ford a river with a pickup and barely made it but the water got into the bed of the pickup and washed the labels off all the canned goods. We spent the following two days looking at the mineral prospect, but we had to open cans by guess and at random for our food.

Another trip was out of Culiacán, Sinaloa. Culiacán has sometimes been called the illegal drug capital of Mexico. We drove about thirty miles on dirt roads to this prospect and were sometimes in the bottom of arroyos, which were ideal ambush sites for unhappy drug producers. We arrived at the prospect and a local employee took me around to look at the mineral showings, which indicated that it was a "doggy" prospect and not of interest. However, in the course of visiting the outcrops my guide, who was a helper not only in mineral exploration but also in narcotic cultivation, showed me marijuana fields. We stopped and looked at a marijuana plant and later went through a poppy field and stopped and looked at the opium bulbs. My friend showed me that some had a razor blade mark, and he said that the juice was drained out of the bulb several times into a glass of water where it collected at the bottom as a heavier separation of the water. I asked would it be alright if I take one bulb with me as a souvenir and he said yes, so I put it in one of my twenty bags of rock outcrop samples. On this trip I was using my airplane, which I had left at Culiacán, and at the end of the day I flew back. When I talked to American Customs I had expected to just tell the Customs inspector that my twenty bags contained mineral samples, but unfortunately, he decided to look into the twenty bags. I became increasingly nervous as I counted the bags he had looked at, but when he finally got up to eight bags he decided that I was telling the truth about the mineral samples and never did find the opium bulb.

In 1958 I was on a trip way back into the Sierra Madre Mountain range to visit a mineral prospect near a small town. The hotel I stayed in was rather primitive and consisted of about ten rooms built around a patio with a garden in the patio, and I was treated to a partial striptease performance in the hotel. I had gone to my room to get cleaned up to go to dinner and it was almost dark. The room had a little balcony and I sat on the balcony and on the opposite side of the hotel was another room with a dim light on and a young lady in the other room began undressing. I followed this with rapt attention as she took off some of her outer garments one by one, and I decided afterward that it was a staged performance for my benefit. When she got to a critical stage in the disrobing she turned the light out, and I went to the bar and had a drink.

On a later occasion, around 1967, I traveled with Clark Arnold, a geologist I often worked with who held a PhD from the University of Arizona, to look at a mineral prospect in Mexico, which was a long distance to reach by ground transportation but was relatively near a village with an airstrip. This was before I used my own airplane for this kind of trip, so I chartered a small plane in Arizona. We flew down and located the town and landed on the airstrip. I succeeded in finding some horses and a guide, and there was a small hotel for the pilot. Unfortunately, he spoke no Spanish and no one in the hotel spoke any English.

Clark and I had our own problems. When it got dark we hadn't reached the prospect, so we found what appeared to be a clear area and laid out our sleeping bags. It was dark and we didn't see that we were in a cow trail, but in the middle of the night we felt thuds in the ground and woke up. Clark had a flashlight and shined it around and right into the eyes of cows, going down their trail in the dark.

Back at the hotel, however, things were not going very well either. Our pilot was a good-natured, outgoing sort of fellow, but had problems understanding the hotel arrangements. The hotel was run and probably owned by a very pleasant plumpish middle-aged lady who was also the cook. She was assisted by a plumpish teenage daughter. Both were amazed at having an airplane and a pilot turn up in their town and hotel. The pilot finally made them understand that he would eat whatever they gave him for dinner, but the next morning he was determined to get ham and eggs for breakfast. When communication broke down he acted out being a chicken laying an egg and, on all fours, being a pig saying "oink, oink." He said the girl laughed so hard she fell on the floor, but he got ham and eggs. Clark and I succeeded in not being stepped on by a cow, and the horses didn't get away, and we found and sampled the mine. We found our comical pilot, paid the bill, and flew back to Tucson.

While I was vice president—and most of the staff—of Southwest Ventures, another senior exploration manager of Ventures Limited met Tony Barranco in Mexico, realized his potential, hired him, and assigned him to work in a tungsten exploration project near Alamos, Sonora, where Tony met Hilda, a very enterprising and attractive girl whose family lived in Navojoa, Sonora. They had been recently married when I met Tony, and with the help of Ventures Ltd., and later me, he immigrated to the United States. I grabbed him and he worked in my office in Tucson for several years as secretary, accountant, office manager, and, on occasion, field assistant. Once, we arranged to be dropped by a helicopter at a very isolated place in Yavapai County called Lion Mountain. Tony was by nature a very clean, fastidious sort of guy, and

Tony Barranco begging to be carried away from his assignment at Lion Mountain with the scorpions and rattlesnakes.

Antonio Barranco: A Very Competent Man of All Work

Tony Barranco's father was Mexico's consul in New York City and his mother was a German immigrant to the United States. They met and were married in New York City. Tony inherited the Mexican charm of his father and the German industriousness, organization, and determination of his mother. He grew up in Mexico City and had a good secondary school education and spoke English. Tony made a voyage of discovery to the United States by joining the American Bracero Program to bring in temporary agricultural workers and picked berries in California. A *Life* magazine reporter happened by and talked to him, and a photo of Tony's callused hands was on the cover of *Life*, illustrating I guess that some of the Bracero workers were educated and cultured, but worked hard.

our self-prepared food was somewhat hit or miss. We ran out of water in the middle of the three-day stay and had to filter water from a little spring through a sock to get the miscellaneous stuff out of the water. Tony had done some laundry, and he had a ball of underwear that he was taking back from the spring when he discovered there was a scorpion on the ball of laundry. He didn't want to drop the recently laundered shorts and so he rotated the ball of laundry and the scorpion had to race around the ball and Tony yelled very loudly until I came to assist in the scorpion problem. When the helicopter arrived we left Lion Mountain, and as we were leaving Tony posed for a picture in which he was pleading with the pilot to take him in the helicopter.

The time Tony worked for me was one of the few times in my career when I had a well-organized office. Tony was stolen from me by a large mining company and later had an amazing series of promotions and was an important executive when he retired. He was and always will be a nice guy.

Quite a bit of mineral exploration was being done in southern Arizona in the early 1950s, and a lot of my work was either at Copper Basin or other porphyry copper prospects. During this time I became very interested in porphyry copper geology and began to educate myself on the subject. By 1959, when I left Ventures and went to work for Utah Construction Company, one of my credentials was knowing quite a bit about porphyry copper deposits, and I started developing a rudimentary new porphyry copper model. This education was based on reading articles, visiting mines, looking at prospects, and talking to geologists. Later in my career, in the 1960s, I set out on a premeditated program to try to visit every important porphyry copper deposit in the world. I thought at one point that I had been to more than half of them. The two days I had spent in the field at Copper Basin with the legendary Thayer Lindsley in 1957 was true inspiration. Here was a flesh and blood Great Man who was polite and considerate to a young engineer but whose brain and initiative had produced very large and valuable mining operations. This was the stuff of demigods!

My tour with Ranwick and Southwest Ventures was somewhat hit or miss, but my experiences were generally very valuable. Later in my career, I realized that independence in the explorationist tends to improve the chance of success. I didn't find a mine during that tour, but I found new ideas that produced later success.

Geologist and District Geologist, Utah Construction Company, 1959–1961

In 1959 I was offered a job by Utah Construction Company in San Francisco as a senior geologist, with the understanding that I would soon be returning to Arizona as a Utah Construction Company district geologist. The offer came from Wes Bourret who was VP in charge of exploration. I later had relatively little contact with him and the person I reported to during most of my time with Utah was Hollis G. Peacock, the chief geologist. The company was then called Utah Construction Company, later changed to Utah Construction and Mining, later changed again to Utah International, and finally becoming the copper branch of BHP, an Australian multinational mining and petroleum company, which has become the largest mining company in the world. Utah was an important heavy-construction company, and they were also important in mining, principally iron, coal, and uranium. My familiarity with uranium as well as copper was responsible for my offer of the job in their exploration group. I took the job at Utah Construction because I sensed that the Ventures funding was beginning to run out for our program in the Southwest. The deciding factor for me was the promise that I could return to Arizona as a district geologist to try to find a new porphyry copper deposit. The deciding factor for Edith was the perceived security of working for a large company. We were both to be disappointed. The move to Arizona was delayed, and when it did come there was little independence, strategy was dictated by the head office, and no ore discoveries occurred. Edith discovered that there may be less security for an exploration geologist in a large company.

We moved from Tucson to Palo Alto, California, once again, where Utah had a temporary office at the time. Our office was next door to a psychiatrist's office, and Dick Ellett, one of the geologists with whom I was associated, amused himself by turning a glass with the open end toward the wall and putting his ear against the closed end of the glass and listening to the psychiatric conversation. At one point he said,

"They've fallen on the floor!" While we were in Palo Alto, Edith and I socialized a good deal with Don and Betty Peterson and with Rep and Nancy Repenning.

Our office was soon moved from Palo Alto to Utah's corporate office on California Street in the San Francisco financial district. Holly Peacock, my boss there, probably taught me more exploration geology than any other person in my total career. Most of our staff found Holly to be a little bit abrasive. He was a very fast thinking, kind of ironic, hard-to-joke-with type of fellow. I was almost the only one in our department who really appreciated Holly. He was very productive, and was almost in the genius range as far as intelligence.

I began to commute from Palo Alto to San Francisco. One of my fellow Utah geologists was Paul Riddell, another second-generation miner, whose father was a professor at Michigan Tech and invented the Riddell Clamshell Mucker. Paul and I lived close to each other in Palo Alto, and we shared rides and commuted together to the office in San Francisco. Paul had a home brewing operation going, and when he was out of town on fieldwork at a critical time and I was in the office, I had to tend his batch of beer. We were a symbiotic team in the commuting process, because I was a more capable driver to get to the station in the morning and he was more capable coming back at night. (He had problems like forgetting to put a belt in his pants and leaving the car lights on and being late and whatnot.) We drove to the Palo Alto train station and took the train to the San Francisco station and either walked or took a bus to the financial district.

I did much the same sort of work for Utah that I had been doing in Arizona, with a lot of air travel to places, evaluating mineral prospects, and an occasional drilling program. My projects were mostly in the western United States and Mexico. I don't remember getting out of North America. On one occasion I was drafted by a Utah Construction project estimator to estimate the hardness of the rock and the amount of water that would drain into a long railroad tunnel, seven miles long, that Utah was bidding on. I think I was given this assignment because I was both a geologist and mining engineer, but it struck me as being a problem without an answer. I made my best guess as to how hard the rock was going to be and how much water was going to run into the tunnel. The bids were opened late on a Friday and I called the estimator, whose first name was Johnny, early Saturday morning. I said, "How did we do, Johnny?" and he replied, "We did beautifully." I asked, "Did we get the contract?" and he said, "Oh no, we were third from lowest in a field of seventeen bidders."

I was working for Utah Construction Company in January 1960 when the company airplane crashed. Several people, including middle management from the San Francisco office, were flying, I believe, to visit mining operations in Utah. I had nothing to do with those mining operations, but someone in the office had mentioned that the Utah Company plane was going and asked me if Dick Ellett and I would like to go along to see the mine. This sort of thing is commonly done in the mining business, to allow staff members to visit mining operations just for general information. I had another little job come up that it would have interfered with, and this would have been kind of a monkey-business trip for me anyway. The other job was something that I felt responsible for completing, so I bowed out on the trip. Dick Ellett was also unable to go. The crash happened near the Iron Springs Mine, near Cedar City. The airplane was a converted military airplane, a Lockheed Lodestar—a very high powered airplane, not up to the normal civilian airline company standards of safety and built for combat-type conditions. I don't remember the circumstances of the crash, but J. A. Mecia, general vice president and manager of the Mining Division, and Homer Mann, manager of Mining Services for Utah were both killed. Four others were injured. Dick Ellett and I have gotten together several times since to marvel about our good luck.

In late 1960, after working for over a year for Utah Construction in California, I was invited to go to Arizona to open a branch office in Tucson, which had been the original understanding with them. I did work on several copper prospects. One was in the Sacaton area, where ASARCO was in the process of developing the Sacaton deposit. Other work was in the state of Utah in the Eureka district near Cedar City.

In the summer of 1961, toward the end of my employment with Utah Construction, the company participated in a joint project with Stan Ward, who was at the time a geophysics professor at the University of California, Berkeley, working together with a geophysical group from Toronto, Canada, to test the AFMAG geophysical method of exploration, an airborne prospecting device that depends on natural earth telluric currents, which are theoretically distorted by buried sulfide orebodies. The area of the test was in the Wasatch Mountains near Salt Lake City, Utah. I did the preliminary geological work to identify a prospective area to test with the AFMAG survey.

The technique involved a helicopter towing a "bird"—a bomb-shaped device about eight feet long containing the geophysical sensor—and in the helicopter was a console of instruments that we read, flying the traverses. The working group consisted of Stan, myself, the helicopter pilot, and Erik Kirschner, a ground technician who was a German immigrant to Canada who didn't fly with us. We had a Hiller Model 12-E helicopter. The nominal elevation of our survey lines was 12,000 feet, and the helicopter was capable of flying reliably to about 11,500 feet (its operating ceiling), which presented an immediate problem because we had multiple crashes of our bird hitting rocks and pine trees and so forth. Whenever that happened, another one had to be sent from Canada. We finally got down to the last AFMAG bird in existence on our survey.

I was navigating our profiles, which had been plotted on an enlarged aerial photograph, and the bunches of pine trees and rock outcrops that could be recognized on the photo were going by at 70 mph only fifty to a hundred feet below and once, in my effort to navigate, I found that I had climbed out on the skid without a safety belt.

At one point, the helicopter engine stopped at 12,000 feet. The elevation was higher than the elevation at which the helicopter could autorotate, so it immediately started to change from a flying machine to something like a rock dropping. But there was momentum stored up in the spinning rotor, and the helicopter pilot, who was a veteran of military helicopter flying in Korea, tipped it over and dived for the ground and came in at a tangent. There were lots of sparks and loud noises and a certain amount of damage to the skids, but no one was seriously hurt.

We had another incident in which part of the rotor flew off into the bushes when we were warming up to take off, and it would have been a fatal accident if it had occurred in the air. Finally, by mutual consent of everybody involved, including the helicopter pilot, we all shook hands and went back to our respective home bases.

I carried out a beryl reconnaissance for Utah Construction Company in 1961 and visited a number of sites looking for evidence of a large deposit. Beryl is a mineral often associated with granitic pegmatites, mica schists, and limestone, and emerald is gem-quality beryl. Utah Company was not looking for gemstones, but for the free element, a metal often used to increase hardness and resistance to corrosion when alloyed to some other metals. One site we visited was on Mt. Antero in Colorado, at 13,000 feet elevation, another was in southern Utah.

The Utah site had been explored by a long adit (a horizontal mine working with only one entrance). The adit was about 1,000 feet long, had been recently driven, and was in part in "heavy ground." I was working alone and had a sandwich and bottle of water in my pack. I had been examining the adit wall as I entered when I noticed it was noon and I sat down with my back against the wall and started eating the sandwich. A small rock the size of a pea fell and hit my knee. From long habit acquired in underground mines, I automatically got up and moved fifty feet to another spot where the back looked more solid. I had almost finished my sandwich when there was a loud noise and dust temporarily filled the air. I had previously concluded that the adit represented sloppy work, and I jumped up and looked around with my light to see what had happened. There were several tons of caved rock where I had been sitting, and depending on how quickly the collapse occurred, I would have been killed or badly hurt if I had not moved. I looked carefully at the site of the rockfall; it looked reasonably stable so I went on to the end of the adit and left without wasting any time.

It was a promotional prospect and not an attractive beryl showing, and in retrospect I think I should not have gone into the adit when I saw it was not safe.

When I was assigned to look for a beryl mine for Utah Construction I had one problem. I have a slight speech impediment, which makes it difficult for me to pronounce words like "Lowell," "cattle," and "beryl." Paul Riddell, a senior geologist in our office, commented, "Why should we believe what you tell us about beryl when you can't even pronounce the word?"

BOOK II, 1961–1972

Consulting work with considerable freedom to plan exploration, three discoveries, and one partial discovery

CHAPTER ONE

Initial Development of the Porphyry Copper Model

The published Lowell-Guilbert Porphyry Copper Model evolved over several stages. From 1957 to 1959 my observation had been that central disseminated copper deposits contained quartz and sericite and pyrite and chalcopyrite in the primary ore, which was usually light gray. The orebody was surrounded, first by a bleached zone (later called quartz sericite or phyllic alteration); this in turn was surrounded by a larger greenish zone (later called chlorite epidote, or propylitic alteration).

Over time, between 1959 and 1965, I read an occasional article and I became more and more familiar with the various types of alteration. An important thing to understand is that during this period, while porphyry copper research was going on furiously in the laboratories of Anaconda, Kennecott, the U.S. Geological Survey, and in Japan and elsewhere, and while all these groups were busily subdividing and sectioning the individual components, they hadn't noticed the broader pattern. I think I was the only person to have recognized that there was always a concentric pattern and the concentric pattern of the lateral and vertical alteration zoning could be a huge advantage in *finding* porphyry coppers. What's more, I proceeded to apply the theory, twice, at Vekol Hills and at Kalamazoo. The association with John Guilbert about a year later, around 1966, brought in the complex explanation of chemical phases and temperature and pressure zonation and such.

The two of us felt this model was some kind of breakthrough, and we began a literature research program that involved tabulation of twenty-seven porphyry copper deposit descriptions. These deposit descriptions varied in the accuracy of describing the alteration zones, but all twenty-seven specifically supported our original premise if viewed in the right context.

The discovery of the Kalamazoo orebody was based on my ideas about concentric zoning of porphyry copper deposits. There was also a structural fault displacement interpretation and 70-degree tilting of the orebody that was important, but the more important part was realizing the concentric zoning idea and identifying evidence of it, first in the San Manuel orebody, which was a mirror image half of the Kalamazoo orebody, and then finding evidence of the same zoning in old drill holes and outcrops in the vicinity of the location of the Kalamazoo orebody. John Guilbert came into the project a few months later. I felt that the deposit required more theoretical documentation than I was able to supply. John Guilbert had worked in the Anaconda research laboratory at Butte, Montana, for a number of years and, although he was a few years younger than I, he was already an expert on silicate alteration and had seen a number of porphyry copper deposits. I asked him if he would care to do consulting work for Quintana on the theoretical aspects of Kalamazoo, and he agreed.

John is a very enthusiastic, energetic fellow and is an inspiring teacher. He became the stand-out ore deposits professor of the University of Arizona and was well known internationally. Among his many accomplishments is his significant contribution to the eventual development of Bajo Alumbrera in Argentina. He was also the senior author of *The Geology of Ore Deposits*, which became the standard college text. In the course of our meetings on the documentation of the description of the deposit, we decided to compare notes and build the Kalamazoo example into a composite, general model of porphyry copper deposits, using, as it were, his academic background and my experience background because at that point I had looked at many porphyry copper deposits in the field. And so we decided to write a joint paper.

A Consultant on Five Minutes' Notice, 1961–1969

In the spring of 1961 Hollis Peacock had visited my Utah Construction office in Tucson. The first thing he said to me was, "Dave, I have good news for you. You will be transfered to Vancouver where you will be in charge of Utah's Canadian Exploration Division and you will have five geologists reporting to you. It will be a big promotion!" I said, "Holly, I am unwilling to go to Vancouver" (knowing Edith's heart would be broken to leave Tucson after being overjoyed to move back). Holly said, "In that case you are fired." I said, "Okay, I will become a consulting geologist. Why don't you pay me a retainer to be a listening post in the Southwest?" Holly thought a minute and said, "Okay, I will pay you for two days a month." That is how I got in the consulting business on the basis of a five-minute conversation. Edith was very happy she wasn't leaving Tucson, but very worried about not having any security or food for her babies.

I had thought a little bit about becoming an independent consultant, but this was very much a spur-of-the-moment decision. When my regular job at Utah Construction ended, I informed all my friends that I was available to do consulting work, but I didn't know whether I would have any work at all. Edith took immediate action by trying to get her teaching certificate. She was very anxious to get qualified and get a job to support us, which, as it happened, was not necessary, but neither of us knew that at the time. I was thirty-three years old in 1961 and younger than normal for beginning a consulting career. Susie was eleven years old, Bill nine, and Doug five, and I had a lot of family responsibilities, but I was healthy and optimistic. I began hustling around, not knowing what to expect in the consulting business, but I did have this relatively small retainer from Utah, which was a couple days a month of work.

To my surprise work started coming in. I worked for Kern County Land Company on several projects. One was a choice assignment in Death Valley, California, in July and September, managing some drilling projects for borate deposits of the sort mined by U.S. Borax. The

Lowell family
Christmas card
photo, 1962.

mineral was not borax but colemanite plus another borate mineral. Death Valley was so hot I had to wear gloves to pick up rocks from the ground surface, and the drillers wore aluminum hard hats that were so hot they had to wear gloves to take them off. A little bird came and perched on the drill rig looking for water to drink and the drillers poured some water in a dish for the bird and when they moved the drill rig to the next hole the bird flew over the drill rig with them.

I stayed in Death Valley Junction Motel. Much of the population of Death Valley at that time was made up of the flotsam and jetsam of the U.S. population, and an act of violence occurred while I was there. The cook in the motel was a retired Marine Corps cook and very tough and hard-bitten, and his wife, who was the postmistress, fit the same description. A triangle formed consisting of the cook and the postmistress, who were married, and the vice czar of the area, who had a house of ill repute not very far from Death Valley Junction. The cook caught the postmistress and vice czar in a compromising situation and shot them both with a pistol. The vice czar then wrestled the pistol away from the cook and shot him. Somebody called the nearest hospital, in Lone Pine, California, which sent its lone ambulance to the site of the violence; all three participants of the triangle had to ride together to Lone Pine. In another incident at Death Valley Junction, a couple of the children living at the motel there broke into the place where the beer was kept and got intoxicated. In a third incident, the hotel manager, Slim, caught a little sidewinder rattlesnake in a quart mason jar, and in playing with it Slim got bitten on the end of his finger and he also had to go to the hospital in Lone Pine. Death Valley Junction was a small but active place.

The way consulting work actually materializes is through word of mouth and personal contacts. Much of geological consulting work is really more contract work than consulting in the sense of advice. People look around for someone available who they think can do the work. And that's how it happens. It's kind of a chicken and egg thing. You do difficult work to develop a reputation, but you can't develop it unless you get some chances to do the work. I think in my career I created the chances, with premeditation, by using some of my own time to become knowledgeable about known ore deposits in North and South America and elsewhere. The principal advantage was probably more for my own education than in the contacts. It's a talking point to say, "Gosh, I have visited fifty porphyry copper mines," but the more important thing is that some ideas have gradually seeped into your head from seeing similarities and differences between a large number of examples.

My next job was a project for Kern County Land Company and Duval Corporation near Navajo, Arizona. I was hired by Kern County because the chief geologist was Wayne Wallace, who was a friend of mine in Tucson. The Navajo, Arizona, potash work involved drilling relatively deep diamond core holes looking for a sylvite (potash) bed. (Potash is the common name for potassium-based salts used commercially in fertilizers.) It was basically a twenty-four-hour-a-day job, because the drill rig was running twenty-four hours, but on one occasion I was called in the night and went out to the drill site. They had hit high-pressure gas, which was blowing the drill mud out a hundred feet from the drill rig before the trajectory caused it to hit the ground, and no one knew what the composition of the gas was. I had no experience with flammable gas but was able to understand that it might easily burn up the drill rig if anything was done while the gas was blowing out. I found a bottle with a lid on it and managed to get it into the trajectory of the gas coming out of the hole, put the lid on the bottle and took it a safe distance away from the drill rig with a box of kitchen matches and tried to light the gas. It was not flammable, and there was no danger of burning up the drill rig.

The curious thing for me was that within a few hours of intersecting the high-pressure gas, professional petroleum property leasers started to arrive in the middle of the night, thinking it might be natural gas or, in that district, helium gas, and there would be an opportunity to make money by getting a lease on the ground or nearby ground. Eventually the project was finished, and it seemed to me that it may have been successful in finding potash ore, but I was not experienced enough in the potash business to know whether that was true.

When I was working for Utah as a consultant I made a visit with Don Hansen, a Utah geophysicist, to a mineral prospect in the Black Canyon area of Arizona. It had some underground mine workings and had been offered for purchase to Utah. I got in trouble by trying to be a nice guy. The owner of the mine had offered to pump out a winze (an interior shaft) that was full of water so we could see the geology and mineralization below the water level. He had an electric sump pump that weighed a hundred pounds or more, attached to a steel cable. But he couldn't make the sump pump work. It wouldn't raise the water, and he was trying to lift it up and down to get the pumping process started. I was about ten feet above him in the mine drift; I asked him what he was doing and he said the pump was too heavy to lift and told me what he was trying to do. I climbed down onto the staging (a timber platform) in the shaft and got hold of the cable with him and we pulled together. Unbeknownst to me, the staging hadn't been put in very well and when we pulled hard on the cable, everything came loose and the mine owner and I and a bunch of heavy pieces of timber all fell down the shaft together.

We fell about thirty-five feet and hit the water, then went a long way below the surface. I had a little ordinary flashlight in my hand, which continued shining underwater. I looked around, and I saw this other fellow floating underwater. I grabbed him and swam back up to the surface. He was unconscious and I draped him over one of the timbers. The whole shaft was full of pieces of timber, some of which were ten inches square, big pieces of wood. We had to hang onto the timber. Don Hansen had expected to meet me, and when I didn't show up, he came looking. I was able to yell to him as he went by and he found a ladder and got it hung in the shaft, which was no mean trick. In the meantime, I noticed that my shirt was bloody and I found that I had broken my elbow when I hit the side of the shaft or a piece of timber had hit me on the way down or after I was in the water. It was a chip fracture of the elbow. It was painful, but not particularly debilitating. I was able to drive home after getting out of the shaft. It's a good example of why the safety rules should be followed.

Right after my Black Canyon Mine incident in Arizona, I was hired to do a mapping and drilling job in Idaho for the Newmont Mining Corporation. I had been contacted by Bob Fulton, Newmont's VP for exploration, to do this job about the same time I was doing the potash drilling for Kern County in Navajo, Arizona. He called me because I had developed a small reputation at that time in porphyry copper exploration work, and Newmont was really more of a holding company than a mining company. They operated a number of large mines, but as partly owned subsidiaries. The company itself had a very small exploration staff and used a lot of consultants and independent geologists like me. They owned the large Carlin gold mine in Nevada where they had geologists working, and they owned the O'Okiep and Palabora mines in South Africa and at least one other important mine at that time. Bob Fulton and one other geologist worked out of New York, and they had a research center in Massachusetts and a couple of people in Vancouver who worked mainly in Canada. Unfortunately, I had a broken bone in my left elbow from the mine accident. The orthopedic surgeon said it was not a serious break, and he didn't remove a loose fragment of bone but did give me an L-shaped aluminum splint because I was in significant pain.

Equipped with my splint I flew to Carlin, Nevada, to pick up the Exploration Department's Dodge Power Wagon, which the company provided for me to use in Idaho. A Power Wagon resembles a Sherman tank much more than it resembles Ford pickups with soft seats and nice suspensions. I was essentially a one-armed man and was a little paranoid about having to drive the Power Wagon, but I managed. And when I met Bob Fulton in Carlin he looked at the vehicle with admiration and said, "I like Power Wagons; they have a lot of iron in them."

We examined the maps for the project and met with a plump field assistant Bob had borrowed from the Carlin Mine. The prospect area was in steep, mountainous terrain with scattered pine trees. The ground was mostly covered with a thin layer of snow, which had thawed and refrozen as ice, and a lot of loose rocks coated with ice created very treacherous footing. It was especially hard on me, with only one usable arm. I fell several times and once, just in passing, observed that it hurt quite a bit falling on a broken elbow, but this didn't elicit any sympathy from Bob. He loved to hike (and I suspected, loved to suffer). After a while the field assistant from Carlin (who had earlier told me that his real profession was bartending), who had also had some nasty falls, said to Bob Fulton, "Mr. Fulton, I don't do this type of work," and he turned around and hobbled back in the direction of the vehicles. Bob Fulton outranked the field assistant by about nine Newmont pay grades, and was amazed. He said incredulously to me, "Have you ever seen anything like that?"

Eventually Bob and I agreed on the scope of the mapping problem and I volunteered to hire a field assistant in Snowville to replace the plump gentleman from Carlin. Snowville is a small town a short distance away across the state line in Utah, where I intended to stay. Bob and I were already well acquainted, and he left knowing that I do everything that I agree to, pleasant or not.

In Snowville I thought I noticed the results of a generation or two of polygamy. The people were pleasant, likeable, and intelligent, but they all resembled each other. This was a summer dry-farming commu-

Robert G. Fulton

Bob Fulton was vice president of exploration and development of Newmont Mining Corporation when I first began consulting for him. He was my most important consulting client for several years early in my consulting career. He had a very different personality from Chuck Pillar, who I worked closely with later in my career, but they agreed on the importance of honesty and truthfulness and *getting the job done*. Bob Fulton was in the habit of using consultants more than most companies do; I got along very well with Newmont and spent most of my time for a couple of years working for them. Bob Fulton was one of the most impressive people I've known. He was a very intelligent, determined, decisive man, but economical with words in both his conversation and his letters. I received one letter from him that consisted of only four or five words. He had been a distance runner in college and liked to hike long distances when reviewing exploration projects with me. He was grimly determined to get any job done and not inclined to accept excuses. Bob later became president of MacIntyre Porcupine Mines in Canada, where I again did consulting work for him at Madeleine Mines in Quebec.

nity, and there was little to do in the winter. I found and hired a middle-aged fellow named Mr. Cutler as my field assistant. He was a good assistant, except on one occasion when we drove to the place where we had stopped mapping the day before and a slow rain was falling. We sat in the cab of the truck for about an hour. The rain was still falling when I said, "If it's OK with you Mr. Cutler, let's get out and get started." He said, "Usually when it's raining I just go inside." I couldn't very well tell him about Bob Fulton's work rules, but we put in a good day's work, and in a couple of weeks had finished the mapping and sampling.

In Snowville in the early 1960s there wasn't much to do, and I took my meals at the same restaurant every day. I had the same breakfast every day, and asked for the same two ham and cheese sandwiches to take for lunch, and for dinner had systematically started at the top of the menu and moved down one space every day. I was served by the same pleasant, nice-looking girl every breakfast and dinner. Other patrons were mostly locals, with a few truck drivers who were easy to spot. I don't know what was going through my waitress friend's mind, but I suspect she viewed me as Escape From Snowville. Anyway, one day she told me, "I have made a little cake just for you!" I thought this was pretty serious, and wondered to myself, "What if we get some encouragement, and this gold project drags on six months? Twelve months? Two years?" Fortunately, it didn't.

We brought in a bulldozer and a Cat skinner to build drill access roads and drill sites where I planned to drill a few exploration holes. I can't remember the Cat skinner's name, but he was an artist with a D7 Caterpillar tractor. He told me he had been a prisoner of war for a couple of years at the end of World War II. He learned some Japanese and became good friends with a guard in the warehouse complex where he was working. Toward the end, food was running out for both the prisoners and the guards. He and his friend worked out a way to stay alive. There were narrow alleys between the warehouses, and he and the Japanese guard would start at opposite ends of an alley and meet in the middle. If there was a cat in the alley they would catch and eat it. In icy conditions, bulldozer treads are equipped with "ice grousers," or cleated track, to grip the ground. On one occasion I was at the crest of a ridge with my vehicle at the bottom, and my Cat skinner offered to give me a ride down, which I accepted. I climbed up on the seat and we started down over a long stretch of frozen ground. As far as I could see the ice grousers didn't help at all, and the thirty-ton machine ran down the slope like an Olympic skier, but my friend was totally relaxed so I thought there wasn't a problem.

In due course the project was finished and I said a fond good-bye to my Cat skinner, my field assistant, and my waitress, and I hope life has treated them all well.

In the mid-'60s and early '70s I took a wide variety of consulting jobs. I evaluated mineral prospects and did geologic mapping in Arizona and Nevada. One of these jobs was a little bit of work at the San Manuel Mine as a guide for Newmont geologists in a short course on porphyry copper geology. I took two groups of Newmont visitors to San Manuel, where there were also a number of geologists working for Magma Copper Company. I took the same groups of geologists to other copper deposits in Arizona and gave them a short course in the district geology. I did that twice, and on one of the tours was accompanied by John Livermore; he was in charge of Newmont's work in Canada, and he came with a group of Canadian geologists. The other group was multinational; they came from Africa, Australia, and other places. The San Manuel visit later turned out to have a significant effect on my career.

I spent several months in the early 1960s doing geologic mapping for Newmont Mining Co., first in the Eureka District and, the next spring, in the Elko District. Newmont had selected the areas to be mapped, possibly based on the locations of geophysical anomalies. I usually worked alone, but sometimes hired a local field assistant.

At Eureka my area included the outcrop of a massive fault called the Roberts Mountain fault. Usually faulting does not disturb the original sequence of sedimentary beds, with the oldest formation on the bottom and the youngest formation on the top. However, in my map area the sequence of beds was like a deck of cards that had been shuffled. Sometimes the youngest would be on the bottom or in the middle of the pile, which made the mapping very difficult and also made locating drill holes difficult. Newmont had hired a small, weakly financed drilling company; my hole locations sometimes intersected unexpected and difficult formations to drill and the company eventually went broke.

The Elko map area was in a very flat outcrop area. The mapping was scheduled to begin June 1, to take advantage of good weather. I arrived a day earlier, but it was snowing. The geology was difficult to map under the best of conditions because there were only occasional windows in the soil where outcrops of bedrock could be seen, and with a couple of inches of snow no geological features could be seen. On my first visit to the area to be mapped I noticed someone had skinned a coyote and left the body in a cardboard box with one leg sticking straight up. I used the leg as a snow gauge while it snowed every day for a week, and finally only the paw was visible.

I had gotten very tired of sitting around in the motel, and I heard an announcement on the radio about a big party scheduled at the steakhouse. I imagined beer and steaks sizzling and laughter and merriment, so I asked someone in Elko where the steakhouse was located, and they said, "Why the Stake is located at the Mormon Church, of course." After a week I called Bob Fulton and he agreed to put off the mapping project.

There is a volcanic plateau that extends ten miles east from the town of Superior, Arizona, which is post-ore in age (younger than the fifty-five- to sixty-million-year-old period of ore formation in the district based on isotopic age dating). Based on various geologic evidence, part of which I had developed earlier, it looked hopeful that there might be a porphyry copper deposit hidden below the post-ore volcanic sheet. Newmont asked me to make a study of the area and Bob Fulton (the former distance runner) came down and we made a twenty- to twenty-five-mile joint reconnaissance walk over rough country. I made my study, and Gordon Wieduwilt, a Newmont geophysicist and good friend of mine, ran an induced polarization survey (a geophysical imaging technique used to identify ores and other materials underground), and we later drilled several unsuccessful holes. The interesting thing is that Kennecott Copper found a very large relatively high-grade copper deposit called the Resolution orebody close to our target area about twenty-five years later.

The Kalamazoo Discovery

Out of that work for Newmont came, indirectly, the Kalamazoo discovery in 1965. I had been skeptical about the description of the geology of the San Manuel Mine before these visits. The San Manuel, located north of the Santa Catalinas in southern Arizona, was originally mapped by a fellow named Schwartz. This was back in a time when copper was a strategic war metal, shortly after World War II. Schwartz had logged a number of churn drill holes, most of which passed through the San Manuel fault into the San Manuel orebody. In his report he was uncertain about the origin of the San Manuel orebody. I think Schwartz did a good job on his study. He was working for the USGS when he did that.

Then around 1960 USGS had another study done in the district by Cy Creasey, who was more academic. He mapped the San Manuel fault and the geology of that quadrangle in the San Pedro Valley. Creasey described the San Manuel orebody as a "typical canoe-shaped deposit," which puzzled me because I didn't know of any other canoe-shaped orebody in the world, especially a porphyry copper deposit. San Manuel is a kind of trough-shaped deposit with essentially barren material in what would be the inside of the trough. Cy Creasey explained that as a barren intrusion into the deposit. He explained the San Manuel fault, which dips to the southeast and cuts off the top of the southwest San Manuel orebody, as a strike-slip fault; in other words the fault had displaced the missing part of the orebody laterally rather than vertically. By this time I had visited quite an impressive list of copper occurrences in North America and other places, and it didn't seem to fit with my ideas about concentric zones of porphyry deposits. Creasey's conclusion seemed illogical.

So during these two Newmont tours we had maps and I made a point of collecting rock specimens in a fence across the orebody both times, which was somewhat difficult because most of the San Manuel underground mine walls had been grouted with high-pressure concrete and there was only an occasional window where you could actually see the rock. However, I was able to piece together the fence of specimens and took them back to my office and brooded over them and over the mineral assemblage and silicate alteration assemblage. I came up with an alternative thought about the geometry of the deposit, which was that it was half of what it had originally been—a vertical cylinder that had first been tilted and then sliced by a gravity fault, displacing the missing segment down the fault. I didn't really think much about it at that time, but I talked to Bob Fulton about this and I said, "Why don't you let me do some work on the west side of the deposit? There might be a target over there to find the missing piece of the orebody." He turned me down partly because he didn't want to ruffle the feathers of the geologists working at San Manuel.

At that time I didn't have a sense of the movement of the fault, whether it was a normal gravity fault or a reverse fault, but in this extensional terrain where the earth's crust is being pulled apart, usually you get normal faults. A few months after my second visit to San Manuel, a Texas independent oil company, Quintana Petroleum Corporation, came into the picture. The company had been advised to diversify away from oil production and get into the mining business. This was a popular idea among oil companies at that time, and in a kind of a sheep mentality most of them did the same thing at about the same time; it turned out disastrously for almost all of them. I believe Quintana contacted Kenyon Richards and Harold Courtright with ASARCO to ask who they should hire for a local consultant to manage some copper exploration for them in the Southwest, and Quintana was given my name. Kenyon Richards was arguably the best mine-finder of his time.

The Quintana group arrived in Tucson and it was more like a Middle East monarch arriving. It was (and still is) a family company, owned and run by super wealthy members of the Roy Cullen family from Houston, Texas. The general manager or president at that time was Corbin Robertson, who was a son-in-law of Roy Cullen. The story of Quintana Petroleum goes something like this: There was an oil driller named Roy Cullen, who also dabbled in oil leases. In one area considered favorable for oil production, no one had been able to drill holes through a formation that was called the Heaving Shale. Roy Cullen decided that he could do this, and he acquired a big block of ground and succeeded in drilling holes, and some of them were enormously productive in oil. I guess almost overnight the family became very wealthy.

The Quintana Petroleum Corporation contributed $150 million to the Houston University Medical Center, which at that time was the largest individual gift ever given to a university in the United States. Robertson was known as Corby. Corby had married the youngest daughter of Roy Cullen, whose name is Wilhelmina. I visited them several times at their home in Houston and got well acquainted.

So in 1965 Corby arrived with his money-handling man, his lawyer, his geologist, and his drilling manager, and I met with them in one of the fancy hotels in Tucson. They agreed to hire me on a retainer basis for a limited period of time. They had already in their files some mineral prospects that they wanted evaluated in southern Arizona, which other people had submitted to them for consideration. I looked at a couple of these. One was on the other side of the San Pedro Valley, past San Manuel. I spent a day looking around. It was a geophysical anomaly, and I decided that it didn't look very interesting, as indicated by the geology with which the anomaly was associated. Most geophysical anomalies have no real significance, and this was one of those. But coming back, I drove through Mammoth and Oracle. My friend Ted Johnson worked for the Department of Mineral Resources and lived in Oracle, and in the course of driving over and back I got to thinking about San Manuel and thought, well, these oil people have money enough to drill some deep holes, and I wonder what the status is of the property next to San Manuel?

I knew the property was owned by a lady named Martha Purcell, who had just died. She had been married to a dentist in Tucson, and one side or the other of the family had a significant amount of money. Martha Purcell's interest was in having a churn drill company. I never met Mrs. Purcell, but I heard from a San Manuel geologist who had met her that she wore bib overalls and was a big, beefy, loud, aggressive woman. She had acquired this group of mining claims adjacent to the Newmont claims at San Manuel and had held the claims for many years, like fifteen or twenty years, I suppose. She knew a little about ore deposits and was advised by geologists.

Anyway, she set out to personally drill deep churn drill holes on the Purcell side of the boundary. She had unbelievably bad luck. A churn drill, technology-wise, is kind of like using a stone axe. It's just banging a bit on the rock, and you get a penetration of maybe ten feet per twenty-four hours. It's a very hard way to get a hole drilled. But it had been more or less standard technology for some time, particularly for water wells. She drilled five holes, some as deep as 3,000 feet, which involved drilling for almost a whole year on one hole. She personally ran the machine herself, but with a crew. She had the bad luck to have located one hole over the Kalamazoo orebody that wasn't deep enough and another one that was deep enough that wasn't over the Kalamazoo orebody. The Kalamazoo orebody is a mirror image of San Manuel, which has a shape like an overturned tilted canoe, so it's got a high point on the east end that is relatively easy to reach with a drill hole. All these drill samples were saved and dutifully logged by the San Manuel geologists, who were interested in being Johnny-at-the-rathole if an orebody was found. Martha was getting free geology done from her most obvious purchaser or joint venture partner if she was successful.

As I was driving back through Oracle I did stop and talk to Ted Johnson. As local representative of the Department of Mineral Resources, he covered a good part of southern Arizona. I had talked to him before about the San Manuel area, but this time I asked him if he knew anything about the availability of this property next door. He said, "Well, as a matter of fact, Mrs. Purcell died just a month ago," and the estate, he thought, would be open to selling the claim. Mrs. Purcell had a nephew who was a lawyer. I called him and he said, "Well, go see Frank Salas, who is our watchman on the mining claims." Frank Salas had been a miner at San Manuel for many years. So I talked to Frank Salas, and he said, "Well, I'm more the owner of the ground than Mrs. Purcell's heirs, who haven't paid the assessment work, and I did the assessment work, more or less, and have been living on the claim. I would be willing to make a joint deal with Mr. So-and-So," the lawyer. But he said, "But there's a promoter whose name is Jerry Bell, who has overstaked our valid claims since Mrs. Purcell died." Jerry Bell had been some kind of associate of Mrs. Purcell. Anyway, this was all a legal snarl. It was a little bit hard to tell who was in the right among the group at that point.

Newmont hadn't done anything about it, which is an important fact because they should have gone in and acquired the property, just on general principles, long ago. And so I talked to the lawyer nephew, and I talked to Frank Salas, and I negotiated for Quintana a reasonable deal on their claim. And then Jerry Bell showed up, maybe hearing about the activity, and said, "You can't make a deal with these people. These are really my claims and not theirs." I think he then filed a suit against the Purcell estate. Quintana hired the most highly perfumed law firm in Tucson to represent them. They said they thought the Purcell family's title was better than Jerry Bell's. But by then the lawsuit was under way. I, in the meantime, had undertaken a study of the evidence. This consisted of evaluating the published data on San Manuel and looking at the Purcell drill samples.

One thing I did was plot the elevation of the pierce points in the San Manuel fault of the original drill holes noted in the published Schwartz report on San Manuel, and then I made a contour map of the surface of the fault coming down from San Manuel toward Kalamazoo. The map showed a giant mullion structure, a rolling surface of parallel grooves and ridges that strongly suggested that the upper plate of the fault had moved through these grooves down toward the Kalamazoo orebody.

The San Manuel mullion structure and concentric alteration were so huge you have to put your observations down on a map and then view the map. You can't see it very well on an individual outcrop. Both these features were missed by the USGS geologists who spent months or years studying the area. Both the concentric zoning and the mullion structure in the San Manuel fault were obvious if you were looking for them, but they weren't obvious if you weren't looking for them.

All the Purcell churn drill samples had been put in labeled paper bags and stored in a short tunnel adit on the property. The adit had previously been a powder magazine where dynamite was stored. It had a wooden door, and a hive of wild bees on the inside of the door had to be removed. Over the years, groundwater from rains had dripped from the ceiling of the tunnel and caused these bags to weld together. The numbers were still visible on the bags, but the bags weren't intact. And so I hired a graduate student from the university, Will Chester, and gave him a new set of bags and a spatula and a brush to excavate these bags like an archaeologist, one by one, and rebag them. At about this time I hired another graduate student, Clark Arnold, to work on the project on a part-time basis.

I already had the logs that had been made by the Newmont geologist for the churn drill holes and given to Martha Purcell. However, they hadn't logged the information that tied in to my approach to determine the concentric zoning of a porphyry copper deposit—things like the silicate minerals, chlorite, epidote, sericite, potassium feldspar, and quartz; and sulfide mineral information, like percent and ratio of pyrite and chalcopyrite.

We relogged all the samples. It was quite a significant job because there was probably 10,000 feet of drilling represented in two thousand samples. When that was finished—eureka! It all fit into this picture of this pyritic halo around a chalcopyrite-pyrite ore shell and silicate zon-

---

Clark Arnold

Clark worked for me for more than fifteen years, and our association ended when my consulting activities began to phase into strictly Latin American projects in Chile and Peru. Clark was a University of Arizona graduate student with no exploration experience when I hired him on a part-time basis to help me on the Kalamazoo Project. He continued to work part time until he completed his PhD in geology and then became full time. Clark learned mineral exploration from me, and I hope some of his people-person talents rubbed off on me. Clark is a very intelligent, outgoing, reliable, and optimistic guy whose skills to some extent were symbiotic to mine. I owe him a debt of gratitude for his help.

ing with chlorite and epidote in the propylitic alteration, sitting outside the quartz sericite or phyllic zone. I supposed the central barren area in the San Manuel orebody was potassic alteration. Later, in the publication that John Guilbert and I did, we actually named some of these porphyry copper zones. We coined the words "phyllic" and "potassic," which are now accepted names. The churn drill information correlated with my fence of samples across the San Manuel orebody.

Since my "Copper Basin School," I had continued to collect porphyry copper information in talks, mine visits, articles, conversations and, most importantly, in consulting assignments. I could now readily fit the mineralogy into the concentric color zones. I had some perception of the expected size and primary and secondary ore grades. I was casually viewing the porphyry copper "woods" while my competitors were busily focusing their microscopes on "trees" and missed the porphyry copper model concept.

With the mullion structures on the fault, and the evidence that the outcrop near Kalamazoo and the deep churn drill holes had intersected symmetrical alteration on the sides of the deposit, and the fault displacement direction pointed in the same direction, I was able to come up with an almost airtight picture of where the orebody was, even though it hadn't been intersected by any of the drill holes. I located a hole that was close to where the shallowest part of the Kalamazoo part was, close to the fault, and went over to explain what I wanted to do to Quintana, and Corby Robertson said, "I don't like that location. If I find an orebody, I want to be sure it's a huge orebody." So he made me move it all the way back to the middle of the orebody.

I drove up over the surface of this ground about this time with Edith, and I said, "You know, if we're lucky, we may be passing over the middle of a multi-hundred-million-ton orebody." I could at that point almost say what the tonnage and grade were because it would be similar to the other half at San Manuel. Then we contracted a drill rig with sufficient depth capacity.

All this time the lawsuit was going on between the Purcell group and Jerry Bell. While we were drilling the first hole, before it had got-

Edith standing on a drill access road at Kalamazoo, 1965. A drill rig in the background is drilling a hole more than 4,000 feet deep.

ten to the depth to hit the orebody, Jerry Bell showed up out on the property, and Frank Salas saw him and went up to the drill rig. Jerry Bell was up on the drill platform, and Frank Salas said, "Jerry, you're going to have to get out of here. You've got no right to be on that drill platform." Jerry Bell turned around and kicked him in the face and cut his nose, and he had to have a couple of stitches in it. When I heard about that a couple of hours later, I called the lawyer and said, "Jerry Bell has kicked Frank Salas, and he's had to have his face sewed up." And the lawyer said, "Oh, that's good! That's very good! That will help our case."

While our project was going on, the lawyer instructed us to hire several samplers who were to establish *pedis possessio*. They had to put their foot on each claim every day and make a record of this, to prove that we were really there, establishing *pedis possessio* on the ground. So we drilled a couple of holes and the first hole had a long ore intercept.

"Jackknife" oil drill rig drilling deep Kalamazoo drill hole.

After that, it was just like shooting fish in a barrel. Every one of our drill holes had an ore intercept. The first one had drilled farther away, as Robertson wanted. If they had drilled where I wanted to, it would have cut the orebody sooner. It isn't often that a geology project gets as exciting as the Kalamazoo Project; it was very dramatic.

The really amazing thing was that I simultaneously had a project going for Newmont, on the Papago (Tohono O'odham) Indian reservation, which also found an orebody, the Vekol Hills orebody, the same week. (I refer to the Tohono O'odham people as Papagos, since that was how we knew them through most of the twentieth century.) By that time the Vekol Hills Project had been taken over by Newmont, which had sent in its own geologist to manage it. I was present every day on the Kalamazoo Project. Logging the core before we intersected the top of the orebody was kind of an agony of suspense. Both of these projects were based on my understanding of the Porphyry Copper Model.

When Utah Construction transfered me from California to Arizona

Aerial view of the Vekol drill area taken shortly after the drill project. The white patches are drill sites, but 50 years later evidence of drilling has almost disappeared.

in 1960, we had moved back into the Rudasill Road house, and I turned half of the garage into an office. The other half of the garage was being used for laying out these trays of samples. The propylitic zone in porphyry copper is green rock, and the phyllic zone is gray rock. The sequence was from green, low-pyrite material to green, high-pyrite material, to gray, high-pyrite with a sniff of chalcopyrite, and then over a short interval into light-gray ore-grade chalcopyrite-pyrite-porphyry-copper ore. So these samples were being laid out in our garage. Edith and the kids were anxiously looking at the color of the cuttings on a daily basis.

I had a sampler bringing the samples from the drill rig to our house. We had a Jones splitter, a special device that divided the drill cuttings, and we were splitting out samples to send to the assay lab. We were using Jacobs Assay Lab in Tucson. The lab was also noticing the ore grades—or the copper grades, which were going from almost nil to 0.03 to 0.05 to 0.20 percent copper. Mr. Jacobs commented that it looked like the grade was going up, and I thought, well, with the lawsuit and all in progress, it's probably dangerous to have the samples assayed in Tucson, because it might get back to the people on the other side of the lawsuit. So when I thought we were about to penetrate the orebody and I could recognize chalcopyrite in the samples, I sent a set of samples to Union Assay in Salt Lake City, which was probably a good idea, but it didn't work out very well because the Greyhound Bus Company lost the samples in Kingman, Arizona, for a week. I was just terribly anxious to find out what the grade was. But when the samples were finally found and the assays were made, it was 0.5 percent to 1 percent copper. Shortly after that, somebody from Quintana negotiated with Jerry Bell and bought him off to get rid of the lawsuit.

Corbin Robertson named the Kalamazoo orebody. He had been a navigator in large bombers flying over Germany and he and Wilhelmina Cullen had been sweethearts during World War II, and this was the era of the big bands. Corbin was a romantic guy anyway, but he named projects after Glenn Miller songs. There was one called "String of Pearls" and this one was "I've Got a Gal in Kalamazoo."

With the assay returns from Union Assay it was pretty clear that we had found the other half of the San Manuel orebody. I was talking with Quintana people every day, usually with Quintana's chief geologist, Ronald Thompson. Ron was a petroleum geologist, but very capable. He picked up porphyry copper geology very quickly and was a pleasure to work with.

This was the first hole Quintana drilled in their whole minerals program, and they probably drilled hundreds or thousands of drill holes all together in the next several years in their minerals program, in which they eventually ended up spending maybe twenty or fifty million dollars. But this first drill hole found the Kalamazoo orebody. They weren't too excited about it. They thought, "Well, this is probably how it is in the mining business." In the oil business, you could expect to find one oil well out of five or ten holes. In the mining business, it's more like one out of a thousand or five thousand. So there was a communication gap there.

I didn't have a finder's fee agreement with Quintana, but they gave me a finder's fee anyway, which I thought was pretty decent of them. The fee wasn't terribly large. I got, I think, $120,000 from Quintana, and they were also paying me well as a consultant. It was a lot of money, and we were very happy about it, but by that time I had really gotten well established in the consulting business, and I was busy almost full time. George Brimhall, professor of geology at the University of California, Berkeley, said that one of the significant things here was that I pulled together two different views on the concentric zoning and the tilted pipe.

I did not get a finder's fee from Vekol Hills. That's one of the dumber things that I've done. Bob Fulton asked me if I thought I deserved a fee, and I said, grandly, no, I was working as a consultant. I could very well have gotten some kind of an interest in it, but since the deposit was never developed, through a chain of unfortunate circumstances, if I had had an interest in the production, it wouldn't have been worth anything.

Both the Kalamazoo and Vekol discoveries occurred during the same week in 1965. I was heavily involved at Kalamazoo for two more years. At that time, we completed an ore reserve calculation and a prefeasibility study. Quintana decided, probably correctly, that it wasn't a proper job for an oil company to develop this large deep underground mine, and they invited various major companies to look at the data, including Newmont, which operated the San Manuel deposit as Magma Copper Company. Newmont decided to make a cash offer for the deposit of $27 million, which in 1967 was maybe equivalent to $150 million now. Quintana elected to sell it lock, stock, and barrel to Magma. Years later, Magma developed the deposit, and for several years it was the principal source of ore for the San Manuel mill and smelter.

The staff at San Manuel had been very friendly to me. Earlier, after we'd drilled a number of holes at Kalamazoo, a funny incident occurred. I talked to the Quintana management and said, "You know,

I think it would be a good idea to let Newmont know what is happening so that they will have some lead time to get their wits together in case they want a joint venture with us on the deposit." At that point, I knew beyond a shadow of a doubt that there was nobody in Quintana who knew anything about mining, and it didn't look like a very good idea for them to jump into a major, deep, difficult mining operation themselves, on short notice. So Bob Fulton and Arthur Brant came to Tucson, and I think one of them had called me and told me that they were going to be here. I met them for breakfast. They knew that we were drilling holes there, and I said to Bob, "I think we've found the other half of the San Manuel orebody." They asked me what we had found in the drill holes and I told them. They said, "What led you to drill in this spot?" I said, "Well, we relogged the Purcell churn drill holes, and I had contoured the Schwartz data," and they both simultaneously said, in horror, "Contoured the Schwartz data?!" and "My God, why didn't we do that fifteen years ago?" So there were reasonably amicable feelings with Newmont. I think they correctly deduced that I was a friendly go-between between Quintana and Newmont, which eventually led to Newmont's buying it. I did at least some consulting work later for Newmont, and they later funded in part my Covered Area Project.

The Kalamazoo discovery was a huge success and a very happy event, but it also had an almost mystical effect which is hard to describe. It was as if a voice somewhere was telling me, "See what we already knew; you are a chosen one who finds and will find hidden treasure." When the same week I learned about the Vekol Hills discovery it was an anticlimax and even more puzzling. I knew the very large odds against one exploration success, and it was almost inconceivable to have two. I am not a superstitious person, but this seemed preordained.

While I was working for Quintana Petroleum I became well acquainted with several members of the staff. These included Corbin Robertson, CEO, Ron Thompson, chief geologist, and Marvin (Tiger) Morris, the land man who, in part, negotiated the Kalamazoo property. I also made a trip to Canada with Corbin Robertson, Jr., who was an

18-year-old University of Texas student, very modest about being an All American linebacker on the Texas football team. He is now CEO of Quintana.

The Vekol Hills Discovery

While I was doing work at the Lakeshore Mine southwest of Eloy, Arizona, I recommended that Newmont acquire Lakeshore and they declined, which may or may not have been a mistake because it later developed into a large copper orebody, but, perhaps because of bad management decisions, it has never made a significant profit.

Through my Lakeshore Project I became familiar with that part of the Papago Indian Reservation, and I suggested to Bob Fulton that I expand my work and do a little bit of regional work, which I did. In the course of doing this, I talked to a fellow named Mo Kaufman, who had a small company, based I think in Spokane, that had obtained some kind of exclusive exploration permit for part of the Papago Reservation. His work was based almost entirely on geophysics, which I have never felt was a very effective way to look for porphyry copper deposits, but they had anomalies and some limited geological and geochemical information in two targets on the Papago Reservation at the time I talked to him. They had decided that neither one justified additional investment, but he asked me if I would be interested in taking over their exploration permit with the Indians.

I looked at the data, and both of these looked mildly interesting so I called Bob Fulton and asked him if Newmont was willing to take over this project, which basically cost them very little but required an immediate decision because the deadline was a week or two later. Bob Fulton was a very decisive fellow. By this time we had had some period of association and understood how each other thought, and he said, "Yes, do it." So I did, and then did a little mapping job. This wasn't a typical big-company exhaustive project. I think the total time I devoted to each project was less than a week of fieldwork. I did the fieldwork by myself, with no field assistant.

The Vekol site was west of Casa Grande, in the southwest corner of

Pinal County. In the case of the Vekol mapping, I slept on the ground in a sleeping bag in an old mine working while I was there. (In the late 1800s there had been a productive silver mine in the Vekol Hills, but it was worked out and closed before 1910.) For me, it was hard-core type of exploration work. At that time I had some, but imperfect, understanding of porphyry copper-silicate alteration and peripheral zoning (the Porphyry Copper Model), and I saw some evidence of that at Vekol. The Vekol orebody is in a quartzite rock, a porphyry intrusion into quartzite, but the outcrop is just quartzite. Quartzite consists of 90 percent quartz (silica), and when it is subjected to phyllic alteration, which is quartz sericite alteration, it doesn't make a very obvious change in the composition and texture and appearance of the rock. So this was a tough one to map. Most of the area was covered by postmineral rocks. In the course of mapping in a very small gully in an inaccessible place, I crawled down the gully and found a postmineral dike, something like a fresh andesite dike. The reactive fresh feldspar crystals in the andesite had precipitated some malachite, a secondary oxide copper mineral. This was the deciding clue for the Vekol deposit. The deposit wasn't coincident with the geophysical anomaly but fairly near it. If exploration drilling had been in the geophysical anomaly the orebody would not have been discovered. This small occurrence of oxide copper indicated that copper was migrating in the groundwater and had been precipitated by the reactive feldspar in the andesite dike. Then I went back and puzzled over the quartzite outcrop, and there was some stockwork of veinlets that looked more significant in view of some known copper. I said, "Let's go for it." I wrote a report.

I turned down the other prospect and wrote a report recommending a drill hole in the Vekol deposit. Newmont sent a geologist who lived in a house trailer in the summer on the Papago Reservation, very hot and very far from town, and he was very unhappy. They drilled a hole that went into a chalcocite orebody under the quartzite outcrop. The Vekol deposit has something like 200 million tons of 0.6 or 0.7 percent copper, and with modern leaching, solvent-extraction electrowinning technology, it would be a medium-sized copper mine. But progressively the

Papago Indians have become more closed and hostile to outside development on the reservation. I think Newmont could have developed a mine at the time, but they let it sit around, by big-company habit, and when they went back in a few years, the Papagos in effect said no, we won't let you develop the mine.

There was an interesting little sidelight to that. When Newmont went back, they had a very carefully orchestrated presentation to the local community council of the Papagos for that district of the reservation. The local Papago government had a community hall, which was, if I remember correctly, sort of octagonal shaped, like a Navajo hogan, in an isolated part of the reservation. The Newmont people from New York and Denver and other big cities had a number of charts and enlarged aerial photographs and film clips, and several different people presented their portions of the proposal for most of the morning, to demonstrate how pleasant it would be to have a mine there and how many Papagos would be employed and how happy they would be and how happy the other Papagos would be with their newfound royalties.

I heard that the Papagos didn't say anything at all, and when the presentation was finished, they got up and walked out. The Newmont group thought they were having a caucus outside, and they waited and nothing happened for half an hour and then an hour, and then somebody went and looked out the door. The Papago council members had gone outside, gotten in their pickups, and gone home without saying a word. And that was the end of Vekol. It was a scientific success, but a practical failure. It was disappointing to me. I think the Indians made a mistake in not allowing the mine to be developed. They had agreed to the exploration contract. One of the arguments I later heard was that one of the council members said that that was a particularly good place to harvest saguaro fruit, and the number of saguaro cactuses in the mine area times yearly production of fruit would be worth maybe one one-millionth of what the value of the jobs and the production from the mine would be worth. I guess they were buying peace and quiet.

One other thing that happened about the same time as Kalamazoo and Vekol Hills was I was selected to be an expert witness on a continuing basis for the Arizona Highway Department in suits involving mineral properties. I ended up being a witness in eight different lawsuits on the side of the assistant attorney general who was defending the suits for the state of Arizona. This was a very different kind of activity from anything I had done before, but it turned out to be exciting and many times a lot of fun.

The assistant attorney general I worked with was Stanley Z. Goodfarb. Stan was a very good trial lawyer, and we won in every suit I was involved in. I felt that the reason for the high success rate was hard work. Stan would rehearse me for a couple of days before the suit and write endless series of hypothetical questions and answers. The answers that I couldn't make I would go to the library and look up, and then I would make hypothetical questions for the other side's expert witness. Every time we got in the court, it was a rout. We knew the answers and

David Lowell and Peter Davies doing fieldwork in Argentina for Kaiser Aluminum, 1969.

they didn't, and so we would win. This was a little side interlude in my mining career.

The Kaiser Project and Bajo Alumbrera

In December 1968, Kaiser Steel contacted me out of the blue to do a porphyry copper reconnaissance of the Argentine side of the Andes. This project began in January 1969, and continued for six months. I probably spent only six or eight weeks in Argentina, but had two people assigned full time, my colleague Clark Arnold from Arizona, and Peter Davies, a mining engineer from Wales, UK, who had previous experience working for Kaiser in South America. The project was largely aerial reconnaissance looking for hydrothermal alteration zones and ground-checking attractive zones with field trips.

The program was divided into two stages. The first stage was a little self-serving on my part and was a calibration of the appearance from the air of porphyry copper alteration zones around known deposits on the west slope of the Andes in Peru and in the porphyry copper belt in Chile extending south to Santiago. The plan was to fly in a small plane from Lima to Santiago, stopping for a number of mine visits I had arranged. I had plotted all the locations on maps of the prospects I knew about in addition to the deposits that were in production. I had done a good deal of library research and had learned a lot by the time the trip was completed.

The known mines and identified deposits in southern Peru were Cerro Verde, Toquepala, Cuajone, and Quellaveco; and in Chile, Quebrada Blanca, Chuquicamata, El Salvador, Cerro Blanco (now called Andina), Disputada, and Braden (now called El Teniente).

The trip began by chartering an ancient Cessna 310 aircraft from a fixed-base operator (FBO) in Peru, which also supplied a moonlighting Peruvian army pilot named Capitan Perez. Before taking off, the pilot crossed himself but did not do a preflight check. The airplane had one engine fail a short distance south of Lima, and we had to make an emergency landing at Pisco, Peru, where we had to spend the night waiting for repairs. Pisco is said to be the place where Pisco Sours, the national drink of both Peru and Chile, was invented. However, Chile claims the drink was invented in Chile. The Pisco Sours in Chile are more sour, and I prefer the Peruvian variation. Pisco is also the site of a very smelly fishmeal plant.

In due course the engine was repaired and we left for an overflight of the Southern Peru Copper Company deposits and Cerro Verde, which belonged to the Anaconda Co., and landed in Tacna, Peru, the administrative center for Southern Peru Copper Co., which then had Toquepala in production and Cuajone in development. Quellaveco was drilled out and was a beautiful example of leached capping after chalcocite and enrichment of a porphyry copper deposit. (Leached capping is a material over a porphyry copper deposit from which the copper has been leached and carried down to form a secondary enrichment blanket.) Quellaveco was nationalized (expropriated) a few years later by the then-leftist Peruvian government. We had begun to get intimations that we might not get a permit to enter Chile with a Peruvian plane and a Peruvian army pilot in spite of his promises to the contrary. In fact, after we left by car for the Toquepala camp, Capitan Perez simply abandoned us and flew the plane back to Lima, but we didn't know this until we finished our ground visit. There was a long-standing animosity between Chile and Peru dating back to the beginning of the War of the Pacific in 1879.

We were very hospitably treated by the Toquepala management and put up in the guesthouse and given good tours of the three Southern Peru Copper deposits before returning to Tacna and learning that we had been abandoned. We first talked to the Southern Peru Copper logistical manager. He was a heavyset Peruvian who laughed heartily, thinking we were Canadian diamond drillers who had gotten drunk and lost our passports. He pulled a stack of passports out of his desk and matched the pictures with our faces and claimed he had acceptable likenesses for both of us. He seemed to be disappointed that we had lost our airplane, not our passports, but helped us find a taxi to drive a relatively short distance from Tacna across the border to Arica, Chile, where we hoped to find a replacement airplane.

Aircraft we chartered in Arica, Chile, for overflights of all of Chilean porphyry copper mines and undeveloped deposits.

There wasn't an aircraft service (or FBO) in Arica, but there was a flying club, Club Aero, that had an almost-new Cessna 182 with a high wing, much better from the standpoint of reconnaissance visibility than our previous 310. The president of the Club Aero was Arthur Heathcote-Paige; he was a compatriot of Peter's from England and "spoke the same language," and they immediately hit it off. He set an attractive rental price on the plane and introduced us to Juan Salmo, the Club Aero instructor, who agreed to be our pilot for a reasonable rate and fly us from Arica to Santiago and bring the plane back to Arica. Juan was a Spanish immigrant to Chile and was also a blacksmith. He was very helpful and cooperative as well as being a good pilot.

We flew from Arica, overflying Quebrada Blanca and Chuquicamata and landing at Antofagasta. The FBO at the airport told us that he would, without any doubt, be back at 7:00 a.m. to fuel the plane. We got up early in the morning and went to the airport in a taxi. We were waiting at 7:00 a.m. and no fuel; eight o'clock and no fuel, then eight-thirty. I called the Anaconda exploration office. I was more fluent in Spanish than Peter, but these telephone calls were far from easy in isolated locations and with no easy way to pay for the calls and speaking another language and so on. I finally got the secretary in the exploration office who spoke English, and I said, "I'm terribly sorry and upset. This fellow was supposed to be here at seven o'clock and it's almost nine." She said, "Mr. Lowell, is this your first trip to Chile?" We eventually got to Chuquicamata and had a nice visit courtesy of Anaconda.

Before we left for South America, I had written to Lou Gustafson, who was the Anaconda geologist at Salvador. I had gotten no reply, so I assumed that we were not going to get a visit to Salvador, but the next day we overflew Salvador and looked at it from the air and then turned west again to Chañaral, a little town on the coast, and checked into the hotel. By the time we got checked in, it was dark. It was a little hotel in a remote location; the lights were poor in the hotel and we couldn't see very well. We ordered a scotch and were sitting there chatting when a fellow walked up to me and said in Spanish, "Are you Mr. Lowell?" I said, "Yes," thinking there is no one in the world—not anybody, that knows that we are in Chañaral. He said, "Well, Mr. Lopez wants to see you down at [some place], and if you can come with me we'll go see Mr. Lopez now."

I thought, "What kind of thing am I getting into?" I remembered the movie *Casablanca* with Humphrey Bogart, but I decided, what the heck, and got in the car; we drove down and it turned out that the place we were going to was Anaconda's office in Chañaral. The village was used as the port for the Salvador Mine. Lew Gustafson had seen the airplane fly over and had deduced from the letter that he hadn't answered that it was me. So he sent this fellow to tell me if I could come the next day, we could get a mine tour.

After the Salvador visit we flew south from Chañaral looking at other prospects. The next stop was La Serena, where we landed with little remaining fuel. I took pictures and studied the color zoning, which reflects the alteration zoning. We finally got to Santiago, where we paid the charter pilot who had done a great job for us.

One of the things we saw in northern Chile was an Inca or pre-Inca temple on a high mountain peak at maybe 17,000 or 18,000 feet elevation. From Santiago we visited Andina and El Teniente by car and back to Santiago. The next day we flew to Buenos Aires then back to Mendoza to begin the recon and exploration that was the second stage of the project.

The second stage of the Kaiser project resulted in my identification of the large Bajo Alumbrera deposit near Belen, Argentina, as a very well-zoned, typical porphyry copper, with a good leached capping and evidence of secondary copper enrichment. All this was at least tentatively confirmed by three very small diameter and poor core recovery "x-ray size" core drill holes, the deepest of which was about a hundred feet. At the bottom of the hundred feet of core was a six-inch-long piece of core which assayed 0.67 percent Cu and 0.6 grams per metric tonne gold. This was ore-grade mineralization. This, together with the other exposed outcrop geology indicated, based on my experience, a good probability of a large orebody, mineable at the then prevailing copper and gold prices.

In 1969 the Bajo Alumbrera site was owned by YMAD (Yacimientos Mineros de Agua de Dionisio), a company that could only happen in Argentina. It was a joint venture of a university, a water company, and a branch of the Argentine military. We hired a lawyer who was not put off by this structure and wrote up a purchase option agreement with terms favorable to both sides. Both sides signed the agreement. I signed for Kaiser. Kaiser had told me they badly wanted to acquire a porphyry copper deposit in Argentina, where they already owned an automobile manufacturing plant and other investments. However, when presented with a signed deal they were horrified! It turned out that they wanted to be able to say they were "looking," but they had no interest in "finding." This kind of mining company psychology is surprisingly common among major mining companies, and it is a formula for almost certain failure in exploration. Because the agreement was only an option, no one had to carry through, and Kaiser didn't.

I don't know what the previous history of Bajo Alumbrera was, but I was probably the first explorationist to have recognized and understood the potential of the deposit. About twenty years later a consortium of three Australian companies led by Mount Isa Mines acquired and developed Bajo Alumbrera, which is now the largest mine in Argentina. It is now in production forty years later and very profitable at present metal prices. The ore reserves are said to be in the range of billions of tonnes. However, Mount Isa is having trouble doing business in Argentina, as are most other investors in Argentina.

In retrospect, when Kaiser turned down the Bajo Alumbrera project I might, if I had known how, as I know now, have formed a junior company and financed a mine at Bajo Alumbrera. However, it is so far in the past that I don't remember the details, and there might have been reasons why this would not have been an option.

We had lots of problems with airplanes and helicopters in Argentina, largely because of poor maintenance and inadequate pilot training and discipline. None of the fixed-wing planes we chartered were equipped with oxygen for pilot and passengers. In the United States there is a rigid regulation that oxygen must be used in commercial flights when cabin elevation exceeds 12,000 feet. In Argentina most of our recon flying was at least 17,000 feet, and we occasionally flew as high as 18,500 feet. On one occasion we were at 18,000 feet for thirty minutes and I was taking notes, but I found after we landed that I couldn't read my own notes.

The wind velocity in the Andes is typically high. On one occasion in Argentina I spent two hours laboriously climbing a high, knife-edge ridge and when I finally stumbled up to the crest the wind knocked me down on my rear end. On another occasion I was flying with Peter in a Cessna 310 twin-engine airplane around the inside of a cirque (a cusp carved by a glacier in the side of a mountain). Peter said, "If you want to see something interesting, point your finger at a spot on the ground." I did, and we were moving backward in a plane with a cruising speed on the order of 140 mph! The counter wind speed was higher than 140 mph, but without a point of reference (the finger), you wouldn't notice that you were moving backward.

On one occasion I was flying alone with our pilot, who was having an earnest conversation with the Mendoza tower, and when we turned onto our final approach, a fire engine and an ambulance were racing down beside us on the airstrip. Nothing in particular happened when we touched down. I put this down to the Argentine love for drama, but I wasn't sure because we had had a lot of previous mechanical problems.

Our game plan was to spot good looking alteration zones from fixed-wing aircraft and return in helicopters for ground checks. The plan was based on a couple of misconceptions. The first was that, while it was relatively easy to get a promise of a helicopter, over a period of months none ever showed up. Our last month we got as close as, "The helicopter will be in Mendoza at 7:00 a.m. Monday." Unfortunately it crashed photographing an auto race on Friday. Later in the month a Hiller Model 12 actually showed up (with a pilot who had less than a hundred hours helicopter time). We met the helicopter at a prearranged site a couple hundred kilometers from Mendoza. The second misconception was that the machine would run. We refueled the machine from a barrel of helicopter fuel in our pickup and a bucket and a funnel. Some part of the fuel got into the helicopter tank and the rest spread over the fuselage and ground, violating a bunch of safety rules. Because of limitations in weight and altitude capability we took off with only the pilot and myself. We flew a relatively short distance up the mountain and the pilot suddenly became very agitated to the extent of shaking violently. I had difficulty hearing him, but finally understood that the electrical system had gone out and we were flying just on the battery. I said (all this in Spanish), "Doesn't the motor continue running with a magneto?" He said, "Yes, but the controls are electrically operated!" At that point I felt like shaking myself, but we got back to the truck and to the pool of aviation fuel, where we left the helicopter, and that was about the last event in Kaiser's doomed-to-failure project.

Argentina is a country with a majority (reportedly up to 60 percent) of Italian ancestry, and the collective personality has an Italian flavor. They are a strong competitor to be the country with the honor of being worst automobile drivers. Our Kaiser driver was named George Malbran, and he had been a professional racing car driver. I once clocked him at more than 100 kph in a 15 kph zone. His habit was to drive at night with his lights out, but he had a button switch on the steering wheel to be able to flash his lights at another car coming from the other direction, or a car approaching on a collision course on a crossroad. The light flashing allowed two cars to play "chicken," or Russian roulette: who is going to slow down first to avoid a wreck? When we were driving cross-country at night this chicken situation occurred frequently.

During much of my work time there I would do reconnaissance flying during the day and drive back to the Plaza Hotel in Mendoza at the end of the day. I could almost always get an Argentinean to drive the car, but on one occasion I had a car at the airport and had the keys and had to drive myself. I almost got in a wreck. The mistake I made was that I drove up to a stop sign and stopped. The car behind was driving at high speed and had no idea that anyone would stop at a stop sign. He braked and slid sideways and barely missed me. That was the last time I drove in Argentina.

I concluded after that experience that I was not enthusiastic about doing mineral exploration in Argentina. The Argentineans, somebody told me at the time, are very good for singing and playing musical instruments and cooking, but they are not very good people to actually get anything done or to do business with. We also found them not very reliable in business deals. The situation in Argentina at that time was stable, with no real political problems nor a particularly unproductive government. I was a little skeptical about the political outlook, even then, and in recent years it has gotten much worse and there have been some serious implications for mining companies working there. In the case of Bajo Alumbrera, for example, Mount Isa made what we thought was a very clear-cut deal, and I think by now they've invested the best part of a billion dollars. Later the officials of the province in which the deposit is located informed Mount Isa, "By the way, we would like something like a 5 percent royalty for the province, in addition to the other terms," which is still being argued about, but if they make it stick it may make the operation uneconomic. There were lots of little problems that we ran into somewhat along the same lines.

Daniel Jackling Award

In 1970 I received the Daniel Jackling Award from the SME division of the AIME (American Institute of Mining Engineers). This award was a result of the Kalamazoo discovery and is the AIME's most prestigious award for a mining engineer or geologist. I gave a lecture entitled, "Copper Resources in 1970," that among other things predicted, not very accurately, future copper production and copper prices.

Photo looking northwest over Kalamazoo drill holes pattern (white spots now overgrown with vegetation) 40 miles north of Tucson, Arizona, 1966. A grid of 26 deep drill holes was drilled and 25 holes intersected the Kalamazoo orebody because the earlier geologic study had indicated almost exactly the location of the faulted segment (page 155).

This was the only helicopter available to charter during the Kaiser Project in Argentina, 1969. During the first hour of flight the electrical system failed and it almost crashed with the pilot and David on board (page 172).

Photo taken en route to a 1973 visit to a prospect in northern Luzon, Philippines, in the Bontoc native territory. The airstrip was originally a WWII Japanese fighter plane strip. From the left are Louis Albarracin, unidentified geologist, Al Faretta, and David Lowell (page 213).

Field work at 15,000 feet in 1974 in the high Andes, central Chile. Most of the precipitation in the Atacama Desert is in the form of snow that falls above an elevation of about 12,000 feet (page 216).

David Lowell with guide on trip to a gold prospect in Sinaloa, Mexico, about 1974 (page 180).

Andes terrain south of El Teniente, Chile, 1975 (page 169).

Harris Drilling Company rig drilling the La Escondida discovery hole in 1981. Visible in the background is an abandoned station on a narrow gauge railroad (page 231).

A 1985 trip to visit a high altitude prospect in Region III, central Chile. Ice had to be melted for the horses to drink and David came back with several frost-bitten fingers (page 220).

Spirit House where the "bones of the people and the pigs are kept." Migilsimbip village near Ok Tedi mine north-central Papua New Guinea, 1987 (page 271).

Papuan man at Grasberg with penis gourd and pig tusk in nose, 1989. Grasberg is in the Indonesian western half of the island of New Guinea (page 270).

Mother and baby at Grasberg, New Guinea, 1989 (page 270).

Trip to look at a mineral prospect in the Chilean Andes, 1985. Some of the horses and mules are conditioned to work up to 16,000 feet (page 249).

Typical camp in Atacama exploration, 1985. Most of the Atacama Desert is accessible with four wheel drive vehicles and much of David's work was done from tent camps (page 229).

David Lowell with Minera
Escondida chief engineer in 1995
visit to Escondida. It was exciting
to see the discovery grow into a
huge operation providing work
directly and indirectly for perhaps
20,000 people (page 248; photo
by Julian Malnic).

David Lowell, on
the first visit to Los
Calatos prospect in
southern Peru, with
chartered Peruvian
Army helicopter in the
background, 1992. Los
Calatos contains 1.3
billion tonnes of ore and
was discovered by David
on a reconnaissance
flight and was acquired
by staking mining
claims (page 300).

Local belles on top of Pierina orebody outcrop at an elevation of almost 15,000 feet, 1996. Partly concealed by clouds is Huascarán, the highest point in Peru, with an elevation of over 21,000 feet (page 316).

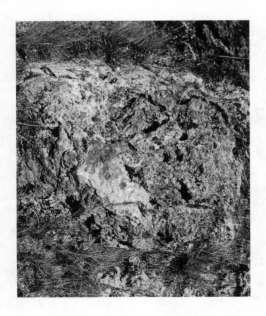

Vuggy silica rock texture in Pierina outcrop, 1996. This texture is typical of one type of epithermal gold deposit (page 316).

Edith riding up the Pierina outcrop from an elevation of 14,000 feet up to 15,000 feet, 1996 (page 318).

This man-portable drill rig had been carried seven kilometers and was being assembled at a drill site in the Warintza orebody in Ecuador, 2000. The terrain is very steep and rainfall here is heavy as in most of the Amazon jungle (page 339).

Edith and David on the Atascosa Ranch in 1996. Most of the vegetation at this elevation consists of three species of oak trees (page 395).

David at Toromocho, 2005. Toromocho is in the Cordillera Central, the central range of the Andes, a three-hour drive east from Lima, Peru. This photograph is at an elevation of 15,000 feet (page 352; photo by Mary Humphreys).

Edith and David about to depart for Canberra in an ancient World War II C-47 aircraft owned by Geoff Loudon. The trip was made to receive the 2009 Haddon Forrester King Medal from the Australian Academy of Science (page 386).

Desert fox 30 kilometers north of Escondida, 2010. A fox patrols an area about 20 kilometers in diameter in the less arid (one rain every five years) part of the Atacama Desert. They are not afraid of people but view them as possible sources of discarded food (page 231).

In 2011 David and Edith went on a Princeton University Egypt tour. This is David, receiving information about the forthcoming uprising, which began two days later, 12 hours after their departure from Egypt (page 420).

Alto Paraná Pilot Plant at the mine site in Paraguay, 100 kilometers north of Ciudad del Este. This mineral separation plant produced four tonnes per 24 hours of clean ilmenite (titanium) and magnetite (iron) concentrate for later arc-furnace testing in Johannesburg, South Africa (page 377).

Alto Paraná Pilot Plant inauguration in Paraguay, 2011. From left, unidentified CIC geologist, David Lowell, mining specialist, Don Hains, Peter Davies, Monica Quintana, Rob Reeves, and Jorge Fierro (page 377).

CHAPTER TWO

Fame and Professional Advancement from the Lowell-Guilbert Porphyry Copper Model

In 1970 John Guilbert and I put together an article for *Economic Geology* titled "Lateral and Vertical Alteration—Mineralization Zoning in Porphyry Ore Deposits." For quite a few years, it was the primary reference for geology of porphyry copper deposits. It has been referenced in other papers several hundred times, has been translated into Japanese, Chinese, and Russian, and has turned out to be a benchmark publication, probably largely because of its timing. There were similar papers published a year or two later, but ours was the first one to pull all this information together. John and I have since collaborated on several other, shorter, less important papers and worked together on other projects. I have authored or co-authored about a dozen articles for *Economic Geology*, but have published more than fifty papers in total. There was a period in the 1970s in which I was part of an informal group of theoretical geochemists that met for conferences once every year or two.

When John Guilbert and I published our paper describing our Lowell-Guilbert Porphyry Copper Model, we expected that it would be of interest in the exploration fraternity, but we were amazed at the reaction that occurred almost immediately. We got many letters, and the paper was translated into three languages. We were both invited to give lectures, and I was given consulting assignments in many parts of

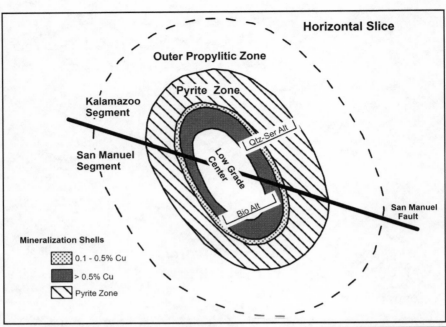

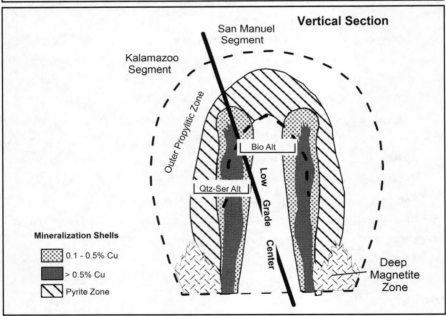

Top: Cross section of Porphyry Copper Model illustrated by San Manuel–Kalamazoo. *Bottom:* Vertical sction of original San Manuel–Kalamazoo Porphyry Copper system (J. D. Lowell and J. M. Guilbert, 1969).

the world. Some of these lectures resulted in discovery of new mines by those attending the lecture. Some of the mines I visited expanded my understanding and contributed to later discoveries I made. I had a humorous experience in November 2013 when I visited a large gold mine in Guerrero State, Mexico. I was with Dave Jones (who is given credit for finding the mine) and Jorge Fierro, exploration manager of Lowell Copper. We met with a group of about eight Mexican geologists to hear an informal talk about the geology of the mine. Dave Jones asked the group, "What do you think has been the most important ore-deposit model in history?" One spoke up and said, "Probably the Lowell-Guilbert Model." Dave said, "Do you know that Lowell is here today?" They didn't and they all turned and stared at me in amazement.

Thayer Lindsley Lecturer for the Society of Economic Geologists

The Thayer Lindsley SEG Lecturer involved giving lectures in universities in the United States. The lectures were at universities in Florida, Colorado, and Massachusetts. The job involves preparing two lectures and giving one or the other of them. I was also given the Society of

---

Helen Hauck

Helen was my first secretary after my consulting business grew large enough to justify having a secretary. She was in late middle age and a sadder but wiser lady. Helen had spent a good deal of her career in the horse racing fraternity. She was intelligent, totally reliable and honest, and a can-do person. On one occasion I was camped in an isolated spot in the Canadian bush when something came up in Tucson that Helen thought absolutely deserved my attention. She called the client and arranged to charter a helicopter that showed up where I was camped and loaded me up and took me back to the city (at a cost of several thousand dollars).

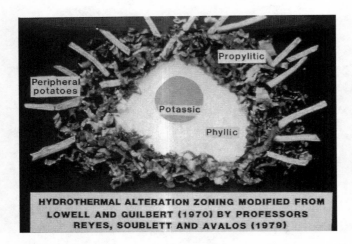

Joke Lowell-Guilbert Porphyry Copper Model created by Pancho Ortiz during the Atacama Project in Chile.

Economic Geologists' Silver Medal for excellence in mineral exploration in 1983 as a result of the La Escondida discovery.

Canadian Mining and Metallurgical Society Distinguished Lecturer

The Canadian Mining and Metallurgical Society Distinguished Lecturer involved giving lectures at universities in Canada. I wrote these lectures myself. They were all related to porphyry copper geology, which was in vogue at that time. For many years, it was a painful process for me to give lectures because I'm not a talented public speaker. I have given talks in lots of different parts of the world: the United States, Canada, Australia, New Zealand, China, Japan, Mexico, Peru, Chile, France, and England, and finally have partly learned how to give a lecture.

Consulting for Bethlehem Copper and the JA Orebody Discovery

In 1970 I was invited by Bethlehem Copper, a midsize British Columbia, Canada, company, to advise them on mine geology and district exploration in the Jersey open pit mine in Highland Valley, British Columbia. I reported to Henry Ewanchuk, who was mine superintendent and also served as Bethlehem's chief geologist. Henry, or "Hank," was a geologist, but did a first-class job operating the mine and also organized a relatively small but active exploration department. Hank is a smart, energetic, enterprising engineer of Ukrainian descent with whom I enjoyed working.

I also worked at the Endako molybdenum mine, and the Gibraltar and Cragmont mines, all Placer Development mines in British Columbia, Canada. In the course of my later work at the Marcopper Mine in the Philippines, the word got around that I was helping Placer Development, and the managers from almost all the other companies invited me to do work on the same trip for other mines.

I worked as a long-term advisor for Bethlehem Copper Company in Canada, which had indirect association with Asian mines. Bethlehem was one-third owned by Sumitomo Company, and I met a number of Sumitomo people at that time. I also visited Japan twice and met people there. The Japanese porphyry copper number one expert was a fellow named Shunsho Ishihara, who came to visit me a couple of times in Arizona. He worked mainly for the Japanese Geological Survey and one of the universities. When I became associated with Bethlehem Copper it had two large shareholders: the Sumitomo Company from Japan, and ASARCO, and later, Newmont from the United States. There were also smaller shareholders.

My work went well, and I was able to suggest mine geology and mine development strategies I had learned in other porphyry copper operations. I visited four other mines in Highland Valley and, based on similarity of the district with other porphyry copper districts in other parts of the world, recommended a district exploration program. This program was very simple. The locations of the four known deposits and their respective peripheral alteration zones were plotted. Also plotted was the area of postmineral cover where the ore-deposit geology was not known, and whether there was room for another hidden orebody that might be present below the cover. I suggested that this hidden area be covered by a wide-spaced grid of "scout" drill holes, close enough together to find any hidden undiscovered orebody. Bethlehem accepted the suggestion and carried out this plan. I did not locate or log the holes, but the project was successful in finding the JA orebody, which was the same order of size and grade as the Jersey deposit, but deeper, producing a higher stripping ratio. The stripping ratio is the volume of waste rock that has to be removed compared to the volume of ore that this exposes in an open pit mine. Considering costs and the price of copper, this made the JA submarginal, but now, or in the future, with a higher copper price it may become mineable.

This discovery is in the category of maybe-I-was-responsible-for orebodies A, B, and C. The human personality in mineral exploration always rationalizes that your contribution was the important part, so there always are many more discoverers than discoveries; I was a member of the team that found the JA deposit.

During one of my Bethlehem visits, in about 1972, a Russian trade delegation visited the mine and was entertained at a lunch to which I was also invited. There were interpreters, and first jokes in English were translated into Russian, then the head of the delegation told a Russian joke. "Two Russians were driving cars which collided at a road intersection. Both drivers leaped out of their cars and one pulled a pocket flask of vodka out and offered it to the other driver, saying, 'Comrade, let us drink together to celebrate surviving this terrible wreck.' The other driver drank a large swig and handed it back to the first driver who put it back in his pocket. The second driver asked, 'Aren't you going to have a drink?' The first driver answered, 'No, I am going to wait until the police arrive.'"

I made exploration trips for Bethlehem to Mexico and Australia, where Bethlehem was a partner with Sumitomo and with a private company from Denver, Colorado, in a syndicate being operated by an Aussie group that held a number of mineral prospects in several Australian states. Our party consisted of myself, the Bethlehem chief geologist, Robin Anderson, a geologist from Sumitomo, a geologist from Denver, and one or two Australians representing the syndicate.

We did a lot of traveling and visited prospects that varied from "doggy" to "very doggy." I noticed the Japanese geologist, whose name was something like Ichihara (we called him Itchie), made notes about

David in Queensland,
Australia, in 1972.

each prospect we visited. If the prospect was only moderately unattractive, Itchie made only one or two pages of notes, but if it were a totally hopeless prospect he might write five or six pages. The outback of Australia is not densely populated, but two or three times on the trip local Sumitomo representatives met us to debrief Itchie.

We spent several days at a place called Sandstone, West Australia. Sandstone consisted of just one building, a two-story hotel that had been partly destroyed by a cyclone (hurricane) a few years earlier. There were no bathing facilities in the rooms, but a bathtub had been built in a patio surrounded by the hotel on two sides. Unfortunately the cyclone had removed two of the four walls of the tub enclosure, and it was a tricky business to fill the tub and take your clothes off and look for Peeping Toms in the twenty or so windows on the exposed side of the bathtub. The truth probably was that nobody was interested in peeping at me.

The main feature of the hotel was the bar, which had a number of nude photographs and a sign that said, "Sandstone Sporting Bodies." Every evening a number of people came from some mysterious locations out in the desert and drank in the bar. I heard a snatch of conversation between the two barmaids: "Where is he?" answered by, "On the floor behind the bar." The tone suggested that this was a stable solution for the rest of the night. One morning there was a little herd of big kangaroos in the hotel patio, and altogether lots of similarities to *Crocodile Dundee*, but that's why I love Australia.

Associate Editor of *Economic Geology*

I attended several meetings that were in the form of Gordon or Penrose conferences. In the course of these meetings I became acquainted with Brian Skinner, who was the editor for many years of *Economic Geology*, and he invited me to become a member of the *Economic Geology* board, which I did for five years. It consisted of reviewing papers submitted to *Economic Geology*. I also wrote reviews of other publications in other journals.

BOOK III, 1973–1991

Launching new enterprises with more freedom to plan exploration and significant finder's fees, seven discoveries

CHAPTER ONE

Exploration in the Canadian Bush and a
Unique Career Formula

In the early 1970s I was asked to visit two porphyry copper prospects in the Atlin district near the British Columbia–Yukon Territory border. My son Doug was fourteen years old, and I asked him if he would like to go, since it sounded like an interesting trip. We spent several days flying in a helicopter in the bush, and it was during the salmon run, which is also when grizzly bears congregate on salmon rivers. The first day we flew into a sport camp for the mineral prospect visits. We saw six grizzlies from the air before landing. The pilot landed on an island in the river a hundred yards from the camp instead of on the riverbank. When I asked why, he said grizzlies sometimes tear up helicopters and the theory is that they remember being chased by helicopters and when they find their enemy on the ground, they get even.

There were no fishermen in the camp, only a guide and a cook. The guide had had a frightening confrontation with a big sow grizzly shortly before we landed, and we heard hours of bear stories. Doug borrowed a fishing rod and thrashed the water, and the fishing was exceptionally good. He got up to start again at dawn while I was still mostly asleep. I heard what sounded like pigs grunting, then a shout, and then a little later the same sequence of sounds followed by a shot. At this I piled out of my tent in my underwear to see what was happening. There was a little (300 pound) dead grizzly bear at the edge of camp, the guide was holding a .30-06 rifle, and Doug was climbing down from a pine tree. Three yearling cubs had walked into camp on the riverbank. Doug ran up a tree and the guide yelled at the bears, which first ran into the bush but reconsidered and came back out in their fighting stance, walking on their knuckles. The guide shot the lead bear between the eyes and the other two ran.

In 1973, indirectly as a result of the Kalamazoo Project, I hit on a career formula that I followed for all of the next fifteen or twenty years: the formula was to keep one foot in the consulting business but also to do contract exploration. This formula was, and maybe still is, unique in the industry. The plan was, first, to spend nominally 50 percent of my time doing contract projects and, second, 50 percent doing consulting. I followed that plan between 1973 and 1987.

I had done consulting work for about twenty major companies that were hoping to find a porphyry copper deposit but were not working in the right way in the right place. It occurred to me, without talking in advance to a given major corporation, that I could design an exploration program in a location favorable for their requirements, but to be managed by me. I would be paid my normal consulting fees plus a success fee or small carried interest. An advantage to the corporation would be that any failure would not be their fault. About half the eight companies to whom I made this proposal accepted, and four discoveries resulted: Casa Grande West, Arizona (which was not developed); and Escondida, Zaldívar, and Leonor, which are all in production in Chile.

The Covered Area Project and the Casa Grande West Discovery

This consulting and half-time contract work started in 1973. I put together a program we called CAP, for Covered Area Project. It continued for about five years, but the intensive part lasted three years, from 1973 to 1976. Newmont was the original funder of the CAP, about eight years after the Kalamazoo discovery. Newmont originally signed

Casa Grande West drill hole and Francisco Grande Hotel, 1975.

the contract with me. Then they asked to bring in Hanna Mining Company to split the risk. A year later Newmont essentially got totally out of the copper business, and they bowed out of our project, as it happened, only a couple of months before the Casa Grande West discovery, which might have changed their mind.

Hanna Mining Company brought in Getty Oil Company, so the CAP was originally Newmont, then it was Newmont-Hanna, then it was Hanna-Getty. Getty paid their bills, but there is some question in my mind as to whether it was good luck or bad luck that they became involved in Arizona and then later in Chile, because they tended to be a "disorg," or uncooperative partner, in Arizona, and to a greater degree in the Atacama Project in Chile. Getty had the same deficiency that Quintana had of almost total ignorance about the mining business. But the Quintana people were basically intending to be friendly and cooperative and fair, and learned quickly.

The logic for the project was to use a mapping technique to project silicate alteration zones and geochemical anomalies from premineral

Jenny Darling Brown

Jenny worked for us for a couple of years in Tucson as secretary until her husband got a job in another town. She had grown up in the Cananea, Sonora, Mexico, mining camp. She was completely bilingual and knew quite a bit about mining and had a good English education. Jenny was a very well disposed person. There were usually four mining engineers and geologists in my office, and the first thing she did in the morning was to speak briefly with everyone to be sure we were all feeling cheerful and positive. If not, she had a routine to get everyone on track. It involved smiles and cups of coffee or hot chocolate, and in very serious cases, a brief neck rub. She was also a good secretary and office manager, and it was a sad day when she left Lowell Mineral Exploration.

outcrop out into areas of postmineral cover, and then drill scout holes on wide spacing to see if the alteration zone could be extrapolated. The annual budget was $750,000. We operated very cheaply and efficiently, I think, and we had drilled twenty CAP prospects in the two years from the time the contract was signed until the Casa Grande West discovery project. We had drilled twenty targets, and we had drilled 120 individual drill holes that were deep but low-cost air rotary drill holes at that time. We had one strong smell of mineralization but no hits. The twenty-first project was the Casa Grande West Project. It was based on the fact that we were aware that ASARCO's Sacaton orebody was bottomed on a flat fault, a large displacement, low dip-angle fault, along the lines of the San Manuel fault, but almost horizontal in dip. Part of my knowledge dated back to earlier work in the district for Southwest Ventures and Utah.

We were aware that farmers had found pebbles of oxide copper mineralization in quite a number of water wells in the valley. The Casa Grande West work related back to my first published article about mapping stream directions in sedimentary rock. Our exploration at Casa

Grande West was about the fifth exploration program in the area. It wasn't a new idea that there might be another piece of this orebody. A number of other companies had worked in the district. A typical habit of exploration geologists is after they try something themselves and it doesn't work, they chat with their friends about it afterward. That's where the first part of the information came from.

But our project was predicated on drilling scout holes. We had a little project to compile all the information we could get on this area. It was actually one of our earliest projects in the Covered Area Project. Each of the twenty previous projects we drilled were the ones that at any given time we thought were the most favorable, and so this project kept dropping to somewhere in the middle of the pile but not being rejected. We finally got around to the Casa Grande Project, and we compiled all the information we could get from scuttlebutt and published information. On that project, we even went so far as to go to the county recorder and develop a chronological history of when mining claims were staked and where and by whom in that area, so that we had a historical record of where the other company's interest was— for instance, after ASARCO found that the Sacaton orebody was bottomed by a fault. ASARCO was the individual company that had been most interested in that target area and had done the most work there.

Then I went back to my experience on the Colorado Plateau in mapping ancient stream directions. We had a program mapping along principally the east boundary; this was the east side of the Santa Cruz River drainage. The Santa Cruz River dies out in this district and goes into a distributary network. It probably originally connected with the Gila River near Gila Bend but doesn't now; it just flows out into the valley and stops.

We mapped stream directions, and in the course of doing that I talked to a friend named Spade Cooley, who was a USGS geologist based in Tucson for a while. I knew that he had worked in the vicinity of Casa Grande, and I compared notes on stream directions with him. The age of the mineralization there is approximately sixty million years old, and there are outcrops of rocks that range from modern streams to streams maybe fifteen million years old in that district. Spade told me something very surprising: that his work suggested that the Santa Cruz River had reversed direction twice in its history, that it had originally flowed from south to north, then it flowed from north to south, and now it flows from south to north again.

So I took this information and went back to our mapping and the plotting of the locations where the copper pebbles had been found in the water wells, which had not formed a very obvious pattern based on a south-to-north flow, but they made a very neat pattern, a wedge-shaped pattern, based on a north-to-south flow. So on this basis, we went out to the key area and acquired property. Some of the ground that we staked had originally been staked by ASARCO, and they had allowed their claims to lapse. They later said, well, we were interested in this area all along, and you're just unethical latecomers and so on. But the evidence really didn't support that, because they had allowed their claims to lapse.

We went to this key area and drilled several holes and immediately found evidence of porphyry copper mineralization. The first hole intersected some leached capping. But there was no ore—we found weak copper mineralization but no strong mineralization. We moved around. The trail got hotter and colder and hotter; we were six miles from the nearest outcrop of premineral rock, so geologic mapping was of no use, but subsurface interpretation was what we were doing. While we were doing this, the "jungle telegraph" operated in the opposite direction, and ASARCO heard we were drilling out there, and they got excited and came back out and started competing with us.

Our fifth hole was near ore grade, and our seventh hole was definitely ore grade. It became apparent that one quarter section of land might be the center of the orebody and was possibly available property. This was land in which the surface owner owned both the surface rights and the mineral rights. The owner was a congressman from Dallas, Texas, who had bought the land for speculation purposes, not for mineral but for real estate.

The CAP had borrowed Bill Mounts from Newmont Mining Company, and then Bill elected to resign from Newmont, when they dropped out, and work for me. We had borrowed a land man from Getty named Don Nichols, a retired Marine Corps fighter pilot and a very aggressive sort of guy. Most of his land work had been done in the oil business, but he was a good negotiator. We called this congressman, who was kind of a self-important, successful politician, successful

---

Charles Pillar

Chuck was the epitome of a hard-boiled, tough guy, mine-manager type of mining engineer. He'd worked his way up in Magma Copper Company earlier in his career, joining Placer Development Ltd. in 1965, where he worked for about ten years. After he was appointed vice president in charge of operations of Placer Development Company, he offered me a consulting retainer to review and supervise the mine geology work at four large open pit mines in Canada and the Philippines. We agreed perfectly on how to run a mine and later on joint consulting assignments. We were both strong-minded people but we never had an argument. Chuck was a very experienced and competent mining engineer, a 1935 graduate of the Colorado School of Mines. He held the rank of major in the Air Force when World War II ended. He was a very honest, determined, decisive person, with a genius for solving mine development problems. More than anyone I have known, he was able to separate the important parts of a problem from the unimportant and put his finger on a specific, often very simple, solution. It was very valuable in my professional development to work with and to observe Chuck Pillar's thinking and management skills. After leaving Placer Development in 1975, Chuck moved back to Tucson, Arizona, where I was already an established consultant, and suggested we join forces in a mining consulting firm. I agreed, and because at that time he was more senior, I suggested we call it Pillar, Lowell, and Associates. We worked together for several years and I think a little of his wisdom rubbed off on me.

Exploration Strategy

I have a number of exploration rules that I follow.

1 Ore is rock which can be mined at a profit. Low grade is sometimes mineable, and high grade sometimes not.

2 Mines are found in the field, not the office.

3 Mines are now almost always found by drilling holes, so if no part of the budget is spent on drilling there is almost no chance of success. (Pierina was the rare exception.)

4 Exploration is a cost/benefit business. Expensive high-precision core drilling is often used when low-precision low-cost rotary drilling would suffice. In the Atacama Project we spent $3 million on wide-spaced rotary drill holes. If we had used core holes our budget would have run out when less than half the holes were drilled including those that found the Escondida and Zaldivar orebodies. The same logic applies to all other exploration costs.

5 High-tech devices and geophysical surveys are very rarely of value in mine discovery. There should be an almost metaphysical communication between the rocks and the successful explorationist in which the rocks talk to the explorationist. If he turns part of this job of geological mapping over to a high-tech gadget, he may look good to uninformed management, but he is less likely to find a mine.

businessman, and he wouldn't talk to us, so I asked Don to make a trip to Dallas to see the congressman. Don went to his office and explained to his secretary who he was and what he wanted to see Congressman Joe Blow about, and the secretary talked to the congressman, and the congressman said he was too busy, go away. So Don sat down in the chair in the reception room, and he waited there all day until this guy came out, and then he buttonholed him and, with his charm, was able

6 It is important for the explorationist to have a good understanding of the target he is looking for, including understanding some mining engineering, metallurgy, mine finance, and mineral economics. He is not looking for a scientific curiosity; he is looking for a mass of rock which can be made into a mine. I believe my mining engineering and mine production work has been very important in my exploration success.

7 Mineral exploration, like inventing new blockbuster drugs, has a very low probability of success. Only one out of three hundred to five hundred attractive targets becomes a mine. You have to accept the fact that you will usually be wrong. I'd guess that only one out of thirty well-trained exploration geologists ever actually finds a mine. However, if an explorer has found one mine, statistically he is likely to find others.

8 Finding mines is a high-risk business. In addition to the geological risk are the political risk, the metal price risk, the mine financing risk and the timid, incompetent management risk. Success is the summation of a list of well-evaluated risks.

9 My last factor, which you don't find in training manuals or classrooms or mining articles, is the freedom to plan your own exploration project without interference of company rules or traditions or interference by supervisors who are not as good a prospector as you.

to talk to him and make a deal. We got this quarter section of ground, which turned out to contain something like 500 million tons of 1 percent copper, in one quarter of one square mile. We drilled through 1977. My experience on a number of occasions is that when some prize is found in a project like this, a major company develops an almost irresistible urge to take the project over themselves. Hanna and Getty said thanks very much, but we'll continue the development. Hanna was the operator of the project. We had spent about $2 million on the whole Covered Area Project, but they spent $20 million drilling at Casa Grande West, which was an excessive amount to spend. They drilled it out on too close spacing, drilling many more holes than necessary, trying to bend over backward being overconservative and avoiding the decision on whether to develop a mine.

They should have sunk a shaft early on. The shallowest part of the orebody was about 1,000 feet deep, which would be an expensive shaft, but they could probably have done that for what they spent on close-spaced holes, and they would have had the start of a mine. Instead, they drilled an excessive number of drill holes and were never able to make the hard decision to go underground. This was partly because Hanna was not a copper company and didn't have copper experience, and Getty was almost totally ignorant about mining. The net result was that they sat around and agonized for years, and in the meantime real estate development encroached, and the environmental movement became stronger and stronger. It finally was no longer practical to try to develop the copper mine there, and the orebody may be lost forever. At the time it was the most important copper discovery in Arizona in the last forty years. That's the long, sad history of the Casa Grande West Project.

My contract said that a bonus would be paid when a mineable deposit was found, and we had a long argument about whether or not this was a mineable deposit. It is "beauty is in the eye of the beholder"—an aggressive company would have thought it was mineable, and a timid company would not. They ended up paying part of the bonus payment in my contract. I think if Newmont had still been involved, and if they hadn't changed their policy about mining copper, they would have probably gone ahead and developed it.

Moving out of the United States

When I began the Covered Area Project in southeastern Arizona and southwestern New Mexico in 1973, the United States was in the early stages of a transition from an industrial society to an information society, which, it was thought, would maintain our high standard of living. The worst interpretation was that we were converting the United States from a producing society to a consuming society, which borrows some of the money to pay for what we consume. Mining's part in this was that concentrators and smelters were "smokestack industries" and were bad. People thought electricity didn't come from burning coal; it came out of a socket in the wall. A big copper mine in the United States is bad and will destroy the environment, but the identical big copper mine overseas seems to be okay and won't hurt anything.

I was not thinking for the U.S. Chamber of Commerce, or for Newmont or Phelps Dodge—just trying to save one little exploration consultant named Dave—when I came to two conclusions: (1) I seemed to be able to find new mines a great deal better than the major mining companies. Therefore, it was logical to try to charge them for this ore-finding skill by way of some sort of success fee in addition to a fee for my professional and administrative talents. (2) Maybe it was also time to think about getting out of Dodge City (where they profess to hate mining) and move my dog and pony show to Chile, or Peru, or the Philippines, where they say they love mining and would be delighted to have a new mine and a higher standard of living.

I didn't stop the Covered Area Project and have a bon voyage party. I did, however, start asking for finder's fees in those projects I planned and managed, like CAP. I found four new mines in Chile and then, around 1993, largely gave up consulting work, concentrated on owning some kind of equity in future discoveries, and worked mainly in South America. This usually entailed taking over most of the planning and management, with financing coming from a private or public company. The CAP continued until about 1975 without another discovery.

I visited Iran on two occasions, in 1970 and 1975. The first trip was for Kaiser Aluminum Company based in Oakland, California, and the second was for McIntyre Porcupine Mines of Canada. In both cases my assignment was to make a reconnaissance of Iranian sites for porphyry copper deposits.

The first trip began with a search for an interpreter and expediter,

Massoud (Mac) Moezzi, guide, interpreter, and expeditor whose father was commanding general of the Iranian Gendarme force. Mac was a graduate of the Nevada College of Mines and worked in Lovelock, Nevada.

and I found an ideal person. His name was Massoud Moezzi, and he was a Persian with a geology degree from the University of Nevada. He was working for an industrial minerals company in Lovelock, Nevada. Massoud's English name was Mac and he was, and I hope still is, a people person. He was chairman of the Lovelock Democratic Party and a grandson of one of the Shahs of Iran, but as he pointed out, he is one of over a hundred grandsons. More important for our trips was the fact that his father, General Moezzi, was commanding general of the Iranian Gendarme force, the Iranian army under the last Shah, Mohammad Rez Pahlavi. This was sometimes very useful in the logistics of our trips. Mac went with me on both of my trips to Iran and was pleased to have a chance to visit his family again after several years of separation.

Edith, who is an anthropologist, agreed to go with me on the first trip and was able to visit Persepolis and Isfahan. We spent about three weeks in Iran and en route made brief visits to Spain and Greece. The plan was to go from Iran to Thailand to the Philippines, where I had another consulting job, and back to Arizona, for a round-the-world trip. There were a couple of hitches to this plan. The first was that with crossing a lot of time zones and trying to see too much on the first trip, I got the first and only case of total insomnia of my life.

When Mac and I went from Tehran to Kerman I had not slept for three days. Kerman at that time was a small town of maybe five thousand people in the middle of the desert. The "best" hotel had about a dozen rooms in a ring around a patio in the center. There was a bazaar in the town, the Persian equivalent of a shopping center. Artisans in one area of the bazaar were making copper pots, beginning with a lump of copper metal and, in a painstaking process, hammering out a handsome pot or bowl or tray.

Mac also found a small man with a large white beard who had an apothecary shop in a kiosk with a floor space of about eight by ten feet. Mac addressed him in Farsi, the Persian language, as follows: "Sir, my friend comes from a place very far away, and he has very deep thoughts so important that he cannot sleep. You must give him a potion which will allow him to sleep." The white-bearded apothecary replied, "If you will answer three questions I will give him the potion. The first question is, What is this place very far away from whence he comes? The second question is, Why does he have these deep thoughts? And the third question is, What are these thoughts that are so important they prevent him from sleeping for three days?" Mac answered, "I will answer your three questions if you will answer my three questions. How do we know that your potion will cure my friend? How should my friend take this potion? And if your potion kills my friend, is there any place in Kerman where we can bury a Christian?"

This went on a little longer, and I learned I should go to bed first, then take the potion, which was a harmless looking round white pill about the size of the head of a wooden match. The bearded apothecary expertly wrapped the pill up in a small square of newspaper and charged us the equivalent of US10 cents. We returned to the hotel, where I climbed into bed, sat up and swallowed the pill, and was asleep before my head hit the pillow. I slept ten hours. If this gentleman could expand his market into the United States he would make a fortune, but I am sure the People Who Know Best would squash this insomnia cure, especially if the odd patient did die.

In Kerman we rented a very ancient Russian Volga automobile, complete with driver, and first drove out to see the Sar Cheshmeh copper deposit, which at that time was owned by Selection Trust, a large British mining company carrying out an exploration diamond drilling program. The Brits were very hospitable and obliging and arranged a tour through the Sar Cheshmeh underground workings for me. It was a genuine large, typical, relatively high grade porphyry copper deposit.

I have always been interested in artifacts and archaeology and asked the manager if there were any ancient sites near Sar Cheshmeh. He said that when they did their first work they found the remains of eight one-shot copper furnaces. These are rock domes about eight or ten feet high with an opening at ground level for some sort of bellows. They are "one-shot" because they were carefully constructed with a thick layer of charcoal on the bottom over which there was a layer of oxide copper ore, and they may have mixed in some kind of flux like quartz or limestone. A hole in the roof allowed the smoke to escape. When all was prepared they lit the charcoal, vigorously operated the bellows, and finally a big puddle of molten copper metal collected on the floor. The problem was when they arrived for the Sunday picnic there were nine one-shot furnaces instead of eight. Someone had stolen a ton of ore from Sar Cheshmeh, built a furnace, smelted the ore, and taken the copper to the bazaar to pound into copper pots.

We visited several copper prospects in our ancient Volga, none of which were interesting. I occasionally inquired about artifacts, and in one village where we stopped, someone told me about a buried pot we might be interested in. We were in the Silk Road, which had been going for a few thousand years, and there were ruins of forts and habitation sites that might have been three hundred or three thousand years old. When we arrived at the nearby pot site the guide removed a flat rock,

Old fort along the Silk Road in Iran.

exposing a thick-walled buried pot probably four or five feet deep and two or three feet in diameter. Someone three hundred or three thousand years ago had stored something there for future reference. Water? Grain? Gold? (not likely). Anyway, it wouldn't fit in my suitcase and might be an important clue to Persian history, so we put the flat rock back and left.

Farther along we were driving on an almost deserted paved road. I was sitting in the left rear seat admiring the countryside when I noticed an automobile wheel passing us on the left. I tapped the driver on the shoulder and pointed. He, perhaps unwisely, braked, and the Volga tilted and lurched and squealed with sparks and dust and finally stopped, somewhat tilted. We looked over the hub and jacked it up, and I walked a half mile back up the highway looking for lug bolts and found only two. With the combined wisdom of three non-mechanics in two languages we decided that the Volga's medical condition penetrated deeper into the axle and differential than just the lug bolts. Mac located us approximately on a map, which indicated we were twelve miles from the nearest place where there might be people and a rescue vehicle. The obvious guy to hike was the driver, and he set off with a list of instructions in Farsi, which I didn't understand.

In about a half hour we heard a motor noise and saw a little ten-passenger bus traveling in the same direction we had been going. Mac leaped out and flagged the bus down, and we packed our suitcases, bags of samples, and ourselves and putted on down the highway, picked up our driver, and finally reached a town. Mac had made an agreement with the bus driver whereby other arrangements were to be made for transporting the other five or six bus passengers (with poorer aristocracy credentials), and we proceeded ahead for two days with our hijacked bus. We then spent two days sightseeing in Isfahan and Persepolis and one day visiting another uninteresting mineral prospect.

One of the things the Shah had done (in addition to hundreds of schools and hundreds of clinics and thousands of miles of highways) was the renovation of the Shah Abbas Hotel in Isfahan, where we arrived with our minibus. We were planning to meet Edith at the hotel. She had been on a personal tour of Isfahan, Shiraz, and Persepolis that had been arranged at our hotel in Tehran. The Shah Abbas Hotel was not large, with perhaps fifty or one hundred rooms, but it was very beautiful and decorated with many fine Persian carpets. It had been built about three hundred years earlier during the reign of King Sultan Husayn of Safavid. Mac and I found we had regular rooms, but Edith had something like the bridal suite, and we discovered it was because her reservation was made in the name of General Moezzi.

We visited Mac's father, General Moezzi, and his mother, a very pleasant plump lady of about sixty years (who was smoking a water pipe). Then it was time to say good-bye to Mac, and we were off to Thailand (vacation), the Philippines (consulting work), and home.

The day we arrived in the Philippines, Edith left the hotel and strolled around in Manila and there were Filipino gentlemen sitting on the doorstep with shotguns in most of the stores near the hotel. She didn't think she liked the Philippines very well, and she also had a premonition that something might have happened to our youngest son, Douglas, so she caught an early flight home. When she arrived in San Francisco she was met by our daughter, Susan, and asked how everybody was; Susan hesitated and said, "Everything is fine and Doug isn't badly hurt." The details were that Doug had ridden his motorcycle off a cliff and landed hard enough to scrape the paint off the top of his helmet, but he was okay other than some sprains and bruises. I went on to Marcopper.

My second copper reconnaissance trip to Iran five years later was similar to the first, but was for a different mining company, McIntyre Porcupine. For part of the trip I traveled with Robert B. Fulton, by that time president of McIntyre Porcupine. Since I had worked with Bob Fulton a number of times, we were well acquainted. We were also fortunate in obtaining the services of Mac Moezzi again as interpreter and expeditor. This time he also arranged for an aircraft to do fairly extensive aerial reconnaissance of the districts.

The results of the second Iran visit were again negative, partly because porphyry copper systems are not as numerous in Iran as in Arizona and Chile. I thought the lack of success was also partly because of lack of courageousness on the part of management to begin an expensive exploration program in an exotic part of the world. However, events in Iran since 1975 have certainly contradicted my conclusion that it was a quiet, progressive, well-run country. I think the interference of the United States and others had a detrimental effect in Iran in the late 1970s.

The first part of my trip was with Bob Fulton and Mac Moezzi, visiting mines and mineral prospects. I remember after a number of days in the field we got to Isfahan, which is an important historical center. Bob wanted to spend one or two days sightseeing, which surprised me because he had a grim, driving, taciturn personality and worked long hours and hiked long distances. I hadn't visited Persepolis on my first Iran visit but did this time with Bob. The site is an Old World wonder, with beautiful statues and rockwork. I took lots of pictures, but they were all ruined by being x-rayed in Customs when I left.

The second day Bob heard about a place where you could watch a Persian carpet being made and invited me to go, but I declined and instead shopped for some presents to take back home. Bob said he was taken to the carpet place by a taxi driver who spoke a little English. It was in a basement, where a number of children were tying knots in several carpets being made. A young lady about sixteen years old who spoke a little English became Bob's guide. They sat on a bench at the edge of the work area and she took his hand and showed him how to play finger games. Bob, in an effort to change the subject, asked her how much the nearest carpet would be sold for. He rapidly converted this in his mind to U.S. dollars and came up with the figure of $12.75; he decided she was not talking about the price of the carpet and scuttled back out to the street.

For the reconnaissance flights in Iran I was flown in a twin-engine American aircraft, something like a Beechcraft Queen Air. The pilot was a small Iranian with a great sense of humor. Most educated Iranians I became acquainted with were very charming people. He had become a pilot when he was in the Iranian army and had been sent to a U.S. Air Force base in Nevada for advance training but was a civilian pilot when I flew with him. His nickname was Kamikaze, but in our flights he was unwilling to fly any closer than twenty kilometers from the Russian border because the year before the Russians had shot down an Iranian plane, inside Iran but close to the Russian border. I had had some previous experience identifying from the air peripheral porphyry copper alteration zones, but didn't find any with Kamikaze.

On the ground we visited a qanat, which is an ancient system of developing water in the desert. In Iran, the rainfall is typically less than five inches a year. The first qanats were probably built in Persia by the Romans. In a typical valley, the ridges on each side are rock outcrops and there is a gentle gravel slope down to the middle of the valley and up the other side where the rock surface again emerges. The qanat system takes advantage of a perched water table at the rock/gravel interface. If there is sufficient water above the rock basement, then a line of ventilation shafts are constructed, with picks and shovels, every three hundred to five hundred feet, leading to a flat area in the middle of the valley. The water is collected at the buried bedrock surface by an almost

Top: Qanat shaft in Iran, 1970. David Lowell with shaft sinking workers who allowed him to go down the shaft as a professional courtesy because he was a mining engineer. The shaft is part of a gravity water development system probably invented by the Romans. *Bottom:* An oasis created with water from qanat, which supports cultivation of large pistachio farm.

horizontal tunnel which eventually emerges at the ground surface. This tunnel delivers water by gravity to create an oasis. In our recon flying we saw piles of gravel dug out for qanat shafts in lines that were sometimes thirty miles long, representing a whole generation of work to create an oasis and pistachio farm.

When the crew at the collar of the qanat heard I was a mining engineer they invited me to go down their shaft since it wasn't very deep, and I accepted. It was about eighty to a hundred feet deep and penetrated only partly consolidated gravel. I put both feet in a sinking bucket attached to a reel, and held the hemp rope that held it with both hands. This type of untimbered shaft is inherently unsafe because a pebble or cobble-sized rock could at any time fall out of the shaft wall and by the time it had dropped to the bottom would be a very dangerous missile. At the bottom of the shaft was a bed of saturated gravel with a trickle of water flowing, maybe two or three gallons per minute. It was very humid and stuffy and dank. I did not attempt to crawl either way in the tunnel, which was only three or four feet high.

One of the tricks in designing a qanat is the slope of the tunnel carrying the water. From my mining experience I assume the slope is about one-half of 1 percent grade: steep enough for the water to flow, but not steep enough to have a tendency to cut into the floor. I have no idea how these qanat artisans calculate and control the slope. Many of the long-established qanats are populated by white, blind lungfish, but no one seems to know where they came from. As arranged, I climbed back in the bucket and tugged three times on the rope, the signal to pull me up. The shaft was so small I could have easily put a hand on each wall, and it would have been very unpleasant for a person suffering from claustrophobia. They answered my tug, and pulled me up with no mishap.

I finished my aerial recon with Kamikaze after several days, each night in a different town where we could land. We found no obvious porphyry copper peripheral silicate zoning indicated by color. On the way back we stopped in Tehran, and one of our associates took us through Iran's equivalent of Fort Knox. Rather than gold, Iran's currency was based on the Royal Jewels stored in the basement of a bank. There were literally buckets full of diamonds and emeralds and crowns set with jewels. The Peacock Throne, a golden throne inlaid with precious stones and captured, I believe, from India, was there. There was very strict security, with a maximum of twenty or thirty visitors, who were locked up in the room with the jewels in the cases for a twenty-minute visit.

My experience on both trips to Iran was very pleasant and truly interesting from a historical standpoint. One of my companions from Kaiser was an Alexander the Great buff. We once drove over a ridge bordering a large valley and my friend became very excited and said, "This is the very valley that Alexander's army marched through on his way to Persepolis." Every Iranian I met from all levels of society was pleasant, considerate, and courteous, and it is hard to believe that the country was soon taken over by ruthless religious fanatics.

Adventures in the Philippines

The 1970s held several exotic adventures for me. I did a lot of work in the Philippine Islands for Placer Development Company, Benguet Corporation, Atlas Consolidated Mining Company, and Lepanto. I worked at least once for most of the large companies working in the Philippines on porphyry copper deposits. While I was there, I learned that law and order in the Philippines has not been very good since World War II, although it gets better and worse. I had various exciting experiences.

There was a Philippine group called the NPA or New People's Army, a Communist insurgent terrorist group, not as bad as Sendero Luminoso in Peru but with some of the same ideas. I remember once on a trip to look at a Benguet gold prospect on Masbate Island I found that the Filipinos tend to be sneaky about telling you only what they think you ought to know and not what they think you want to know. On this occasion, they took me out in an NPA training area, where they had some kind of a truce arrangement with the insurgents. They didn't tell me where we were going until we were already there. We drove over a Jeep trail in the jungle for an hour or more to look at some prospects, then at the end of the day we drove back out.

We had come through a dip. It was a dirt road, but a cement dip had been built to provide a crossing of a stream. There was an open area on the other side of the dip, and on the trip back we drove down to the dip and stopped. The driver stopped just before going into the dip. I was sitting in the right front seat, and there were several other

David Lowell and the Benguet helicopter at Davao City, Mindanao, Philippines, 1973.

Filipino geologists; it was a Toyota Land Cruiser automobile. Nobody said anything, and nobody got out. Probably a full minute went by. I said, "Why did we stop?" And the driver said, "Well, somebody has put a log across the road." Then I noticed there was a big coconut trunk across the road.

What had happened was that these Communist insurgents had put this across the road, knowing that we were there, to make us stop. Nobody knew what the next step in the play was. Finally, two of the Filipinos got out very slowly and walked very slowly through the dip and very slowly moved the log off the road, but there were undoubtedly some people with automatic rifles in the tree line, watching us while this went on. We never saw them, and nothing happened to us, but it was a worrisome experience.

We drove on to the next town. We were supposed to go to the end of the island to visit a gold mine. The plan had been to drive up the highway to the mine. We were a little behind schedule, and when we got to the town, one of them told me, "We think it might be nice to go to the mine in a banca canoe." I said, "Why is that? Isn't there a paved road all the way?" And they said, "Yes, but it's our policy not to drive on that road after dark. This is because of the possibility of being attacked."

We hired a motorized banca canoe, a hollowed-out large tree trunk with an outrigger—a typical Philippine boat—and we had to go maybe half a mile out to sea and then up the coast. The water was fairly rough, and we all got totally soaked. My suitcase was soaked, and we came in at the mine camp, which was on the coast. I guess they called ahead, and somebody was there to meet us. But it was a little bit like the movie *The Time Machine*, where the Morlocks come out at night.

On another occasion in about 1975, I went to the Lepanto mining camp with its chief engineer, Roger Concepcion, a very competent Filipino. Lepanto had a guesthouse that was quite nice, where I had stayed before. The second night Roger said, "I'm not going to be able to stay with you tonight. I'm going to stay with friends." He said, "They have made up a death list for Lepanto and I'm one of the names on the list. My policy is to stay in a different place every night." I decided at about that point that life is too short to continue doing a lot of work in the Philippines, but I did return several times to work on projects where personal safety seemed less of a problem.

I worked twice on a Benguet prospect called King King on Mindanao Island in the Southern Philippines. On my first visit, in the early eighties, Benguet had their helicopter and it was about a twenty-minute helicopter ride from Davao City. The drill core from King King was stored in an abandoned sawmill a similar distance but toward the interior of the island. They asked me whether I wanted to see the prospect first or the core first, and I asked to visit the deposit first and we flew to visit King King. At breakfast the next day I read an article in the Davao newspaper that said NPA bandits had held up a bus containing forty passengers and lined them up and made them strip naked to find all valuables. I asked Louie Albarracin where this attack had taken place and he said, "Oh that's the abandoned sawmill." I have thought many times what it would have been like to be one in a line of totally naked bus riders.

I returned to King King about five years later with the Benguet manager. The political situation had gotten much worse and two men had been killed. The helicopter landed near the deposit and the manager said, "Take anything you will need because the helicopter will be moved to the top of that hill." It was a hot, very humid day. I was not very anxious to hike up a hill at the end of the day and I asked why the helicopter would be moved. He replied that he had a policy to never land the helicopter in the same place twice. Presumably there might be a guy waiting with an AK-47.

Once while I was working at Marcopper, a drainage tunnel was being driven under the open pit by one shift of workers, but at the end of the day shift they did not come out of the tunnel. It took a couple of hours to determine they were missing and organize a rescue party. The tunnel shift were found sitting on the ground at the face of the tunnel. When asked why they didn't go home one of them said, "Well, we started out and someone saw some of the Little People and we just decided to stay in the tunnel." "Little People" are malevolent-type elves that live in the jungle and aren't to be messed with.

A more tragic experience happened to my friend Al Ploesser, who spent most of his career in the Philippines. He was managing a mine in the interior of Mindanao Island, a hotbed of NPA and of "Morros," who were even more dangerous. It was generally agreed that the "bad guys" owned the night, and Al was commuting daily back and forth to the mine from Davao City. On one occasion he had not quite finished his work and violated his own rule by staying a little late. It was raining and the road was covered with slippery mud and he was in a hurry to get out of the jungle. He passed a Jeep that had slid into the ditch and he stopped, thinking it was his duty to help the other motorist. He backed up beside the Jeep and saw to his horror that there was a bullet hole in the windshield, with the driver slumped over the wheel, dead. Al panicked, thinking the killer was nearby, and roared off, but his wheels were spinning in the mud and he soon skidded into the ditch. For a while he thought he would not be able to get out but he finally did and made it back to Davao City.

A water buffalo in a threatening pose near its owner's Nipa hut.

I was once walking through the jungle with three Philippine geologists and we passed a thatched "Nipa hut" with a water buffalo outside in a mud wallow. Water buffalos are very tame with their owners and you often see a five- or six-year-old child riding happily on a buffalo's neck, steering him with a small stick. However, they are also very territorial and this one erupted from his mud wallow and charged us at high speed. We all ran as fast as we could in four different directions and the buffalo, satisfied that he had defended his homestead, went back to his mud wallow. It took us a little while to reorganize our expedition, and at the end of the day we returned by a different route.

I enjoyed my work in the Philippines and liked the people, but over time the dangerous incidents seemed to occur with greater frequency. I didn't decide overnight to stop working in the Philippines, but accepted fewer and fewer jobs in favor of working in safer places. I was involved in a peripheral way in two ore discoveries in the Philippines. In neither case was I really directly responsible for the mine. The first was a Dizon project for Benguet Corporation. I was working as a consultant

David with a community of Negritos. Most of the individuals in the picture are adults. The photo was taken near a copper prospect on the slope of Mt. Pinatubu, about three years before the huge volcanic eruption that deposited up to 200 meters of ash on this site in 1982. It's not known whether these Negritos escaped.

for Benguet when the Dizon Project was submitted to Benguet. It had already been explored briefly by the Nippon Mining Company, who had driven a short adit and drilled several holes.

On my first visit I felt it looked encouraging, but the Benguet chief geologist disagreed, and we had a debate that lasted for a week or more about this. The Benguet management decided to take my side of the argument, and they acquired the property and began a drilling project and drilled out a porphyry copper orebody that has developed into a large open pit mine and was very profitable for the company. I believe that had this not happened exactly this way, some other group would have eventually done the same thing at Dizon.

My original job in the Philippines was for Marcopper, a mine operated by Placer Development Company. For a period of several years in the early 1970s, I was Placer Development's in-house advisor on mine geology, and I worked in all their mines at that time, with the resident

Portal of the adit previously driven by Nippon Mining Company in the Dizon orebody. This was a significant meeting during which I identified Dizon as a porphyry copper, rather than a subcommercial "contact metamorphic" occurrence as had been thought by Benguet's staff. Benguet accepted my opinion and went ahead with an exploration project followed by mine development. From left, Burl Worley, Louis Albarracin, two unidentified Benguet geologists, David Lowell, Earl McCarthy, and Al Faretta, 1972.

geologists, reviewing the systems used to collect geological information, ore-grade information, and drilling technology and so forth.

At Marcopper I had a small, very indirect input in expediting the development of the San Antonio orebody, which was found by Geoff Loudon, the resident geologist. Geoff is Australian. The thinking that resulted in the discovery was entirely Geoff's, but I was able to support him in getting the deposit drilled out and accepted by the Placer management later.

I worked several times for Atlas Consolidated Mining Company, which operated a large open pit copper mine on Cebu Island. This company also produces San Miguel Beer, a brand popular in Asia. On one of my visits to Cebu the company assigned a company sedan and driver to me to get from the guesthouse to the engineering office and to the pit. The first day I rode in the car I noticed a piece of heavy conveyor belting installed inside the rear window. I asked the driver why the belting was there and he replied, "Look above the window beside you." There I saw a vertical line of small holes in the upholstery spaced about two inches apart, as would be produced by an automatic rifle. He said this car had been previously assigned to the company comptroller who at present was in the hospital recovering from a bullet that had passed through his pancreas. The driver said that the Israelis had found that conveyor belt was very effective in stopping small arms fire and that belting had also been placed inside the doors of my vehicle and others.

This made me a little less eager to enjoy looking out the window at the flowers and mango trees and pretty scenery. It also was one of those incidents that made me wonder exactly why I was working in the Philippines.

Fieldwork in Luzon

I also had several unpleasant experiences in the field in the Philippines, and most were the result of steep, often jungle-covered terrain with a lack of access roads. On one occasion I hiked with a Filipino geologist to look at a copper prospect on Luzon Island. We planned to return before dark. However, it rained all day and the rocks were slippery, which slowed us somewhat, and when dusk came we were still some distance from our vehicle. We each had a light rain jacket but by the end of the day we were soaking wet, tired, and hungry. We came upon an unoccupied Nipa hut. This is a standard Philippine native residence, with walls and floors made of split bamboo, typically about five or six inches in diameter before splitting. The roofs are thatched, and the most expensive item in the construction of a Nipa hut is the nails. We were happy to get out of the rain but had nothing to eat. There were no beds. We slept in our wet clothes on the floor lined with rounded bamboo splits, but it wasn't too bad.

On another field trip in Negros Island we were crossing a sizable stream by jumping from rounded boulder to rounded boulder. I slipped on one and broke my tailbone, which took about six months to heal. It's a far cry from most geologic fieldwork in North America.

There is a very inaccessible area in the northern part of Luzon Island that is known as "the Igorot country." It has some mineral potential, but to the best of my knowledge all the prospects are unexplored and undeveloped, although I don't know what has happened in the last few decades. According to Philippine laws this area is open to claim location, but there is a reason there are no claims: the Igorots don't want people messing around in Igorot country and everybody knows they are tough hombres.

A number of centuries ago Spain ran into the Igorots and came out second best. About a hundred years ago the United States tried using more diplomacy but had the same result. Then in World War II Japan tried using brute force and killed a lot of Igorots and the Igorots killed a lot of Japanese and the Japanese gave up their invasion.

In the mid-1970s Benguet Consolidated Mining Company had heard about attractive mineral targets there. They assumed they could use diplomacy and that the Igorots had become docile and friendly. An exploration trip was organized with a total of about six people, including two gringos. They arrived unexpectedly at a village near the mineral occurrence and the Igorots, as a first step, invited them to move onto the second story of a two-story guesthouse. They then had a community meeting to decide what to do with these uninvited pests and decided to let the women deal with them. When morning came and the Benguet group started down the ladder they found a solid layer of glowering Igorot women lying down around the ladder. They were held prisoner until noon when they were told to come down and leave.

The area around the village consisted of rice paddies, and the Benguet people marched off in single file and eventually were walking on a narrow trail on a dike between two paddies. One of the gringos, a somewhat overweight geologist, was panting along in the rear, when an Igorot woman caught up. She wanted to pass and she began to grumble. He didn't understand and he ignored her. She then came up behind him and delivered a huge kick, which landed him in the rice paddies on his face. Thus ended the most recent Igorot War.

"Godfather" of Lepanto's Far Southeast Orebody

I selected the location of most all the deep drill holes drilled in what Lepanto called the Far Southeast orebody. In modern times, the success or failure of an exploration project on a site with mineable ore is normally the result of whether or not holes are drilled in the right place. Orebodies are almost always found by drill holes, so it's very important that the right logic is used in planning the drilling.

At some point, Lepanto hired a geostatistical firm in Vancouver to perform an ore reserve calculation on the holes that had been completed. Far Southeast was very deep. It was 1,000 meters (over 3,000 feet) minimum depth below the surface. Each drill hole was very expensive. At that point, it still missed being a definitely mineable deposit.

A meeting was arranged in Vancouver. I came from Arizona, where I was working at the time, and Roger Concepcion came from the Philippines. We looked over the data, and I think the Lepanto general manager, Art Disini, was there also. The geostatisticians presented their data, and they said, "We have deduced that the grade of the orebody is decreasing with depth."

We had previously reviewed the drill core and the assays of the cores for copper and gold and molybdenum content. It was obvious to me that the grade was not decreasing in depth; it was increasing. I had looked at the actual cores. I will not get off into a technical description of the geometry of the orebody but I was sure that the grade was not decreasing. I was able to convince the Lepanto manager that that was the case. This was a case in which statistical analysis suggested something that was untrue, which I think may happen fairly often. As a result of this meeting, they decided to drill deeper holes and they found a larger and higher-grade orebody, which is now being developed into a mine. Later, the president of Lepanto referred to me as the "godfather of the Far Southeast Orebody." Not the one who found it, but the one who saved it.

CHAPTER TWO

Consultant for Codelco's Mines in Chile

In the period following the overthrow of Salvador Allende in Chile in late 1973, the Allende government left the large, state-owned mines, which had earlier been expropriated, in shambles. They had done a very poor job of operating the mines. The average age of the average mine manager, I was told, was either twenty-four or twenty-five years old. Apparently there was a great shortage of people who both had studied mine engineering and were also Communists. They collected some of these young political-type mine engineers and made them managers of mines like Chuquicamata and Braden, and it didn't work.

When Gen. Augusto Pinochet took over, the mines were practically destroyed. The Pinochet government hired a large number of consultants and contractors to come in to put things back in shape. There were contracting firms from half a dozen countries at any given time working at Chuquicamata, and a lot of different engineering and geology consultants. I was the principal ore deposits consultant for Codelco in Chile for six years between 1974 and 1980.

I would probably never have been Codelco's ore deposits consultant, and would never have organized the Atacama Project, which found the Escondida and Zaldívar deposits, and never indirectly been involved in the later San Cristobal and Leonor discoveries but for a decision by Alexander Sutulof to invite me to Chile. Alexander, or Alex, was a refugee from Communist Russia. His father had been a general in the tsarist army who fled I believe to Yugoslavia, and Alex, in turn, fled to Chile. Alex moved to the United States when Allende took over. He taught metallurgy in the University of Utah. Alex was the author of a number of books, and in the process of rebuilding the Chilean copper industry, his research identified me as the porphyry copper expert they needed. He later became a close friend.

During my six-year retainer as mine geology and exploration consultant for Codelco, I worked in all the large Codelco mines. These had been nationalized from the Kennecott, Anaconda, and Cerro de Pasco companies. I offered criticisms and advice regarding development plans and exploration techniques. However, there was a built-in difference of viewpoint.

Exploration geologists are divided into "lumpers" and "splitters." I think my career had been successful because I am an unashamed lumper, and corner-cutter, and risk taker. The Chilean geologists at that time had accepted the splitter philosophy of the Anaconda Company, which previously operated Chuquicamata and El Salvador. Their professors in Chilean universities also were 100 percent in favor of high-tech exploration methods and hairsplitting geology descriptions. I was hired because I had worked on fifty porphyry copper systems and at that time had found four new porphyry copper mines.

One of the Codelco deposits I worked on was El Abra, roughly eighty kilometers north of Chuquicamata on the Falla Oeste (West Fissure) ore trend. El Abra, which is now in production as a large mine, was at relatively high elevation, with much of the outcrop above 4,500 meters (15,000 feet). I was familiar with the roads and geology and ore grades, and also knew the watchman who lived in a cave excavated in the side of the hill where the locked entrance gate was located. The cave had a door and a window. At the time of this visit the Codelco exploration was shut down and the watchman was alone at El Abra.

There is a convention in the mining industry of reciprocal hospitality toward visitors to your mine or project, and when Codelco was approached by an Australian company asking to visit El Abra on short

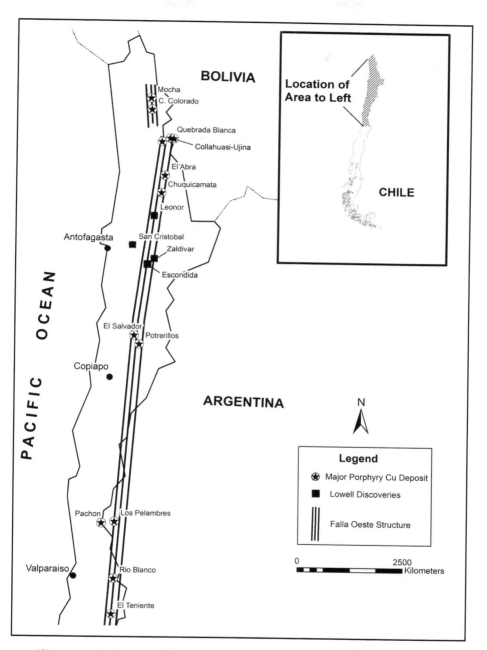

Alignment of Chilean Copper deposits along the Falla Oeste Structure at the start of the Atacama Project (J. D. Lowell, 1978).

Visit to El Abra Prospect (now a large mine) in 1976. From left, two unidentified Codelco geologists, Don Carlos Ruiz, David Lowell. Don Carlos had
been Director of the Instituto de Investigaciones Geológicas, the Chilean
Geological Survey. Don Carlos was a close friend and co-author with David of
two published articles.

notice they agreed, but Codelco was unwilling to organize a visit on
Sunday and suggested that the three Australian geologists contact
me, since I was at the time working out of Calama, the town near
Chuquicamata and the jumping-off point for El Abra. They called me
and I agreed to go as a favor. I told the visitors that it would be a poor
idea to drink very much in Calama the night before the visit. Their
answer to this was "Any Aussie knows how to hold his liquor," and they
disregarded my suggestion.

We met the next morning at their hotel and left for El Abra, but
there wasn't much conversation and I thought they looked a little "triste"
(under the weather). By the time we got to the watchman's cave they
didn't have anything at all to say and were just staring straight ahead,
looking very triste. The watchman came out and looked them over, and
we decided that only one of the three was up to driving around El Abra.
The watchman brought out two cot-sized cotton mattresses and laid
them on the road, and we laid the two worst cases of altitude sickness

on their backs on the mattresses staring up at the sky. It looked like a double wake. I drove the third geologist around El Abra, and he got to see the geology and drill sites and collect a few specimens. When we got back to the gate the first two were exactly where we had left them, but we were able to get them in the vehicle and back to Calama. Calama isn't exactly sea level; its elevation is about 12,000 feet. However, my three friends survived.

During that time, I had an opportunity to work in every one of the Codelco mines and visit in the field almost every copper prospect in Chile. The principal copper mining area in Chile is the Atacama Desert in Regions I and II, which is the northern part of Chile. I had begun the CAP in Arizona in 1973, exploring below postmineral cover. It became obvious, visiting prospects in Chile, that Chile was a more favorable place than Arizona for this approach to exploration.

The ideal geological situation for my exploration techniques was the

Cristo de las Vetas, Copiapó, Chile, 1977. Copiapó is a small mining town and the residents say in this statue Christ is showing how wide his vein is.

David with "Indi," a tame vicuna, at Quebrada Blanca camp at over 14,000 feet before development of the mine, about 1982.

presence of a narrow structural belt in which all the orebodies occurred, and this geology is present in northern Chile, and with a ratio of about 50:50 between postmineral cover and premineral outcrop. In premineral outcrop it's possible to map alterations and sample to find the edges of geochemical anomalies in the 50 percent of premineral outcrops and extrapolate this anomaly into postmineral cover where there may be a hidden orebody.

The Atacama Project

In 1978 I decided to just go ahead and launch a postmineral cover exploration of the sort described, and I put together a plan and budget and approached several major North American companies, including Utah International. Bob Wheaton, whom I had known a long time and was a classmate in college, was at that time the exploration manager

A typical Atacama scout drill hole, 1980. The average hole depth was about 300 meters (1,000 feet), and over 18 months of drilling we averaged, including moving the rig, about 250 meters per 24 hours, about one hole completed per day.

there. I had proposed a budget of $1.5 million a year for three years and had a series of steps involving reconnaissance geologic mapping and reconnaissance geochem sampling covering a 500-kilometer-long and 35-kilometer-wide block between El Salvador and the Chuquicamata Mine.

Bob Wheaton agreed to fund it. And then, unfortunately for both of us, he decided that $4.5 million was a pretty large expenditure for Utah, and he came back and asked me if I would agree to bring Getty Minerals in, which had lots of oil money and was looking for joint venture projects. I agreed (and lived to regret it), and the Atacama Project was set up. We did reconnaissance and compilation of geologic mapping, and after several months I hired a Chilean chief geologist, Francisco Ortiz. Through most of the project, the staff was entirely Chilean, with the exception of me and Bill Mounts, the drilling consultant, who spent a good part of his time in Chile. We hired several uni-

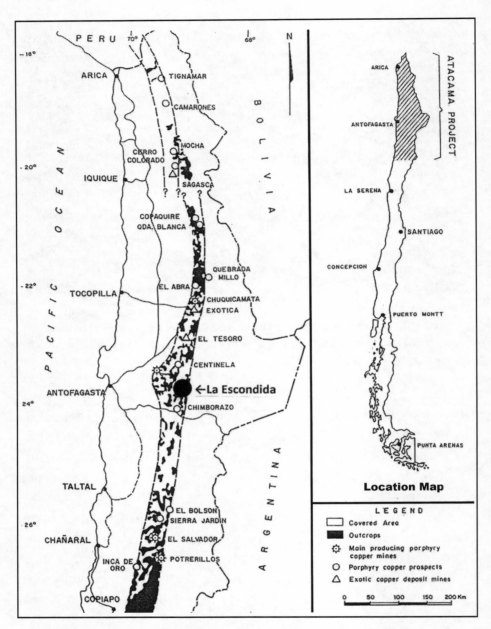

Map showing areas of postmineral cover from which the Atacama Project was selected. This section of porphyry copper belt with 50/50 postmineral cover and premineral outcrop was favorable for the Atacama Project exploration strategy and for the La Escondida and Zaldívar discoveries (J. D. Lowell and L. Clark Arnold, 1978).

versity professors in Chile to assist in compiling the geology, and they did some fill-in reconnaissance mapping. At a point early in the project, I filed mining claims over the whole 500-kilometer-long belt. One of these claims covered most of the Escondida orebody, as it turned out later, and another covered about half of the Zaldívar deposit.

The Atacama Project started off with a couple of things I did right and a couple I later regretted. The first correct move was the planning of the project. It ran smoothly and efficiently, and the two large copper deposits we found were in ground we acquired by staking. With more cooperation from Utah and Getty I think a third deposit could have been found. The second thing I did right was to have the agreement written at my own expense by the best corporate law firm in southern Arizona. It was airtight.

I also made two mistakes. The first was in agreeing with Utah to invite Getty to participate in the Atacama Project. The second was in agreeing to accept a finder's fee of a carried 5 percent interest, but with a $3.75 million cap. I am sure I could have had a 3 percent with no cap, which, in the case of Escondida, would have netted me at least a billion additional dollars.

The whole Atacama Project encompassed 17,500 square kilometers between El Salvador and the Chuquicamata Mine, a strip thirty-five kilometers wide and five hundred kilometers long. The first target, only partly explored due to property problems, was El Tesoro (The Treasure). This was an "exotic copper deposit" (copper transported late in geologic history by rainwater). An unsuccessful effort had been made forty years earlier to mine oxide copper ore on a small scale. Exotic copper deposits contain copper that has been transported horizontally, usually only one or two kilometers from the source, and the source is usually a porphyry copper system. The presence of exotic copper is obviously a strong indication that there may be a nearby porphyry copper.

El Tesoro had two very large handicaps. The first was that it was immediately adjacent to part of the huge strike-slip Falla Oeste fault that cuts off the west side of the Chuquicamata orebody and could have a horizontal displacement of as much as 125 kilometers. This makes the

El Tesoro Mine looking west. Host rock is highly sheared Jurassic sediments.

El Tesoro geology very complicated because of fault displaced segments. The second obstacle for us was that El Tesoro was owned by Andronico Luksic, the richest man in Chile with a reputation of always, one way or another, coming out on top of every business deal. I became well acquainted with Andronico (who was born on the same day of the same year as I was). I tried for a long time with many different formulas to make an option or joint venture deal, but was not successful. We had staked a block of claims to the east of El Tesoro and our drilling found part of a hidden porphyry copper system and indicated several hundred million tonnes of 0.25 percent copper. This grade was only half of commercial ore grade in 1979, but under the current copper price would be nearly ore grade.

We contracted a little bit of drilling with a local drilling company that was a branch of Boyles Brothers drilling company called Boyles Geotech. Their drilling costs were substantially higher than what we

David Lowell with Andronico Luksic, the wealthiest man in Chile but not the easiest to deal with.

had been paying in Arizona, so in consultation with Bill Mounts, I did a search for a North American company that was willing to go to Chile, and we found a company called Harris Drilling Company, who had done a good job in projects for us in Arizona.

Hugh Harris, the manager of the Harris Drilling Company, had his office in San Diego, California. We made a deal with him to bring the drill rig, all the supplies and spare parts, pickups, flatbed trucks, and camp, and it was all loaded on a ship in Houston and hauled down to the port of Antofagasta. The Harris group unloaded their drill rig and assembled it and unloaded all their supplies, drove over a hundred kilometers out in the desert, and had finished their first drill hole two days after coming in sight of Antofagasta. And they got everything through Customs, which under the Pinochet government was relatively easy. Drilling proceeded fairly smoothly through the rest of the project. We had one drill rig running continuously almost 365 days a year. We drilled an average of something like 800 feet per twenty-four hours through two years.

We drilled a huge amount of footage. Our drilling costs per foot were almost exactly 50 percent of what we had been charged before. The deal involved our paying for the mobilization and for the shipping cost of equipment, but we were to be reimbursed for this amount over eight months, so after eight months it had cost us nothing to have the new drilling company in Chile. They are still there and are one of the principal drilling companies in Chile, with eight drill rigs operating in 2010. They have recently merged with another company.

We tried to complete a geochem survey in which there would be one rock geochem or stream sediment geochem sample every kilometer in east–west profiles about 35 kilometers long, which had a north–south spacing averaging about five kilometers between profiles. We started off planning to do this out of helicopters. Pancho Ortiz, our chief geologist, and I tried for two or three days to establish a protocol for the helicopter sampling, and it became pretty obvious that it would be both dangerous and expensive.

Chile, at that time, had a safety regulation that helicopter fuel could only be used out of new fifty-five-gallon barrels. This required us to bring in a large truckload of barrels from Santiago, about a thousand kilometers to the south. The charter cost of helicopters was about US$1000 per hour and the standby cost more than $500 per hour, so it was very important to keep to a schedule. We had arranged for the barrels to arrive two or three days early, but they didn't arrive, and we launched an all-out search. We found that the truck driver had a girlfriend halfway to our exploration site, and they were happily having a romantic interlude in Copiapó.

We had several samplers, including me, in the helicopter test. If the helicopter would carry the pilot and three samplers, the pilot would drop a sampler and then fly a kilometer further and drop a second sampler and fly a kilometer further and drop a third one. They would collect samples, then the pilot would turn around and fly back and

Helicopter pilot and David Lowell on flight into high terrain in Region III about 1976. A few years later when David tried to hire him for a charter flight he found he had been killed in a crash as had the other pilot. David thought he was very competent. The combination of high elevation and strong wind make helicopters very dangerous in the Andes.

pick up the first and the second and the third sampler, and drop them father along. It was a leapfrog process. This kind of utilization of helicopters wasn't a new idea. It's commonly done in various parts of the world where there is not good road access. But we ran into a problem because the first area, which was fairly representative of our whole project, was at an elevation of about 12,000 feet, where the performance of a helicopter is significantly decreased. The Andes are famous for being a windy part of the world, especially in the afternoon. The pilot was having trouble making quick landings at each point on our traverse at that altitude, with those wind speeds. It began to look distinctly dicey to do it.

After two or three days, I said, "Forget it," and we sent the helicopter back to Santiago and did the sample collection from Jeeps or on foot. A lot of the sampling was done by driving to one end of a

Trying to pitch a tent in the usual afternoon high wind, 1985. Site is in a *salar*, an evaporite interior drainage lake which contains water at rare intervals.

35-kilometer traverse and dropping the sampler and then driving to the other end and picking him up at the end of the day. The job involved walking thirty-five kilometers or about twenty miles a day, sometimes carrying thirty or forty pounds of samples. It's fairly easy walking in most of the desert, but it's also pretty strenuous walking that far at that altitude. We had a problem getting somebody physically able to do this. It wasn't working very well, and somebody told me about an American geologist named Tyler Kittredge, who lived in Panama and was kind of a Rambo-type fellow. He had been shot three times in the chest in Viet Nam and had then throttled the fellow who shot him. I called Tyler on the telephone and asked him if he was interested in this job, and he said he was, and he did all the sampling. He actually personally collected about 2,500 samples. The samples were surface samples from whatever was present at the 1-kilometer interval. If there was a rock outcrop of premineral rock or a sediment sample of sand or gravel we sampled it, and we found this worked well. The stream sediment samples correlated well with adjacent rock outcrop samples.

So that was one of the rings of the circus, this sampling program. We had some land problems also, but we started out with an assembly line of drilling prospects that were represented by geochemical anomalies or other geological evidence of a possible porphyry copper system.

We had one Chilean engineer, Donaldo Rojas, who was our land guy. His brother, Nivaldo Rojas, was a geologist. Nivaldo may have been the best exploration geologist that I had in Chile during this project. He has since worked for BHP and has been in charge of their work in Argentina. Nivaldo was not a university graduate. He graduated from a two-year technical school in Copiapó, Chile. At one point, I tried to talk him into going back to the university and offered to pay a half-time salary while he was in the university, but he had a family and decided he didn't want to do that. It didn't hold him back at all. He has done very well, and his brother also was a very competent guy in the land work and surveying.

La Escondida, the Largest Copper Mine in the World

Each land problem is a separate problem. They most commonly revolve around trying to negotiate option deals with landowners. The bulk of the land work in Chile is in determining the land status. Records in Chile were not very systematically kept, and it was sometimes very difficult to find out who owned what property. Some of the records were kept in Santiago and some locally in the province (region), and that's part of the difficulty.

We had drilled four prospects in the Atacama Project. At the first one, El Tesoro, we got some suggestion of an orebody, but nothing in the second, third, and fourth targets drilled. The fifth we named La Escondida (The Hidden One), and that's part of the story. Escondida

This is a typical Atacama field camp, 1987. In this case it's in an area where there is rain every few years as indicated by sparse vegetation, and the ground surface is a mudflow. After a rain there is usually not enough water to form a flood, but mud moves down drainages like a lava flow.

had been acquired and looked at by five other companies that walked away. We were the sixth company to do work at Escondida. None of the previous five companies had even found anything encouraging enough to drill a hole in, but we did. And it's now the largest copper deposit in the world. I looked at it the first time with Pancho Ortiz, who is also a very capable, smart geologist. Pancho has a master's degree from Stanford University and did some work toward a doctorate at Colorado School of Mines, and he also has a degree from University of Chile. Nivaldo, Pancho, and I made the first visit to what would become the Escondida Mines. It fit part of the criteria for one of our projects. We found some of the right kind of hydrothermal alteration, and there was concentric zoning, including lead-zinc occurrences and scarn in the outer edges of the system, and a couple of weak showings of oxide copper in places on the surface. The leached capping wasn't typical; there's a whole science in interpretation of leached capping, and this leached

First visit to La
Escondida, 1980.

capping didn't look very favorable, but the occasional piece of it did
look good. Later, in a stream sediment survey of the area, we found
a clearly defined copper geochemical anomaly and also a molybdenum anomaly. This alone justified drilling the prospect. I also collected
150 leached capping specimens, which I sent to Harold Courtright, a
leached capping expert in Arizona.

The Atacama Desert has the driest climate in the world. This super-
arid climate leads to "super leaching," a process named by Hans Langer-
feld, a Chilean geologist working for Anglo American Company. Super
leaching happens only in the Atacama Desert. That leaching process is
probably the result of capillary migration of water from deep levels to
the surface of the desert, where it evaporates, but it has carried salts in

Outcrop of Cerro Colorado and Colorado Chico during first visit to Escondida, 1980.

solution that crystallize when water evaporates, and the crystallization causes an expansion. It's a diurnal variation, expansion-contraction, in the rock. Super leaching has the effect of plucking limonite out of the leached capping, so instead of having all of the limonite and the right textures, you end up with part of the limonite and a sort of a melting of the silicate textures, in which the original pyrite pseudomorph cube shapes become spherical, like scoria, which is a rock that has little spherical cavities in it.

I understood something about this process and had dug pits to identify and sample the vertical zones. I was also an expert on conventional leached capping and porphyry copper concentric zoning. At Escondida I was more impressed by the porphyry copper zoning and concentric geochemical anomalies. There was a very large area at Escondida that represented concentric bands of rock that would have been typical of a big porphyry copper system. Harold hadn't visited Escondida, and he didn't have exactly the same understanding or opinion of some of the

In dry parts of the Atacama Desert it may rain only once every 5 or 20 years, but when it does, plants sprout and flowers bloom as in this photo.

other features laid out in the Lowell-Guilbert Porphyry Copper Model. All he had was a collection of 140 pieces of rock.

He wrote a report and said, "In my opinion, the rock does not represent secondary enrichment of chalcocite. It may represent high-level vertical zoning over primary ore at a depth of maybe 1,000 meters." Harold was wrong on both points here, but might have made the correct assessment if he had visited Escondida. All the ore we found in this area was high-grade secondary enriched chalcocite. My decision to drill in this area was on the basis of my different interpretation of the leached capping plus strong copper and molybdenum anomalies in a stream sediment geochemical survey of the area. The five companies

Building made out of blocks of salt, indicating the infrequency of rain.

who had previously held the property, including Phelps Dodge and Codelco, may have come to the same conclusion as in Harold's written report and for that reason dropped the property.

The Colorado Grande hill where the leached capping was exposed was held by a Chilean lawyer named Pedro Butazoni, who was an acquaintance of mine. He was deputy minister of economy of Chile in an earlier administration. We approached Pedro and asked if we could make some kind of a deal with him on his property. This property was held as an exploration permit; at that time there were four levels of validity of claims: *concesión de exploración* was the least valid; the next one was called *manifestación*; the next one was called *manifestación constituida*; and the last one was called a *mensura* (meaning "measured"). This *mensura* is analogous in the United States to a patented mine claim, where you own surface rights and mineral rights. It has been measured by a Perito, who is equivalent to a U.S. mineral surveyor. He's an officer of the government. It's a cadastral survey—a legal survey that defines the boundaries of land for purposes of title and ownership. They are done very precisely. Pedro's title to the ground was pretty flimsy with

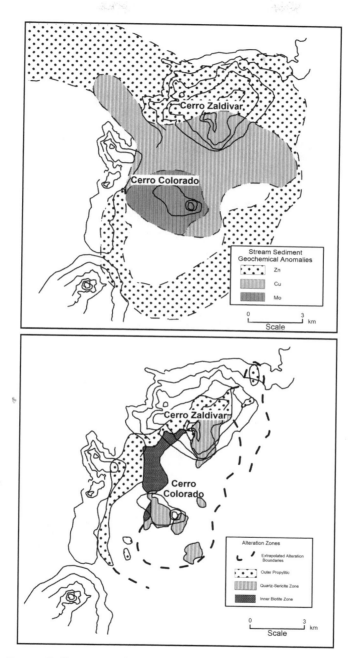

Top: Stream Sediment Geochemical Survey made before Escondida Drilling Project. *Bottom:* Distribution of alteration at the Escondida Prospect (J. D. Lowell, 1997).

the type of claim he held, but we offered to buy it, and he said, "No, it's not for sale at this time."

We had overlapping *manifestaciónes* that overlapped his claim. I won't go into a long explanation of Chilean mining law, but there are various *tramites*, red-tape things you have to go through. If you have a claim and somebody stakes over you and starts through this process of going to a *constituida* claim and publishing their results, and if you don't follow suit, even though you have priority in time, the other person gets title to it. Chile is one of the few places where this kind of regulation is in force. This is a loophole that we decided to try to follow. We had a late-night meeting and, with a bottle of scotch, sat around a table until something like one o'clock in the morning in our office in Antofagasta trying to come up with a strategy to acquire this prospect. Present were Pancho Ortiz, Donaldo Rojas, and myself. The two people with the strongest votes in this at that point were Donaldo and me. I was responsible, and Donaldo was the guru of Chilean mining regulations. At that time, companies had to submit a survey with Universal Transverse Mercator (UTM) coordinates that would clearly indicate the location when they were published. Publication in the *Diario Oficial* was a mandatory step in staking the claim. But if you were a small miner, you could just describe it, "I see over to the northwest the Cerro Blanco, and I'm close to what they called the Quebrada Negra," and so on. So Donaldo said that what we should do is write up a claim in the language that a small miner would use. We talked about that, and I said, "Why don't we call it the San Francisco claim?" Donaldo said, "No, no. A small miner is more romantic than that. He wouldn't call it San Francisco. He would call it something like La Escondida, The Hidden One." I said, "Okay, you know more about it than I do." So that was where the name came from, even though the claim itself didn't ever become valid.

We wrote up a claim notice in the name of our janitor, who was a retired miner, a very nice old guy. The claim notice said, "I, Manuel Torres, miner, single man, have found a claim which I call La Escondida, and it's in the Augusto Victoria district, and I see in front of me generally to the south a black hill that is sometimes called Cerro Negro, and I see to the southwest a red hill that is sometimes called Cerro Colorado." I've forgotten the exact language of this, but it was something like that. It was a relatively modest sized claim, but it was right on top of this leached capping, and on top of Pedro Butazoni. So we filed it—it's like putting a fishing line out. Pedro, or Pedro's man, was alert and caught this and went to the next step in his process which saved him from being trumped by Mr. Torres' claim.

We didn't give up. We had another conference, and either Pancho or Donaldo came up with another strategy. This strategy was to do this detailed *mensura* survey. We went out in the field and with a Perito turned all the angles and taped all the distances and had a finished claim ready to go. We published it something like the day before Christmas. We did this on one of the claims that we had filed a year or two before when we staked the whole belt. The published claim fit the requirements for a *mensura*.

We went through all these steps in rapid-fire order. We filed the claim, got it published in a day or two in the *Boletín Minero*, and by the time the New Year's holiday was over, we already had this nailed down. Then Pedro Butazoni sued Minera Utah, which was the name we were operating under, and in his brief he said, "This work was done with unseemly haste during the holiday season and not according to the traditions of mining in Chile." But he lost. He didn't really lose because he eventually got paid $6 million for part of his other claim, which covered part of the Zaldívar deposit.

Zaldívar, Another World-Class Deposit

The Zaldívar outcrop had phyllic alteration, and the Cerro Colorado, where the leached capping was, had phyllic alteration. We constructed a hypothetical zoning picture since these were just little islands of outcrop with gravel between, and we assumed that the strongest alteration would be between the two. It would go from phyllic to potassic, back down to phyllic. So our first five holes were drilled in a line across this covered area. They intersected phyllic alteration and a lot of pyrite and some copper mineralization. One of the holes averaged a quarter of 1 percent copper, but far less than our target ore grade.

What we didn't know was that the Zaldívar deposit was a separate occurrence and not contiguous with Escondida. But the sixth hole was in the Cerro Colorado area, and it intersected a long interval of chalcocite mineralization that the Chilean geologist sitting on the drill rig didn't recognize. He thought it was manganese. The samples that night went down to Antofagasta, where Nivaldo Rojas happened to be. He wasn't directly involved in the project, but he poked through the samples and recognized that it was a chalcocite zone.

I had been in Chile when the drilling started at Escondida, but was gone when it was completed. We had drilled nine holes, and the sixth and seventh and ninth all had good ore intersections. It was an average of 150 meters of 1.4 percent copper average. That wasn't good enough to be part of the Escondida ore reserves for the early production years because it was so much better farther to the south. At the time, on the basis of those holes, I was able to infer an ore reserve of 250 million tons of 1.4 percent copper, which was already a world-class copper deposit.

Jim Bratt was hired to replace me as manager of the project. As it happened, it was bad luck for him because he couldn't claim any authorship of the project because the discovery had been made the day he was hired and before he ever visited the project. Also, as it happened, none of the Utah or Getty geologists or other employees had ever been to Escondida. It was only our group that had selected the target and done the work. The new team immediately took the project away from me, and I didn't get any chance to participate in the fun part of it, which was getting the spectacular ore intersections. Bratt almost immediately terminated the drilling contract with the fast, cheap contractor and brought back the slow, expensive contractor. Such are the ways of large companies.

The ore grade during the first couple of years of mining at Escondida was 3 percent copper, or about five times the grade being mined in Arizona. It's a beautiful orebody. I had the contract with Utah and

Getty for three years. I had laid out the three-year plan but neither Utah nor Getty followed it after the discovery. They never found another ore-body in Chile after that. I think we would have if they had lived up to their contract.

I think of Escondida and Zaldívar as being the same target because they are nearby and both within the same large propylitic alteration envelope. Zaldívar was drilled, and the history of that is also kind of amazing. Utah drilled several holes on the claims that we held, and Pedro Butazoni filed another suit against them with respect to his original claim, which covered half of what finally became the Zaldívar orebody. By the time the suit was settled, it had become apparent that Escondida was a multibillion-ton orebody. When the Utah manager—I think his title was president of Minera Escondida at that point—talked to Pedro Butazoni, Butazoni said, "Well, I've won the suit, but I'll give you my interest in Zaldívar for one million dollars." The Minera Escondida manager said, "Listen we have all the reserves we could possibly use, and I'm not interested in buying it." A little later, Pedro Butazoni sold his interest for $6 million to Pudahuel Mining Company, and then Pudahuel sold the same interest to a bank, and it was sold by the bank to Outokumpu for $28 million. A little later, Outokumpu sold a half-interest in it to Placer Dome for $100 million. Later still, Minera Escondida had to buy water rights from Zaldívar for a very high price.

I was hired a number of years later by Fluor and Placer as a geological consultant in the Zaldívar feasibility study. By the time Escondida was developed, it became obvious they had a space problem and needed the Zaldívar ground for their surface plant. They had saved a million dollars but lost probably several hundred million dollars.

Minera Utah and later Minera Escondida were afraid of making an investment in Chile. Escondida was the first big mine development in Chile after the Allende period. Utah made a policy decision that they were going to hold out for project finance; in other words, get financial groups to invest up to 100 percent of the investment, and they wouldn't risk anything. That was a mistake—a mistake that cost on the order of tens of billions of dollars in the long run. They did multiple feasibility studies in order to justify sitting on this large natural resource. They continued doing feasibility studies before they finally lined up what was then Rio Tinto Zinc and a group of Japanese companies in a consortium, and the World Bank also put in some money, so as to get 100 percent of the financing. They gained in the area of finance, but they lost several ways. The biggest one was they lost in time. The net present value of a project depends on when the annuity from the project starts to flow back, and in the case of Escondida they lost something like five years of time. If you calculate the effect on the present value of putting the production off for five years with Escondida, it's a huge amount of money. They also lost about 35 percent of the ownership by getting partners in to put up part of the finance money. So that was also part of the comedy of errors.

Another little criticism viewed from the outside: the original Escondida mill (concentrator) was 40,000 tons a day. The orebody is the largest copper deposit in the world. I asked the Escondida chief engineer how they had hit on a 40,000-ton operation. It seemed to me they might very well have started with 100,000 or 200,000 tons. He said, "Well, it was perfectly logical. We were operating the Island Copper deposit on Vancouver Island at a 40,000-ton rate, and we had the plans for the mill already in the file." This is for a development that cost a billion dollars or so, and the plans might have cost a few million dollars. Another penny-wise decision.

Just a side note about controversy in successful exploration projects: I've now been involved in between fifteen and seventeen discoveries, and in almost every case there has been a controversy about who gets credit that has ranged from a mild argument to a very acrimonious argument. In the majority of my discoveries, and also others that I know something about but was not involved in, there also is some kind of litigation about ownership. It's my feeling that it is the syndrome of *The Treasure of the Sierra Madre* movie—when something of great value, from a standpoint of money or fame or status, shows up, people's normal ethics disappear, and they scrap like dogs over a bone.

Several years after the Atacama Project, I returned to El Tesoro on behalf of Niugini Mining and identified and optioned the Leonor deposit, which contained 50 million tonnes of 1.5 percent leachable exotic copper ore. Most of the credit for finding the Leonor orebody should go to a Chilean mining engineer named Claudio Segura. Andronico Luksic later used the Leonor block as the core of the El Tesoro Mine, which also included lower grade exotic ore from his own property. A second deep porphyry copper was found a short distance to the south by geologists of Luksic's company after the El Tesoro Mine was in production.

The first conflict in the Atacama Project occurred while we were exploring near El Tesoro. I had a contract that gave me total authority for planning and managing the Atacama Project. Disregarding this contract and disregarding my previous success in finding large copper deposits, Getty complained that I was wasting Utah and Getty money exploring at El Tesoro. The Getty Manager tried to stop the El Tesoro Project, where two orebodies were later found and developed into large mines. With more patience we might have found one of them during the Atacama Project. Something similar later happened in the La Escondida area, where Getty ignored the contract and campaigned to have the Atacama Project shut down a month or two before I found the Escondida and Zaldívar mines. In the Escondida area we found those two large mines in spite of Getty's efforts to stop the project.

I assumed in managing the Atacama Project that I was better able to evaluate the mineral outcrops and better able to locate the position of the exploration drill holes than other geologists in the Atacama Project. I visited every critical outcrop myself, wearing out a pair of Chippewa field boots. I located or agreed to the location of every hole drilled in the project. The discovery holes at Escondida were a line of holes crossing the middle of the molybdenum anomaly on Colorado Grande hill; they had been plotted on Harold Courtright's map and were the obvious drill locations to test the outcrop of the molybdenum anomaly, so I approved those. After the Escondida area was later drilled out by Minera Escondida, it became obvious that a hole drilled anywhere in a two-by-three-kilometer area would have intersected chalcocite ore and the precise location of the holes was immaterial.

A few years before the Atacama Project someone had calculated that the average exploration cost of discovering a new porphyry copper mine was over $100 million. This number was derived by adding up all the recent porphyry copper exploration budgets and dividing by the number of mines found. The cost would now be much higher, perhaps $300 million. In the Atacama Project I spent a total of about $3 million and found two mines. It was a huge bargain for Utah and Getty; each discovery cost only about 1 percent of the industry average.

I had a contract based on the total amount spent, and it was not to my benefit to waste project money. Utah International had the handicap of having an agent of French nationality whose job was to be a sales agent in Chile for Utah's coal and iron ore in Chile. He loved rules and bureaucracy and knew that the more of my money was wasted, the more important his job would be. I imported a whole drilling company into Chile to cut the cost per meter in half—and to have twice as many meters to find orebodies with. I also on occasion bypassed the normal procedures by using cash and credit cards to pay for things directly. There was a complicated set of regulations connected with getting a business visa so I just used a tourist visa. I was the only expatriate working on the project.

All this worried Paul Gondaneau and, to a lesser degree, Pedro Deutsch, who was the managing accountant and vice president of Price Waterhouse. Pedro is a very impressive person. He has both law and accounting degrees, speaks about six languages fluently, and has a wonderful sense of humor. He was smart enough to understand exactly what I was doing, but still wanted me to follow some of the rules. I was following most of his rules by the end of the project.

Two Partial Medium-Sized Discoveries, San Cristobal and Leonor

San Cristobal is a gold deposit in northern Chile between the towns of Antofagasta and Calama. San Cristobal was found by a small com-

"Not Perfect, But Adequate"

During one of my projects in Chile I had a meeting with three lawyers including Pedro Deutsch. All were bilingual, but the hour-long meeting was in Spanish. At the end of the meeting Mario Diaz said in English, "Dave, your Spanish is getting better." Pedro Deutsch turned to me and said, "Is that the language you were speaking?"

We had a Chilean friend named Ginny Chamy, who had a degree from the University of Illinois and taught both English and Spanish in Santiago. Shortly after Pedro's joke I made a deal with Ginny to come to my office and teach me Spanish for an hour every day. I gave up lunch for about three months and was confronted by a bewildering array of new tenses and constructions. I already had a good Spanish vocabulary, but my previous Spanish professor in Mexico, Chimin, who himself was a graduate of grade three, was not overly concerned with tenses or gender or construction. Ginny decided, correctly, that I had forgotten my English constructions and started teaching me what adverbs and prepositions were. She was heartless about homework assignments, and I became a conscientious student and after sixty one-hour sessions my Spanish grammar was greatly improved. I have since given talks in Spanish in Chile, Peru, and Paraguay with not perfect, but adequate, Spanish.

pany that I was a partner in called Minera del Inca. It was formed as kind of a lark at a cocktail party in Santiago in 1985. Two people I was acquainted with were at the party. One, the principal force in Minera del Inca, was a lady named Julia Aspillaga. She is still in Santiago. The second was Pat Burns, a Canadian geologist who had worked for me for a short time at the end of my part of the Escondida Project. I had hired Pat as a drill superintendent to supervise the American drillers

Julia Aspillaga

Julia has, at different times, been a friend, advisor, and business associate. She is a very charming Chilean lady, but at the same time very intelligent, and as good as anyone I have known at getting very difficult things done. She is a very powerful force with very good intentions. She counts congressmen, ministers, presidents, humble Mapuche Indians, and me as friends. Julia is an unusual person. I think of her as a small steamroller, a very effective executive accomplishing amazing things by a combination of charm and force of personality and intelligence. Over the years Julia has worked herself into an important position in the Chilean mining industry as an associate in the small miners association and an associate of Hernán Büchi, former Chilean minister of treasury and finance, who now works as a consultant to several other Latin American governments. She has represented Chile in international mining investment meetings.

in the Harris Drilling Company. At the cocktail party we were talking about the fact that at that time, there were no junior mining companies in Chile, but some attractive opportunities. This was in the early part of the gold boom in bulk low-grade cyanide-leach gold deposits, which had already seen extensive development in Nevada and Australia and various parts of the world. In the course of the evening, we talked about how this might be possible in Chile, and somebody said, well, why don't the three of us form a company? Julia, who is a very assertive person, immediately hustled back to her office and in a day or two had a specific proposal for the company.

When our company was formed in about 1985, Julia had been working for Anglo American Company and Bernstein and Thompson in Chile, who had been responsible for developing at least one mine at that time, El Indio Mine. They had also found several gold occurrences which developed into mines in the Maricunga district in northern

The owners of Minera del Inca and the San Cristobal Project. From left, Chuck Croft, Julia Aspillaga, and David Lowell, 1985, shortly after the discovery of the San Cristobal orebody.

Chile. She is a very intelligent person, and had a business degree. She knew a lot about mining finance and accounting and Chilean mining regulations, and knew many of the important mining people in Chile.

When she said, "Well, I've made the preliminary arrangements for a new mining company," it was a surprise to me. We looked around for somebody to put money into it. A friend of mine, who is an entrepreneur in Vancouver, Canada, and had various interests, is Chuck Croft. He had owned the Tonto Drilling Company, was in the soft drink business and real estate and oil and various things, and is a chartered accountant by education. We talked to him and he agreed to put up $96,000 for a one-year budget, which is a subminimal-size exploration budget, so I agreed to contribute some of my time, and I worked in the planning and evaluation and managed the work. Julia did the office part of it and much of the negotiating, and Pat Burns agreed to do some fieldwork. As it worked out, he wasn't too interested in the project, and he eventually bowed out of the partnership.

We looked at a number of prospects. One was a prospect the Anaconda Company had been looking at in the San Cristobal district in northern Chile. Anaconda was in their final death rattle at that time, and this was the last prospect they looked at in Chile. They didn't carry their work as far as optioning the property. The prospect was disseminated gold in a porphyry intrusive body. It was just simply an interesting outcrop. I learned a couple of years after our project started that the actual identification of gold mineralization at that site had been made by two Anaconda geologists who were working at the Chuquicamata Mine about thirty years before. When we learned about their having worked there, Anaconda had already abandoned their project. We did a minimal amount of geologic mapping and a systematic sampling. We made more than four hundred hand-dug pits about one and a half meters deep on fences of pits across the deposit and in the course of that work found a second, parallel anomaly, which turned out after drilling not to be ore grade. We drilled twelve shallow diamond-drill holes at San Cristobal with our meager budget.

The holes were a maximum of a hundred meters deep and averaged about eighty meters deep. I believe that seven of the twelve holes had ore intersections at about the same grade as we had found on the surface. On this basis, we decided to shop this around and see if we could find somebody who would buy the property from us and complete the exploration. We made a deal with a small North American mining company, Glamis Gold, which operated a mine called the Picacho Mine near the Arizona-California border, in California, near Yuma, Arizona. They did a more extensive drilling project and did some test leaching, and then Niugini Mining Company from Australia took over their position, and also bought out the Minera del Inca ownership.

At about that time, we hired Bob Shoemaker as a metallurgical consultant. Bob Shoemaker is a very well known metallurgist who was president of the Society of Mining Engineers. I had worked with Bob in projects with the Bechtel Company. I worked on a number of Bechtel projects over several years. Two of my feasibility studies with Bob were at Chuquicamata. One was at a place called Quartz Hill in Alaska, and another was Stillwater Mine in Montana. Bob Shoemaker came down to offer a metallurgical opinion on a couple of the prospects we were looking at, one of which was the San Cristobal Mine. Part of the work we did was negotiating property deals. There were two owners on parts of the San Cristobal orebody that we outlined on the surface.

Chile has a different attitude toward bad debts and bad checks than the United States. They had something analogous to debtor's prison. If you don't pay your debts, carabineros come and collect you and put you in jail until some family member or friend pays up for you. There was a local Chilean in this position, who owned one of these claims and a key part of the property. They hadn't captured him, but he was in a position where he would have to go to jail if he was found because of nonpayment of mortgage debts. So we had a cloak-and-dagger deal to get in contact with this fellow through friends. He once showed up for a meeting in the back of a van where he couldn't be seen. There were various clandestine arrangements to talk to him. After we made the deal, he was able to get together enough money to become legitimate again.

When we encountered the problem of this property owner who was delinquent and in hiding, but at the same time trying to saddle us with unfair, possibly crooked, property terms, we decided to look for a local lawyer accustomed to dealing with such individuals. We found an ideal man. He was "headquartered" in a town in the same region as San Cristobal, but it was more complicated than that. He was the owner and the pilot of an ancient, single-engine airplane, and he had offices in two other towns in the region. He not only had three offices, but he had three families. Dealing with an avaricious, not very reliable claim owner in hiding from the law was child's play compared to ordinary run-of-the-mill domestic problems. He got us a not-too-favorable purchase agreement, and the last we heard he and all his families were doing well.

The deposit at San Cristobal had a mineral fabric that made it very difficult to control the grade of the mill heads. It was relatively easy to calculate grades from drill hole interpolation and extrapolation, but it was much harder to maintain the necessary grade from the pit. Niugini had limited mining experience and was unable to cope with this grade-control problem. This problem finally resulted in their mining a larger tonnage but lower grade ore than had originally been calculated in the feasibility study, and this had a serious impact on the return from the Niugini Mining operation.

My return from San Cristobal was a relatively modest profit. The Minera del Inca operation turned out to have been a somewhat chaotic and not totally successful experience.

The María Rosa Project

The María Rosa Project is in Region II of Chile at elevations ranging from 4,000 to 5,000 meters (13,000 to 16,000 feet). It is near a small copper prospect called Queen Elizabeth, which had been known a long time. Ernesto Egert and I visited this prospect during a joint venture I had with Kennecott Copper Company in about 1983. We left Iquique early in the morning and arrived before lunch at Queen Elizabeth and looked at it briefly and confirmed its small size potential. Because of

David and Ernesto Egert near Quebrada Blanca, Chile.

Horseback trip in the Andes, elevation 4,000 meters, about 14,000 feet.

my habit of trying to fit prospects into the Lowell-Guilbert Porphyry Copper Model, I decided we should climb higher on the mountain and there we found, to my surprise, leached capping after chalcocite mineralization in sandstone rock, which was an almost unique mineral occurrence. Time was not available to explore what turned out to be a virgin discovery of a new porphyry copper occurrence. We had sleeping bags and a small tent and decided to camp and explore the prospect the following day. Wind in the Andes comes up in the afternoon, and that day it averaged about forty miles per hour when we set about pitching our tent. It required more than an hour to set up the tent, a job that could have been done in five or ten minutes except for the wind and the altitude. We then had a cold sandwich and spent a miserable night, but the tent protected us against the wind.

The next day we climbed higher on the mountain and found attractive outcrops, but were impeded by the wind and the altitude. It sounds easy but is very difficult to climb from 4,000 to 4,500 meters. We were

Tracks made by oxcarts carrying ore are incised into volcanic tuff more than 100 years ago. Site is near the large Ujina porphyry copper deposit in Region I, northern Chile.

able to estimate coordinates for acquiring claims by GPS, which was done soon after. We had learned through the grapevine that Queen Elizabeth had been visited previously by several major companies, but they apparently had driven from a comfortable hotel at low elevation, spent a couple of hours at Queen Elizabeth, and returned to the comfortable hotel the same day without finding the real target. Additional work and a drilling project later indicated the deposit was a moderately large, partly leachable, porphyry copper enrichment blanket, but the combination of grade and tonnage and stripping ration indicated it to be submarginal.

We bought an old three-room lumber house and moved it to the site for protection from the wind during the drilling project. One of the geologists, Art Ona, who was from the Philippines, had a thermometer and determined that the house may have actually lowered the twenty-four-hour temperature. Art had grown up at almost sea level and had a particularly severe case of altitude sickness with hallucinations in which

Guanacos in Region III. These are wild camelids related to llamas and alpacas.

he thought he had become a llama. We had to move him right away down to sea level, but he had no serious aftereffects.

There was an Indian village a few kilometers from María Rosa where a benevolent Chilean businessman in Iquique on the Pacific Coast had financed some charitable improvements. These consisted of a two-way radio connection, medicine, and facilities for a small clinic managed by an Aymara lady with minimal nursing training. There was a small elementary school also with an Aymara teacher with adequate education who also taught the Aymara language to the children. Last was a one-ton truck for hauling supplies and passengers back and forth to Iquique, which was about three hours away. The effect of all this was amazing. The village citizens were polite but very self-confident, and seemed to think of their high-altitude village as an independent kingdom. Wildlife in the area included viscachas, a chinchilla-like animal about the size of a rabbit with a long furry tail, which either rolled up in a small roll or unrolled about ten inches to assist in balancing while making long jumps between boulders. There were also rhea, a South

American ostrich-like bird, and pink flamingos in a salar, or natural interior drainage small lake.

We were very disappointed that María Rosa turned out to be a scientific curiosity rather than a new mine. Not long after that I had another small joint venture project with Amax. It was a small-scale, largely reconnaissance project with a little bit of drilling done. We were

---

Nicolas Tschichow

Nicolas Tschichow, like Alexander Sutolof, who first invited me to Chile, was a Russian immigrant to Chile. He was born in Leningrad (St. Petersburg) about 1936. Both his father and mother were professors in the University of Leningrad, and his father became an unwilling officer in the Russian army and was wounded in the siege of Stalingrad in 1942. Stalin had an order to execute any Russian caught behind German lines. In the shuffling of German-Russian lines during the battle, Nicolas and his mother and father were caught behind the German lines and then had to become displaced persons; they progressively migrated across Europe, and at the end of the war immigrated to Chile. Nicolas (Nic) was something of a prodigy and obtained a chemistry degree in Chile and an MS in metallurgy in the United States. He went to work for Codelco and was rapidly promoted. He fled from Chile when Salvador Allende, the Communist Party candidate, was elected in 1970. Nicolas was given a job as a mill superintendent in the United States by Hecla Mining Company. When Pinochet took over in 1973, Nic was hired as general manager of the Chuquicamata Mine, then the largest copper mine in the world. He managed Chuquicamata for a number of years before taking a job as manager of the Disputada Mine for Exxon. I first met Nic when he was working for Codelco; we later became close friends and went on many trout fishing trips together in southern Chile. Nic was my closest friend in Chile.

looking for gold deposits in the Cordillera of the coast in western Chile. We found several apparent small deposits but nothing large enough to be of interest to Amax.

In the mid-eighties I also participated in a Kennecott regional exploration project in Chile for a year or two as a consultant with a finder's fee arrangement. We were unsuccessful, and I didn't collect a finder's fee. The project had an aspect of the tail wagging the dog problem. It was originally set up as a project based largely on geology and geochemistry, but it ended up, because of Kennecott's interference, being based almost entirely on geophysical surveys and was unsuccessful. On the geologic side we found the María Rosa chalcocite enrichment blanket, which was almost mineable grade.

Following the Amax work, I did similar work for Niugini Mining Company. This association came about because of my longtime friendship with Geoff Loudon, an Australian geologist. In the early seventies, when I was Placer Development's in-house consultant for geology in their mining operations, I was to some degree Geoff's supervisor and mentor since he was chief geologist at the Marcopper Mine in the Philippines. I was impressed by Geoff because he was an independent thinker and a confirmed maverick. He was entirely responsible for the discovery of the large San Antonio orebody near Marcopper, where he drilled the discovery hole in violation of instructions not to drill in an area which had been certified by Placer's exploration department in Vancouver to contain no ore and in which they were building a tailings pond. The tailings later had to be removed. Predictably, when the discovery was made, the exploration manager came back and claimed credit. I was on the editorial board of *Economic Geology* at the time, and arranged for Geoff to publish a paper on Marcopper and San Antonio. Geoff went on to find two more large mines for Placer in Papua New Guinea and Australia. He later branched out on his own, and as president of Niugini found the large Lihir Island gold deposit in Papua New Guinea in a joint venture with Kennecott. He has a good exploration track record. In the late 1980s he asked me to put together an exploration program in Chile, and he also bought the San Cristobal deposit.

Staff of Leonor Project: from left, David Lowell, Ernesto Egert, unidentified driver, and Guillermo Contreras.

The Niugini work resulted in one orebody, Leonor, which I brought to Niugini. It is in the El Tesoro district, where I had long been interested in ore possibilities.

The problem at Leonor was another property problem. We had a clear title in the Leonor claim, but the orebody extended to the borders of Leonor, and the surrounding ground was held in part by a Chilean captain of industry, Andronico Luksic. I was well acquainted with him, probably to my detriment, as you may remember from my accounts of earlier projects in Chile. Soon after we began drilling at Leonor, it became pretty obvious that it was going to be an orebody, and we started negotiations with the majority owner of the adjacent ground, in which Luksic owned a minority interest. That adjacent claim was called the Sorpresa—Surprise. There is a story that I'll tell later about the relationship between Leonor and Sorpresa.

The Sorpresa claim has a horseshoe shape surrounding Leonor on three sides. The majority interest was held by Mrs. Camponetti, a long-time Chilean family of Italian descent. Mrs. Camponetti agreed to terms for a sale of her property to us, and an agreement was signed by her lawyer as her agent. The night that the agreement was signed to sell the property to us, Mr. Luksic paid the lawyer something like $230,000 cash and paid Mrs. Camponetti something like $800,000 cash for her interest in the property. Mr. Luksic acquired the property, and we lost out. I looked into the possibility of the lawyer being disbarred from practice but was discouraged from trying to do this, and so we lost the Sorpresa claim through dishonesty.

In any case, that made mining the Leonor deposit difficult. Mr. Luksic's company eventually entered into a partnership with a company that inherited from Niugini the Leonor property, and he had a majority interest in the composite mine, whose ore reserves were larger than ours but lower grade and less profitable. I optioned and drilled Leonor, but major credit for the discovery of the Leonor should properly go to one of the owners, Claudio Segura, from whom we bought the claim, who sank a decline into the orebody and also drilled a hole that intersected the mineralization.

I made nothing out of Leonor and neither did Niugini. Niugini at that time was a subsidiary of Battle Mountain Gold Company. Battle Mountain Gold hired a consultant who wrote a report which concluded that 50 million tons of 1.5 percent leachable copper was not economically feasible, which was ridiculous, but it was an excuse to not get involved in the development. Another factor was that the stock market puts a relatively high price-to-earnings ratio on gold mining companies and lower ratio on copper companies: if a gold company opens a copper mine, their stock price tends to drop, and Battle Mountain didn't want this to happen.

Getting back to the history of the Leonor and Sorpresa claim, Mrs. Camponetti's husband was a partner with another Chilean in the Leonor claim. They had an informal arrangement that any ground that either partner staked in the district would be jointly owned. But Mrs.

Camponetti's husband decided that there was nothing written, and so he staked the horseshoe claim around Leonor, which he called the Sorpresa, or the Surprise claim. "Surprise, I've cheated on our agreement." The other partner responded to this by getting a pistol and going to see Mr. Camponetti and killing him. And so Mrs. Camponetti became a widow and for that reason was an owner of the surrounding ground when we were doing our exploration project.

CHAPTER THREE

Stories from Chile

Bill Mounts was employed almost full time as a drilling expert/supervisor/consultant on the Atacama Project in Chile. He deserves a lot of the credit for the success of the project.

Our first significant drilling project was in the El Tesoro District. It was a short enough distance from Antofagasta that we decided to commute and not set up a tent camp as we usually did. There was a Carabinero checkpoint in Baquedano between "Anto" and our project, and all vehicles were stopped and car and driver's license and destination recorded. To understand this story you have to know something about Carabineros. They are an elite national police force with some elements of the Royal Canadian Mounted Police, the Australian Patrol Officers in Papua New Guinea (before PNG was, very unwisely in my opinion, given its independence), and in the United States the former FBI. Anyone stupid enough to offer a bribe to a Carabinero would go straight to jail, no questions asked. The Carabinero patrolman is a graduate of a two-year police college and officers are graduates of a four-year course. In Chile it is an honor to be a Carabinero, and small towns typically have one patrolman who supplies Law and Order and Discipline.

In the early part of the Atacama Project while we were drilling El Tesoro Project there were usually two or three geologists and Bill Mounts running the drilling project, and we all crawled into whatever vehicle, usually a king cab Toyota 4x4 pickup, happened to be going to Anto. One day it was Bill's pickup so, as the driver, he had to talk to the Carabineros at Baquedano. We all to some extent dreaded being interrogated (what if they knew about you playing hooky from school in the third grade?), so when Bill got out of the driver's seat and shambled across the highway looking down at the road we all watched with interest. When he was halfway across the road he said something to the Carabinero, who waved both arms with an unmistakable order to go back to the vehicle and leave. This had never happened to any of us, and when he got back I immediately asked, "Bill, what did you say to him?" It was about 6:00 p.m., and one convention followed religiously by even the most ignorant person in Latin America is to say "Buenos días" until 12:00 noon, and at 12:01 p.m. say, "Buenas tardes." Bill said, "I didn't say anything special, I just said 'Buenos días.'" The Carabinero must have said to himself, "Life is too short to try to interrogate a dumb gringo who shambles when he walks and says 'Buenos días' at 6:04 p.m." He would have been right about everything except "dumb." Barrick regularly sends Bill halfway around the world to spend a day straightening out a drill project.

Another Carabinero story occurred when Jimmy Toller, manager of our drilling company, discovered that a ring of people were stealing gasoline from his company. He asked the local Carabinero office to look into it. Two patrolmen arrived. They are always dressed perfectly in their uniforms and speak very formally. Jimmy asked if he could participate in the questioning and was told, "No thank you, we would prefer to do it in private." Twenty minutes later the culprits and the Carabineros emerged from the conference room and the Carabineros had copies of signed, detailed confessions regarding the gasoline theft.

I was once driving south of Concepción on the Pan-American Highway to visit a mineral prospect. The road sign for the availability of a restaurant is a crossed knife and fork. The road sign for a Carabinero checkpoint is crossed carbines (a short rifle used by cavalry). I was driving along at 20 kph over the speed limit and passed one of these signs, which turned out to not be a table setting. The checkpoint consisted of one patrolman and one whistle. No squad car, no siren, no backup, but in Chile it was more than sufficient. I backed up to the place where the one patrolman was waiting. I had been mentally rehearsing a totally convincing excuse. He had been reviewing all the infractions. On his form there was a rectangle about four by five inches in size labeled "infractions committed." He started writing with very small letters so he could get everything into the small rectangle. I started talking in a low penitent voice (by this time I spoke Spanish fairly fluently and with a slight Chilean accent). I remember touching on the difference in driving customs between countries and about why there should be hands across national borders and how we were all really brothers at heart. My speech almost brought tears to my eyes. His answer was, "I imagine you have been here quite some time. I will keep your driver's license. You take this form to the municipal judge and pay your fine and get your license back from me." The judge was a young lady who was more susceptible to the "hands across the border" line and only fined me about US$30, as I remember.

On one occasion a longtime friend and associate and a distinguished exploration geologist from Arizona (let's call him Clark) was doing some work on my Atacama Project in Chile. He was in Taltal on the Pacific coast in Region II in a pickup with a Chilean driver. He is a "people person" who likes people and has a distinct talent for communicating with people. On this occasion it became a handicap. He and his driver had just bought gas in a service station and were still stopped when a moderately attractive young middle-aged lady walked briskly up to the passenger side and tapped on the window. He started to roll down the window. The driver, seeing the situation, tried to stop him, but he being a nice guy opened the window to practice his Spanish on this nice lady (who the driver had already identified as a gypsy).

Several things then happened in rapid order: The lady asked him for money. He declined, speaking slowly so as not to hurt her feelings. She responded by quickly sticking her hand into the cab, unzipping his pants, and grabbing his private parts! This tipped the argument strongly in her favor, but the driver put the car in gear and started to move off.

My friend howled to the driver in English and Spanish to stop and the gypsy yelled her intentions and the driver yelled at the gypsy and my friend grabbed her arm to save his private parts and somehow they escaped across the filling station ramp.

Later, after the Atacama Project was completed, I had an office on the third floor of a small building on Providencia in central Santiago. There was an elevator, but I always climbed the stairs for exercise and the Chileans always thought I was crazy. It gets very cold in the winter, and I collected an assortment of heaters for my room, but the Chileans felt that summer was hot and winter was cold and a reasonable person just put on another sweater, so they named my office The Arizona Room.

Julia Aspillaga, who was our administrative manager at the time, had saved a little Mapuche Indian boy named Sergio whom she hired as office boy and trained in many office skills. She bullied him into buying an apartment and getting a mortgage and a wife (and climbing up into the middle class). One Christmas I was away in Arizona and two friends each gave me a bottle of scotch whiskey, which sat on my desk for a week before I remembered to take them back to my apartment. Sergio came into my office while they were still there and asked (all conversation in the office was in Spanish) if I had any scotch I would give him? I said "No," thinking that was a surprising request to give your boss. When I reported this to my secretary, María Elena, she laughed and laughed and said, "Sergio was looking for scotch tape."

I once organized a little project to study the Falla Oeste or West Fissure fault in Chile. This fault with parallel faults probably controls the location of most or all of the large Chilean porphyry copper deposits. I hired Professor George Davis from the University of Arizona to help me in the study (and provide the technical smarts). George is a world-class structural geologist who has published a structural geology textbook. He is a nice guy, very modest, but has administrative talents and was once president of the University of Vermont. We visited several widely separated outcrops of the Falla Oeste to collect oriented samples of the fault zone to determine the sense of displacement. It

Chuqui West fissure, 1976.

is a strike-slip fault in which the left lateral displacement is horizontal. The "left lateral" means if you step across the fault the other side moved left (maybe tens of kilometers!). The oriented samples are large rock samples marked with a felt-tipped pen with a horizontal line and north–south and east–west lines. These specimens were taken back to George's lab and the direction of displacement positively determined.

One collecting trip for specimens was to Mansa Mina, a Codelco-owned deposit apparently (but not certainly) sliced off the west end of the Chuquicamata Mine. When we visited there was nothing going on at Manza Mina, but there were lots of underground workings where we could select a site for our sample. Our group consisted of George, myself, and Edith. Edith was invited to go into the mine with us, but politely declined, remembering many other mine visits, sometimes climbing greasy ropes or dirty ladders or wading in mud or being dropped 800 feet in an open bucket. Also present was a big gray dog with a generous dusting of mine dust. He was typically generic, representing eighty or a hundred years of mixing dog breeds to produce a "Chuqui Dog" with long ears, the sweet disposition of a bird dog, and a watchdog's broad face. You may think I have spent too much time discussing The Dog, but you will find out he played a key part in our visit.

When George and I went into the mine (which I was already familiar with, so we didn't need a guide), Edith was sitting in our truck reading a book and the truck door was open and the dog was lying companionably near. George and I changed our clothes and left our other clothes in the "Change Room," which was open and visible from the truck. We put on underground "diggers" and rubber boots. There must have been a watchman, but we didn't see him. It took us about an hour and a half to collect the specimen and carefully pack it in a box, and then we had to change clothes again in the Change Room. I didn't have any trouble, but George said, "I can't find my left shoe." So we started carefully looking through the rather large Change Room. No one else was around, and George was hopping on one foot and, over a thirty-minute search, was getting increasingly anxious about catching our plane in Calama and wondering how he would look on the plane with one shoe. I finally looked outside the building, and The Dog helpfully trailed along. I found Professor Davis's shoe where The Dog had been lying when we arrived!

I have a friend whose name I won't mention who has been very successful and is a lot like me, but maybe even more of a maverick. Let's call him "Andy." Andy was doing some work near the northern border of Chile, not many kilometers from Peru. Andy needed some topographic maps, but the Chilean government had restrictions on the sale of maps near the border, fearing invasion (or so they said). In about 1877 The War of the Pacific occurred, with Chile on one side and Peru and Bolivia on the other. It lasted several years and Chile won in spite of having a much smaller population. One hundred years later all these countries appear to be still about as mad at each other as they were in 1877.

Andy had to go to a Chilean Air Force office where these maps might be obtained if you first convinced the officials you were not a

Peruvian spy. Here is where Andy's strong maverick streak caused him some trouble. I was also working in Chile at about that time, and we were both annoyed by having to frequently give our passport numbers. Andy had developed the habit of just making up a passport number. He did this in the Air Force front office, but in one of the sequence of later steps they asked for his passport, and the next people he met were a couple of mean-looking military police who led him away for two hours of interrogation around the general question of, "Why are you a Peruvian spy trying to collect information for an invasion of our country?" It turned out they had compared the number from the front office with the number on the passport. My friend speaks Spanish very fluently and is a guy whom most people like, and he finally talked his way out of this jam. I suspect the reason they let him go was that the Chilean officers knew that it was a silly regulation in the first place when anyone could obtain Landsat satellite images which were probably a lot better for planning invasions.

In 1985 I went back to my habit of doing independent exploration projects. A good part of my work was in joint venture or strategic-alliance-type joint projects with Rio Tinto, an English company, which is one of the largest mining companies in the world. They own Kennecott Copper and U.S. Borax in the United States and various companies in other parts of the world. They are now a part owner in the Escondida deposit, having about a 30 percent interest in it. My contact with Rio Tinto came through people I know who were with Kennecott Copper. The principal one of this group was Tom Patton, vice president in charge of exploration for Kennecott and later Rio Tinto's exploration manager in South America. I had two projects under way in which Rio Tinto was contributing part of the financing. One was in North America, mostly in Arizona and Sonora, Mexico, looking for porphyry copper deposits; the other one was in northern Chile in South America, also looking for porphyry copper deposits.

Most of the people working for me in both places were longtime former employees. Ernesto Egert is an old associate and friend who participated with me for twelve years in the projects for Kennecott, Amax,

In a Chilean field camp, 1987: from left, Lee Mun Kit, Malaysian geologist, unidentified, Nic Tschichow, Ernesto Egert, David Lowell. Nic at that time was general manager of the Chuquicamata Mine, then the largest mine in the world. People in photo are from Malaysia, England, Russia, and the United States.

and Niugini. Ernesto has a degree from the University of Chile and an MS from Stanford University. He was a geologist with the Instituto de Investigaciones Geológicas and mapped several Chilean quadrangles and also taught at the University of Chile. When he left the Instituto he worked for multinational mining companies. He is a highly respected, very honest member of upper-class Chilean society, as is his wife, Valentina, and is one of the most competent exploration geologists I have worked with anywhere in the world.

María Elena Aspillaga, our Santiago office manager, had worked with me almost as long as Ernesto and is also both an associate and a friend. Everyone, without exception, likes María Elena. She is a member of a Chilean upper-class family that was ruined by the Allende government through expropriation of almost all their property. She is a very intelligent person who taught herself first to be a first-class secre-

An adit we drove in the Regalito project in central Chile.

tary, and then to be an office manager, accountant, property expert, and highly skilled computer operator. María Elena is married to an attractive man and has three bright children.

Sergio Bulganio has a two-year degree from a mining technical school at Copiapó, Chile. He is a competent, serious, industrious field geologist who identified a couple of key outcrops in our project. He also had worked more than five years in our group. Our project was blessed by a staff of four who were somewhere between very competent friends and close family members.

The projects we worked on were low-budget, low-profile, low-technology projects of the sort I've always done. We were optimistic that we would find an orebody somewhere, one of which, I thought at that time, might turn out to be sort of a swan song for me. However, almost thirty years later, I have had six more discoveries in different categories and different countries.

Tales from Honduras to East Asia

I've made about eight trips to China and Hong Kong and for a while was a special advisor for a company called Zen that was trying to develop mines in China. Later I negotiated a sale of the Toromocho Project to a large Chinese mining company, Chinalco.

I gave a number of talks in China in about 1975. We had a Chinese interpreter named Mrs. Chin, who was a very bright, well-educated gal. She had been assigned the job of shoveling coal into a furnace during the Cultural Revolution and almost died as a result. On our first trip to China Edith got something like pneumonia, and she had to be dropped off at a hospital. Mrs. Chin stayed with us to help out while Edith was in the hospital for two days. Mrs. Chin seized on the opportunity of getting a pregnancy test. It was positive, but some of the Chinese red tape made it more favorable to become pregnant a month or two later, so she couldn't discuss this exciting subject with anyone but me. I had always preferred to think that babies were brought by the stork, so in this case I had to suffer through all the technical details with Mrs. Chin. First and last, we got very well acquainted with Mrs. Chin. She's written letters to us a number of times, and we get pictures of her little boy and Christmas cards.

The second trip was for DuPont about ten years later. I participated in a symposium sponsored by DuPont in Chindao, I think at Bob Shoemaker's suggestion. As I mentioned in my account of the San Cristobal Mine, Bob and I worked together for Bechtel on feasibility studies, and we have since had other projects in common. Bob was one of a couple of people who went over to China as metallurgical specialists for DuPont. I wrote a paper called "Geology and Mining of Gold" for the symposium and gave a talk. DuPont sells cyanide to China for gold metallurgy, and most of the people attending this symposium were from the Chinese Gold Corporation.

We had talks for two or three days in Chindao and then went out and visited gold mines and plants and so forth. One of the DuPont people with me was a young fellow named Tom Kuo. Tom was a super

David Lowell and Chinese engineer visiting gold mine in China for DuPont, 1985.

impressive American of Chinese ancestry and had degrees from Caltech and MIT and was a very charming fellow. He was a grandson of one of Chiang Kai-shek's generals in the civil war in China. He took Edith and me to see (from a distance) Chiang Kai-shek's summer home at Chindao. He still had relatives in China and Taiwan, and he was able to give us insight into the evolution of the Chinese political situation and the relationship of offshore Chinese to people living in China.

Between 1975 and 1978 I spent time on Viti Levu, the most populated of the Fiji Islands. It is a beautiful island, and when I was there, about equal numbers of indigenous Papuans and East Indian immigrants lived there. The land was owned by the Papuan natives, but in general the East Indians, who had been brought in originally to do agricultural work, were better educated, more energetic and ambitious, ran the businesses, and were typically the clerks and lower government officials. I remember seeing a jail work gang going out to cut brush in the jungle. About eight large, powerful prisoners (who had probably been arrested for drunkenness) were laughing and joking and obviously enjoying the outing. They each had a machete (called a bolo knife) and were guarded by a small skinny, sober East Indian with a nightstick.

I was reviewing the exploration project being carried out on the Nymosi porphyry copper deposit for Conzinc Riotinto of Australia (CRA), a large Australian mining company. The road to the project passed by a small village where a local alcoholic drink could be bought. This drink is made in a sort of religious event in which a number of men sit on logs around a large wooden bowl chewing a bean which they spit into the bowl. After being chewed it is fermented into a sort of beer. Just hearing about it made my digestive system conjure up awful symptoms.

I was staying in the Nymosi Guest House in Suva, the capital of Fiji. An engineer working on a temporary basis on the Nymosi project was also staying in the Guest House, and he took me one night to the Purple Dragon Bar. The South Pacific Games happened to be under way, and in the Purple Dragon were members of athletic teams from places as diverse as Papua New Guinea and French Polynesia. There was also a Russian ship in the harbor with really hard-bitten looking sailors, and some kind of British warship supplied some wildly homosexual sailors to the bar crowd. The engineer asked me, "Have you seen *Star Wars*?" You probably remember the scene in *Star Wars* of an intergalactic crossroads bar with a collection of people with lizard tails or lion heads, which wasn't very different from our Purple Dragon crowd.

I also worked several times in New Guinea, which had a very primitive society. The most violent and dangerous spot was not one of the isolated villages where they reputedly killed each other for entertainment and were practicing cannibals (which some tribes still practice). Rather, it was Port Moresby, the Papua New Guinea (PNG) capital, where Western companies supplied a bodyguard for staff members who had to walk down the street. I once spent a night in Geoff Loudon's apartment in Port Moresby. It was on the fifth floor of a building; at ground level was a razor wire fence surrounding the building and a mean-looking set of twenty-four-hour-a-day guards. I was surprised to see that Geoff, who is an old PNG hand, felt it prudent to add five deadbolts to the apartment door.

In July 1990 I was asked to visit the large copper-gold Grasberg Mine in the Indonesian portion of the island of New Guinea. This Indonesian territory was called West Irian at that time. I was accompanied on the trip by Edith who, being an anthropologist, was very interested to meet Papuan natives. We took a commercial flight from Cairns, Australia, to the Grasberg Airport at Timika and from there to a mining camp called Tembagapura by vehicle. We checked into the staff dormitory at Tembagapura. I got a geologic briefing from Barry Gillies

David Lowell at the outcrop of a massive copper skarn deposit at Ok Tedi, New Guinea.

and Tom Collins on the day we arrived and spent a total of three days in the field and in the office. I was able to compare some of the geology of the Chuquicamata, Ok Tedi, and Lepanto Far Southeast deposits with Grasberg, which may have been helpful to the staff. Grasberg at that time had published ore reserves of 399 million tons of 1.53 percent copper and 1.97 grams per ton of gold. The reserves are now much larger, making it one of the largest gold reserves in the world and the largest reserve of copper plus gold in the world. My fieldwork consisted of surface and underground visits and a number of very interesting helicopter reconnaissance flights.

On our return we landed in Cairns, Australia, and went through Australian Immigration and Customs. The Customs inspector was very dubious of allowing some of the artifact treasures Edith had acquired, which had obvious slime and mold. He asked how long these objects would remain in Australia. When told two days only he decided the country could stand that much exposure.

In the mid-eighties, prior to my visit to the Grasberg Mine, I had been to the Ok Tedi site. I worked twice on the Ok Tedi Project before construction started there. It is in the Star Mountains, in the central part of the island of New Guinea, and at that time was an extremely isolated location. It's near the Fly River, a huge river. When I was there they were doing water monitoring in streams, as a preliminary to building a plant. It's a real jungle area, and had the highest rainfall of any weather station in the world that year. Traveling around was difficult, and we moved mostly by helicopter. I became acquainted with the hydrologist who was checking weirs to measure water flow in creeks and rain gauges. I had inquired if it would be possible to see a native village while I was there, and the hydrologist invited me to go with him on a helicopter trip one day to visit the only village that was near Ok Tedi. Papua New Guinea was not by any means densely populated. The jungle is a very unproductive place for human habitation, and there were only small villages, widely scattered, in that part of New Guinea.

The village we went to was called Migilsimbip. They had had their first view of white people something like eight years before I was there.

David Lowell and indigenous group in village of Migilsimbip near the Ok Tedi Mine in the center of the island of New Guinea, 1987. The lady farthest in the back has an elongated breast and my guide explained that she was suckling a pig. The inhabitants of the village had their first contact with outsiders about 10 years earlier and were still cannibals.

It is possible that they were still practicing cannibals, as some tribes were. As far as clothing goes, they were not totally naked but largely so. We took along an interpreter who was from that village and who spoke pidgin English as well as the local language. He showed us something called the boys' house, where boys are put to live when they are six or seven years old. They stay there until they become men and they're taught to be warriors and do all the things that warriors are supposed to do. There were around fifteen buildings in this village, but only one building that was painted. I asked the interpreter what that was, and he said, "That is the Spirit House where we keep the bones of the people and the pigs." The pigs were a food source, but they were also considered sort of part of the population. We saw some women that had one elongated breast. The interpreter said that that was caused by suckling pigs.

In my various trips, the only sort of threatening natives I ever saw were on Bougainville Island, which is politically part of New Guinea but is really a different culture (Melanesians?). They looked like pretty mean customers, sort of glowering and threatening. I was with a Bechtel engineer, and saw a fellow going down the street with an umbrella in one hand and a bow and arrow in the other hand. I said, "Stop. I would like to take a picture of him." I thought it was kind of a humorous picture. He said, "Oh, I wouldn't advise you to do that." He said, "I tried to take a picture of a fellow with a bow and arrow once, and when I got the camera focused he had the arrow notched and pointing it at me." Later the same group rebelled against authorities and took over the mine, and CRA has never gotten the mine back.

The chief geologist at Ok Tedi was an Australian named Leake. He and his wife were living in a wall tent and using steel "patrol boxes" for furniture. A patrol box is a metal box about two by two by three feet in size with a waterproof lid and hoops at each end through which a pole can be inserted so that it can be carried in jungle treks by two natives. The Leakes had a baby less than a year old and seemed content, in spite of the almost continuous rain and life in a camp where there were active cases of amebic dysentery, malaria, and dengue fever. Helen Leake was a professional artist and painted an acrylic painting for me depicting the creation myth of the Papuans emerging from a carst hole in the jungle. It is very beautiful and is displayed in our home in Tucson.

My first trip to Costa Rica in about 1992 was for an American nonmetallic company ambitious to find a copper mine and get into the copper business. The exploration project was in heavy jungle and steep terrain that was only accessible by helicopter. It was about fifty kilometers southwest of Limon, Costa Rica's most important Atlantic port. I flew to San Juan's international airport, then took a feeder flight to Limon, where I was picked up by helicopter for a flight to the company's exploration camp.

The camp was a building typical of the tropics, made of 2x4s, plywood, grass mat curtains, and a corrugated iron roof. It was divided into a dormitory with six or eight cots, an office with maps and drafting equipment, and a rudimentary kitchen with a Servel butane refrigerator. There was a butane stove and a small water tank on the roof to service a kitchen sink. The shelves were stocked mainly with canned goods.

The camp was located in a clearing in the jungle, on a small ridge about a hundred feet by trail from a nice stream of water about twenty feet wide. The trail passed through high grass on both sides. When I arrived I was assigned a cot that was said to be, based on my importance, the best sleeping site. I don't remember why it was the best, but it was something like the center cots were farther from the entrances (and the snakes). I had lived a good part of my life in rural Arizona with a population of rattlesnakes. I knew the statistics—that most bites were ankle height or lower and fewer than 5 percent of bites were fatal—and I spent very little time worrying about snakebites. I soon learned the snake situation in our camp in the jungle was a different ball game. Our Arizona rattlesnakes were typically only three or four feet long, but the ones in Costa Rica were up to ten feet long. In Arizona, I was familiar with and had often seen rattlesnakes of one kind or another, which are venomous, but in this camp in Costa Rica the staff told me there were nine poisonous snakes (the actual number in the Costa Rica region is closer to twenty). I saw one fer-de-lance snake that was three or four inches thick and about four feet long. Several of the pit viper species have venom that acts on nerves rather than muscles, and bites from these snakes are often fatal. There is also a blood snake that kills by lowering the viscosity of blood so you "bleed from every pore." I tested these wild snake stories by asking a local Indian who was helping me, "Do you actually know anyone who has died of a snake bite?" He thought a minute and said, "Well, there was my brother."

The second night I was in the camp, one of the geologists I thought of as The Professor stripped down to his shorts, got a towel and a bar of soap and said, "I've sweated all day, and I am going down to the stream and have a bath," and he went out. About one minute later he came back in the door and started to put his clothes back on. He said, "I couldn't face going down that trail with the grass on both sides with the chance of nine varieties of deadly snakes lying in wait."

The company had come the previous year and made six or eight helipads by digging into the steep hillside to make part of a flat pad and then cut logs to make support posts and floor to extend the floor out from the hillside. From these sites, trails were built on contour in both directions. These were more trenches than trails and were cut into the side of the hill through the soil layer until they encountered rock, the description of which could be recorded in a geological map and sampled to determine possible metal contact in a geochem map. I was asked to look at and reinterpret the results of the geology and geo-chemical anomalies, and spot-check the geology mapped in the trails. This involved first cutting the brush and grass that had grown up in the helipads in the course of a year in a rain forest environment.

The day after I arrived, a helicopter was sent to the helipads carrying a crew of two Indian laborers. The pilot hovered over the helipads and the laborers climbed down on the skids and jumped down onto the pad and then cut the brush with their machetes. One helipad, however, had been taken over by a fer-de-lance snake. The snake had some territo-rial feelings about the helipad and chased the two Indians around in a circle while they frantically whacked at it with their machetes, the pilot watching from above. One finally hit the snake.

The Professor was not a rough-and-tumble Indiana Jones. He was a very knowledgeable ore deposits geologist, but not cut out for this assignment. He told me that after one of the trails was completed he went in to map it and sample it. He was walking down in the trail when his Indian helper bent over and said, "Señor, a tigré" (a jaguar, which, in contrast to mountain lions, does sometimes eat people) "has walked down the trail." He continued to watch the trail and a little later grabbed the Professor's arm and showed him a big cat's print and a little cat's print, and said, "Look Señor, Mommy has taken her kitten with her!" At this point the Professor was examining with every step both sides of the trail and the limbs above. The Professor said the Indian helper didn't show any fear, just great interest, as anyone would have on a good nature walk. The lack of fear made the Professor even more nervous. They proceeded ahead until they came to a large puddle and the Indian got down on his hands and knees to see better and said, "Look, Señor, Mommy has picked up her kitten and carried it across the water! Do you see where his little toes dragged in the mud?" and "Get closer, you can see the water running back into the track! She must be right in front of us." The Professor announced, "This territory belongs to her, not me. I am going back."

He told me another story, which was confirmed by the other geologists, about wildlife in Costa Rica. The company camp is about one hundred miles southeast of San José, and between the two points there was a large oval area marked on the map as *unexplored*. The reason for his designation was a combination of almost impossible terrain and access. The Professor and another geologist set off for some reason on a trip to San José, the capital of Costa Rica. Somewhere in the middle of the unexplored area, the engine began cutting out, but the pilot was able to set the machine in an open area on top of a ridge without any injury. They were out of radio range and in an area where they had almost no chance of walking out. They had a survival kit that contained, among other things, a signal mirror and a tube tent about eight or nine feet long and four or five feet in diameter. It is designed for one or two people, but all three in the crash somehow climbed in when it got dark. The Professor took his shoes and socks off and his tube tent position left his bare feet exposed at one end of the tent. In the middle of the night he woke up and something was sniffing, or licking, the bottom of one foot. He assumed it was the mother tigré, or her local relative, and he screamed and tried to crawl over obstructing miscellaneous body parts to a position in the middle of the tube tent, where he would at least not be the first one eaten. His two companions had been awakened from sleep, in the dark, in a claustrophobic situation, not sure where the exits were and not sure they wanted to exit if the Professor's screams about being attacked by a jaguar were true. They probably thought the Professor had lost at least a foot, or maybe half of a leg. In due course, everything was sorted out, but I can't think they had a very comfortable rest of the night sleeping in their clothes on the ground with an imaginary jaguar outside. The next day they built a signal fire and one member climbed up on the highest point with the signal mirror. He saw a search plane in the distance, but the plane didn't see the mirror or the smoke. This went on for two days until they were spotted by a plane and later rescued by a helicopter. Once, they said, a bird had tried to land on someone's head because it had never seen a human being.

My second Costa Rica assignment was also kind of wild and woolly. A major mining company asked me to look at a copper prospect near the Pan-American Highway about a hundred miles south of San José. The company development manager wanted to participate in the visit, possibly because he thought it would be a nice junket, but he had little to contribute on geology, or operation in Latin America, or speaking Spanish, so I made all the plans and decisions. The company had some kind of a Costa Rican representative, but he was strictly a white-collar guy. I had originally planned to find a vehicle and a driver and drive down the Pan-American Highway then east a short distance and visit the prospect with someone who knew the way.

Things started going wrong almost the moment I arrived. The company development manager was scheduled to arrive a day later, giving me time to arrange the visit first, but within a few hours of my arrival a large earthquake occurred, with its epicenter near the highway south of San José and, according to the maps, north of the prospect. This turned out to be incorrect. The government closed the Pan-American Highway, and I decided the only chance for visiting the prospect was to charter a small plane and land on an airstrip shown on the map and take a chance of finding someone with a four-wheel-drive vehicle to take us to the prospect. The problem was the governmental edict didn't do much to help, but seemed to prohibit almost everything. This included chartering the airplane, landing on the airstrip, visiting the project, and so on. Here's where the company's white-collar administrative guy came in. He started off on the bottom of the ladder and worked up to the president's office. The president was out of town, but we got a letter on Office of the President of Costa Rica stationery that detailed all our problems and said the *presidencia* was in favor of helping us on each problem, but didn't actually give us permission to do anything. However, I and the administrator agreed we could go ahead, and see what happened.

We chartered the plane, and the fixed-base operator and the pilot were fine with the idea of landing on the airstrip. They knew there were a few houses near the strip, so we put on our boots and bought some bottled water and sandwiches and charged off. We landed, and the pilot helped me find a fellow from a farm with an ancient open Jeep, and we started off. The pilot stayed with the plane; I think there were three of us including the owner/driver in the Jeep. Within a half hour we arrived at a village of about thirty or forty houses, made with rock and adobe walls. About half the houses had been largely destroyed by the earthquake the day before and a lot of people must have been killed or hurt. A vigilante committee had been formed, and they were semi-hysterical and had guns that they pointed at us. The owner/driver, whom they knew, talked to them, and I showed them my letter, more or less from the president, and finally they let us go on. We drove on to a Jeep trail that went up to the mineral prospect. The Jeep trail went about two or three miles, a lot of it uphill, and it turned out to be almost a two-hour walk from there to the prospect. I asked the owner/driver if he would drive us to the prospect. He said, "No, there will probably be another earthquake, and it will cut the road and trap my Jeep." I thought to myself that it was a terrible burden to be ignorant and not know anything about earthquakes and, like the vigilantes, cause more intelligent people to suffer. By this time it was noon, and we hiked and sweated, and just before we reached the prospect, I heard what I thought was thunder in the distance. This copper prospect was easy to diagnose. It had no chance of being a mine, but I took enough samples for assay to confirm this. We set off hiking back and made fast progress because it was mostly downhill. When we got to the big hill a half mile from the

Jeep and the owner/driver, we saw big nasty earthquake fissures cutting the road, which hadn't been there two hours before. Some of the openings in the road were a foot wide. The noise I had heard was the second earthquake, but we had been walking and did not feel the ground shake. It destroyed the Jeep trail. It would have trapped the Jeep. So much for who was ignorant and who was intelligent.

When we drove back to the village of the vigilantes we had a second problem. They seemed to think that we had gone up on top of the mountain and in some way generated a second earthquake just to persecute them. When I got out my letter, more or less from the president, they seemed to think the president might have been part of the collusion to hurt them. I thought this was very unreasonable at the time. We finally got through the village, got to the airstrip, and flew to San José. A day later, I flew back to Arizona. It is very hard to find a new mine.

Mules, Grizzly Bears, Elephants, and Cobras

Explorationists who work in the "bush" tell tall stories about dangerous animals that usually cast the teller in a heroic light. If the fieldwork is in Latin America, the dangerous animal is likely to be a mule, or maybe a poisonous snake. In Canada and Alaska the animal of choice is the grizzly bear, although it's also possible to be chased by a black bear. However, in Thailand there are even more dramatic animals, like wild elephants and king cobras. Anyway, these are some of my tall bush stories.

I have made many muleback trips into the mountains in Mexico, the Dominican Republic, Honduras, Ecuador, and many trips in the Andes of Peru and Chile on mules and horses. Horses are dumb and excitable and buck you off and fall on you (I have a fourteen-inch stainless steel plate attached to my right femur as proof), but mules, while being less inclined to buck and more intelligent, are also mean. They are vindictive on the basis of indignities suffered up to years earlier, or perhaps harbor some sort of ancestral vindictiveness about being domesticated.

In the late 1960s I made a trip to Honduras to look at two copper prospects in Tegucigalpa owned by Bill Lady, a prospector and owner of an airline company. Bill was a very nice guy but, as I learned, had a bad temper. He also was very proud of his bush lore and told me about his expertise in mule handling and mule riding. This was also bandit country, and Bill carried a very large revolver on the trip we took together. We went to the jumping-off point for one of the prospects, and Bill rented two mules from a little ranch and we started off. It was immediately clear that the mules were only half broken. My mule, at one point, spun with me on a narrow trail with a cliff on one side, and I made many revolutions before I was able to jump off on the uphill side, but I managed to ride him all day. Bill's mule caused constant problems and finally succeeded in banging Bill's knee very painfully on a boulder. I was fifty feet ahead on the trail and Bill jumped off and hobbled after the mule in a fury. He pulled out his revolver and cocked the hammer and said, "I'm going to kill you, you dirty son of a bitch." This alarmed me, not through any benevolent desire to save the mule's life, but because I was in the line of fire. I asked Bill to wait a minute until I climbed a few feet up the slope, but by this time his knee hurt a little less and he decided not to shoot.

In the early seventies I had a consulting assignment to look at some copper prospects in the Dominican Republic in a combination helicopter-mule expedition in the mountains. I was dropped by the helicopter at a ranch in the jungle where some mules had been lined up, and together with Vreeland Johnson, the claim owner, and a Dominican *arriero* (mule handler), we were to ride all day visiting a prospect and would be picked up late in the day in a clearing on the other side of the mountain where the helicopter would land. I made several mistakes that day, and the first was confidently admitting I was a good mule rider, which resulted in my getting the worst mule. From my first move to mount he went through his bag of tricks, which included biting, kicking, spinning, and bucking. We had a who-is-in-charge tussle for the first half hour and then settled into a clippity-clop trot on a trail in the jungle along a riverbank.

It was a warm morning, and I had begun to daydream when I saw something out of the corner of my eye. When I looked to the right there was an attractive young Dominican woman, bare to the waist, washing clothes on the riverbank! It took a second or two to bring this picture into proper focus, but that was plenty of time for the mule to realize my guard was down and swerve off the trail toward a tree with a limb about six inches higher than the saddle. When he broke into a run I felt the acceleration and saw the limb and threw my legs up and lay back on the mule's rump and slithered under the limb, but for a while couldn't get my feet back in the stirrups and galloped by the partly clad lady rotating in horizontal circles on the mule. I have wondered since what she thought of the performance. I was able to get back into the saddle without falling off and we continued clippity-clopping on.

The prospect was in a little mountain range, and in the afternoon we were going down a steep trail when the *gurapera* on the saddle broke. This is the strap on a mule saddle under the mule's tail that keeps the saddle from slipping forward over the mule's shoulders, which is necessary because a mule's shoulders are narrower than a horse's. I didn't realize that the gurapera was broken until I noticed that the mule's ears were almost in my face. I then climbed frantically backward until I could grab the mule's tail. The mule was unable to bite, kick, spin, or buck because he was just as anxious to not fall off the cliff as I was. We came to a condition of equilibrium with the mule's legs spraddled out and me lying backward with a death grip on the tail. The arriero observed in Spanish after this second performance, "Señor, you are a very agile gringo!"

In the course of our adventures during the day, our package of ham and cheese sandwiches had been totally mashed into a flat tortilla of homogeneous ham, cheese, bread, and waxed paper, and we declined to eat it at lunch, but when we arrived at the clearing and the helicopter had not arrived, we cut the mess up into three pieces and ate it. About dark the helicopter arrived and we flew to a small airport with a one-room terminal building, where a car was waiting for us. When the pilot circled to land next to the building, Dominican soldiers ran out of both doors waving their arms and pointing to a spot on the airstrip. I asked the pilot what that was all about and he said, "Oh, that area must have been mined because there is a current threatened invasion by another Caribbean country."

Vreeland Johnson was an American who owned a Dominican flying service and had spent his entire career in the Dominican Republic. He was killed in a helicopter crash after I knew him. I asked Vreeland how he happened to settle in the Dominican Republic. He told me that during World War II he was a Navy amphibious PBY pilot assigned to a base in the Aleutian Islands, an area said to have the worst weather in the world. He said it was a miserable life with no feminine companionship and nothing to do. He said they took off from the base in the middle of blizzards and flew out over the ocean in bad weather looking for Japanese ships, and on the rare occasions when they found one, they were shot at. On their return flights they had great difficulty finding the base and often also landed in a blizzard. Vreeland said a questionnaire arrived from the Navy Department and one of the questions was, "In what capacity do you think you could be of most value to the United States Navy?" Vreeland filled it out like this: "As a military attaché in a Caribbean country." The other pilots laughed, but two months later he was transferred to Santo Domingo, and when the war was over, he stayed.

Around 1982 I made two trips to Thailand to work on porphyry copper and disseminated gold deposits near Loei. I worked with a Thai geologist named Wat, and when I arrived he gave me an orientation that included how to deal with dangerous animals, which in that district included wild elephants and king cobras. Wat said there were three things you could do if chased by an elephant. If you were in a flat area and there was a nearby bamboo grove, run into it because elephants break the bamboo shoots and the sharp broken shafts puncture their pinkies so they don't chase geologists into bamboo thickets. If you are in an open flat area look for a big tree too big for the elephant to push over and run around it close to the trunk. An elephant, with his wide wheelbase, has to run farther out on a much longer path length and tires out sooner than a terrified geologist. If you are chased by an elephant on a steep hillside you must remember that the elephant can run much faster than you uphill or downhill. However, with his wide wheelbase he cannot run horizontally or he would roll down the hill, so you must run along the contour line. King cobras, according to Wat, are encountered in tall elephant grass and normally rise suddenly to confront you at eye level. They can travel faster than a man and, if you run, will chase and kill you, so what you do is stand perfectly still and stare into the king cobra's eyes. After a while, according to Wat, the cobra will get tired and drop down and slither off. I wasn't so sure about Wat's stories, but we did once see some huge, dinner-plate-sized tracks, which made me nervously try to remember the three sets of elephant instructions.

We ate breakfast every morning in Loei in a little greasy spoon restaurant and were served by a pretty young waitress. The last day I was in Loei the waitress and Wat had an animated conversation, and when we left I asked him what they were talking about. Wat said she had observed that winter was coming on and that a man would suffer from the cold at night if he didn't have a warm female to sleep with. Wat said he told her he thought he would just buy a blanket!

CHAPTER FOUR

Independent Illegal Miners throughout the World

Gambusinos (Mexico), *pirqueneros* (Chile), *mineros informales* (Peru), *petroleros* (Ecuador), *guayanperos* (Brazil), *illegals* (Philippines), and *high graders* (United States): all these names connote independent small miners who remove and sell ore without owning the mineral rights. They are all stealing the ore from the legitimate owner, whether an individual, a mining company, or a government. The interesting thing is that there is a wide difference in the amount of guilt felt in different situations. In some countries with socialistic politics the illegal miners feel the claim system is morally wrong and the ore belongs to whoever mines it. People with this idea are likely to violently resist the legitimate owner trying to reclaim his property. In some countries, such as Mexico, Ecuador, and Brazil, the small miners have some rights written into the mining code, and these may relate to the size or ore grade or situation—for example, the right to scavenge remaining ore after a mining company has made a first pass of mining.

I have had many encounters with these people and have usually felt a lot of respect for their courage and independence, even when they are creating a problem for me. In Chile they are called pirqueneros. In the Atacama Desert a *pirque* is a hut or windbreak made by stacking loose rocks into walls sometimes only three or four feet high and sometimes with no roof or a temporary roof made with a tarp, plastic sheet, or

This is a *pirque* or shelter without a roof, 1980. This one was a way station for Inca runners on an ancient road south of Caracoles, Chile.

cardboard from large boxes. It may rain only once in five years or once in twenty years so it doesn't have to shed water, but it does offer some protection from the wind. I know because I was a few times happy to put my sleeping bag in a pirque.

The Chilean pirqueneros are typically looking for narrow, high-grade gold veins. Usually there is no chance to get proper assays from a laboratory and they have worked out another way. When you visit a pirquenero mine you can usually find a "laboratory stone." This is some kind of hard, resistant rock with a flat upper face about a square foot in area. A sample is cut across the vein in the mine with a pick and then pounded into powder on the flat face of the laboratory rock using a hammer. Then an effort is made to select a representative sample by carefully separating the sample that was cut. The final "lab sample" is measured in a standard measure and the preferred measure is a metal pop or beer bottle cap. This sample, which is about a half teaspoon, is dumped in a peruña, which in Chile is made from a goat horn about

Trapiche showing grinding stones with amalgamation plates lining walls. This one was powered by a diesel motor turning a shaft that rotated arms dragging large stones. A key part of the process is activation of amalgamation plates. Different, sometimes secret, activators are used. The *pirquinero* told David that the best activator was a virgin's urine!

seven or eight inches long and cut lengthwise, then softened in boiling water and carefully shaped into the precise form which works best for gold panning. In Mexico the technology used by gambusinos is different. A cow horn, not a goat horn, is used and a proper peruña must have a black spot in the right place to provide more contrast to be able to identify the "chispas," or specks of free gold.

All this sounds primitive and inaccurate, but when your pirquenero or gambusino tells you how many grams per metric tonne of free milling gold the narrow vein contains, and then you cut your own sample, and you send it off to ALS for a precise analysis, and you wait two to four weeks for the assay returns, you realize how good the pirquenero or gambusino is. In this discussion, the "you" is not a recent graduate from a widely admired university whose vein sampling technique may

David at old gold stamp mill in Peru, 1995.

be totally unreliable; "you" is a sadder but wiser veteran of many campaigns, and many mistakes, and countless nights sleeping miserably on the ground, and not a few meetings, not with Montezuma, but with his Revenge. "You" understands that "ore is rock which can be mined at a profit," and "you" know that mines are almost impossibly hard to find, and almost everyone is lined up in ranks to prevent you finding a mine, and in the front rank fighting fiercely to prevent you finding a mine is the top management of your own company. If you can qualify in all these tests and are still desperate to find a mine you can go ahead on equal terms with the pirqueneros and gambusinos.

Gaby and the 1,400 Petroleros

Around 1985 a friend told me about a gold anomaly that he had found in Ecuador and that his company had abandoned. I was able to relate his prospect description with the Lowell-Guilbert Porphyry Copper Model. The apparent gold content was within the range of a viable bulk, low-grade gold deposit, and there was some recoverable copper. I sometimes make spur-of-the-moment decisions and in this case decided to visit this prospect at my own expense ASAP. If it were not for the 1,400 petroleros making a subsistence living while making the bulk of one of Ecuador's assets unmineable, this story might have had an outcome much better for me.

The first step in the expedition was lining up someone who participated in the original geochem survey and knew where the anomaly was located and arrange a meeting in Ecuador. The second step was the trip to Ecuador. Edith normally does not accept invitations to trips to exotic places where she has to stay in a hotel while I clamber through a mine or mineral prospect, but she had not seen Ecuador and signed on for

Checking a *petrolero*
pit in Peru, 1994.

This is a gold prospect in southern Peru where several hundred *mineros informales* are mining gold in shallow primitive mines. The shacks in which they live are visible in the hills behind David.

the trip. Ecuador is a beautiful country, but doesn't have a very beautiful society. The level of corruption is relatively high and the people have a lower standard of living than they need to, as a result of their government's problems. We saw some of this on the Gaby visit. Guayaquil and Quito are the two large cities in Ecuador. Quito is in a beautiful setting in the mountains, but Guayaquil is almost at sea level with hot, humid weather and mud and mangroves and some malaria. We stayed in an old hotel on a riverbank and found that at some point the hotel had tilted and threatened to slide into the river. A ball placed on the floor of our bedroom rolled vigorously across the room. We left early the next morning. Our driver pointed out that about half the homes had illegal connections with water mains, and a significant fraction also have free connections with natural gas lines. He said the gas connections had to be made with a welding torch and if not done correctly resulted in large fires and damage to the gas thief.

Our road ran parallel to the ocean beach, but a hundred yards inland. There had just been a big flood and a lot of cows were standing on their little hummocks and surrounded by water. We drove about three hours to the Gaby jumping-off place, where four mules were waiting. There was also a small primitive restaurant, but we found that everything was dirty: knives, forks, and plates, and the food was in awful condition too, so we didn't eat. The *arriero* (mule manager) who brought the mules said that nothing in the camp was appropriate for a visit by Edith and she and the driver went on to the next town where there was a reasonable hotel. The four of us then left on typical small, beaten-down Ecuadorian mules. It was raining and appeared to have been raining all day. We were climbing steadily and the mud appeared to be getting thicker so I decided to branch off from the group to ride up the crest of a ridge where there was some rock outcrop and less mud. I got off my mule to tighten the cinch and I saw a huge white grub worm. It was about one and one-quarter inch in diameter and about eight inches long. The jungle produces some strange creatures.

My navigating turned out to be okay, and I met the *mozo* who was the camp watchman. The camp consisted of two one-room buildings made of thatched walls and corrugated iron roofs. One building was totally open on one side with the kitchen in front. Inside the building were about three platforms cut into the soil so several people could sleep on ledges at different elevations. Sanitary facilities consisted of a latrine in unspeakable condition, partly because of the rain. The second building was also of thatched walls and corrugated roof; it was built in two stories, with the bottom room used as a storeroom and the top room with a door and a window and a ladder, but it appeared to be used as a chicken coop for the watchman's twenty-odd chickens.

The stove was built of cement, like a primitive woodstove with a sort of open oven. I had never seen one like it, and it may be an Ecuadorian invention. It was cool when I arrived and I sat close to the fire to try to dry out. I waited a half hour and then an hour for the others to arrive. Finally, assuming something was wrong, I saddled my mule and was just leaving camp when I met them. They all looked like they had been in a mud-wrestling match—they were mud from head to toe. They told me two of the mules had wallowed into the mud up to the level of their bellies, and then my three companions had to get into the mud themselves and bodily lift the mules out. Since the mules probably weighed 800 or 1000 pounds the operation sounded impossible, but the mules may have helped by trying to swim out. I felt a little guilty having missed the mud bath, but happy to have been on the ridge top.

Cooking dinner consisted of heating various pots with a wood fire below a grate in the cement stove and then putting them on the cement to cool off. The chickens, however, watched the process, and when a pot became cool enough they perched on the pot lip. This didn't improve the hygiene of the meal, but eventually some food was passed out and eaten. The next event was to prepare my bed chamber. I had been determined to be the most important visitor and therefore in line to sleep in the second-story room with the chickens. The caretaker climbed up the ladder and threw all the chickens out into empty space amid a lot of cackling and wing flapping noises. A problem developed when the chickens noticed that the window was open and did a 180-degree turn and came back in the window. This went on for thirty minutes, until it started to get dark and the chickens finally abandoned my elegant chamber until daybreak. However, I visited my bedroom and complained that I wouldn't sleep in the chicken droppings. This was solved to some degree with a broom, and I climbed in and slept like a baby. Early the next morning we had some more of the Gaby cuisine and left on our mules to ride over to Gaby. There was lots of evidence of disseminated gold and lots of evidence of the petroleros, who had dug pits and trenches and incline shafts up to twenty-five feet deep vertically. We also ran into two groups, both armed with machetes and giving us very hostile looks. When I thought we had developed an idea of the size of the deposit and also collected a number of indicative samples to estimate approximate grade, we rode back to the five-star restaurant on the highway and found Edith and the vehicle for our return to her hotel (which looked like paradise).

We then made a trip to the capital, Quito, to see whether we could acquire Gaby mineral rights. There was a small three-story building dedicated to business the government had with the mining industry. The bottom floor was open to the public. The second floor was not open to the public except rarely, and the third was like getting into a King's inner sanctum. I had lined up a young lawyer to help on the government visit, and we went to the three-story building. We first went into the first floor and then tiptoed illegally up to the second where my friend knew one of the important secretaries, who had an important secret document that could get us invited to the third floor, but which my friend could read for only five minutes while the secretary looked out the door and up and down the hall, very worried. The cloak and dagger worked, and we were invited past a guard up the stairs. By this time I had developed a mental picture of the Mining Chief. I had him very formally dressed sitting behind a huge desk with an important somewhat cruel expression and being assisted by one or two frightened helpers. What we actually found was a friendly guy about twenty-five years old without a necktie and apparently bored and happy to meet us. He had decorated the walls of his office with photographs cut out of *Playboy* magazine attached with scotch tape. When I asked about staking the Gaby property, he said, "It's open to location and we can give you the papers to fill out." When I asked if the government would help us with the 1,400 mean-looking petroleros, he said, "No, just tell them to leave."

I remembered a story I had heard from a Chilean geologist working for Placer Development Company (a large Canadian company), who told me about visiting a prospect in Ecuador. He and another geologist made the property visit in a helicopter. The helicopter landed in a clearing and the geologists had walked a little way away when a group of petroleros burst out of the jungle throwing rocks at the helicopter, which immediately took off without the geologists, who ran for their lives down a *quebrada* chased by machete-waving petroleros. The pilot watched where they had gone and was able to pick them up several hours later, but it didn't sound like trouble-free exploration, and I decided not to go ahead with Gaby.

King King, Where There Were 3,000 Illegal Miners

King King is a porphyry copper-gold deposit located across the bay from Davao City, the largest city on Mindanao Island in the Philippines. King King was found and explored by Benguet Consolidated Mining Company. Benguet operated two fairly large underground gold mines near Baguio on Luzon Island and for fifteen or twenty years they also operated the Dizon porphyry copper-gold mine on Luzon where I played a part in identifying the orebody and planning the exploration. I had no part in finding King King, but was twice asked to visit it for Benguet and give advice.

High Graders in the United States and the Saga of Fraction Brown

The mining convention in the United States about stealing ore has been a little different than in Latin America, for a couple of reasons. The first is that the American Mining Law of 1872 clearly defined mining claim ownership. The second is that the American political system has been free-enterprise democracy without significant moves toward socialism or communism, and there has been no question that there might be community ownership of minerals. This did not entirely prevent outsiders from removing ore from a claim that was owned by someone else, but when they did both parties knew the ore was being stolen and this was supported by the courts. This theft usually involved taking easily accessible small blocks of high-grade ore that were likely to be in pillars of the vein material supporting the upper "hanging wall" side of the vein. Sometimes when the pillars were removed the whole mine collapsed, so the "high graders" were not popular in the mining industry.

Another variety of poaching involved studying the public mining records, or even conducting surveys, to identify "fractions," small areas not covered by existing claims through the oversight of original claim stakers. If such a small, open wedge could be found and staked, the nuisance claim could be very high if it was in the middle of an orebody. There was an expert in this practice in Pima County, Arizona, who was popularly known as "Fraction Brown." He had held up several previous companies over claim fractions, and around 1965 he identified a small fraction in the middle of the large open pit Mission Mine southwest of Tucson. Arizona mining regulations required, when staking a claim, the excavation of a six-by-six-by-eight-foot-deep "discovery pit." Mr. Brown rented a bulldozer and walked it up to the main gate of the ASARCO Mission Mine, and the guards assumed the bulldozer belonged to ASARCO and opened the gate. Fraction Brown then chug-chugged down the spiral haul road, dodging big haul trucks, to the bottom of the pit where his fraction was located. He dug his discovery pit and put out his location notice and his claim stakes and then chug-chugged back up the road and out the gate. ASARCO's lawyers found lots of issues on which to base lawsuits, but eventually had to pay up.

BOOK IV, 1992–2014

Total freedom to plan exploration, more innovation
and risk taking with ownership, six discoveries
and large financial return

CHAPTER ONE

Los Calatos Discovery in Peru and Inadequate Financing

In our early, self-financed exploration, we did a pretty thorough first-step reconnaissance of the southern Peru copper belt in the course of the first year, as well as the extrapolation of the belt south to the border of Chile and north toward Lima, where we acquired Los Calatos by staking. We identified one prospect that we called Los Pinos, near Cañete, Peru, that we acquired by an option agreement. We filed claims covering a large number of porphyry copper style alteration zones in the southern Peru copper belt and in the southern projection of the belt.

During this period we didn't establish an office in Peru, we didn't have a bank account, and we didn't hire any service employees other than field assistants for the senior geologists, who were working almost entirely in the field. I paid all the bills in cash, or with a credit card or, on some occasions, a U.S. check.

We accomplished a lot during that period. At a cocktail party in Chile, I became acquainted with Catherine (Katie) McLeod. Catherine was a professional mine finance person from Canada with a commerce degree. She was sent down to Santiago to open an office for a Canadian brokerage firm that had intended to get its foot in the door in the Chilean mining industry by acting as a broker to finance Chilean mining companies. She was there for less than a year and resigned from the company she was working for. I had known her only casually, but

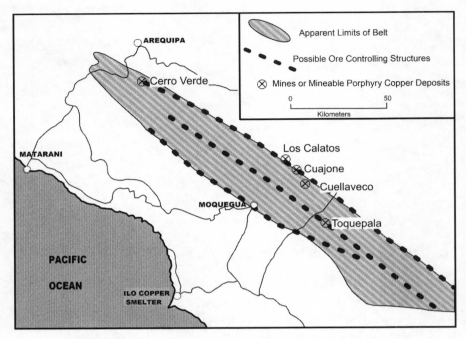

Southern Peru Porphyry Copper Belt showing location of Los Calatos deposit (J. D. Lowell, 1979).

she had heard through the grapevine that I had started an exploration program in Peru, and she also knew I had an outstanding track record for finding mines. She then came to Peru to try to talk me into forming a company. At that time, in 1992, I was not interested in forming a Canadian junior company and declined her proposals. In the meantime, I had, at about the end of the first year, formed a company called Acuarios Minera y Exploradora in Peru, only for the purpose of holding mining property. It was a wholly owned company. About a year after beginning the project, we were flying between known targets south of Arequipa and north of the Cuajone Mine, southeast of Moquegua, Peru, and I personally noticed a concentric color anomaly out the window of the airplane. This was not a unique event, because we had found by then twenty or more, but this area had better-developed concentric alteration. The aircraft was equipped with a GPS, and we had an

David on first visit to Los Calatos hydrothermal alteration zone. Sandy looking material is volcanic ash from eruption during historic times 200 to 300 years ago.

arrangement for finding GPS coordinates on the map by programming them into the aircraft GPS instrument. When we found something of interest, we would ask the pilot to punch it into the machine, and then we would later pick up these coordinates from the aircraft's instrument, and that's what we did on this occasion.

This prospect turned out to be the deposit we named Los Calatos, from a geographical name on the map, meaning "the bald ones." It's in a very dry desert environment, with almost no vegetation except for a few cacti. It's in a very inaccessible place, and it was open to staking. It required a full day's walk to get to Los Calatos in the beginning. Early in the project it appeared to be a copper deposit that probably contained a minimum of 50 million tons of 1 percent copper in a sooty chalcocite-style mineralization, which is leachable, that would result in a smaller capital investment because it is a less complicated concentrating plant.

Helicopter on phyllic alteration with leached capping at Los Calatos, 1992.

We did a detailed geochem survey on Los Calatos, and later, because Acuarios Minera lacked funds, we negotiated a joint venture agreement with Phelps Dodge Corporation to explore Los Calatos. Phelps Dodge did a lot of geophysical work and relatively little geochemical work or surface geological work, which are the two techniques I have emphasized in my porphyry copper exploration.

The country manager of the Phelps Dodge exploration was Jorge Benavides. Jorge is a nephew of Alberto Benavides, the dean emeritus of Peruvian mining and a friend of mine. He has a graduate degree from Harvard and was at one time the chief geologist at Cerro de Pasco Corporation; he is a very intelligent, capable guy. As I write, he is president of Buenaventura Mining Company, which is, I believe, the largest Peruvian-owned mining company in Peru.

His nephew is also a very well educated fellow and was picked as Peru manager by Phelps Dodge Corporation. In the middle of the

Charter flight during which David looked out the window and discovered the Los Calatos concentric porphyry copper alteration pattern that led to staking the target, 1992. The area was open to location.

Phelps Dodge project at Los Calatos, a scheduled airline flight, something like a 727 airplane, crashed in the ocean near Arequipa and everyone was killed, including the project manager of Los Calatos and two of the geologists working on it. This stopped the project for a month or more and also interrupted the momentum of the project. Partly as a result of this the exploration wasn't properly completed. There were only two drill holes drilled in the orebody itself. The rest of the drilling was in IP (induced polarization) anomalies that had been found by the geophysicists and which turned out not to be related to copper ore (as is usually the case). The geochemical anomalies we had found were not drilled by Phelps Dodge but would have led to the large deposit later found. Los Calatos was acquired from Barrick Gold in about 2008 by an Australian company, which has since announced over a billion tonnes of marginal grade copper ore, and it will probably be mined in the future. (Barrick inherited Los Calatos when they took over Arequipa

Different opinions about the height of the Incas' gold placed by Atahualpa in Cajamarca, Peru, room.

Resources in 1996.) It turned out to be a serious error on our part to farm the prospect out to Phelps Dodge.

In about the middle of 1993 a flood of foreign companies began coming into Peru, and most of the southern Peru copper belt was blanket-staked by these big companies. It pretty much shut down our regional exploration in the southern part of the country. Our work was based on looking for alteration zones and then acquiring them by staking. After everything was staked, we couldn't continue with this strategy. We weren't sufficiently financed to enter into a lot of option agreements in which substantial cash payments had to be made.

In the course of our work, however, I had begun to appreciate the fact that there was a regional structure analogous to the Falla Oeste in Chile, with a possible extension on the order of a thousand or more kilometers of strike length. The structure was defined by the Incahuasi fault to the northeast and the Incapuquio fault to the southwest. It was represented in the south of Peru by the southern Peru copper belt and appeared to be aligned in the north of Peru by the recently discovered Yanacocha gold deposit of Newmont, and other deposits that formed a northwesterly trending gold belt near Cajamarca, Peru, including deposits like Maqui Maqui, Tantahuatay, and the Michiquillay porphyry copper deposit originally owned by ASARCO, among others.

Further Exploration in Southern Peru

On the border of Chile and Peru, the continental margin abruptly swings from basically north–south to a northwesterly direction. The porphyry copper belt in Chile parallels the continental margin, and the southern Peru copper belt also parallels the new alignment of the continental margin. For my type of exploration, this is another obvious target, looking for new deposits within the narrow belt in Peru.

This belt is marked by the Incapuquio fault on the northwest side and the Incahuasi fault on the northeast side. There are four known large deposits there: Toquepala, Quellaveco, Cuajone, and Cerro Verde. Our Los Calatos discovery will be the fifth. This relationship of belts occurred to me in my first reconnaissance trip in 1969 and had stuck in the back of my mind ever since. In 1985 I returned on a little reconnaissance trip to southern Peru and determined at that time that it looked pretty hopeless from the political/foreign investment viewpoint to invest any time or money in Peru. This was during the first Alan Garcia administration in Peru, and in some residential sections in Lima the garbage was being dumped in the middle of the streets.

During the period of roughly 1975 to 1990 Peru had a series of bad governments, ranging from far left to military to very corrupt, and sometimes various combinations of these. Superimposed on these in the 1980s was the horrific Sendero Luminoso, a Communist insurgent guerrilla organization in Peru, and the bad but less horrific Túpac Amaru Revolutionary Movement. These forces were a real obstacle to working in Peru, but I used a listening post—a Peruvian resident who kept me informed—to follow the political situation and terrorism danger in Peru. I also read whatever showed up in the Chilean newspapers, which was quite a bit, about the political situation in Peru. I had been watching Peruvian politics with the hope of finding a porphyry copper deposit either south of the southern Peru copper belt or north of it. The brutal terrorism by the Sendero Luminoso reached a peak probably around 1988 or 1990, and in 1990 Alberto Fujimori was elected president. The outlook was good for a free-enterprise government. In January 1991 I decided it was a strategic time to begin an exploration project in Peru, and I began an exploration project financed solely by me.

In early 1991, I made a trip to Peru and set about exploring the southern Peru copper belt. At this point, I was very much in the vanguard of foreign exploration there. I was almost the only one doing work in Peru. Although the situation was better than it had been a couple of years earlier, the country was still in a very chaotic condition. When my team began this exploration program there was a car bomb exploding on average every one to two weeks in Lima. The hotel I stayed in on my first trip was called the Hotel Condado, and before I returned the second time, it had been blown up by a car bomb and some of the clerks were killed. It was surprising that it was possible to continue doing business in Peru in spite of the political problems.

For this project, I had hired three Peruvian geologists. It was easy to get experienced exploration geologists at that time because there was a shortage of jobs and the country was in a very poverty-stricken condition. Salaries were low, and I hired everybody on the basis of salary somewhere above the going rate, plus an incentive discovery bonus, a finder's-fee type of arrangement, which appealed greatly to some of the Peruvians. Peru had been a socialistic country for the twenty years prior, and many of the people—many of the professionals—really had only a dim understanding of capitalist arrangements; finder's fees and shares and options and all that sort of thing. I paid them in U.S. dollars. (I have a 5,000,000 sol bill I acquired during that period that was equivalent to US$1.50.)

The geologists I hired were a pipeline into scuttlebutt in the industry, and we began by identifying a number of prospects in southern Peru. We investigated the literature, and we looked at and sampled and did aerial reconnaissance on a large number of prospects in the first year. We began a regional geochemical prospecting program in which teams collected wide-spaced rock, geochem samples, and stream sediment samples. This was in the north end of the Atacama Desert, and in some areas there were horses and mules available but usually not, because there wasn't enough vegetation and water to use horses.

In Chile most of the area is accessible to four-wheel-drive vehicles. In southern Peru most of the area is not accessible, for two reasons. One is that the terrain is rockier and is dissected by large *quebradas*, steep canyons. The other is that Chile is a more developed country, with a higher standard of living and more advanced government; the result of this is more road construction by the government or by private individuals. In Peru it was kind of catch-as-catch-can as far as access goes. The availability of aircraft and particularly helicopters is also poor in Peru. We used helicopters a number of times, and it was pretty obvious each time that we were risking our lives. Most of our helicopter chartering was from the Peruvian Air Force; the maintenance of the helicopters was poor, and the capability of the pilots was also uncertain.

I was actually involved in another brush with death in a helicopter in Moquegua, Peru, in the southern Peru copper belt. It was a Bell Model 212 helicopter with two turbine engines. The automatic fuel control device malfunctioned and the engines stopped, but the military pilot was able, in a matter of just a few seconds, to use a manual control and restart the helicopter. We made an emergency landing, but we had to scramble around to get transportation back to Moquegua, which took about one day in various vehicles. That malfunction, like my helicopter accident in Utah years before, was another situation in which it was questionable that autorotation would be possible. It was also at high altitude. The Chilean geologist who was with me commented that when the engines stopped "it flew like a Stillson wrench." My experience is that helicopters are very dangerous machines; I've known three people who have been killed in helicopters and quite a few others who have had experiences like mine of nonfatal crashes.

Later, a British company called Dollar Helicopters came into Peru with three high-altitude Lama Helicopters. In the course of a year all three crashed, and the company elected to leave Peru at that point. The maintenance and piloting was much better in the British company's operation, but also not conducive to a great deal of confidence.

Even though the Sendero Luminoso was by this time on the decline because of the effective efforts of the Fujimori government, there were still some areas in northern Peru that were distinctly dangerous. Our policy was to talk to the counterterrorist people in the Peruvian army. I also went to see their counterparts in the American Embassy, but they did not seem interested in helping Americans. We had one major in the Peruvian army counterterrorism branch as a contact guy we got information from. I thought about accepting the offer of the army to provide soldiers as guards in our fieldwork, but we decided that was not the most effective solution. Another North American company did accept the offer, and one of the army guards fell and his rifle went off, shooting off part of the geologist's ear.

What we actually did was send somebody to a new district in advance to talk to the storekeepers and the mayor of the town to find out if there was suspicious activity going on, and they always had a lot of information. In a couple of cases, we elected not to work in a district because of this problem. In one district, the geologist came to me after we began doing work and said, "You know, I really don't feel comfortable." They were talking to the local people, so I said, "Well, forget it. Let's go somewhere else." This happened to be a place where a geologist working for a Canadian company, maybe even on the same prospect, was killed just a short time afterward. So this was a logistical problem for our project.

Peru has a National Geological Survey. It is not as well financed as the USGS, and the geologists are probably not as well qualified on the basis of education, but it is a similar organization. A geological survey is also present in Chile, called Sernaciomin; their earlier one was called Instituto de Investigaciones Geológicas and was modeled after the USGS. Two USGS geologists spent several years in Chile helping get it started.

The Peru mining literature is surprisingly good. The Peruvian Geological Survey has published bulletins and mapped quadrangles that cover most of the part of Peru that's interesting from an exploration standpoint, and there have been various mining congresses with a number of published mining geology articles, so there is quite a bit to look at. Around 1989 or 1990 they had published a metallogenic map of Peru that is probably one of the best in the world. There is no similar map I'm familiar with in the United States, and there is not an equivalent map in Chile. The Peru metallogenic map showed all the principal known ore deposits, and all the principal known prospects were also located on the map, with a reference, which would make it possible, beginning with the map, to go back to the library and get a running start on exploration in this given district.

When my Peruvian exploration project was operating during 1991 and 1992, with cash supplied by me, there was a problem transfering $15,000 per month to Peru. I was using wire transfers to a Peruvian bank in Lima. The exchange rate at that time was about three million sols per U.S. dollar. Government regulation required that the claim-staking fees be paid in cash in sols, and the country wasn't well geared up with hundred million and billion sol notes. On one humorous occasion we needed the sol equivalent of about $25,000, which worked out to a package of currency about twenty inches long, a foot wide, and eight or ten inches thick, given to me at the bank wrapped up in newspapers and tied with twine. Peru was very unstable and crime was rampant at that time. I witnessed two robberies or attempted robberies during the 1991 to 1992 period, and it would not take a genius to translate the size of the package into value in sols. I had been dropped off with a promise to be picked up in front of the bank in fifteen minutes. I nervously left with my package, trying to look very casual. I went out the door of the bank and immediately nipped behind a large pillar about thirty inches in diameter where I could hide my package but get an eye out anxiously looking for our car. I was surprised to see a short middle-aged Peruvian woman behind the next pillar with a newspaper-wrapped package a little smaller than mine, but still large. The next eight or ten minutes passed very slowly. I remember that it was said you could arrange a murder in Mexico for $500 but in the Philippines for only $150. I wondered what the price would be in Lima. I did the mental arithmetic for how many murders $25,000 would pay for and how this would affect the strategy of a Peruvian bad guy who had seen me scuttle from the door to the pillar. With my one observation eye I tried to analyze the character of anyone who seemed to be loitering in front of the bank. Then the car arrived. I have to admit that it took very little time to get down the steps and into the car and away.

The second year of my Peruvian exploration, I took in as a partner a friend I had known for a number of years who was a mining executive. He offered to match my investment in Peru but wanted to keep his name confidential. This didn't worry me at the time, but it later became an issue after the Canadian junior company, called Arequipa Resources, was formed. One of the reporters from a Canadian scandal sheet–type mining newsletter, *Stock Watch*, made a big point of trying to find out who the partner was. It was never divulged, but there was nothing illegal or unethical about it. Our arrangement was unbelievably casual. The money was delivered to me, with no written agreement of any sort. I spent it, and my partner had confidence in my honesty and it turned out very well for him. His investment was multiplied by five hundred times! Under this new partnership, we continued the Peruvian exploration project. The steps we had begun in our first year with library research, aerial reconnaissance, geochem work, and ground geologic mapping continued. We filed claims covering prospects and did ground reconnaissance and geochem sampling. We planned to follow up with test drilling, and we did some of that, but most of it was done by major companies later, on a farmed-out basis, due to our limited finances.

Around the beginning of 1992 I had declined to form a Canadian junior company, but the money that I and the partner had put in to the Peruvian explorations project (which at that time did not have a name) began to run out later in 1992, and in 1993 I agreed that a company be formed. The structure was a private placement by several individuals in Canada and a total of $2 million Canadian was put into the new company, which would buy a 50 percent interest in my portfolio of properties in Peru. There was a provision in the arrangement that, with the agreement of both sides, a merger would later be made with Acuarios, and the other 50 percent would go into Arequipa Resources.

I didn't personally receive any of the $2 million Canadian, which at the time was about US$1.5 million. It was all spent in exploration expenses in Peru. At the time of the merger, other underwritings were done in Canada to supply additional funds.

Step by step, we began to resemble a conventional company, with secretaries, larger offices, accountants, and so forth—and with lower efficiency. The Los Calatos farm-out had been a big mistake, and our financing was never very secure. On two occasions I had to pay the payroll out of my own funds. Several times I have wondered whether the junior company was my best financing solution.

Exploration for Gold in Northern Peru and the Discovery of the Pierina Orebody

Between the 1000-kilometer-long belt of known deposits in Peru—gold-copper deposits to the north (Yanacocha and others) and copper deposits in the south (Toquepala, Los Calatos, and others)—was a long gap. I began another library research and reconnaissance project to define a gold belt in northern Peru. I identified almost all the known gold deposits in Peru on maps and noted the concentration of belts in a band north and south of Cajamarca and plotted the location of Calpuy volcanic outcrops. I then did the same sort of exercise that we had done in copper reconnaissance: doing a land status investigation to determine areas open for location and identifying the owners of the ground that was held, compiling the existing geologic reports and geology from various maps, and following up with some aerial reconnaissance. The aerial reconnaissance was not as effective in northern Peru because the area has changed from the Atacama Desert to an area with more vegetation and soil, which is not favorable for identifying by aerial reconnaissance the types of features we were looking for.

We were working on the west side of the Andes and had also shifted gears from porphyry copper geology to epithermal (low-temperature) gold geology. These bulk, low-grade gold occurrences are common in Nevada and to some extent California, but show up in various parts of the world. The Yanacocha deposit was one of these, as was Tantahuatay

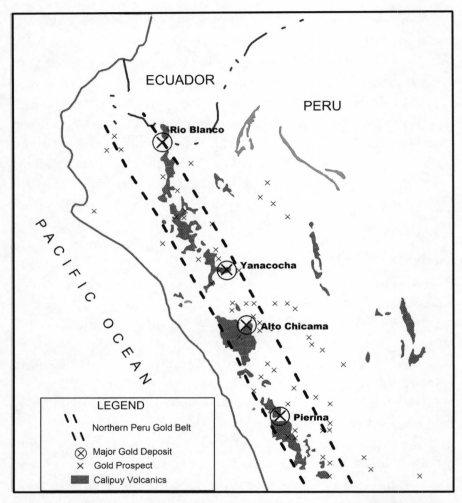

Northern Peru Gold Belt put together by David Lowell in 1994 (J. D. Lowell, 1994).

and Maqui Maqui. I was the only one in the group at that time who had any experience with epithermal gold deposits.

We moved into a district between Huaraz and Caraz, which is a graben structure, a down-faulted large block bordered by northwest-trending faults on both the east side and the west sides. This is called the Yungay Graben, or the Callejon de Huaylas valley. On the east side of the valley is the Cordillera Blanca or White Range, which contains the highest topographic point in Peru. It is called Huascarán Peak. There is also a string of glaciers and snowfields in the Cordillera Blanca. A beautiful area, it's very popular for international mountain climbers to visit, to climb some of these peaks. Huascarán has an elevation of around 22,000 feet.

There was a devastating earthquake in the Yungay Graben less than a hundred years ago. The town of Yungay was buried by a mudflow, and twenty thousand people were killed. A church steeple and some palm trees still project out of the mud. The west side of the graben is another mountain range called the Cordillera Negra or Black Range. The Cordillera Blanca is a white-looking mountain range, and the Cordillera Negra is a black-looking mountain range.

One of the geologists who worked for me had worked for Centromin, a Peruvian government corporation formed to take over the nationalized Cerro de Pasco and other mining properties. He had done work in this district for Centromin, and he pointed out hydrothermal alteration zones which were very obvious even from the highway and which occurred in both the Cordillera Blanca and the Cordillera Negra sides of the valley. The district fit precisely my preconceived model for exploring the gold belt. It was on the projection of our Northern Peru Gold Belt with large structures and abundant Calpuy volcanic outcrops. There were porphyry copper outcrops in the bottom of the graben and overlying alteration zones.

Compared with porphyry coppers, epithermal gold deposits have relatively low formation temperatures and formed nearer the surface at the time of the mineralization and have a different mineral assemblage. The exploration techniques are different. I had already had some experience with this type of exploration, so it was not a totally new problem. My previous experience with epithermal gold deposits in Nevada, California, Malaysia, the Philippines, Ecuador, and Chile had never been for more than a few days at a time, and never with the same focused effort as in my porphyry copper self-education, where I made more of an effort to understand the theoretical basis. Epithermal gold-silver deposits (the gold deposits also contain silver) are typically an order of magnitude smaller in area than porphyry coppers and more erratic and less predictable. There is some peripheral alteration zoning consisting of quartz, alunite, clay, disseminated pyrite, chlorite, and so on, but it is not as homogeneous and predictable and reliable as the porphyry alteration zones that we documented and quantified. Epithermal deposits are usually flat-tabular deposits, likely to be found at the surface or at relatively shallow depth. Porphyry deposits, on the other hand, tend to be vertical cylinder-like in shape, sometimes with a vertical dimension of as much as 20,000 feet. We use geologic mapping and broad-scale geochemical surveys and grid drilling to find porphyries. Our competitors use geophysical surveys and remote sensing, which are stylish but seldom successful. Epithermal gold exploration uses geophysics somewhat more successfully but relies mostly on close-spaced drilling and geochemical sampling and recognition of silicate alteration assemblages. Luck and persistence are the most important techniques, together with many, many drill holes.

The first deposit we visited in the Huaraz-Caraz district was called Parón, on the east side of the graben. We did some sampling and determined that there was at least a limited amount of epithermal microngold-type mineralization. We eventually negotiated a tough option deal with the owner, but the business relation with the owner was not a very happy one. We found that he had been untruthful several times in what he had told us. He was a Peruvian and a friend of Luis Montoya. This was the point where I became aware that Luis Montoya had been working both sides of the street with property owners, including the Parón owner, so I had to let him go, but this didn't interfere very much with the project. We continued to operate efficiently; in fact, much more efficiently and reliably with Norberto Socolich as Peru manager. But I was very interested in the significance of elongated hydrothermal alteration zones which related mineralization to regional structure. The known occurrence of epithermal gold mineralization at Parón became very exciting at that point. This was probably the first time that epithermal gold mineralization had been recognized in the district.

South of the Parón Mine, on the east side of the Yungay Graben, a

Norberto Socolich and Pat Hilliard on Pierina outcrop shortly after discovery.

gold prospect called California Cuatro had been found sometime before our first visit. It was a weak gold anomaly covering a relatively large area elongated in a north–south direction parallel to the graben. We negotiated an option agreement with the owner, which I believe was a small private Peruvian company, and then laid out a geochemical grid. Part of the target area was on claims we staked. The rock exposures were poor, but we did a recon geologic map and collected geochem samples. The results were not encouraging, and we gave up the prospect, but from a genetic point of view (regarding origin of the deposits) it was encouraging to find a relatively large area with low-grade gold occurring associated with silica and alunite alteration. This indirectly added encouragement to our exploration of Calpuy volcanics on the west (Pierina) side of the graben.

Also very interesting was a major archaeological site in the California Cuatro claim. It appeared to be pre-Inca age, with some massive multiton rocks built into walls. The main site appeared to be a fort, or possibly a temple, surrounded by three concentric walls. No excavation had been made and I saw no pottery shards. Unexcavated sites of this sort are common in Peru.

We had heard that a couple of major foreign companies had recently visited the Huaraz-Caraz district, which provided a time urgency in the availability of property, so on the spur of the moment I decided to do extensive and expensive claim-staking in the district. We filed claims on all the known alteration zones, which were almost all open to location. All the known gold mineralization was on the east side of the graben, in the Cordillera Blanca, but from a genetic standpoint, the west side contained a dozen large alteration zones and a number of mineral occurrences, and also looked permissive for the occurrence of epithermal gold deposits, so I elected to file claims covering all the alteration zones on both sides of the graben.

Parón was on the east side, in the flank of the Cordillera Blanca. Pierina was on the west side, in the Cordillera Negra. The elevation at Parón was about 4,000 meters or 14,500 feet. At that time I was in my late sixties, and I found it pretty strenuous to climb the hills at 4,000 meter elevation. There was a road almost to the Parón deposit, but some of our other prospects on the east side of the valley were only accessible by foot or on horses. We eventually found three occurrences of epithermal mineralization on the slope of Cordillera Blanca in a northwest–southeast belt, and we had a continuous line of claims about 40 kilometers long in the Cordillera Blanca belt. We did surface sampling and mapping at Parón and later had a small drilling project with a hand-carried diamond drill. We found that the grade at depth was significantly lower than at the surface and that the deposit was a manto-type occurrence, a subhorizontal tabular deposit, and we gave up our option. Part of the reason for not continuing was the business difficulties we had encountered with the owner.

There were three of us, Rigoberto Soto, Fredy Huanqui, and me, working out of the helicopter, covering, on wide-spaced points, the entire Huaraz-Caraz district. We got some anomalous samples, and the next step was a follow-up program of ground-checking the anomalous samples, and some of the alteration zones were of interest because of the existence of other known mineral deposits. This work was during 1994, and near the end of 1994 we chartered a high-altitude Lama helicopter operated by the British company Dollar Helicopter. We took a few wide-spaced samples in every one of the alteration zones. These were calibration samples to get an idea about the distribution of mineralization. We had our analytical work done in Lima, in a couple of Peruvian labs, and we sent pulp samples to Bonder-Clegg in Vancouver, Canada, via FedEx, and they faxed back the results. We had a turnaround time of a week to ten days.

Two samples were anomalous in silver and zinc; neither of these was our target metal, gold, but these elements are often associated with epithermal gold deposits. These samples were north of an abandoned mine called Santo Toribio. Santo Toribio is about eight miles from and almost due west of the town of Huaraz, a sizable community of 60,000 people. During the next several months we held the claims we had staked, but we didn't get back to the regional reconnaissance. We did a BLEG survey, a type of regional gold stream sediment geochemistry that was developed in Australia. We didn't find any BLEG anomalies that turned out to be significant.

In the summer of 1995 I felt that our fieldwork was not going as fast and as systematically as I had hoped, so I decided to add another geologist, a gringo from North America, to the Peruvian staff. His name is Pat Hillard. Pat is a loner type who has a large tolerance for unpleasant living conditions and mountain climbing. He had done a lot of work in Papua New Guinea, Spain, and Patagonia in South America, and is a good exploration geologist. When Pat arrived on our project in August of that year, I asked him to push the follow-up surface work for the claims that had been staked in alteration zones. At the top of the list I gave Pat to work on were the samples in the vicinity of Santo Toribio, which I thought were somewhat more interesting than any of the other weakly anomalous samples. Pierina is on the west side of the graben. Pat worked with Fredy Huanqui. Although their stories differ on how they

Access road to Pierina orebody being bult by local community members.
Employment was rotated among five communities in order to provide some
money for each group.

actually found the first anomalous gold samples on the Pierina claim,
I'm certain they did it by hiking and riding on horseback long distances
and systematically collecting wide-spaced samples and looking at the
rocks as Pat reported.

I was on the outcrop of the Pierina orebody shortly afterward,
which was very interesting because it was very nondescript looking,
kind of a gray, gnarly, siliceous rock outcrop; but, looked at closely, it
had epithermal vuggy silica texture. There wasn't a pit or an adit or a
cut or evidence that a geology hammer had ever broken a rock on the
outcrop. It was a totally virgin outcrop, which is very unusual. This was
because the gold grains were micron size (one-millionth of a meter),
and the gold could not have been panned by an Inca prospector or a
Spanish prospector or a Peruvian prospector, and the outcrop had never
been previously found, contrary to what Fredy Huanqui and others
later suggested.

There was an area about 400 by 600 meters of strongly anomalous gold mineralization. The first sampling indicated a gold grade averaging about 1.6 grams per metric ton, which is above minimum bulk low-grade gold mining grade, which at that time was usually about 1 gram. In my experience surface grade is not a reliable indication of the grade at depth, because gold can either be leached out of the surface by a solvent such as humic acid, or it can be enriched at the surface by the physical concentration of gold as erosion planes down the original deposit. My experience in other parts of the world suggested that the second process is more common than the first: that it's more likely you'll find better surface grade than what is present at shallow depth, but it could be either way. By trial and error, I had determined that the best first-stage exploration technique in the Andes was to make hand-dug pits deep enough to get below this surface effect. So I insisted that some pits be made. By this time, it was late in the fall. Fourteen wide-spaced pits, about one and a half meters deep, were dug, and the samples were sent out shortly before the Christmas vacation. The results came in on December 28, 1995, and I happened to be the only person in our whole group working at that time.

I was in Arizona when I received the assay return by fax. The fourteen samples averaged about 7 grams of gold, or more than four times the grade at the surface! I made a copy of the assay return and wrote a penciled note on it that said, "Pat, do you believe this?" I faxed it to him and he was just as surprised as I was. We both thought that was probably an assay error. As soon as our fellows went back to work after New Year's Day, I sent them back to resample the pits. The second set of assays came back the same as the first. We then did a detailed pitting of the outcrop area, and we dug ninety-two pits. They were dug deeper, all a minimum of two meters deep. Those came back with pretty much the same grade. They averaged between 6 and 7 grams, and there was only one pit that was below 1 gram. This is unusual because gold mineralization is usually very erratic.

We could still work in the winter, but found the climatic obstacle was rain, not snow. The bottom of the snow line was around 4,500

Driving one of the two Pierina adits in 1996. These adits exposed a third dimension of the orebody before exploration drilling was possible.

meters (15,000 feet), but December through mid-April is a heavy rain season that interferes with road building and, to some extent, with diamond drilling. So in January 1996, when we realized that this was very probably a major gold deposit, we couldn't begin road building until April or May. However, in this district there was cheap hand labor and also good small-scale mining expertise, so I arranged a contract with a small contractor in Caraz to drive two adits, which we called Tunnel 1 and Tunnel 2.

Access to the site at that time was by horseback and by foot, and the contractor got a small air compressor there by hiring forty Quechua Indians who towed it with ropes. We began driving the two tunnels about the beginning of February 1996. The advance was good, considering the rock conditions and the access problems. One of the tunnels eventually went in a distance of 176 meters (577 feet). We assayed the rock on one-meter intervals as the tunnels were driven. They were both in continuous ore-grade mineralization. Both of them averaged 5 to 6 grams of gold, which is high-grade bulk gold ore.

At the same time, we were putting in the pits and arranging for road building to begin at the end of the rainy season. Using hand labor, we had a road completed in late May. At that time, drilling equipment was hard to contract in Peru, and there was a shortage of drill machines. We had one drill contractor who performed very badly and had to be replaced with a second one, and we eventually completed nine drill holes on wide spacing.

Early in the exploration work I laid out a possible future mine in order to have some idea where and how big an area might be required for pit, waste dumps, leach pads, precipitation plant, pregnant solution ponds, and camps. These estimates weren't very accurate in detail, but overall they were pretty good. Surface rights had to be negotiated with five different Indian communities. We began right away with a community relations program, which involved fixing the roofs on a number of churches and building pipelines from springs for drinking water. With the intention of putting money into the communities, we devised a work plan of using hand labor instead of mechanized equipment to build roads and drill sites. The plan involved rotation of workers from each of the five communities so some money flowed into every family. We got along very well with the indigenous folks.

Unfortunately, at the Pierina site we were unable to get the geologic mapping done up to my standards for a drilling project. But the mapping really should be done before the drill sites and the drill access roads were completed. In the beginning of June, I finally lost patience with my guys working on the mapping and laid out a pattern of drill sites on hundred-meter grid spacing. This was a 333-foot-square grid between drill sites, which was a revolutionary way to drill epithermal gold deposits, because they normally have an erratic nature and the holes have to be closer together and based on detailed mapping. I judged, based on the continuity of the mineralization that had shown up in the surface samples, pit samples, and adits, that this was an unusual sort of deposit and that we could go to wide spacing. The decision to proceed with this approach was predicated in part on limited financing and time urgency. The terrain we covered was mainly a

Pierina in 1997 after Barrick Gold development.

steep slope ranging from 4,000 to 4,500 meters. The grid was based on horizontal distances, but of course going uphill the collar elevations of holes varied considerably. In any case, we were able to build these drill sites and get a total of nine holes completed, all but one of which intersected ore.

Most of the holes were vertical holes, although I think a couple of inclined holes were in that group. Eight of the nine holes had significant ore intercepts. But the geologic mapping turned out to be a very large obstacle. It was hard to do and required some background knowledge of epithermal geology, which none of the geologists had. In any case, the game of going to a broad-spaced grid of holes probably resulted in a very significant increase in the sale price of Arequipa Resources when Barrick made a hostile takeover a short time later. If the drill spacing had been fifty meters, for example, in the limited time and drilling capability we had, we would have been able to develop only one-fourth as many tons of reserves, and Barrick's offer might have been hundreds of millions of dollars lower.

I concluded afterward that I had made a mistake in not moving to Huaraz myself for the several months of the drilling project, but I thought that I would be able to do it by remote control from Arizona. In the early stages of corporate organization I had appointed a Canadian engineer I had known for a long time, Henry Ewanchuk, to be president and run the office in Vancouver. In a way, Hank had the same problem the gringo geologists had of not really understanding how to operate in Latin America. He had had a very successful career in exploration and mine management in Canada. He is a very competent person and had been president of Bethlehem Gold and other Canadian companies, but he was at a handicap in Latin America. Catherine (Katie) McLeod Seltzer, whom I had met some years before, had a little understanding of the problems of Latin America operations after her tour in Chile, but she had had no mining experience. Her father had been a miner, not an engineer or geologist, and she had grown up in Canadian mining camps and listened to mine talk at the dinner table all her life. After Arequipa Resources' first year of existence, I asked her to take over as president in Vancouver, in charge of company shareholder and government regulation work. I had the title of chairman of Arequipa and managed all the Peruvian activities.

The legal code in Latin America is Napoleonic law, which says you're guilty until proven innocent and that a verbal agreement has no basis in law. Not even a written letter of agreement is valid: it has to be an agreement that is rewritten and recorded by a *notario*, who is a lawyer and is basically an officer of the court. The other dimension of difficulty for gringos working in Latin America is that the philosophy, ethics, and customs of Latin Americans are much different than those of Anglo-Saxons. This is a fundamental difference. This is not to say that Americans are honest and Chileans are dishonest; you could almost make an argument on the other side. But in doing business, it's quite a different ball game.

At times we made verbal agreements with property owners and followed up with a letter saying, "We'll just write out these terms. That's a $20,000 payment on signing and $50,000 at the end of a year, and

$200,000 at the end of two years." If we agreed, he said yes, so we both signed the letter. This was a mutual agreement. Then we would turn this over to a lawyer to write up and record an agreement, and the property owner might then say, "Well, you know, I believe that this agreement should say a $50,000 down payment, and I believe the agreement should say a 4 percent net smelter return royalty." The lawyer and we would say, "Well, gosh, Pablo, you signed this other thing." He would say, "Yes, but I talked to my brother-in-law and he said he didn't think that was really very fair. Take it or leave it. I'll have to have $50,000." This, in part, is related to Napoleonic law, where to be valid it has to be written and recorded. No baloney about "his word is his bond." Hank Ewanchuk wasn't able to understand this very well and might say, "Well, this guy is a damn crook, and I sure don't want to be any part of dealing with him. What do I tell the shareholders?" But in Rome, do as the Romans do. You have to understand the philosophy of the people. Your letter of agreement is worthless.

Earlier I mentioned the story about the lawyer who took a bribe in order to give our property to Andronico Luksic. When I talked to the

---

David De Witt

Dave De Witt came well recommended, and I hired him to represent me personally when I faced having to swim with the sharks, and I agreed to be CEO of my first Canadian junior mining company, Arequipa Resources, in 1993. He did save me and he was later available to save me again with the second company that had a less competent and more problem-prone board of directors. Dave dropped everything and flew to meet me in Taipei, Taiwan, in 2007 when I received a call from Chinalco that they were ready to buy Toromocho. I feel that Dave and his family are more like close family members than just friends.

other Chilean lawyers, they said, "Boy, he's really a crook. We'll agree to that. But there's no question of disbarring him or having him charged with a crime." That may, in a nutshell, be the difference.

Katie did a good job in Canada. The operations in Peru were entirely under my management, while she did most of the corporate part—communication with shareholders and prospective shareholders, negotiation with underwriting companies for financing, filing reports with the securities commissions, going on road shows to visit prospective investors, and attending trade shows. She probably talked to hundreds of financial institutions. Shares in Arequipa Resources were held mostly by institutions—retirement funds, banks, mutual funds, and the like. The percentage owned by individuals was relatively small. Katie was also very helpful in negotiating joint venture agreements, but this sometimes backfired, as at Los Calatos, and in retrospect I should have disregarded some of her advice. That's how the corporate part worked. I didn't throw my weight around much in the corporate part until the last weeks of the Pierina story.

On one occasion Katie and I were in England together talking to representatives of several institutions. One was Harry Oppenheimer, who headed a large mining empire including the De Beers Group. We met in his paneled office and he had a lunch brought in, but I had to give a talk about Arequipa and was too tense to enjoy the lunch. One of his engineers had visited Pierina, and Mr. Oppenheimer offered to invest $10 million, but we decided it would be awkward to have a major as a relatively small minority partner and we declined. Oppenheimer invited us to visit the De Beers Diamond Company display room in the same building. We were shown the diamonds by an elegant English gentleman with no sign of security (although there must have been elaborate measures). We saw hundreds of millions of dollars' worth of diamonds, including the largest in the world of some classes and colors, mostly loose so that they could be handled. The manager passed Katie a cupful of large cut stones, and she let the gems dribble through her fingers into a plate. I watched closely to be sure they all ended up on the plate! There was one uncut diamond the size of a small hen's egg from which, when you held it against your cheek, you could feel the unusual rapid-heat-transfer property of diamonds.

Our policy regarding Pierina was that we probably would not end up developing the mine ourselves; we would end up as a partner in development by a major company or would sell the deposit or the company to a major company. For that reason, before we started to drill we invited everybody who was interested to visit the prospect. Around forty mining companies sent teams to look at it, because it was pretty obvious that the Pierina site was going to be an important gold mine. We had good surface sample information, and we had a third dimension represented by the two adits that I had had driven into the mountain. It was an ideal spot for people to inspect because they could go collect their own samples in the pits and in the adits. When we began drilling we stopped the visits to the project because of the insider information problem.

We weren't allowing companies to visit the drilling operation, but we were announcing the drill results as they came in, which excited the prospective investors, and the price of the stock went up from about $1 a share to over $30 a share when nine holes were completed. The stock had originally been on the Vancouver exchange, but it was later listed on the Toronto exchange, which is a more conservative and prestigious exchange. With nine holes completed, we had an annual meeting for stockholders. The share price was about $32. I gave a fifteen-minute talk about the results of the exploration. I had insisted that we be conservative in all our announcements, and my talk was relatively conservative. There were a number of brokers in the audience, and I noticed that they started getting up and leaving. Fifteen to thirty minutes afterward, Katie told me she had heard that our stock had dropped from $32 to $15. I had expected it would go up because it was good news, but it was good news presented in a reasonably conservative way, and the Canadian stock fraternity assumed that everybody was going to lie and exaggerate. The stock soon went back up.

On another occasion in July 1996 the events were even more dramatic. I usually traveled with Katie on these road shows; I believe we twice traveled to England and once to France, as we had shareholders in both countries. On this occasion we went to talk to the Royal Bank of Canada, which was one of our shareholders, and several other mutual funds and brokerage houses in Toronto. These were really exhausting trips. We might have eight meetings in one day. This time, we had had some meetings the day before, and we had a breakfast meeting with one of these groups in the King Edward Hotel where we were both staying. Before the meeting we got a call from Bill Biggar, vice president in charge of finance for Barrick Gold Company. Barrick at that time was the largest gold producer in North America and the second or third largest in the world. It is now the largest in the world.

Bill Biggar asked if he could talk to us. We told him our schedule was completely filled up. He said, "How about breakfast?" And we said, "We're having breakfast with so-and-so." He said, "Where are you having breakfast?" We said, "In the Prince Edward Hotel." He said, "Well, it won't take very long. Could we meet you in the lobby when you come out from breakfast?" We said, "Yes." We thought that was a little bit odd. In the lobby after breakfast we found Bill Biggar and Alan Hill. Alan Hill was vice president in charge of development for Barrick. Bill Biggar, who is more suave than Alan, was the spokesman. He said, "Well, could we sit down here in the lobby in a place that's a little bit private?" We sat down, and he said, "I don't know exactly how to tell you this, but we have launched a hostile takeover for Arequipa Resources. We have offered to buy all the shares of Arequipa Resources for twenty-seven dollars Canadian per share."

Barrick Launches a "Hostile" Takeover

And, he said, "Peter Munk wanted me to tell you that this is technically a hostile takeover, but we actually want it to be as friendly as possible." Peter Munk was the chairman and CEO of Barrick. The success of their takeover depended on more than 50 percent of our shareholders accepting the offer. This immediately presented a huge problem for me because if we advised the shareholders to accept the offer and it turned out that the deposit was really worth forty dollars a share instead of the twenty-seven, our shareholders could sue us for having been incompetent. On the other hand, if we advised the shareholders not to accept $27 and that turned out to be a generous offer and it killed the deal, then they could sue us for incompetence in that direction. As chairman of Arequipa Resources, I was in the hot seat for the first time. Bill Biggar said Peter Munk, who was a legendary figure, had said he would be happy to talk to us that morning.

Our lawyer was with us on this trip, but I have always been a little bit suspicious of lawyers and I said, "I don't want a lawyer along. I want to make this an informal conversation." So we met with Peter Munk, and he brought in Bob Smith, who was president of Barrick at the time, and we discussed the Barrick offer. It was a very friendly, amicable conversation. Peter Munk said, "The thing I admire most about you is your insisting that no lawyers be present."

We then called a meeting of the board of directors of Arequipa Resources, who had been almost totally inactive in the company until then; there were several directors who had very responsible mining jobs. One of them was Tony Petrina, who had been CEO of Placer Dome Company; another was Chet Idziszek, president of a substantial Canadian company. We had an immediate meeting of the directors by conference call on the telephone, and then convened a face-to-face meeting in Vancouver of everyone who could be present. There were seven directors altogether, including Katie and me. As a group, we decided that we might squeeze more than $27 out of Barrick, so we advised the shareholders not to accept the $27 and not to tender their shares to Barrick.

I immediately launched an intensive drilling campaign to try to drill as many holes and develop as many tons of ore as possible before the time ran out for this hostile takeover. The time frame was prescribed by regulations in the Toronto Stock Exchange or the Ontario Securities Commission. It was about thirty-five days. This fast-track drilling was a risky move, because we were not sure the ore was there, but we succeeded in completing forty holes before the deadline, and all but one intersected ore. When the deadline neared, we had another directors meeting in Toronto. We had hired the top corporate lawyer for mergers in Canada, with three or four law firms involved by this time. I had retained one of these expensive lawyers to represent me personally because of this liability issue. Our directors meeting lasted about four days. On one occasion we met for fourteen hours without eating anything. It was very stressful stuff. At that point, I took over firmly as manager of the directors' activities because I had the legal liability myself. We were getting messages about what various friends of friends had reported that the Barrick people were doing, and there were various little clues as to whether they might increase their offer or not.

We were meanwhile receiving counteroffers from other major companies; a total of six companies had made proposals. The biggest perceived threat to Barrick was Placer Dome, whose head office is in Vancouver. Our chief guru, David Jackson, was a lawyer in Toronto—an elderly, white-haired, overbearing sort of guy, but very smart. In the middle of one of these sessions, in the middle of a sentence, he said, "I think we should all go, right now, to Vancouver and continue the meeting there, and Barrick will think that Placer Dome is about to close a deal with us." This was partly true, but not entirely. So we decided on the spur of the moment to move our directors meetings from Toronto to our little company office in Vancouver. We checked airline schedules and rushed to our hotels and grabbed our suitcases and checked out of the hotels. It's a fairly long trip to Vancouver. We flew to Vancouver and got started again with the meeting in our office.

In the meantime, we were getting under-the-counter communiqués from the Placer Dome office. Placer Dome had called a spur-of-the-moment directors meeting that week because of this Pierina deal. One of their directors had come all the way from Australia, and some had come from the United States, and Placer was having their meeting. We got under-the-counter reports from somebody in Placer's office about who had arrived and what the rumor was that they were doing. They were probably getting under-the-counter news about us.

David Jackson said, "I predict that Barrick will show up here tomorrow." I thought this was taking a lot for granted. We started our meeting early in the morning. We were really kind of frantic. We didn't know what would be the best thing to do. I got a phone call at about 7 a.m. and the voice on the other end of the line was slightly garbled. "Hello, David? This is Bob Smith." I said, "Hello, Bob, where are you?" He said, "Well, I'm on our corporate jet, and we're going to arrive in Vancouver in forty-five minutes." The Barrick group had left in the middle of the night and flown to Vancouver. So then we had another meeting, and Placer Dome was said to be agonizing about a counter-offer, but we had not heard from them.

Consummating a Billion-Dollar Takeover

We had a meeting then with Barrick in their hotel. The meeting was just between Bob Smith, Katie, and me. We talked for a couple of hours, and he offered to raise the offer to $30 from $27. Katie and I had a little huddle, and I said, "Okay." The $30 translated into a little over $1 billion Canadian. Bob Smith, when we shook hands and left, said, "Well, Catherine, thanks a million." And she said, "No, Bob, thanks a billion." That was the end of the Arequipa story. The crash drilling project probably added $100 million or more to the sale price. The shareholders signed up at just about 100 percent. I later did some consulting work for Barrick and took two trips to Pierina in a Barrick jet.

We had an option to receive part of the payment in Barrick stock, and Barrick asked me to do that. They didn't demand that I do it, but they said it would be helpful to them if my particular ownership was in the form of cash plus Barrick shares because it would help, image wise. It would be a vote of confidence in Barrick. I did that, but I soon after-ward sold the shares, which turned out to be a lucky break because gold stocks went down after I sold.

I was a director of the project for a couple of months, but this was only a temporary arrangement. I participated a little bit, but in a very minor way, in the planning of their work in Peru. I think they did a very good job on the mine development. The mine went into produc-tion quickly. The first gold was poured in November or December of

1998, which is some kind of a record for speed in a large mine of this sort. The production costs of the gold were by far the lowest of any large gold mine in the world. It cost less than $50 an ounce to produce the gold. The total reserves were about eight million ounces. Barrick calculated that their purchase price would result in a break-even operation at three and a half million ounces, so it turned out to be very profitable for them.

When Barrick finally purchased Arequipa Resources, including the Pierina deposit and all other prospects owned by the company, in August of 1996, there were still some loose ends to tie down. The Barrick contract included a two-year consulting retainer for me at a high, sweetheart consulting daily rate. I initially did not understand that this was really a noncompetition arrangement. I had been happily planning to tell Barrick's exploration department what they were doing wrong, but didn't have that opportunity. And everybody lived happily ever after.

A little postscript to the Arequipa story: Because of our finder's fees arrangement, the Arequipa Pierina discovery and the sale to Barrick created quite a number of millionaires in our group. I think the total was seven or more people who worked in Arequipa and finished up with a windfall profit. One of them was Katie McLeod. She ended up with a big house on a golf course in Vancouver, with her very nice husband, two sons, and a Labrador retriever. She became director of a number of different Canadian companies and CEO of one. She was recognized in the *Financial Post* as one of Canada's most powerful women. I had a windfall but it actually didn't really change my standard of living or affect my life too much. Some aspects of it have been fun and some kind of worrisome, but it was an exciting experience.

Fredy Huanqui, who had claimed he had known for years that Pierina was a large high-grade orebody, elaborated a little after high-grade assays began to come back. His story changed to his having named the claim where the orebody was located, and the orebody itself, after his daughter, Pierina. As it happened, the Pierina claim was several kilometers away and contained no gold ore, but someone in the Peru office, believing Fredy, started calling the deposit "the Pierina orebody," and the name stuck.

Katie McLeod had a friend named Joey Freeze who had the credentials (as had I and lots of other geologists and engineers) to sign 43-101 reports, a sort of government certification of the discovery. Katie asked me if it was okay to use Joey to write and sign the 43-101 report, and I agreed. We gave Joey all the data and she did no fieldwork and rewrote it as a 43-101. She then claimed credit in a newspaper for the discovery! Neither Pat Hillard nor I knew of any contribution whatsoever that she made to the project. Such is human nature.

A couple of years after Pierina went into production I was in Lima working on another project when I received a phone call in my hotel room. It was from a lawyer in the law firm representing Barrick in Peru, and he told me a long complicated story involving a Peruvian geologist who had worked for me but had been terminated before the Pierina discovery. The story was that the family of the owner of the Parón property, which we optioned and drilled, had told Barrick they also owned a majority interest in the Pierina orebody. My former employee also testified that this was true, and gave a detailed account of a meeting (which never took place) in which I was said to have participated. They had a signed agreement. The story was that I had admitted that I didn't know much about the geology of the Yungay Graben. They said the prospect owner (who was not an engineer or geologist) did know there was a very large gold deposit (Pierina), which he had not bothered to stake; that he had given me the location; and that I, in turn, had given him a majority interest in the property, which his family was now willing to sell to Barrick for about a billion dollars. However, he had died by this time. Barrick prepared an affidavit, which I signed the next day, saying all this was untrue, as it was. However, the property owner's son was a lawyer, and he and my former employee had crafted a clever story that they thought would hold up to produce a substantial payment from Barrick. The legal wrangle dragged on for about a year, and periodically the legal firm would update me. They had brought in an expert who had determined that the signatures had been forged. They had had the case transfered from the civil court to the criminal court, but there had still been no clear resolution.

Our sale contract with Barrick required us to give Barrick our Arequipa Resources files. The files in Vancouver were transfered and our lawyer's files were turned over to Barrick, but I had kept my own files, which were in poor condition and were largely rough drafts and geologic reports. As it happened, Barrick had lost all of the two sets of files we sent them. When the fraud developed I went through my files, but found nothing pertinent. But I have a custom of burning files five years out-of-date in a bonfire. One of these burning dates came up, and we assembled twelve boxes of dead files next to the bonfire site and started the fire. I personally fed in the file folders for a last check, and on this occasion I noticed several folders which might relate to Barrick's problem and set them aside. After the file burning was completed I looked at the papers I had saved, and to my surprise and delight found a signed, smoking-gun letter, which I then sent to the Lima law firm. I hoped this would result in getting the lawyer and the geologist a lot of time in jail, but in Peru you never knew. In any case, it was a satisfaction to help Barrick, who had treated us fairly.

Over the years, I have found that there are usually loose strings connected with a major discovery, and people trying to steal some of either the credit or the money. In the case of Pierina, it was both.

Doctor Honoris Causa at Universidad Nacional Mayor de San Marcos, Peru

I had worked a lot in Peru during the period when there was a great deal of Sendero Luminoso (the Shining Path terrorist organization) activity going on. When I began my project in 1991, we were able to do our fieldwork and other activities with a fair degree of confidence.

The Sendero Luminoso had become pretty insignificant in Peru as a terrorist problem around 1993, but I have noticed in other Latin American countries that it's a fairly easy transition for an idealistic, Communist terrorist to become a practical capitalist bandit, and there are a lot of those in Peru and lots of robberies and quite a few kidnap-

Doctor Honoris Causa ceremony in Lima, August 14, 1998. From left, two University deans who are members of the *claustro,* David Lowell, and Rector of Universidad Nacional Mayor de San Marcos, oldest university in the new world, formed in 1551.

A toast to David Lowell at Universidad Nacional Mayor de San Marcos, Peru, ceremony.

David breaking bottle of wine at Universidad Nacional Mayor de San Marcos ceremony inaugurating the construction of new classrooms.

pings. During one of my visits to Peru, a gentleman I had met who was president of the Hochschild company was murdered and his son kidnapped the day before I arrived in Lima.

In 1998, when Edith and I traveled to Lima for me to receive an honorary degree, a Doctor Honoris Causa, from the Universidad Nacional Mayor de San Marcos in Lima, I realized that I might be a prime target. It occurred to me because the honorary degree had gotten newspaper publicity, and lots of people in Peru knew that I had collected a large amount of money from the sale of the Arequipa Resources company. So for the first time in my life, I lined up a Peruvian security firm to furnish cars and security planning and some bodyguards to accompany myself and Edith in the trips around Lima for the two days we were there. It was probably unnecessary, but I think it was a wise thing to do under the circumstances.

They insisted on giving me the academic robe, and the ceremony involved a colored ribbon and a medallion hung around your neck which makes you a member of the university *claustro*. It's called a clois-

In 1997 shortly after the 1996 sale of Pierina to Barrick Gold, from which
he received a substantial payment, David decided to make a contribution
to Peruvian mining through the Escuela de Minas of the Universidad
Nacional Mayor de Marcos. The donation of US$200,000 produced four new
classrooms and an administration office. A second donation a few years later
added more classrooms and an auditorium partly built with student labor.
This obelisk dedicated to David was included.

ter in English; *claustro* in Spanish. Edith, who is better informed about
things like this than I am, said that it had a kind of a religious group
connotation. In the conversation in the ceremony, they said something
that indicated that now that I was a member of a claustro, I could participate in similar ceremonies as one of the robed, serious-looking gentlemen standing in a row. I received a diploma or certificate on parch-
ment, certifying me as being Doctor Honoris Causa, and there were
lots of photographs taken by three professional photographers. It was a
very exciting experience.

Election to the National Academy of Engineering

In 1999 I was elected to the National Academy of Engineering in Washington, DC. It was different in that I was not required to give a talk. I also found that 40 percent of the NAE membership was from academia, and these were delighted to have the honor and to participate in NAE activities, and 60 percent from industry. Many from industry had research and development backgrounds, and most of the members had PhDs. I felt after getting acquainted with a lot of members that they were bright, competent people. The mission of the NAE is to offer advice to the United States Congress by way of reports.

2000 Society of Economic Geologists Exchange Lecture Tour in Australia

In 1999 I was nominated to be the 2000 Society of Economic Geologists Exchange Lecturer. I was allowed to select the country in which to lecture and I selected Australia, where I had worked twice and where I felt at home. Professor Pat Williams from the James Cook University arranged my visit to Townsville, New South Wales, where the university is located. He devoted hundreds of hours and made at least a hundred phone calls organizing the details for a fast, smooth-running itinerary that included a total of fourteen lectures in eleven sites. Bill Lacy, who for several years was head of the Geological Engineering Department at the University of Arizona and passed away in January 2014, had participated at James Cook University in putting together the "Professional Masters" program, encouraging graduate engineers and geologists to return to a university to study on a part-time basis to earn an MS degree and become "retreaded" with modern computer and other skills. A decade or more later, in company with Mary Poulton and Mark Barton, I participated in transplanting this idea to the Lowell Institute of Mineral Resources at the University of Arizona. Bill Lacy's son, John Lacy, is a mining lawyer in Tucson and a personal friend.

The Exchange Lectureship was successful in talks at twelve Australian universities, as well as one in Tasmania and one in New Zealand. I had been advised that the talks would be easy using a Power Point presentation, which had recently been developed. The combination of my poor computer skills and the variety of projectors available caused mechanical problems in most of my talks, but the Australians were very forgiving and totally hospitable.

CHAPTER TWO

Zamora River Project in Ecuador, 1999–2014

In about 1980, I had a joint venture exploration project in Arizona with Billiton (the minerals arm of Shell Oil Company). Shortly after Arequipa Resources was sold, I was approached by Billiton, which had carried out several years of grassroots exploration in the Zamora River district of southeastern Ecuador. The access was very difficult, and there are no roads in much of the area, which is Amazon jungle, with high rainfall, very steep terrain, and a variety of poisonous snakes. Shuar Indians inhabited much of the exploration area; historically, these tribes had been headhunters and headshrinkers, with the last record of this activity in 1987.

Billiton had operated too much like a big company, with lots of different varieties of geophysical, remote sensing, and geostatistical studies. They were overstaffed with high-salaried expatriates, but in spite of all this they had done a pretty good exploration job and had found three large Jurassic-age copper-molybdenum porphyry deposits. Unfortunately the deposits were a little subcommercial, considering access problems and the metal prices of 1997. Billiton proposed that I take over management of the Zamora River Project. We first talked about my finding financing for the project and I declined, but in retrospect, I probably should have organized a new junior company and done this. Their second offer was that if Corriente Resources, another

Canadian junior company that had some cash but had never found a mine, would finance the exploration, I would manage the exploration and the ownership would be split three ways. We all agreed on the second alternative. This turned out to be an important error on my part.

I interviewed the staff and decided not to keep any of the expatriates but to hire Luis Quevedo, an Ecuadorian who was a second-level supervisor in the Billiton Project. Luis had a local engineering degree plus an MS from a British university. He was smart and hardworking, and a competent explorationist. However, the Ecuadorian geologists he hired were less capable. We leased two 4x4 pickups and bought some exploration equipment and got some from Billiton. In the early part of our project I visited fifteen or twenty areas with Luis—all the mineralized prospects that had been identified by Billiton.

The Warintza Discovery in Ecuador

I began a screening process to prioritize the explorations, which eventually narrowed the list down to two areas. The one called Warintza was attractive to me because although little work had yet been done, there was evidence of at least some chalcocite mineralization suggesting secondary enrichment and higher-grade ore than that yet found by Billiton. The second deposit was a large area with no known orebody, but which contained disseminated pyrite and quartz sericite hydrothermal alteration. There were also some small gold vein occurrences and some larger areas anomalous in disseminated gold, but well below commercial grade. We called this area Mirador.

We began in the Warintza district, and the topography was a very difficult obstacle. There was heavy, two- and three-canopy jungle cover and very steep terrain, sometimes inclined 60 to 80 degrees. In our best-looking area there were two *quebradas* (steep canyons) that we named after staff members, and I, with great expenditure of effort, managed to climb up a third by holding on to tree roots and climbing up a creek bottom so steep it was really more of a waterfall. Luis named this one Quebrada David. Gradually, over a period of months, we defined an area with chalcocite mineralization, but we didn't have a clear under-

David Lowell at the Warintza Project, Ecuador, in 2000. A trail has been dug into jungle floor and exposes copper and molybdenum ore.

standing of the geometry of the deposit because of the jungle cover. At this point we organized a drilling project with a British Columbian drilling company called Kluane International Inc.

Kluane sent in two Canadian drillers, a man-portable drill rig, and camping gear. There was a grass airstrip 400 meters long (later lengthened by us to 500 meters) in the Shuar village of Warintza, about six or seven kilometers from our drill area. There was no road connection to Warintza village, but the town of Macas was about thirty kilometers by air from Warintza. From Macas there was slightly uncertain scheduled air service from Quito. There was also a Jesuit order that operated a charter air service to many small churches or missions such as Warintza that had small airstrips. The bishop was the air service manager, and there were about three short-field aircraft, all Helio Curriers, a super-short-field six-passenger airplane that had gone out of production ten or twenty years earlier. The Jesuit order had found a place—it might have been in Atlanta, Georgia—that rebuilt Helio Curriers. The pilots I flew with were all Ecuadorians but were held to strict rules by the bishop and were good pilots.

Our fuel, repair parts, food, and mail came in first to Macas, then by charter flight to Warintza, then were hand carried or sometimes carried by mules to the drilling project. The final two kilometers climbed about six hundred vertical meters. The heaviest piece of the Kluane drill rig weighed 1,600 pounds, which was about the maximum cargo weight for the small plane, and was hand carried by sixteen Shuars to the drill site.

The drill rig was a diamond core rig that used special thin-walled drill rods. It was hydraulic powered, with the power coming from a small gasoline- or diesel-powered pump. If the hole was deeper than about 400 meters, the drillers used two pumps in series to increase the hydraulic pressure. The drillers operated with two twelve-hour shifts and camped miserably in a small nylon tent, often in driving rain. The penetration rate of the drill was good and the core recovery was good. Our deepest hole was about 500 meters deep. I have nothing but admiration for both the air service and the drilling operation.

Corriente Resources did not participate in the geology or exploration, but had some control by periodically cutting off funds, which significantly hurt the effectiveness of the project; for this reason they were not good associates. We managed to drill about thirty holes which indicated a little less than 100 million tonnes of 0.9 to 1 percent copper equivalent ore which included both copper and molybdenum. At a lower cutoff the deposit contains about 200 million tonnes of copper equivalent to 0.7 percent mineable ore. The surface exposures gave us hope that this reserve could be doubled if we could get permission from the Shuar and the Peruvian government to finish the project.

There were many little interludes in the Warintza Project: reversals of policy by the national government; reversals of Shuar acceptance of agreements; attacks by Shuars. The first attack by the Shuars was supposed to be a two-pronged attack on the Panantza Camp (one of Billiton's original submarginal deposits) and on our camp. The Indians made the mistake, however, of arranging the logistics for the attack by fax, and we got a copy of the fax and arranged to have eight heavily armed policemen protecting the camp at Panantza when the Indians came over the hill. If the fax had been invented before the battle at Little Big Horn, it might have been much better for General Custer. The second attack had the same two prongs, but without the fax it was a complete surprise. The Shuars beat up but did not kill a couple of our employees, and stole everything of value from the camp. It succeeded— at least in lowering the Warintza Shuars standard of living, education, health care, and nutrition.

In Ecuador the indigenous tribes have been treated well in the sense of not being required, in general, to obey the laws and regulations, but badly in not being educated and given medical care. This often leaves them in a situation where they are generally too ignorant or illiterate to participate in running the country and are poor and diseased. They can be and are taken advantage of by unethical self-interested foreign companies and organizations of all kinds—including environmentalists and NGOs and meddlers. I once saw a collection of pamphlets in Spanish made in Belgium for educating Ecuadorian Indians. The titles were: "Why Oil Production Should Not Be Allowed in Ecuador," "Why Logging Should Not Be Allowed," "Why Fish Farming Should Not Be Allowed," "Why Shrimp Farming Should Not Be Allowed," "Why Mining Should Not Be Allowed." I read the mining pamphlet, which said, "The first thing a mining company does when it comes into a community is rape all the women and poison all the wells." I heard the same line from a Catholic priest. This pervasive ignorance makes Ecuador ripe for foreign activists. We tried to counteract this in the case of Warintza by organizing tours for groups of Shuars to visit recently developed mines in indigenous areas, several in Peru, and one in Brazil. What the local Peruvian Indians told the Shuars about increased standards of living, better health clinics, schools, and so on was very convincing. I think some progress was made.

Warintza camp built with lumber made at the site at a total cost under US$15,000, 2000.

At Warintza the mineral rights were acquired by us from the national government and were not owned by the Shuars. When we began work there were no Shuars living in the area, but they later moved in to try to develop nuisance claims. When our Warintza drilling project was being planned we built a nice camp with a dormitory for thirty to forty people, a mess hall, a kitchen, a recreation hall with a television set, bathrooms with running water, toilets and showers, and an office and drafting room. There was a core storage and core logging facility. All this was constructed out of lumber made on the site using chainsaws. Roofing was sheets of corrugated galvanized iron. It was a really good job, and the total cost was between US$12,000 and $15,000, including development of a water source and a septic tank.

We used local workers to do unskilled work on the camp and the trail construction. We imported carpenters from Macas to do skilled work. They earned about 30 percent more than the Shuars. The terrain was so steep that long sections of trails had to be carved or blasted out of near-vertical cliffs. I shipped in an Atlas Copco gasoline-powered percussion drill which would drill blast holes up to 1.5 meters in depth. At the beginning of the program we made a contract with the village of Warintza, with various terms intended to be attractive to the locals. They signed it and got an advance payment. In less than one month they came back and said, "We have decided we don't like the agreement we signed and want a new more generous one with a new front-end payment." They first demanded a pay rate equal to the Macas carpenter rate, but a couple of weeks later came back and demanded a 100 percent increase in pay rate, which we refused, but our negotiations had something of the air of trying to make an important deal with a gang of children. Later in the project the Ecuadorian government put a clause in the mining law that said, in effect, that a company developing a mine had to get the permission of the people in the nearest town. A little later, in 2001, our project was attacked by the group of Shuars that beat up our employees. They stole radio equipment and various things including our Atlas Copco drill and the corrugated roof from the camp building. We have had endless negotiations with the government and Shuars and with Codelco (a Chilean government mining company), which is interested in Warintza and would like to make some arrangement to complete the Warintza exploration project. Such is life in Ecuador.

The Mirador Discovery in Ecuador

After one of these events we decided to shift our attention to the Mirador area. This project originally had a very difficult to pronounce Indian name, and I asked Luis to find a new name gringos could pronounce. He came up with Mirador, which means "lookout" and was a local place name. Mirador was very near the Peruvian border where the Cenepa War had taken place a few years earlier, and border guards were still jumpy. But it being Latin America, the guards let us detour into Peru, getting back to Mirador on a better jungle road. This part of Ecuador apparently had more poisonous snakes than the Warintza area, and we ran across a number of venomous pit vipers variously called *fer-de-lance* (iron lance), *hojas podridas* (rotten leaves), and *equis* (Xes, from the pat-

343

David Lowell in a rainstorm at the Mirador Project near the border with Peru in 2002.

tern of the skin). Two people in our extended group were bitten by these snakes. In a very small village near Mirador where our crew lived, a twelve-year-old girl was bitten and died. One worker was bitten on the back by a snake on a tree limb. Luckily, we carried dry antivenin powder, a vial of sterile water to mix it with, and a hypodermic needle. He got the shot very quickly and lived, but his back turned black for a month.

Another incident occurred when Billiton was running the project. There are some weird animals in the Zamora River area and one is a large, bright purple tarantula. Billiton had brought in an attractive young lady geologist who was an expert on the fracturing of rocks. I don't understand how this specialty would have been important to the project, but she arrived and stayed a couple of weeks. Everyone in the

David Lowell at a copper prospect in Jamaica in 1977. It was very hot and humid and involved a long walk and the photo was taken during a successful negotiation to rent the mule (without saddle and with rope-around-nose bridle). Everyone including mule were in agreement with terms.

Amazon jungle wears rubber boots, and she had left hers beside her bed when she went to sleep. When she got up the next morning she put a bare foot in one boot and felt something inside, so she put her hand in to remove it. It was a large purple tarantula, and she emitted a loud piercing scream which brought the male members of the crew from all directions. Tarantulas are venomous, but not deadly, but this lady got the full treatment, antivenin, high-voltage electrical shock (a debunked but once popular treatment for snakebite), and a helicopter trip to the nearest hospital. She came back the next day with her arm in a splint but the purpose of the splint was never explained.

We began at Mirador with stream sediment surveys, taken with some difficulty in steep-sided creeks full of boulders. We found weak gold anomalies and drilled several holes without success. Our first sampling had covered several square kilometers, and in a high area with very difficult access we found some anomalous copper results following

From left: horse tender, Vicente, Carlos, driver, and broken-rib patient
David at Mirador.

the same strategy as in the Atacama Project. I felt that I was the member
of our group most likely to recognize a porphyry copper in a jungle setting, having seen them in New Guinea, Guadalcanal, Jamaica, Panama,
and Thailand. Assessing the area involved a lot of pain and suffering for
several days, but it paid off because I recognized some familiar features.
The last day we climbed down the almost vertical side of a ridge. Because
the jungle was impenetrable we were following a small stream, when I
slipped and fell down a waterfall for about twenty feet. My head hit a
water-smoothed rock face and made a sound like a hammer blow on a
melon, and I landed in a heap at the bottom with some aches and pains
but no broken arms or legs. I had worried initially that I might have a
brain concussion, but the pain in my head stopped quickly. However,
I discovered that two ribs were very painful and determined that they
were broken. Luis Quevedo had also sprained his wrist during the day.
We hiked (or stumbled) back to our vehicle and drove to the closest
small town and asked if there was a doctor. We found there was not,
but there was a combination chiropractor-mortician. We didn't think

any of his skills could help us, so we instead went to a small, poorly stocked pharmacy and bought a little tin of liniment with the picture of a dragon on it. There wasn't much to do to treat either broken ribs or a sprained wrist except talk about the porphyry copper leached capping we saw that day, which later became the Mirador copper-gold deposit.

We began a geologic mapping and grid sampling program, which found a well-defined copper-gold anomaly and was followed by a grid pattern of core holes from which a representative composite metallurgical test sample was sent to a lab in Nevada for testing. We defined a large copper-gold deposit. No one from Corriente Resources had visited Mirador up to this point, but they later announced that they had discovered the deposit. Success has a hundred fathers, but failure is an orphan. They also changed the name Zamora River Mineral Belt to Corriente Mineral Belt.

Around 2002 I made a trip to another gold prospect in south central Ecuador with a Chilean geologist employed by the owner of the gold property. It involved a long hike, and the route crossed a sizable river on a swinging bridge. A swinging bridge is usually made with two heavy support cables about a meter apart connected by short cross-planks laid out as a floor between the support cables. Two lighter-gauge cables are stretched about a meter above the floor cables as handrails. The problem with this bridge, known as "the Indiana Jones Bridge," was that one of the floor cables was broken and some of the floor planks were gone and you had to teeter across on one cable. It wasn't too bad crossing the first time, but coming back was really scary because you knew exactly what to look forward to. The bridge was no problem at all for the local Indians, who just skipped across chattering to each other as they went.

The gold prospect turned out to have a number of small veins and mineralized shear zones too small to be of interest to me, but possibly related to a large hidden bulk low-grade deposit. The fatal flaw was the presence of a total of about five hundred illegal *petroleros* (independent miners), who in Ecuador are almost impossible to deal with because the government is unwilling to enforce their own mining law. My only consolation was that the bridge crossing might have cleaned a good deal of plaque out of my arteries (if I had plaque), especially on the return trip.

Rafael Correa, elected president of Ecuador in 2006, had a PhD in economics from the University of Illinois at Urbana. While there he apparently did not develop any love for the United States or for free-enterprise democracy, but he did develop some leftist, socialist ideas, and became an admirer of Fidel Castro, Hugo Chavez, and Evo Morales, and received support from Chavez in his political campaigns. As finance minister of Ecuador in 2005, he didn't support a free-trade agreement with the United States, and didn't like the International Monetary Fund. In the mining and petroleum industries, the regulations he instituted as president caused confusion and slowed production. People I know have talked to people on committees and commissions who have been appointed to these posts but have no training in the specialty or knowledge of the previous history of the problems. They sometimes have good intentions but do not know what to do. All in all, it is very difficult to do business in Ecuador.

Meanwhile, while we were there in the early to mid-2000s, the copper and gold markets had gone up and down in a pattern that didn't match Ecuadorian politics. In the Zamora River Mineral Belt, we were at the mercy of Corriente's ability to raise money and promote the project, which complicated and slowed the exploration. Finally, I was informed by Billiton that they would like to drop out but hold a 2 percent NSR royalty (NSR is the Net Smelter Return from the concentrate sold to the smelter). Corriente proposed that the property be divided between me and Corriente. In retrospect, I made a mistake by asking for Warintza. The price of copper had gone up, but the price of gold had not yet run up. The Ecuadorian political situation was "same as always," and the profit margin of Warintza looked higher than Mirador. The way it worked out, however, was that the road access to Mirador was much better, and there were no Shuars living near the deposit, which significantly improved that problem for Corriente.

Soon after the division of properties, the copper price moved up as high as US$4 per pound and the submarginal Billiton copper deposits

The ceremony in which David Lowell received an Honorary Doctor of Science from the University of Arizona, with University President Peter Likins (left) and Dean of the Colleges of Letters, Arts, and Science Joaquin Ruiz, 2000.

suddenly became viable, at least to the Chinese, who were better able to cope with a shaky third world government. As a matter of fact, I don't think the Corriente Resources business plan mentioned "British fair play" and Corriente was able to work out a sale of Mirador to a Chinese company, while Warintza remained bogged down with government hostility and Shuar efforts to cope with business and mining problems totally foreign to their Amazon Basin traditions.

University of Arizona Honorary Doctor of Science Degree, 2000

This degree resulted from my success in mineral exploration; by 2000 I may already have had the best track record in the world, and I had also contributed to the science of exploration with my part in the porphyry copper model. In addition, I had helped the University of Arizona in many ways prior to 2000.

Robert M. Dreyer Award

I knew Robert Dreyer, who was an industrial minerals consulting geologist. He set up the Robert M. Dreyer Award to be the premier mineral deposit discovery award in the world, which included a cash prize. I was the first winner in 2000; I gave a talk and received a cash award of $30,000. I was on the Dreyer Award Committee for several years after that, and I had the impression that there was a continuing war between industrial geologists (who seldom make a glamorous discovery) and ore deposits geologists who typically get more publicity.

Mining and Metallurgical Society of America Gold Medal

I received the Mining and Metallurgical Society of America Gold Medal in Denver in 2001 at the MMSA Annual Meeting in conjunction with the American Institute of Mining Engineers and the Society of Mining Engineers Annual Meetings. I gave a talk and received a five-ounce high-purity gold medal (worth $6,200 in January 2014). It's a beautiful medal. The original mission of the MMSA was to advise the U.S. Department of Mines, but during the presidential tenure of Bill Clinton it was abolished and its duties were turned over to the United States Geological Survey, who were less capable of dealing with the mining industry.

CHAPTER THREE

Toromocho Discovery in Peru, 2002–2006

In 2002 Warintza appeared to be temporarily stalled, and I proposed a new investment idea to several of my associates from the Arequipa Resources Pierina Project, David De Witt, Geoff Loudon, Marcel de Groot, and Catherine McLeod Seltzer. I proposed we identify and acquire a large known copper deposit with established ore reserves in which there was a possibility of applying copper leaching techniques not known when the reserves were originally developed.

Copper is usually concentrated from copper ore in one of two ways: flotation or leaching. The flotation method requires crushing the ore followed by grinding the ore in ball mills or autogenous mills, then separating the mill slurry, sometimes by gravity methods but usually by a flotation circuit that separates the sulfide grains into a copper concentrate. The concentrate is later refined in a furnace. Leaching oxide copper ore consists of stacking either mine run (coarse) ore or ore crushed to smaller-sized fragments on an impermeable high-density plastic membrane. The ore heaps are periodically saturated with sulfuric acid, using either sprinkling or a drip irrigation system. The pregnant acid solution runs off the membrane and goes to an SXEW plant, which produces very high purity cathodes containing 0.999 percent Cu (SXEW stands for "solvent-extraction electrowinning"). In general, leaching (which requires ore with acid-soluble copper) costs about half or less of both capital and operating costs compared with flotation system cost, considering that smelting and refining costs also become unnecessary. Some technological advances in leaching had occurred in the years prior to 2002, which sometimes made leaching applicable not only to oxide copper ore, but also to sulfide ore in the form of secondary chalcocite ore and sometimes even to incipiently leached primary chalcopyrite ore. I had training and experience that made me reasonably well informed about this technology.

One-Year Due Diligence Study

My proposal was that I review known deposits with ore reserves predating the development of the new technology. My review was in the literature, sometimes in my own files, and, if necessary, in trips to the field. I did not charge consulting fees to my associates, but did charge expenses. I began with a list of eight possible targets and culled the list down to two possibilities: Taca Taca in Argentina and Toromocho in Peru. Taca Taca was eliminated because of acquisition cost and because it was in Argentina where, for many reasons, it is hard to do business.

Toromocho had been identified as a porphyry copper deposit in about 1940 by Cerro de Pasco Corp., a U.S. mining company that was, at that time, the largest mining company in Peru. Cerro did some drilling in Toromocho in the 1960s and also did underground exploration in "levels" cutting the orebody with tunnels or "drifts" and "crosscuts" at several different elevations. The property was "nationalized" in about 1970—really expropriated, because the compensatory payment made by the leftist Peruvian government was small. Most of the mines in the country, with the exception of Southern Peru Copper Company, were taken over at the same time. Toromocho was placed in the hands of Centromin, a government-owned company, which carried out a second drilling project in 1970. Final reserves were calculated to be about 350 million tonnes of about 0.07 percent copper equivalent with relatively poor metallurgical recovery. Kaiser engineers did a feasibility study for Centromin, and there were several reports published by the government. Unfortunately they were all wrong. I suspected this when I

Looking north from Toromocho over nearby lake. Some of these peaks are almost 5,500 meters or 18,000 feet high.

reviewed the deposit, so I decided to do a due diligence study to reevaluate Toromocho and develop new information. Our group contributed money to pay for first-stage work. The government privatization policy at that time grew out of the free-enterprise policy of Alberto Fujimori, elected president and probably the best president Peru had ever had, at least during his first term. He moved the economy toward free enterprise and attempted to privatize everything the previous administrations had nationalized. Prior to our program Toromocho had come up for privatization, but no one bid, which made me hopeful we could acquire it after due diligence work.

It was good luck being able to hire Angel Alvarez, a Peruvian engineer who had worked at Toromocho for Cerro de Pasco and Centromin.

353

Prospect a few kilometers north of Toromocho, elevation 16,000 feet, 2002.

He was a good mining engineer, but didn't entirely understand porphyry copper geology. Angel and I worked together on the due diligence and sometimes hired one or two field assistants. The Toromocho data was stored (badly) in three different places, and the drill core stored in two places, and sometimes the core from the first half of a drill hole was separated from the second half. We found the assays from sampling the underground workings stored in an abandoned mine change room. We had an advantage, in that Angel was very well acquainted with the Toromocho history and where things might be located. We moved literally many tons of drill core and separated and labeled every drill hole. We then relogged every hole, some in detail and some only in general. We also reorganized the assay reject samples and made up composite samples for metallurgical tests and analyses to determine the distribution of trace elements and samples for petrographic anal-

David Lowell with town of Morococha to the left and right and Cerro San Francisco on the skyline. Almost all of the area in the photo is underlain by the Toromocho orebody (photo by Ross Humphreys).

Rig drilling 1,000-meter hole in center of Toromocho orebody, 2005.

Geologists logging the Toromocho drill core in 2004. The core has been split using a diamond saw.

ysis. In six months, by the spring of 2003, I had totally revised the geological data of Toromocho, including the identification of a huge, previously unrecognized, cylindrical breccia pipe in the center of the deposit. Somewhere in the middle of the due diligence I began to have my prickly treasure-finding feeling. I had been able to fit Toromocho into the Lowell-Guilbert Porphyry Model, which indicated the potential for a great deal larger orebody. I had also gotten in touch with Luis "Lucho" Baertl, whom I had met in Chile years earlier when he was manager of the mining department of Chase Manhattan Bank, if I remember correctly. I met him again in Lima, and he talked as though he had a lot of experience in privatization negotiations with the government. With the agreement of my other associates, I invited Lucho to join our group of investors and put up his share of the money and serve as a Peruvian expeditor.

Privatization from the Peruvian Government

As the due diligence work reached completion with encouraging results, I began to plan to move into the privatization phase of the project. Here Lucho Baertl's experience was very useful, although he made some miscalculations. Toromocho had been put up once or twice previously, and no one had bid because of the mistaken general opinion, based on the previous geological work and the published reports, that it was a "doggy prospect" that could not be mined at a profit. We planned to use a lawyer to write a "tailor-made" request for bids for the privatization authority to be sent out in the first stage of the privatization process. My associates were in agreement with this. Coupled with this would be our own later bid. The whole process was very complicated from a legal standpoint because there were hundreds of old mining claims involved, ranging in age from ten to more than a hundred years old, and purchases and sales and nationalizations. Lucho recommended a lawyer who had previously worked on at least one privatization. This woman happened to be in an emotional state as a result of a recent divorce. Through John Lacy, a well-known Tucson mining attorney, I found another lawyer in Lima to cross-check the legal work; she also had some emotional challenges, and as a result, this data checking and bid writing was somewhat tense and took several months.

Our strategy was to write our bid to have good terms for us—but not too good. We did not want to take advantage of the government. We did not expect a competing bid, but it was certainly a possibility, so we also had to study other recent Peruvian privatizations, and I, starting from zero, had to acquire some familiarity with the process. One detail in all the privatizations was the submittal of a US$2 million cash down payment, which seemed to have some of the characteristics of a surety bond. Lucho waved this off, thinking it was a surety bond. He said,

"Forget about that, it will just cost us US$5,000." Since Lucho had been a banker I assumed he was right, but our bid got into the hands of Sofia Arce, manager of the foreign branch of our Lima bank branch. Sofia found and corrected several errors in our bid and said, "The US$2 million is not a surety bond, it has to be cash on the barrelhead." This was two days before the scheduled date for opening bids. Peru has Napoleonic law, which is totally inflexible. We didn't have $2 million in Lima. I had securities in the United States and immediately began a frantic effort to arrange by remote control a $2 million advance and, even more difficult, get it delivered to Lima. I made a total of sixty-five calls to the United States and by some kind of miracle had the money to deliver when the bids were opened. We were the only bidder and got the option to buy Toromocho on terms that were fair to both sides.

The cost of my six months' due diligence study and the cost of setting up the privatization had been paid in a very informal way. The next step would be more costly, so in 2003 we set up a private company called Peru Copper Syndicate, and passed the hat to get $5 million. Lucho and I were given some financial credit for work we had done, but everyone contributed: David De Witt, Lucho Baertl, Geoff Loudon, Catherine Seltzer, and myself. The $5 million was to cover the cost of drilling five confirmation drill holes to partly test the new geologic theory, to check the accuracy of the old assays, and to determine the percentage of leachable chalcocite. We had already established that the arsenic content was much lower than predicted and was not a serious problem. This was confirmed from assays of composites of old assay reject samples.

Untrained exploration geologists find it difficult to recognize hydrothermal breccia in core holes cutting porphyry copper deposits, and a huge breccia pipe and vertical ore fabric in the center of the deposit had not been recognized before my due diligence study. It was important in two ways: the breccia ore was higher grade, and the porous texture created by brecciation allowed the supergene enrichment solutions to migrate downward to great depth—approaching 1,000 meters—producing very large ore reserves.

Marcel de Groot

Marcel de Groot was chairman of Luna Gold Co., which has a very successful gold mine in Brazil. Luna Gold's Aurizona Mine is an example of the saying "Mines are made, not found." I have had a pretty good view of this mine, and I think it owes its existence to Marcel. When he was in high school he bought several fields of corn from farmers, harvested them, sold the corn, and made thousands of dollars. In 2012 he was voted by his peers to be one of the five best mining finance people in Canada; Canada is the mining finance capital of the world.

Marcel is the Johnny-come-lately of our Lowell-De Witt-de Groot threesome. He has only been associated for ten years but, like Dave De Witt, is totally reliable and totally honest. The three of us have three different specialties. We run complicated enterprises with conference calls, and the decisions made with thirty minutes of conversation—based on three-way respect and confidence—are often better decisions than major mining company decisions based on six-month conversations by multiple committees. It gives us a tremendous advantage.

We drilled the five holes close to key old holes, and the pairs were therefore called "twin holes." In a general way these holes confirmed our conclusions from the old holes. We had much better core recovery than in the original drilling and recovered more of the pulverant chalcocite. The quality of the assaying was better, and we confirmed the presence of the large breccia pipe. As more information accumulated on extensions of the orebody and on process metallurgy possibilities, we realized that chalcocite acid leaching process would not recover the significant molybdenum and silver credits in the ore, and that the leaching option would be impractical.

At this point we began organizing a public company and selecting a board of directors. We were fortunate to have David De Witt as a director because he understood exactly how to "go public." As it turned out, most of the people on the board of directors were fine for stock and shareholder communication problems, but not very good with problems related to developing a large mine in a Latin American country. My Arequipa Resources board had been better suited to that task.

120,000-Meter Drilling Project and Detailed Geological Analysis

The team of eighteen geologists Angel hired worked hard and performed well with consultant John Hunt's training and Angel's supervision. We had eight large diamond drilling machines drilling deep,

Old Cerro de Pasco Toromocho Tuctu staff camp, which was rehabilitated as Peru Copper Camp. The flat area behind Tuctu was a golf course listed in *Ripley's* as the highest golf course in the world.

Ticlio Pass on the Central Highway between Lima and Toromocho. Sign says elevation is 4,818 meters or 15,900 feet and that this is highest railroad grade in the world. In this 2006 photo from the left are Ross, Anna, Susan, and Mary Humphreys and Edith and David Lowell. (Anna is now Anna Humphreys Finn).

large-diameter diamond core holes twenty-four hours per day. We recovered a high percentage of drill core using devices like triple tube core barrels and split tube inner barrel, and using water pressure to push the core out of the barrel. The main reason for all this emphasis on core recovery was to get the chalcocite into the core sample. This chalcocite was soft, crumbly, sometimes sooty, but we recovered almost all of it. Barrick Gold was kind enough to lend me Bill Mounts. Bill spent a week at Toromocho and solved most of our drilling and core recovery problems. The average elevation of our drill sites was about 4,500 meters, or 15,000 feet, and the average hole depth was over 500

Tuctu Camp at Toromocho built by Cerro de Pasco in about 1940.

meters, sometimes 1,000 meters. Another fortunate event was that I was able to hire John Proffett for a two-week review of the Toromocho geology. John may very well be the best ore deposits field geologist in the mining industry, and he identified two important additions to our understanding of the geology.

I have been involved with dozens of drilling projects, but Toromocho might have been the best operation of all. In addition to good management of the drilling, our crew designed and built a large, earthquake-proof core storage building sufficient to hold over 100,000 meters of core. We used an old camp originally built by Cerro de Pasco in about 1940 called Tuctu. It had a small golf course we were too busy to try, but which was in the record books as the highest in the world, as was a section of railroad in Ticlio Pass coming into Toromocho. This is the highest railroad grade in the world. Several times while mapping near Toromocho I worked at elevations of about 5,000 meters (16,000 feet), which is about my personal capability limit.

Increase in Ore Reserves by Ten Times to Over 2.2 Billion Tons of Ore

On one occasion I wanted to visit an old Cerro tunnel to see the rock texture and hydrothermal alteration. It turned out to be a difficult visit. The tunnel had not been cleaned when it was abandoned, and broken pieces of rock up to a foot in diameter were left scattered on the floor. Then a mud slurry made up of thin mud containing a large amount of soluble copper and zinc and sulfuric acid and other chemicals drained into it. The mud was deep enough to conceal the loose pieces of rock, and when we stepped on a rock it sometimes rolled, and we had a tendency to fall into the mud. I was with two others who elected to give up and go back. I finished the hike but fell once, cutting my knee fairly badly. I worried it might become infected, but in a couple of days it was almost completely healed, and I wondered if the mud couldn't be bottled and sold as super cut and abrasion medicine.

Another interesting thing we found in the old Cerro workings were stalactites and stalagmites, like those found in caves, except these were composed of chalcanthite, a beautiful blue, translucent, water-soluble copper specimen. I have several chalcanthite specimens painted with a transparent covering which prevents them from giving off their water of hydration and collapsing into a pile of white powder.

The ore reserves we identified steadily increased from the original 350 million to 500 million to a billion tonnes, and the final figure we calculated at the time of the sale to Chinalco was 2.2 billion tonnes, but it will become much larger. Somewhere along the line, the board of directors suggested that if we were trying to sell or joint venture such a large copper deposit it would be appropriate to hire a manager who had been manager of a very large mine, but this plan didn't work. In a way it was like the frogs in a pond who decided they needed a king and selected a heron to be their king. In our case the king didn't eat any of us frogs, but neither was he willing to make any decisions without a committee to study the problem and recommend a decision. We didn't have a big enough staff to form a committee and didn't get any decisions. This happened successively during the reign of two "kings," who had done fine in previous large mines that largely ran themselves and had plenty of committees to recommend decisions.

We had problems such as making a deal with the silver company that had an inferior mineral title occupying roughly the same area we had privatized, and another company with a nuisance claim over a waste dump site. We also had the problem of owners of primitive houses among the 5,000-population Morococho, who had to be bought out in a deal in which they would get a free, modern house in a new town site. All these problems had an obvious and relatively cheap and easy resolution, but neither our "kings" nor our directors were willing to make decisions.

This problem was largely caused by the board of directors of Peru Copper Inc., the company we had incorporated under the Peru Copper Syndicate in 2004. I didn't select most of the directors, who were typically people very familiar with Canadian junior companies and stock trading but not very familiar with developing or running a large mine in Peru. In one incident a large and very unscrupulous Mexican mining company that controlled Southern Peru Copper Co., called Grupo México, went out of their way to damage Peru Copper Inc. Our directors were up in arms, and a majority was in favor of suing Grupo México. There was one problem with this plan. Grupo's net present value was $13 billion, and Peru Copper Inc. had less than a million dollars. A lawsuit would probably have bankrupted Peru Copper, and I had to call every director at his or her home to convince a bare majority not to vote for suing. There were other problems like this, and it was a very unpleasant period for me. During the same period, we had hired UBS, a large Swiss bank, to represent Peru Copper in a marketing program to find a buyer for Toromocho. They went through the motions, but we learned that their attention was really focused on some prospective petroleum sales worth ten times as much to UBS as a Toromocho sale commission.

Sale to Chinalco, the Largest Chinese Mining Company

Several prospective buyer groups had visited Toromocho. One was a group of six engineers from Chinalco, China's largest mining company; the group was headed by Dr. Henlong Lei, who had a PhD from the University of Michigan. There happened on this occasion to be a UBS banker also visiting the project—Virginie Milliet, a young French lady. The other members of Dr. Lei's group went up in another vehicle (remember, this is a two-and-a-half-hour trip on a winding, dangerous, road up from sea level to 16,000 feet elevation). In our car we had a driver, plus Virginie in the right front seat, Dr. Lei in the left rear seat, and I in the right rear seat. Dr. Lei's English wasn't perfect, but he is an intelligent, charming, talkative man. He was talking happily along, then completely stopped for about two seconds, then suddenly vomited in a voluminous discharge!

The driver stopped the car, and we all got out and found an old newspaper to tidy up with.

After the cleanup I began to worry about whether it was motion sickness, or *soroche* (altitude sickness), which can be very serious. I compromised by driving on to our camp and showing Dr. Lei around briefly and then sending him back to Lima. His crew went up 1,000 feet higher and looked at some of the drill core and such. It happened that Edith was with me on that trip and had spent the day in Lima. When I got back to the hotel she said, "Poor Dr. Lei, we should get a doctor to check him in case this is something serious." I thought this was a good idea, and Edith volunteered to call Henlong's hotel and rustle up a doctor. We did, and he was fine, but the incident might have had long-term ramifications.

The UBS marketing program dragged on for a few months without success; I independently decided to just make a trip to China on my own hook and talk to several Chinese companies. Geoff Loudon volunteered to go with me, paying his own expenses, and UBS offered to supply the services of a Chinese interpreter stationed in Beijing. We spent four days in Shanghai and visited about eight companies, several of which expressed some interest without planning concrete action. The hotel we stayed in published a daily ten-page English newspaper. The first day it reported the police had captured three antisocials selling drugs. The next day they reported the three had been tried and found guilty. The third day two had been executed and the third case was being considered. Geoff and I and about ten million people in Shanghai decided not to become drug sellers.

We then went to Beijing, where we had several additional contacts including Chinalco. When we arrived at the Chinalco office, Dr. Lei, for whom I have a great deal of respect, gave me a hug and made a speech to the staff that was complimentary about my career. We met one of the two Chinalco executives and were invited to a dinner at the Peking Duck restaurant with speeches and expressions of affection and so on. He agreed to send someone with me to the airport to get me checked in and to my departure lounge. A PhD Chinalco geologist who was supposed to speak English delivered me to the Beijing terminal, helped me get my suitcase out, and then sped off, leaving me with roughly 100,000 non-English-speaking Chinese people. I first looked for signs in English. No luck. Then I tried speaking English to desk clerks. No luck with the first fifteen, then an enterprising young lady with adequate English offered to help me. She came quickly around the counter, took a firm grip on my arm, and we dashed to the check-in desk and got me check-in coupons. Then we dashed toward the departure lounge and she said, "You owe me twenty-five dollars." I immediately and thankfully capitulated and eventually got off the plane in Los Angeles.

About three weeks later I had a trip planned to Manila and, a couple of days before leaving, got a call from a gentleman who said, in good English, he was Kevin Tai and wanted to talk to me on behalf of Chinalco. When he heard I planned to go to the Philippines and would change planes in Taipei, he arranged to meet me in the Taipei airport for a two-hour meeting between planes. At this point I invited David De Witt to participate in the negotiation.

The meeting logistics were complicated. The Taipei terminal is very large, with few English-speaking staff. Kevin could not penetrate the central part without an airline ticket. I had a large language problem. I found a nice lady who spoke English at the Transit Desk. I had learned the place where Kevin was waiting, and she wrote out in English how to find this place and then, for good measure, wrote it in Chinese. I found Kevin, and David De Witt was already there. In less than two hours we had negotiated and roughed out a deal on Toromocho. Two or three weeks later the three of us met again in Vancouver, and with the help of three law firms in two long days in May 2007 we wrote and signed a contract to sell Toromocho. I was interested that Chinalco had sent only Kevin, who was then thirty-five or forty years old, to make about an $800 million deal. He made frequent calls to Beijing, but had a lot of responsibility and authority and did a very good job. I felt enormous relief. For the next two months there were some loose ends to attend to, but my responsibility was over, and someone else owned all my Toromocho problems.

Roughly six months after the sale I got a call from Elliott Smith, a reporter for *Bloomberg Press* (a business, financial, and economic news organization), who was writing an article about China's hunger for commodities in third world countries in South America and Africa. He made a trip to Arizona and spent a day in my office. He had done a comprehensive job, had several people working in China, and made multiple visits to Peru and other countries supplying commodities to China. His first article was on the general problem of acquiring commodities in third world countries. Then an article was published using the Toromocho sale as a case history of the acquisition by China of commodities. A third article was a biographical sketch of me. I think Bloomberg must have spent a million dollars altogether on these articles.

American Mining Hall of Fame Inductee

In December 2002, at Tucson, Arizona, I was inducted into the American Mining Hall of Fame. By then there had already been a dozen or more previous inductees, whose names were hung high on the walls of the banquet room with letters about six inches high. At the time I was inducted, a David Lowell flag was added to the others around the room, which was a big thrill.

SEG Penrose Gold Medal

I was selected to receive the SEG Penrose Gold Medal in November 2003, and was presented with it in September 2004, in Australia, for unusually original work in the earth sciences. The presentation took place during a Society of Economic Geologists meeting in Perth, Australia, and I was again surprised to have been chosen for this highest award given by the Society of Economic Geologists. The citation was written by Geoff Loudon, a longtime Australian friend and associate.

CHAPTER FOUR

Alto Paraná Titanium Iron Discovery in Paraguay, 2006–2014

The Alto Paraná Project discovered the world's largest known mineable TiO2 deposit with a pig iron coproduct. This titanium deposit was found as a result of a fortuitous chain of events, including the passage of regulations unfavorable to mining in Ecuador and friendships I had developed in the Philippines thirty years earlier. In 2008 all we had left in Ecuador was a small office in Quito and a partly qualified exploration team, but new mining regulations left little incentive to find another potential mine in Ecuador.

Between roughly 1970 and 1983 I had made many trips to the Philippines and had done consulting work for every large mining company operating in the country, some of which I've described earlier. This included about eight companies, but most of my work was for three: Marcopper (Placer Development), Benguet Consolidated, and Lepanto Consolidated. People in the Philippines, both Filipinos and long-term expatriates, tend to be very personal, and I developed a number of close lifelong friends. One of these is Art Disini, who was Lepanto general manager in the 1970s. He later visited me in Arizona and also in Chile.

Around 2007 I had made a trip back to the Philippines to revisit several large known copper deposits, which, because of ownership problems or government regulation problems, had not been put into production while I worked in the country. On part of the trip I was accompanied by Marcel de Groot, and I used Art Disini as a source of new information and contacts. Art had retired from Lepanto and was chairman of a National Mining Committee and was also teaching in the University of the Philippines College of Mines.

What I learned was that thirty years had not resolved the contested ownership of the large known copper deposits and the problems involving the government, or the invasion of mining districts such as King King by thousands of illegal miners (who could vote in national elections and had progressively become a bigger problem). Art arranged for me to visit several nickel laterite deposits, and I developed the idea, which may have been incorrect, that there might be similar undiscovered deposits in the laterites of northern South America.

I had a number of friends in Manila and, in the course of two days of investigation, found that all the four or five large copper deposits undeveloped in 1980 were still undeveloped. "Undeveloped" does not mean "available." I had found my Philippine friends to be bright, hard-working, friendly, and obliging, but very disinclined to compromise in business deals. Art Disini once told me that it takes only three cars in a Manila intersection to make a traffic jam because none will budge to let another go first. It's the same in a mine deal. If each of two people has an ownership angle to prevent the other owner from making a deal, they would both die rather than compromise.

Two of the best copper deposits had been held by the same owner, who was also the owner of a large operation of interisland freight boats. He was said to have twelve bodyguards because quite a few people in Manila had some interest in killing him. We got his phone number and secured an unenthusiastic invitation to see him in his office. As soon as we entered we saw most of the twelve bodyguards in the outer office. They were dressed like gang members and were ugly, mean characters, who I imagined would without a second thought commit any violent act requested. When we talked to him he showed no interest in making any kind of a deal. We threaded our way through the cutthroats sitting in the outer office, and I gave up my plan of acquiring a large overlooked deposit in the Philippines.

A strange symbiotic industry had developed at this time between the Philippines and mainland China. A couple of decades earlier, Chairman Mao had pushed the idea of small "backyard steel blast furnaces" in China. This turned out to be impractical. The furnaces had all been shut down but many still existed. In the Philippines a number of nickel laterites had been found which were slightly sub-commercial because they weren't big enough, or high enough grade, or capital wasn't available to pay for the expensive conventional concentrating plants to extract and purify the nickel in nickel laterites. But somewhere along the way, a smart, innovative person in either China or the Philippines came up with the idea that the nickel laterite could sometimes be partly concentrated by a low-cost process, or maybe in some cases not concentrated at all, and shipped to China and smelted in the unused "backyard smelters," and if the iron/nickel ratio was more or less right, the product could be a probably low-quality but usable stainless steel. I looked at deposits that might have qualified for this purpose, but figured out that it takes two to tango, and there would have to be an international association made with an invisible, unknown Chinese owner of a backyard smelter to make this work, and that I was probably incapable of arranging this. I also did limited due diligence, which turned up a rumor that China might not continue using this great scheme much longer. I gave up the idea of getting involved, which turned out to be lucky because the rumor was right and in a few months the Chinese stopped buying this material. During the same period I learned a little about the bauxite/alumina/aluminum business.

I then returned to Ecuador and organized a large-scale reconnaissance for nickel laterite and bauxite deposits. Our crew seemed to be working all right and generated a steady string of wide-spaced samples, which were analyzed but didn't indicate ore discoveries. However, it wasn't the whole problem. Our team of three or four exploration geologists was made up of all Ecuadorians, with different combinations of capability and reliability. Their supervision was uncertain, and in any case, we didn't find anything in Ecuador.

We then moved to Colombia for a few months, also with no success, and finally to Paraguay. It took real optimism to go to Paraguay because it is a country that has never had a single significant mine, although it does have large areas covered with laterite, which is a fundamental element in the formation of nickel laterite (in which nickel from an ultramafic source rock is concentrated in the overlying laterite) and in bauxite (in which the aluminum from an alkalic source rock is concentrated in layers of gibbsite in the overlying laterite). Assaying bauxite deposits is tricky because of the Al2O3 aluminum oxide ratio; values are just one of the bauxite qualifications. A second is the presence or absence of activated silica.

Laterite is very common in tropical areas and covers vast areas of the world between 30° north latitude and 30° south latitude. It is a product of tropical weathering in hot climates with high rainfall, which forms organic acids that break down most rock-forming minerals such as feldspars and micas and hornblende and such, and produces clay and fine-grained silica and red iron oxides. The bauxite mineral is usually gibbsite, but some clay minerals also contain aluminum which cannot be extracted.

Potentially Largest Titanium Resource in the World

This brings us to the Alto Paraná titanium iron discovery in the Alto Paraná laterite plateau near the eastern border of Paraguay with Brazil. Our team had found some small veinlets of gibbsite, which is not uncommon in laterites. The samples taken were not very encouraging, but the Ecuadorian chief geologist was convinced he had found a bauxite mine. The several samples analyzed were also strongly anomalous in TiO2 (titanium oxide), but our geologist discounted this with the statement that there are no titanium mines in laterite. I did two things: the first was bring in Andy White, an Australian bauxite expert, to look at the weak gibbsite showing; and second, collect a metallurgical sample and send it to Martin Kuhn, a very competent and experienced process metallurgist with a PhD in metallurgy from Colorado School of Mines. I asked Martin to try to separate the TiO2. One of my maxims, as I

TiO2 exploration in laterite outcrop. From left, CIC geologist, David Lowell, Rob Reeves, and Jorge Fierro. A year earlier David had recognized that this laterite was relatively high grade titanium and iron ore.

have said before, is "ore is rock which can be mined at a profit," and I thought a metallurgical study was justified.

Andy White arrived and, after his first look at our outcrop, pointed both thumbs at the ground. He spent two more days looking at outcrops in Paraguay and across the border in Brazil and said, "No chance." Martin came back in about six weeks with a successful process that eliminated almost all the kaolin clay and silica and limonite and produced a clean concentrate of ilmenite (FeTiO2) and magnetite (Fe2O3). We launched a large-scale exploration program, which indicated that the deposit was huge—it eventually contained 22 billion tonnes of ore—and that the original discovery was not in the highest grade part of the orebody. We did library research and hired as consultants experts on

David and Miguel Grau, Asunción, Paraguay, 2012. Miguel is dean emeritus of South American mining lawyers and has done very good work for mining in Paraguay.

titanium who told us that the iron in the magnetite would be recoverable as a pig iron and would almost double the value of the ore. We also learned that titanium arc furnace smelting is very electric-power intensive, and the nearby Itaipu hydroelectric plant on the Paraná River—second largest in the world and underutilized by Paraguay—would be a huge economic advantage.

The project looked better and better, and this was confirmed by an in-house "scoping study" followed later by another outside study by Hains Engineering, which produced a Canadian 43-101 certified scoping study indicating a $1.6 billion net present value and a 23 percent internal rate of return.

We had staked about 400,000 hectares of mining claims and found that the Paraguayan mining code was not conducive to developing a mine. I suggested that we try to get it rewritten. The government was cooperative, and I asked Miguel Grau, a Peruvian mining lawyer with whom I had worked for many years, to go to Asunción, the capital of Paraguay, and discuss this. Miguel worked with senators and congressmen and lawyers, and in a surprisingly short time a new law based largely on the Peruvian and Chilean mining codes was in place, having been approved by the Paraguayan congress and senate and signed by President Fernando Lugo in 2011. Miguel Grau has a reputation for honesty and is the dean emeritus of South American mining law.

After six weeks of test work, Martin Kuhn had developed the new process that produced a clean concentrate of ilmenite and magnetite. Previous attempts to make concentrates from this type of occurrence used gravity concentration, which failed because the microscopic grains of clay were bonded with the surface of the very fine ore minerals. Knowing this, Dr. Kuhn began from the other direction, using clay industry technology to first remove most of the 65 percent kaolin clay

Martin Kuhn in front of
blunger at pilot plant, 2011.

Jorge, David, and group of young ladies who planned and managed the inauguration. About 150 people attended the event, including twelve senators, congressmen, and the vice president of Paraguay.

by breaking the clay/ore mineral bond with a piece of clay industry milling equipment called a "blunger." The underflow is concentrated further with several gravity concentration devices and, finally, with wet magnetic separation. Both magnetite and ilmenite have significant magnetic susceptibility. We call this the Kuhn Process. We reproduced the laboratory process with a pilot plant built in Paraguay that produces five tonnes of concentrate per day and works even better than in the lab.

Mintek, a large research firm focusing on pyrometallurgical testing of titanium and iron ore in Johannesburg, South Africa, did a two-week arc furnace test early in 2012 using 110 tonnes of concentrate produced by the Kuhn Process pilot plant, and the test ran very smoothly at a temperature of about 1,760 degrees. The goal for the test was to produce 86 percent TiO2 slag, but the second week the grade increased to as much as 92.5 percent TiO2 with no operating problems. Mintek said that this had possibly been the best test they had ever run. My guess on this point is that the formation of the ore in a laterite envi-

Pilot plant aerial photo.

ronment may have allowed a preprocessing that removed most of the usual contaminants and left the concentrate in a condition unusually amenable for concentrating and smelting.

When the pilot plant was completed in summer 2011, we held an inauguration celebration at the plant site attended by twelve congressmen and senators and by Fernando Franco, then vice president, and later president, of Paraguay.

Baseline environmental studies and community relations studies began in 2013 at the Alto Paraná site, and a formal negotiation has been undertaken that has produced a long-term price for electricity; a stability agreement is being discussed to determine long-term tax rates and other government/company understandings. To date, CIC Resources, the private company that owns Alto Paraná, has spent a total of about US$25 million. Officers of CIC are Marcel de Groot, President; J. David Lowell, Chairman and CEO; Jorge Fierro, Vice President Exploration;

Federico Franco and David Lowell. At date of photo Federico was vice president and he was later president of Paraguay.

Steven Krause, CFO; and David De Witt, Director. We are proceeding with additional furnace tests and may begin prefeasibility studies next year, followed by bankable feasibility then construction of a plant and smelter expected to cost at least $1 billion. CIC has been approached by several companies and a preliminary joint venture has been agreed upon with a large titanium company.

In the meantime, we had explored and staked a huge area of 350,000 hectares that contains more than 20 billion tonnes of about 7 percent TiO2 and 22 percent Fe2O3, making it the largest titanium deposit in the world. On the basis of a preliminary scoping study the economics look good.

The ownership is generally not for sale and financing is done by "passing the hat" among a group of four to seven investors. Two of my private companies in the past have "gone public," and both have reached market capitalizations on the order of a billion dollars. A lot of this is good luck. During 2011–2013 we did exploration in Paraguay,

David speaking at the Alto Paraná pilot plant inauguration ceremony.

Brazil, Peru, Chile, Haiti, Papua New Guinea, Africa, and Mexico. One of our group, Jorge Fierro, has an office in Lima. Altogether, I have probably worked with one hundred exploration geologists, none more capable than Jorge.

As I write, the Alto Paraná Project has been under way for six years and almost all the preproduction boxes have been checked off. Development cost is estimated to be approximately $1 billion. My two closest associates have worked with me for about fifteen years on this and many other projects, and the association has to be one of the most pleasant and effective in the mining industry. In addition to Paraná we have a number of other projects in process at an early stage.

In China, the largest producer of titanium slag is Pangang Titanium. Titanium slag is a slightly impure variety of TiO2 that has the same composition as the mineral rutile. Pangang needs additional titanium concentrate from which to produce titanium slag, which can be further refined to make titanium pigment. This pigment is used in most of the highest quality, usually white, paint. Titanium has the best strength-to-weight ratio of any element and is twenty times more resistant to oxidation than iron.

In early 2012, at the invitation of Pangang, Marcel de Groot, Nina Wang, Robert Reeves, and I visited their open pit mine and company headquarters at Panzhihua, China. From Chengdu, China, we took a feeder flight to Xichang, where we were met by a Buick station wagon for a two- or three-hour drive to Panzhihua. This was over a brand new, controlled access highway that resembled an American interstate, but with one difference: we sometimes drove fifteen minutes without see-ing another automobile. In our trip through China we went through several new cities with populations of several million, each being built almost from scratch. Most had numerous cranes in place building a half dozen new high-rise buildings. Nina explained these new cities were designed by central planning in Beijing to fill in empty places in the population distribution and to have at least one big city in every prov-ince. In Beijing, during the roughly forty years in which I have made periodic visits, the downtown streets have gone from massive bicycle traffic jams to small motorcycle traffic jams to compact car traffic jams (mixed with some Mercedes-Benz cars). The central planners are antici-pating jammed highways even though the present traffic has been very sparse so far.

In one spot some distance from the nearest village, we saw two high-rise building cranes set up in a goat pasture, indicating there must be plans for some kind of new city. Another interesting feature of the planning was that the east controlled access lane was usually south of the west lane, but when the road alignment entered steep mountain terrain the west-heading highway climbed up above the east-head-ing highway, and it was a two-story, two-direction highway. The city of Panzhihua, population one million, which is the headquarters of Pangang and also the location of their large titanium-vanadium-iron mine, straddles a steep valley, which required the construction of several really huge bridges to connect the two halves of the city.

We visited the Pangang head office there. In the entry room there was a very large plaque on the wall, about eight by twelve feet,

Pangang, China, welcome plaque for the CIC visit.

which said, "Welcome David Lowell for Visits and Negotiation with Pangang," and so on. It looked like it was bronze, but I suspect it was some sort of digital illusion. We visited the mine, the concentrator, the smelter, and the research department, none of which were up to big U.S. company standards, but may have been appropriate for a Chinese company with low labor rates and evolving technology. Negotiations were cautious on both sides. How can a very entrepreneurial, fast-moving, North American company with lots of Latin American development experience make a joint venture with a branch of the Chinese government with minimal business sophistication and almost no experience outside China? One possibility was that Pangang would buy CIC for a large amount of cash but would have no idea how to do business in Paraguay. It made me think of Kipling's poem, "The Ballad of East and West."

In due course, we traveled back to Xichang, China's "Rocket City," where long-range rockets and satellites are launched. A dinner was arranged at a place Rob Reeves described as "a Chinese version of a

Pangang Banquet for CIC. From the left are Robert Reeves, Marcel de Groot, Pangang general manager, and David Lowell. Nina Wang is out of the picture to the left. The restaurant is located in the middle of a river.

country western hall." There were about three hundred mini-banquets going on, with rotating circles on the table on which exotic Chinese dishes were offered to each of ten people around the table. I was very much on guard because I had once been suckered into getting a raw sea slug in my mouth at a Pangang manager's banquet.

Despite my being on the alert, Marcel played a practical joke on me. A group of about eight pretty girls approximately twenty years old, in costumes supposed to represent ancient dress in that province (if short skirts and cowboy hats were authentic), were singing and dancing on a large stage, and while I was trying to avoid getting a slug or miscellaneous different insects in my mouth, Marcel learned from Nina Wang that a beauty contest was to be staged among the eight scantily

Toho of Tokyo. From left, Robert Reeves, David Lowell, and Nina Wang.

dressed performers and the winner was to be crowned according to who was given the most flowers. People circulated through the crowd selling bouquets of flowers. Marcel bought a whole armload of flowers and then tapped me on the shoulder and said, "Dave, would you hold these for a minute?" I stupidly took the flowers and a little later tried to give them back. Marcel said, "No, no, you have to take them up on the stage and give them to your choice of the prettiest girl." I was then stuck. I had to either be a poor sport or look like a fool. I decided to be the fool and went through the crowd and up the stairs with my arms full of flowers to face the eight girls. I decided on the spur of the moment to divide the flowers between the best-looking and the least beautiful girl (who gave me a big smile). All this while the crowd was making a lot of noise and shouting something that Nina told me was "handsome young man," a joke.

After I had stumbled back to my table there was another commotion and singing behind me, and I discovered that the half of my flowers given to the most beautiful girl had won her the contest and the

Marcel de Groot in Toho office in Tokyo, Japan. Titanium sponge in foreground.

troupe of eight were behind my chair singing a sort of serenade. When I turned around they were holding out to me a bowl containing at least a gallon of beer—I had to drink part of it and pass the rest to the people around my table. By this time I was trying to think of a way to get even, but it wasn't over yet. Two young ladies at our table insisted on having their pictures taken with me, one with both her arms around my neck! So much for the Chinese being retiring and nondemonstrative!

We had an opportunity to see on this trip that the Chinese women in cities were better dressed than women in either Tokyo or Hong Kong, which was also a surprise. In my first visit to China forty years ago, both men and women were wearing Mao jackets, and it was hard to distinguish the girls from the boys.

Early in our Paraná Project we had meetings with various Paraguayan department heads and government ministers. On one occasion, after flying all night I met with Federico Franco, then vice president of Paraguay. When I sat down in his office, he stared intently at my foot then got down on one knee and felt my ankle. He said, "I am a medical doctor and I see that your ankle is swollen." In subsequent visits he always checked my ankles. I was impressed by his concern. Later, in another visit during which I told him about out project, he said, "Este es mi Proyecto" (this is my project). The implication was he would help push it through to completion, which he did. He and twelve congress-men and senators attended the inauguration ceremony when the pilot plant was completed.

A meeting had been scheduled with President Franco for Miguel Grau and myself in February 2013 to discuss the electricity price issue. At the last minute I heard that Willem Van Nierkerk, president of our South African joint venture partner, would be in Asunción as part of a due diligence team, and I invited him to sit in on the meeting with the president in spite of his not speaking Spanish. He accepted. My associates were afraid I had made a diplomatic mistake in this very sensitive problem, which might affect both the progress of the Paraná Project and also in some indirect way affect our chances for a joint venture. At this point we had been trying unsuccessfully for two years to get a commitment on a price per unit for the large amount of electricity we will need. The large British mining company Rio Tinto had been trying to get a quote for an aluminum smelter for four years.

In any case we went to the appointment escorted by the president of the Paraguay Labor Association, one of CIC's friends and a friend of the president. The meeting was held in the presidential palace and there were several layers of security to go through. Our party consisted of Miguel Grau, Willem Van Nierkerk, Jorge Fierro, and me, and there were about five presidential assistants at the meeting. We were all seated around an oval table, and when President Franco entered he sat next to me. His first move was to get down on the floor to check my ankles, which he reported to be in good shape (this had become a joke). This totally amazed Willem. President Franco's second move was to say (in Spanish), "David, what is the next step in your titanium project?" I answered, "Mr. President, the next step is to get an electricity price agreed upon." Several seconds of complete silence followed. Then President Franco shouted instructions to several of his aides and the last order was to get Carlos Heisele Sosa, president of ANDE (National Electricity Association) on the phone. Less than a minute later Carlos Heisele Sosa called back. It was a one-way call in which Federico said, "I want you to give Mr. Lowell a price for electricity for his project. Today!"

He asked me if we wanted to study the problem and visit ANDE in the morning. I said no, we want to have the meeting today. Later that day, we arrived at the ANDE president's office and were met by two gentlemen with hangdog expressions. Miguel began the conversation and Carlos Heisele Sosa produced a small piece of paper with a few numbers representing a sliding scale of costs in U.S. cents per kilowatt hour representing, first, the twenty-four-hour price and, second, lower prices with various different amounts of power used during the three-hour peak load period. These rates were satisfactory to us, and we agreed to write and sign an agreement within a few days. This was an opportunity for a new industry in Paraguay, precipitated by my short conversation with President Franco. While leaving the office I was introduced to the assistant to the ANDE president. I discovered that he was the father of one of two Paraguayan students to whom we had given MS scholarships to study at the Lowell Institute of Mineral Resources at the University of Arizona. It happened that Dr. Poulton, director of the Institute, had recently told me that both Paraguayan students were getting good grades, and hearing this seemed to have pleased Mr. Bernal very much.

Getting the electricity price settled was a very important step in the Alto Paraná Project. Our joint venture partner said it was the most important thing remaining in regard to their decision to sign the preliminary joint venture agreements. I felt enormous relief that the meeting with President Federico Franco had gone so well. I am grateful for his help and friendship.

Australian Academy of Science 2009 Haddon King Medal

I received the Haddon King Medal at a dinner presentation in Canberra, Australia, in February 2010. The award is given for research in mineral

Photo taken prior to David Lowell's induction into National Mining Hall of Fame, Las Vegas, 2012. From left, Roger Newell, David, J. P. Roczniak, and Jim Moore.

exploration. The talk I gave was a review of my exploration career, in some respects similar to this autobiography, and several people present said that they were amazed by hearing about my career.

National Mining Hall of Fame Inductee

In September 2012, I was inducted into the National Mining Hall of Fame at Las Vegas, Nevada, as one of the world's foremost authorities on porphyry copper deposits and outstanding exploration geologist and mine finder. The National Mining Hall of Fame is headquartered in Leadville, Colorado, where an elaborate mining museum is also located. The custom of the National Mining Hall of Fame in their award ceremonies is to require formal dress, which for men is a black tie suit.

London Mining Journal Lifetime Achievement Award

In December 2012, I received the London Mining Journal Lifetime Achievement Award at an event called "Mines and Money" in London. It interfered with a sailing vacation we had planned, but we went to London anyway. Delaying the sailing trip required a hard-boiled negotiation with Edith: we had to first attend a stage play in London. This was very enjoyable in spite of getting lost walking back to the hotel in the rain. The second concession was doing the sailing trip a year later—which we did.

It's not possible to accurately compare awards, but this *Mining Journal* award may be the most prestigious in the mining industry. The chairman told me when the award was offered that there would be one thousand men in black tie dress seeing me receive the award, and he was right.

CHAPTER FIVE

Formation of Lowell Copper Ltd.

During September and October of 2013, a new public company was formed with me as CEO and chairman, Marcel de Groot as president, and Jorge Fierro as vice president, exploration. The current worldwide situation in mining finance is disastrous, with predictions that more than half of junior mining companies will go out of business in the next year. Lowell Copper is an exception, with $10 million on hand and the capability of raising large amounts if required.

We have reviewed other juniors in distressed condition, looking for companies we could acquire at low cost that own attractive and mineable ore deposits. We have found several with apparently good copper-gold deposits and are optimistic that Lowell Copper will be a success. We have already considered prospective acquisition targets in nine countries. Our assets include two mineral prospects and a database that allows almost instant access to data on mining companies and their mineral assets. Another large asset is Jorge Fierro's almost unmatched capability to evaluate deposits in the field and the office. Lowell Copper has almost a dream team, including directors and management.

The Warintza Project in Ecuador

The difficulty of doing business in Ecuador has changed upward and downward with changes of administration. It has been particularly difficult since about 2005 and has left the Warintza Project stranded after the discovery of 200 million tonnes of 0.7 percent copper equivalent ore. Surface mapping and sampling gives encouragement that more exploration will double these figures.

The Ricardo Project in Chile

The Ricardo Project was proposed and has been planned by two consulting geologists: John Proffett and John Hunt, both world-class ore-deposit geologists. They worked together on a geological study, isotopic age dating study, and extensive drilling project related to an underground development at the Chuquicamata Mine. In the course of their study they recognized that four faulted segments had been removed from Chuquicamata which have not been found by subsequent exploration. These segments appear from various evidence to have been carried about thirty kilometers south by horizontal displacement of the Chuquicamata West Fissure. This would move them to the area of the Ricardo property now owned by Lowell Copper Ltd. Several other mining companies have unsuccessfully explored this target, but we are hopeful that the two Johns will be successful based on better understanding of the geology.

The Santa Marta Copper Project in Mexico

The Santa Marta prospect is in the State of Oaxaca, Mexico. It is a VMS (volcanic massive sulfide) deposit originally recognized by David Jones, an exploration geologist with a track record of several mine discoveries in Mexico. David's work was confirmed by James Franklin, a world expert on VMS orebodies. Lowell Copper plans to begin an exploration drilling project at Santa Marta in the spring of 2014. The chances are good of finding a multimillion-tonne mineable copper-zinc-gold orebody at Marta, and we are investigating other mineral prospects in the same district.

CHAPTER SIX

History of Our Atascosa Ranch

Edith and I bought the Atascosa Ranch in 1975. An uncle of mine, Jim Cumming, had been co-owner of part of the present ranch back in the 1920s. I never knew Uncle Jim, who died in a horse accident before I was born. At that time the ranch went out of the family, and when we looked at it for purchase, it had had a couple of different owners. In 1975 we were optimistically thinking we were going to make a profit from raising cattle. We did make a profit for a few years, but cattle ranching has gotten less and less profitable with the increasing number of environmental regulations and lower beef prices in the United States through much of the history of the ranch.

I spent part of my childhood on what was then called the Cumming Ranch and is now the National Forest Murphy Grazing Lease Allotment and part of the Atascosa Ranch. The Murphy Allotment is now owned by our son Doug but is operated as part of the Atascosa Ranch. Cattle have probably grazed on the ranch for at least two hundred years, dating back to Mexican and Spanish times.

The first known Anglo rancher on that land was Arthur Peck, whose family was massacred on what is now the Atascosa Ranch by part of Geronimo's Apache band on April 27, 1886. Others were murdered by the same band in the same raid at the Ruby Mine site about ten miles to the west as the crow flies. My grandfather,

David is riding Lucky and Edith is riding Laddie, both Missouri Fox Trotters who didn't win in the Springfield Horse Show but starred on the Atascosa Ranch.

Douglas Wallace Cumming, was on the coroner's jury investigating the killings.

Cattle were later grazed in the area by a man originally from Eastern Europe named Piskorski. One of our grazing leases was originally called the Piskorski Allotment; the canyon was originally called "Polack Canyon," but more recently the name was changed to the more politically correct "Peck Canyon."

In the early 1920s, during the open-range era, cattle were grazed over part of the area by a partnership consisting of my uncle Jim Cumming and Buck Sorrels. Later the Piskorski Allotment, which is the north half of the Atascosa Ranch, was owned by Joe Kane, and the

Ramanote allotment, the south half, was owned by his brother Bob Kane. We also now own about two hundred fifty acres of private land on the east side of the ranch. Altogether a National Forest grazing lease plus private land covers about thirty square miles or, with the Murphy Allotment, about fifty square miles, but almost all of this is National Forest grazing leases. When we bought the Joe Kane allotment in 1975 and the Bob Kane allotment a few years later, owning the grazing lease was almost like owning the land. However, as time goes on the rancher has less and less to say about how the land and grazing will be managed.

The house at the ranch headquarters is a Frankenstein construction consisting of three parts of three distinctly different ages. A center section, built of local rock cemented with low-quality mortar, dates back to about 1890, when it was used as a cowboy line cabin. The north end was two or three rooms built from adobe in the early 1940s. When we bought the ranch in 1975 there were two adobe rooms in a second

Edith and David at Atascosa Ranch, 1993.

David with Brangus bulls in the Wise Mesa corrals, 2000.

Edith with Brangus cattle and dog Ginger in 2010.

story, but between the time we agreed to buy the ranch and the time we closed the deal the house burned down. We brought in an architect, who said it would be better to rebuild without the second story, so we use part of the original second story as a sewing room and overflow houseguest loft. We had not planned to stay full time in the house, but when our plans changed, we added two rooms of frame construction on the south end. At the same time we remodeled an existing ranch building into a ranch and mining office.

During the thirty-seven years we have operated the ranch we have had several different ranch foremen. Douglas Cumming, my cousin who was operating the contiguous Cumming Ranch (now the Murphy allotment), was foreman for a few years. Later his son, Jim Cumming, served as foreman for several years. He was followed by Rudy Acevedo for a few months. Then Manuel Salomon worked for us twenty-six years and is now semiretired. He was foreman for about twenty-five years, with duties divided with Marcia Racine, who was my mining secretary and also handled the ranch business chores.

Simon Escalada, our long-term large animal vet, is a super capable veterinarian and advisor about everything that moves on the ranch: cows, horses, dogs, and cats and sometimes us. I remember helping him in the middle of the night treat a cow with a prolapsed uterus. We hoisted her into a vertical position with her back feet tied to the bucket of a tractor. She thrived after the treatment.

For the past two years, Reed Thwaits has been in charge, with the title of manager rather than foreman, which reflects the advancing ages of Edith and me, who can no longer put in a long horseback ride. Reed is a first-class ranch manager. A number of Mexican American cowboys have worked on the ranch, and Spanish is the most-spoken language.

Many cowboys have worked for us over the years, but Humberto Leal was our most impressive cowboy. Some people have a natural talent for working with animals, and he was one of those. He had taken a short veterinary course in Mexico lasting only a few months, but had learned a great deal. In contrast with lots of Mexicans I've known, Humberto

Marcia Racine: A Near-Perfect Assistant

Marcia answered an ad in January 1986, was hired, and worked for us until 2004. There is a story connected with both her arrival and departure. When she applied for my job she was working part time for my best friend in Santa Cruz County, Cabot Sedgwick. Cabot has passed away, but was a wealthy graduate lawyer, retired U.S. State Department officer and cattle rancher. In 2006 Marcia came back to work on a part-time basis.

She has a high school education, but has amplified this to university level by self-training to become a paralegal in the Connecticut law firms where she worked for nineteen years. She then became a self-taught and very competent accountant. She was also manager of our 250-head cattle ranch for four years while we lived in Chile. She has a photographic memory and a good self-taught background in practical mining engineering and geology. She has the most curiosity of any person I have ever known and can't stand not understanding anything. Working with her entails answering a steady series of questions.

Then there is her reliability and loyalty. When Arequipa Resources was handed a hostile takeover by Barrick Gold, Marcia was in the middle of a vacation in Connecticut, but got back to my office the next day to help me work with three firms of lawyers. I can't count the number of times she has come by the office on Saturday or Sunday or some national holiday to help me. She is a team player. There is also a serious question as to whether she signed on as an employee or as a member of the family. We all love Marcia.

felt a genuine sympathy for horses and cows. He also teamed up with Marcia or with me to form a two-person foreman. On Memorial Day weekend in 1986, Humberto went on a Sunday beer-drinking holiday with friends to the Peña Blanca Lake and was in a skiff that turned over. He could not swim and he drowned. It was a very sad time.

Humberto Leal on the left and David on the right in 1985. Humberto was an expert cowboy and nice guy who drowned in Peña Blanca Lake during a Sunday picnic outing with his family and friends in 1986.

Ismael was a hardworking, tough, somewhat mean, champion fence builder. He built about ten miles of barbed wire fences on the Atascosa Ranch. His level of education was low and he didn't fit very well into the American society. His son, Sergio, to some degree grew up on the ranch and is now married and has children.

Ruben was a bad egg who worked for us about a year and then, we think, robbed our house. He later died in Mexico.

José Gutierrez worked on the ranch for short periods two or three times, mostly as a stonemason. He was very good at what is now largely a lost art in the United States. He could fit rocks together to form a smooth surface with minimal area devoted to cracks, using dry wall construction, without cement. José lived in southeastern Mexico. He would work in the United States for a couple of months, save his

Emma Salazar

Emma Salazar was hired in December 2008, and has worked for me for five years. She was born in Magdalena, Sonora, Mexico, and she and her husband still own a small ranch in Mexico. Emma has a Mexican secondary school education and a pretty good English vocabulary. One of her previous jobs was with a Nogales, Arizona, newspaper, and she has a good graphics background. She also is much more computer literate than I am, and between the two of us we have gone a long way toward computerizing my files, and we can translate technical reports back and forth into Spanish. We are happy to have Emma.

money, and maybe not return for a year. It was a win-win immigration scheme. In those years an employer could not be arrested for hiring an illegal alien. After the law changed, we hired only U.S. citizens or men with proper papers. But the whole border zone atmosphere changed at about the same time, with aliens becoming predominately city people who often did not appear trustworthy to us. The flow of drugs went through a huge increase, and we started finding dead bodies, some of them pretty clearly victims of murder by drug runners. In 2010, six bodies were found on the ranch, including Officer Brian Terry of the U.S. Border Patrol.

Another interesting cowboy who worked at the ranch off and on for about five years was Martin Andrade ("Mar-teen"). Martin was very curious and sharp-eyed and observant. He once came up to me in the yard with a Safeway grocery bag and said (in Spanish), "Do you want to see something interesting?" I looked in the bag and there was a pretty fresh human head. I quizzed him as to exactly where he had found it and then told him to grab a horse and put it back exactly where he had found it. I called the sheriff's office the next morning, and two deputies came out and went with Martin to collect the head. They spent two

hours in an effort to find a body to go with the head, but were unsuccessful. The government later told a newspaper reporter that the head
went with a body found in the canyon at an elevation 200 feet lower
and a distance of one-half to one mile away. I was taught in geology
classes that detrital objects like sand grains, or pebbles, or boulders, or
human heads travel downhill, not uphill, but you have to make some
allowance for political interpretation.

We often ask ourselves, "Why are we here?" I guess the answer is
that as uncomfortable as the ranch sometimes is, with a flood in 1983
that washed some of our possessions—including a pickup truck—a
couple of miles down the canyon, and a fire in 2011 that burned over
eighty percent of our ranch, and plagues of grasshoppers, and chiggers,
and environmentalists, and this year, rattlesnakes (with two dogs bitten
but recovered), it is a lovely, quiet, tranquil, place to live—most of the
time. If you asked our springer spaniel, Ginger, she would tell you it's
Shangri-la!

Two members of the Lowell family in 2013: Spook III on the left and
Ginger on the right.

Mountain lions are relatively abundant here, and there are probably now more than there ever were because of less hunting. They can be a significant economic problem in raising cattle. We had twenty-one calves killed by lions one year, and we probably averaged a few every year in the thirty-seven years that we've had the ranch. Doug Cumming had a pack of black and tan hounds that he used for lion hunting, which happened every time calves started being killed. Twenty-five or thirty years ago I returned home after riding most of the day on our ranch. I got a call from Doug saying that he had wounded a lion that was in a cave up on a very rough part of his ranch. He asked me if I would like to go up with him—we'd have to dispatch it after dark, probably.

He'd had one or two of his dogs with him that had cornered the lion. I guess the story was the lion was first in a tree, and Doug shot at the lion with a little .22 pistol in his saddlebag. He thought he had hit it, and it jumped down from the tree and ran into a cave, where he thought it might still be.

I was already tired, but I got another horse and rode with him. It was a two-hour ride up to the place where the cave was. We shined our flashlights in the cave and crawled in. There was a back door to the cave that he hadn't seen, so the lion hadn't been cornered in the cave—it had run in one side and sneaked out the other. There was no evidence that it had been shot, either, and, as it turned out, it hadn't been. Doug, who was an expert lion hunter, thought it might still be in the vicinity. This first cave was a slab of rock in a slope where a cliff had caved off some time in the past, and there were many large rocks, some of which had spaces underneath that made caves. We had four or five lion hounds, and one little terrier–beagle hound cross named Gypsy, who had come along for the expedition.

We started looking under these other rocks, spread over an area of maybe two hundred yards on a steep slope. It was hard to get up the slope. I carried Gypsy under my arm, and I had a .30-30 rifle and a flashlight also. We had to boost the lion hounds up some of these little cliffs in order to get them up. Each rock we came to I inserted Gypsy's nose under the rock to watch for her reaction, and she didn't react until finally, sometime later, we found a house-sized rock. I was ahead of Doug, and I stuck Gypsy's head under the rock, and she cringed.

I called down to Doug and told him. He said, "Well, that isn't necessarily a lion. It could be a bobcat or a javelina or a coatimundi." And he continued through this list. Then came a noise like "Wrrrraaow." And he said, "But in this case it is a lion." By this time, it was getting dark. We looked under the rock. There were two openings under the rock. We shined our lights and couldn't see the cat. There was a crack in the rock, and Doug got up on top with a lasso, tied a rock to the end of it, and banged it around.

I was at the second opening, kind of cowering behind a little six-inch-diameter oak tree. If the lion ran out that way, I might get a shot at it, but it would pass very close to me. Doug was by the original hole, and the lion would growl when the rock banged around, but wouldn't come out. We did this for a couple of hours. The lion had killed a calf that day that belonged to us, and I finally decided to crawl in the hole with my flashlight and rifle. I crawled in a ways and I could finally see part of the lion. I lined the rifle and the flashlight up and shot it. There was lots of thrashing around, and I scooted out as fast as I could. By that time, it was pitch dark, and we skinned the lion with considerable difficulty. The slope was steep, and we couldn't see anything to guide the horses, but they found their way back without my being able to see even the horse in front of me. We got back at 2:00 a.m.

I shot another lion a few years later. Manuel Salomon had been riding to check cattle in the Aleman pasture and he found a calf killed by a lion, partly eaten and dragged and left against the trunk of a large juniper tree. Once every year or two on average we inherit an orphan "dogie" calf whose mother has died. It is a real chore giving a calf in a pen a large bottle of mixed milk substitute twice a day for months. This dead calf was one of our dogies, which had been named "Sparky" by our granddaughters.

At that time it was legal to trap lions on the National Forest, and I decided to go back to the kill with Manuel that afternoon and set two lion traps we had. Manuel saddled my horse Smokey, a big Missouri Fox Trotter and a very easy riding horse. Just as an afterthought I grabbed a pistol, a .357 Smith and Wesson revolver, which carries a big wallop. We rode about an hour and found the dead calf. I asked Manuel to stay on the mule he was riding and I started to ride around the juniper, which was surrounded by bushes. My scheme was to find a log that could be dragged with a lasso rope from the saddle horn to form the second half of a funnel to guide the cat over the place where I was planning to bury the traps. Mountain lions have a poor sense of smell and are relatively easy to catch in traps, but I thought it would be good to minimize the number of human tracks. As I started around the bushes I saw a small patch of fur between the limbs of a bush and thought it might be a second kill. I pointed my finger and said in Spanish, "Can you see what kind of animal that is?" Manuel leaned down from his mule and answered, "That is the lion!!"

In a split second I decided it was worth risking being thrown off, and I pulled out the pistol, aimed at the fur spot about twenty feet away, and pulled the trigger. Three things happened during the next second: Smokey, who had no idea that a .357 was about to go off beside his ear, jumped straight up a long ways, and I stayed on more through luck than skill; Manuel's mule jumped straight up but executed a 180-degree turn in the air; and the lion shot out under Smokey's nose and raced toward a small canyon about eighty yards across. I landed pointing in the same direction and put Smokey in a lope, then jumped off and sat down to have a rest when the lion emerged on the other slope of the canyon. Pistols are not very accurate and it would not be likely that I would hit the lion running fifty or one hundred yards away. But he never came out of the canyon. Manuel and I walked down the slope and found the lion shot through the chest cavity and dead. Our granddaughters who had named Sparky asked several times about how Sparky was doing but got evasive answers.

The flood of illegal aliens and drug smugglers in the last ten to fifteen years has caused other ranching problems. In addition to having some homicidal cartel people crossing the ranch almost at will, we have multiple barbed wire fences cut every year, tanks drained by punctured pipelines, leaving cattle without water to drink, and other assorted vandalism. These intrusions create dire consequence, but given the little you hear in the public press, we can't help but think that both the Border Patrol and Forest Service are operating under orders to not report critically anything that would put the illegals and smugglers in a bad light.

Around 2006 there was an article in a Tucson newspaper that said each of the seven large wildfires that year in southern Arizona was caused by illegal aliens. For the past two or three years there have been even more and larger fires (including one that burned about 80 percent of the Atascosa Ranch). One was directly blamed on illegal alien vandalism, but most of them are started by illegals.

Our problems with illegal aliens reached a peak in 2010, when there were at least six people killed on our ranch alone. One was a Border Patrolman, and the other five Mexican cartel members fighting members of another cartel. In addition to the six killed, other illegals were shot at and two or three wounded and one other Border Patrolman wounded in the leg. It was a war zone.

Our interaction with illegals has also gradually changed. Twenty or thirty years ago there were only a few crossing, and most of these were from small villages where they were engaged in farming or ranching. If they were hungry or thirsty they knocked on our door and we always gave them water and usually food. They came in groups of two or three and often asked if we had a day or two of work to finance the rest of their trip, usually to a destination in Arizona. At that time employers were not subject to prosecution, and we often found some job like cleaning the yard or cutting wood. We knew that most of them only stayed for two or three months to save some money, because the same group would stop again going back to Mexico. These on the whole were open-faced, relatively reliable and honest people, almost always men.

However, since 2000 or so the game has changed. The number of illegal aliens has increased by probably five times since we bought the ranch. Their origin is now from cities in Mexico and Central America and a lot from China. Statistics I've seen show that 15 percent are felons. Their cost for border crossing is $2,000 to $6,000 each, to be guided from departure points in the interior of Mexico to sites in southern Arizona. The guides, "coyotes," are bad people who leave illegals to their own devices when they can't keep up, and many of these crossers die in the mountains or desert. We have had a number come to the house in terrible shape, and they sometimes ask us to call the Border Patrol to save them. We have had men show up in discarded clothes and shoes that didn't fit who said they had been robbed of everything they had, including clothes, by the coyotes and had picked up their present clothes along the trail.

The recent groups include something like 10 to 20 percent women. I have been told by Border Patrolmen that it is thought that most of these are raped en route if they don't have husbands or men in the group to protect them. Many rape sites are known, one on our ranch, where the coyotes rape the women they are guiding and leave their underwear on a "rape tree" as a trophy. One such site in the Pajarito Wilderness Area a mile from the Mexican border had thirty-two sets of women's underwear. We feel the whole illegal immigration problem has been very badly mishandled by the government.

Beginning roughly in 1910, the Douglas Wallace Cumming family, and later his sons Jim and John, and finally his grandchildren, Douglas Cumming, and Edith and myself have been ranching in the Peck Canyon area. You could also say his great-grandson, Doug Lowell, is part of the succession because he bought the John Cumming Forest Grazing Allotment, which is being run by the Atascosa Ranch crew. My cousin, Doug Cumming, who is now deceased, was married to Peggy Cumming who was a registered nurse and is a charming elderly lady who still lives in the Cumming ranch house in Peck Canyon. Her two sons, Tom and Jim, live nearby.

This period since 1910 spans the change of Arizona from a territory to a state, and of Peck Canyon from being open range to National Forest grazing lease land. It also spans the period during the 1930s and 1940s when grazing was the most important use for the National Forest land and the National Forest was administered in a more practical and less bureaucratic way. The National Forest has become more bureaucratic, with many more employees and many more regulations that inhibit operating a cattle ranch.

A lot has happened since we bought the ranch. We have remodeled and expanded the house and converted a nearby hay barn into a nice office for myself and a secretary. We have a reliable water system, and we paid to have a power line brought in so we now have air-conditioning, computers, and a sophisticated alarm system. We realigned and paved our road so we now have access when the canyon is in flood, and we don't feel isolated even though our nearest neighbor is a mile away.

Most of the cattle work is done on horseback because road building is not allowed on the National Forest. There are few Anglo cowboys employed in southern Arizona, and in general the Mexican American cowboys are more skillful than the available Anglos. We now employ an Anglo ranch manager who speaks fluent Spanish and a Mexican cowboy with proper papers who has worked for more than ten years in the United States. Both are very competent cattlemen.

I was born near the Mexico border and have had many friends and relatives in the border zone. We also lived twice in Mexico for a total of two years and I considered myself an authority—that is, until we bought the Atascosa Ranch and had frequent contacts with the border population. It is important to understand, first, that the border is not the finite line that appears on maps. In fact it is a zone maybe fifty miles wide, and, beginning twenty-five miles below the border, moving northward in the Mexican countryside, you begin noticing an increasing number of people who speak a little English. By the time you arrive at Nogales, Sonora, the large majority of second- or third-generation residents speak poor to excellent English.

The U.S. side is the mirror image, with almost 100 percent of second- or third-generation natives speaking good Spanish in Nogales, Arizona. The quality of Spanish steadily diminishes going northward into Arizona, and twenty-five miles into Arizona people are not likely to be bilingual. I am reasonably fluent in Spanish and I have had some humorous experiences. A number of times I have been unable to buy something in a store in Nogales, Arizona, without speaking Spanish; however, an equal number of times in Nogales, Sonora, a clerk has been completely unwilling to speak Spanish!

CHAPTER SEVEN

I have a number of hobbies and recreations that I have enjoyed over the years.

Collecting Mine Lamps

Human beings are divided into two groups. There are junk collectors and junk thrower-outers. I'm firmly in the category of being a junk collector. I have a large collection of mine lamps that come from Arizona, Nevada, the Philippines, Peru, Chile, and Cyprus, and I have a couple of oil lamps from Iran. It's a hit-or-miss collection. Probably half of my lamps are oil lamps, originally whale oil lamps from the 1800s, and half are carbide lamps. Ignoring the very old Persian lamps, which probably weren't used in the mines, the others range in age from maybe two hundred fifty or three hundred years old to a few years old.

I have a homemade pirquinero carbide lamp from Chile. The lamp was in use at the time I acquired it, made out of two tin cans: a small-diameter tin can in the middle, opening downward, and a large-diameter can opening upward on the outside. The inner can has a small hole as a flame orifice punched in it, and there is a wire hasp, a ring to hang the lamp. You put the carbide in the middle can and the water in the outer can, and there is a stick that can be twisted on the top for adjusting the pressure between the two cans to regulate the flow of water. It works quite well. I have a total of thirty-five or forty lamps, but the jewel of my collection is a dented-up old Dew-R-Lite carbide lamp.

Dew-R-Lite carbide light that saved David's life. The dents are visible from falling down the raise (shaft) after he lost consciousness. This lamp is part of a collection of mine lamps that range in age from about 1700 to 2004. Some of them were whale oil lamps and some carbide lamps.

This is the lamp that saved my life in the Santa Eulalia Mine in Mexico by indicating with its flame that the air contained almost no oxygen.

Lifelong Exercise Program

Beginning in about 1955 I realized that my typical schedule of a number of consecutive days of sedentary office work followed by periods of vigorous field work was not good for me. I found an exercise program developed for the Royal Canadian Air Force that could be done every day in your home or hotel room to keep up a degree of physical fitness. I followed this program for more than fifty years until I began to develop fairly serious lower back problems related to osteoporosis.

At that point I began an intensive medical campaign to control the osteoporosis, which was eventually successful but still left me with curvature problems and dinged-up vertebrae. At one point I had been treated with Forteo for two years, which was a self-injection in the abdomen once a day, and the drug required refrigeration. This was sometimes difficult to arrange because I was working a lot in the field at that time on the Toromocho Project.

Skin Diving and the Gulf of California

My hobby during most of my life, and the subject of many of our vacations, was skin diving along the Sonora coast and the Baja California coast of the Sea of Cortez with one or two other divers. We typically spent the whole day free diving with an inner tube or inflatable life raft as a base and were very successful in spearing fish.

We did mostly free diving with a face plate and a snorkel and a weight belt. We sometimes did tank diving (scuba diving), but it was difficult to have enough tanks to do very much spearfishing with tanks. Most of our fishing was done at a depth of twenty or thirty or, rarely, forty feet, which is difficult to do without a tank, but I once got down to sixty-five feet.

David with 100-pound grouper speared at San Agustín Bay, Sonora, 1965.

Camping on Sonora coast of Gulf of California about 1965. David was awarded (in an election rigged by Susie) the title of most cheerful camper. The pink T-shirt was the prize.

Wayne Wallace, who was a Kern County Land Company geologist and later a Tenneco geologist, often went diving with me. Lee Vought, another geologist who had a business and didn't work as a geologist and has been a friend through most of my life, also often went diving with me. Bob Thurman, the co-discoverer of the Pima Mine went with us a couple of times. There were sometimes other people who went, but the hard-core group was Wayne, Lee, and me.

These were mostly family trips, with kids. Usually the three of us were the only ones who went diving; the kids and the wives didn't. We fished primarily for grouper. The typical size of fish that we got was ten to thirty pounds. On two occasions I got really large groupers, over a hundred pounds. It gets to be a real rodeo to get a fish that big up to the surface, especially free diving.

There was a Vought family camping trip to a small, isolated bay on the Sonora coast. We did not go on this trip, but two sets of other families went with the Voughts. One was a Vought friend who was a curator for the Arizona Sonora Desert Museum, and his family. Also invited was a ten-year-old friend of Lee Vought, Jr.

No people were living near their campsite, but there was a hill nearby with a shrine and large cross on top. The first notable event was when Connie Vought, about fourteen years old, and another teenage girl on the trip had a romantic idea. They decided to climb the hill and burn a candle in the shrine. This went well except shortly afterward the shrine and the cross burned down. This required a hurried trip to Caborca to find anyone who claimed any association with the shrine and would accept money to rebuild it.

The museum curator had volunteered to construct a "john" for the group and set up a tent over the toilet. He also brought a jug of purifying liquid to make the john smell good. Someone used the john while smoking a cigarette and threw the cigarette butt in the john at which point the john exploded because it turned out the purifying liquid was flammable.

Also, the Voughts had a small camping trailer that literally fell apart on the way back to Caborca. When the Voughts got back to Tucson very late at night the ten-year-old said, "Oh Mrs. Vought, it was the best trip I have ever had, with the cross burning down, the john blowing up, and the trailer unrolling—it was a wonderful trip!"

We had very pleasant times camping, cooking our meals on campfires. We used to buy Oso Negro Mexican rum and have rum and Coca-Cola, or Cuba libres. We would sometimes catch shrimp or lobsters and cook them. Back in those days it was quite safe to camp out in the country in Mexico. We had lots of skin diving adventures over the years and look back with pleasure to this period of our lives.

On one occasion our friends Lee and Dottie Vought, who were living near San Diego at the time, learned about a package trip to the town of Loreto on the Baja California peninsula. They called us and suggested we meet them with our plane at the hotel, which was the destination of the package tour. We agreed and in due course met them in Baja California. The Vought's group flew down in a very old DC-3, and when the pilot (who was also the mechanic and tour director) went out to service the airplane Lee went with him. Lee had been a navigator in World War II, flying in B-25 bombers stationed in China, and knew quite a bit about airplanes. The combination pilot, mechanic, and tour director had to put about a bucket of oil in each of the two engines, which Lee thought wasn't too good.

The first night Lee's group arrived they had what the tour director called "messycan night," and the next morning quite a few of the group were sick. A bus trip was planned this second day to the Pacific side of Baja, and one of the tour members approached Lee, who spoke a little Spanish, and asked, "What is the word for 'stop!' and what is the word for 'bush'?"

On many of our trips we traveled in our first airplane, a Cessna 182 with heavy-duty landing gear and a Robertson kit, which was an aircraft modification to enable the plane to fly at slow speeds and land on short airstrips. We sometimes landed on dirt roads or flat terrain without trees, but our vacation trips were usually to sportfishing hotels on the east coast of Baja California. Some of the fun parts of the trips were the landings on fairly short and sometimes steeply inclined airstrips at some of the hotels. Our favorite hotel was Punta Colorada, which had a unique airstrip: the approach was a flat section a hundred yards long on the beach, and the airstrip then went up a slope on a hill another fifty yards and then had three hundred yards at the top of the hill so you touched down on the approach end, ran up the hill, and stopped at the top of the plateau. One of the kicks in flying to the hotels and their little dirt airstrips was that this permitted you to buzz the hotel building and, doing it right, you would approach twenty to fifty feet above the roof of the hotel building and then cycle the pitch of your propeller from high to low to high, which made a loud roar. With this announcement the hotel sent a car out to collect you and your baggage on the airstrip. Hoping to avoid a second buzz job, they were always prompt.

On one occasion we flew to Baja California with our friends John and Nancy Sumner in their airplane. We found the hotel fully booked, but they shuffled people a bit so that the Sumner-Lowell contingent had one small joint room. Shortly after we settled in there was a loud noise and disturbance outside our room. We ran out to see what was going on, and a low-winged Piper aircraft had just landed. By this time the light was poor and the aircraft partly missed the runway and skidded off some distance and almost went back in the ocean. We ran out to see if anybody was hurt. Other people from the hotel also arrived, and we found that there were no injuries but the airplane had been badly damaged. It had been piloted by a professional baseball player. I had observed that hobby pilots from other specialties, like MDs, weren't necessarily very good at flying, and perhaps this held for pro baseball players.

John Sumner was a pilot with 5,000 hours of flying time and had flown as a Marine Corps fighter pilot in World War II and Korea. He was the flight instructor who taught me to fly in 1967. He said once that he liked the Marine Corps training system. They had a joystick instead of a wheel to control the airplane. The student pilot was in the rear seat. When the student did something dumb, John would instruct him to put his head in his lap and would pound on his forehead with the rear seat joystick.

John had been a Marine Corps major when he left the service, but he retained his disciplinarian training and had us organized to get up at six o'clock in the morning and leave early after our joint night in the hotel room. The last thing he picked up when he left the hotel room was his baseball cap on the dresser. We took off to fly to another spot in Baja California that had been our original objective, but after we got to cruising altitude John's head itched and he took off his baseball cap and a little mouse jumped out of his hat and was never found again in the airplane.

Once on a trip to Baja California we were listening to the airplane radio and another amateur pilot from California thought he didn't have enough gasoline to reach the next airstrip. We listened to the dialogue for half an hour. The California pilot got more and more upset and his voice rose higher and higher and finally he started sending instructions on how to distribute his property to family and friends, but the story

Repennings at
Sportsman's
Lodge, Baja
California, in
1975.

had a happy ending when he landed at La Paz. On a trip once with our friends Rep and Nancy Repenning we were in our airplane and stopped at a hotel called the Sportsman's Lodge Hotel, and Rep, who was a vertebrate paleontologist and had a collection of mammal skulls, found a dead sea lion and removed the head with the idea of boiling the skull. He brought it back in a plastic bag that didn't clearly show what kind of object was in the bag and hung it on the rafter outside his room. A waiter came by and Rep, whose Spanish was very limited, pointed at the bag and said "pescadero" to the waiter, whose mouth dropped open in horror. Rep had been trying to say "pescado" because he didn't know the word for sea lion. "Pescadero" means fisherman. Another time we stayed at the same hotel and, a week before, the hotel had been almost totally booked by the owner of Shakey's Pizza, which had just been sold to a larger pizza company. Shakey had lined up a bunch of local residents and friends and relatives, and they had a truly wild time in the

Sportsman's Lodge. There was lots of nude swimming and such. While we were there the locals were happily building a monument to commemorate the Shakey visit to their hotel.

In some of my commuting back and forth across the Pacific, I arranged to stop at Truk Lagoon. I was by myself, but I was able to hire a Trukese fellow who got us some tanks, and we dove for a couple of days on sunken Japanese ships. One of the interesting things he knew about was in the hull of a big Japanese transport. We had a light and went back through stairways and passageways. There was a Japanese Zero airplane stacked between gasoline barrels. I was able to climb with my tanks into the seat of the Zero, ninety feet below the surface of the water. The Japanese had come back after the war and put up a shrine in that ship, as part of the Shinto religion, to commemorate the sailors who died in the ship. Truk Lagoon was fascinating. It was Japan's Pearl Harbor; the American Navy sank sixty ships in the attack.

Edith with a large rainbow trout she caught in Lago Llanquihue in southern Chile.

Edith and David
at the Great
Wall of China,
1982.

Family rafting near Yellowstone National Park, Montana, 2002.

At a bungalow on Fiji during a stopover short vacation en route to the
Haddon King Medal ceremony.

Edith during a visit to Australia in 2010.

I did a lot of reconnaissance flying, sometimes piloting myself and sometimes using a professional pilot. We flew low and slow over the country to map geology and look for alteration zones. We were mapping geology from the air, identifying rock types and sometimes structural features like faults and folds, and also hydrothermal alteration zones, which show up as color zones. There would be somebody with a map and a pencil in the airplane. On some occasions, we would land on a dirt road or a field to get out and look at the rocks, but usually it was all done from the air.

My first plane was a Cessna 182 airplane, which I equipped with a Robertson short-field kit. With the Robertson kit, the ailerons and flaps are geared together so that it makes a flap the whole length of the wing, which allows much slower flight. My original airplane, which had an N number of 8949 X-ray, had oversized tires and beefed-up landing gear for landing in rough fields. This airplane would slow down to a flying speed of 25 mph, quite slow for a fairly heavy airplane.

Over the years, I had others: another Cessna 182 and a Cessna P210, which was a pressurized, six-passenger, high-speed, and higher-altitude plane. It would fly up to 21,000 feet. I didn't have a chance to use that one very much, and I never felt my proficiency was quite up to the performance of the airplane.

I had a 182 when we started spending most of our time in Chile in the mid- to late '80s. It was hangared for a year, and then I flew it for an annual inspection and discovered that I was really no longer a competent pilot. The rule of thumb in flying is that unless you fly every couple of weeks, or at least every month, the edge goes off your proficiency and you become dangerous to yourself and anybody else. So I sold my airplane and haven't had one since.

We had a landing strip at our Atascosa Ranch for ten years or more. It was pretty short and hairy—about 1,400 feet long—and you had to be careful to get down in that distance because there was a cliff on both ends. We later converted that mesa into an irrigated pasture.

Other Recreations and Close Personal Friends

Two of my long-term hunting companions are Gene Kindred and his capable, charming wife, Gerry. We had many adventures including my falling out of a very narrow duck hunting boat while shooting at a duck that flew directly over the boat. Gene and Jerry are professional game bird raisers. Gerry was a speech therapist in schools and Gene a principal. He played football in college and was on the first string. They are close friends and we also owned a Pointer named Rex with them who took many awards.

Before *Sea Cloud* we owned a 50-foot sailboat, *Odyssey,* with Gordon Wieduwilt and his wife, Nancy. We enjoyed many sailing trips with them. Gordon originally worked for Newmont and was an outstanding geophysicist. Sometimes another friend from Tucson, Mary Lou Saegart, would join us on the *Odyssey* and she was the best sail boat captain and ocean companion we ever had.

Hal Lindquist is a person that we originally met when he had a commodity investment company called TAMI (Tucson Asset Management Inc.). They eventually moved out of Tucson, but Hal has remained as a close friend.

Sea Cloud Trips

We first encountered the two *Sea Cloud* vessels, *Sea Cloud* and *Sea Cloud II*, in 2005 when Geoff Loudon was living in London and called us to say that he and Clare had booked tickets on *Sea Cloud II* for the Admiral Nelson 200th Anniversary of the Battle of Trafalgar cruise in the Mediterranean. Both Edith and I were Admiral Nelson fans, and fans of novelist Patrick O'Brian's sea stories, and we signed on for the trip, which included a history professor who gave excellent Nelson lectures. The cruise visited all the Mediterranean sites famous in Nelson's history and began and ended in Barcelona.

Sea Cloud II is a slightly larger modern version of *Sea Cloud*, which is a four-mast square-rigged sailboat originally owned by Marjorie Post, heiress of the Post Foods family. Both boats are luxurious, with excel-

Sea Cloud with full sails spread. She is a square-rigged boat 360 feet long and 50 feet wide which was origi- nally a yacht owned by Marjorie Merriweather Post. *Sea Cloud* carries 55–60 passengers.

lent cuisine. Our four subsequent trips have all been on *Sea Cloud*. Three were in the Mediterranean and the Caribbean and one was a transatlantic trip from the Canary Islands to Barbados. We made the same trip again in November 2013.

The *Sea Cloud* is mostly crewed by expert sailors from the Philippines. Most of the cabin girls and restaurant staff and purser are Germans. On a couple of our trips we were almost the only passengers who were not German. Almost everyone we met, both staff and passengers, were very nice people.

Coming back from the Canary Islands, in the middle of the Atlantic Ocean, the tour director collected a bunch of wine bottles and pieces

Sea Cloud at anchor.

Transatlantic voyage in 2010 on *Sea Cloud*. Departure was from the Canary Islands and arrival at Barbados.

of paper. Edith and many other passengers accepted a bottle and wrote a note and threw it into the ocean. We had almost forgotten about it when, two years later, she got a letter from a Belize lady who owned a small shop next to the hotel beach near Belize where the bottle was found. We even thought about going there on a vacation, but the facilities sounded a little too authentic—like many places I have had to stay in the course of my work. Edith loved the transatlantic voyage because she loves to sail and loves boats and oceans. I loved the trip because I could hide and read a book and really rest up. I was rooted out once for a painting class and painted a picture, which was clearly the best. None of the others had a giant squid, a shark, and an unclothed mermaid, but it is as hard to be recognized as an artist as it is an explorationist.

Our *Sea Cloud* trips have been the low-pressure replacements for the many Cessna 182 vacation trips we earlier took. When we were younger it was fun to study maps each morning and decide where to land at the end of the day, as we did one year on a tour of Mayan ruins in Belize. Now we prefer the ease of the *Sea Cloud*.

CHAPTER EIGHT

Susan Lowell Humphreys and William Ross Humphreys

Susie is a marvel. She was born in 1950 in a hospital in Chihuahua City, Mexico, and with very little argument immediately moved to a mining camp and began riding in an MB army Jeep; not too much later she was going on camping trips. I remember watching her, less than two years old, being passed from Hopi Indian to Hopi Indian up to the roof of a house from where we, almost the only non-Hopis present, watched the Hopi Indian Snake Dance. She was also at Navajo Squaw Dances and other ceremonies where we were the only Anglos.

She started writing "books," which she pasted together, almost before she learned to read and, all in all, was a very happy addition to our family. She was a good student; perhaps "good" is the wrong word. She graduated from Canyon del Oro High School as a National Merit Scholar, earned a four-year scholarship to college, and was a Presidential Scholar. There were only two Presidential Scholars from each state; they were honored with a trip to Washington to meet President Johnson and some of his cabinet.

Susie enrolled at Stanford, where she earned two degrees, including a BA in English and an MA in English and creative writing; after her marriage to Ross Humphreys, she earned an MA and a PhD from Princeton. This required some maneuvering because Ross was completing an MBA at Wharton School of Finance, which was within commuting distance.

The
Humphreys
in Italy, about
2004.

Following the Princeton PhD, Susie taught English and creative writing, first at the University of Texas, Dallas, then at the University of Arizona. Somewhere along the line she started writing books and has published over a dozen, most of which are children's books. They have all been successful, but her best seller, *The Three Little Javelinas,* has sold over a million copies. I even found a copy for sale in the Santiago, Chile, airport. Her PhD dissertation was on the writing methods of Anthony Trollope, and she is now editing and publishing the previously unpublished complete version of a Trollope novel in cooperation with the Trollope Society in England. She and Ross operate a Southwest book distributing and publishing business called Treasure Chest Books, as well as a successful cattle ranch.

Susie and Ross married in 1975. Ross Humphreys is the eldest of five boys in an Army family. He was born in Japan and grew up in Germany. He attended Tufts University and the University of Arizona, earning a degree in chemistry. He worked as a chemist at the San Manuel Mine before he got his MBA at Wharton.

In the Cumming family for a number of generations there has appeared a clearly defined Scottish-clan-style tough, hard-boiled, hold-your-ground-to-the-death personality. In the last three generations my mother and my daughter are type examples, and I might also qualify. Many people have crossed swords with Susie, usually to their sorrow, expecting this nice-looking, very feminine lady to be a pushover and discovering she is actually more of a tiger. Susie is also a generous, loving daughter who has gone out of her way to support her parents whenever a crisis has occurred, and a loving protective mother, always available to help her two daughters, Anna and Mary, and her husband.

Edith and I have a special relationship with Anna, our first granddaughter. Susie and Ross were living in Dallas when Anna was born in 1980, but were planning to move back to Tucson. At the time of Anna's birth Susie developed some medical symptoms that indicated she had a brain tumor. Edith and I went to Dallas to help out. The tumor was benign, but the operation was complicated. While Susie was in the hospital, Edith and Ross and I used an L. L. Bean canvas tote bag to tote Anna into the hospital and up a back elevator to see Susie (with the nurses' agreement). Everything was in a state of confusion. Susie was in the hospital for a couple of weeks, and she and Ross had not had an opportunity to find a house in Tucson.

Edith and I had bought the Atascosa Ranch a few years earlier. The house had burned down shortly before the deal was closed, and we rebuilt the ranch house planning only to spend weekends there. Edith said, "Why don't you and Ross move into our Tucson house, and we will stay at the ranch until things are straightened out?" The Humphreys accepted, and we moved to the ranch, where things were very primitive. The electricity consisted of an unreliable generator, the water supply was not always working, and the telephone service was a cable laid on the ground for two miles. The road access also left something to be desired. When there was a flood in the canyon there was no longer road access, and sometimes not for several days later. None of these things worried us too much then, but probably would now.

Anyway, Anna arrived in the middle of all these problems, and she visited at the ranch often in her early years. Edith and I developed proprietary feelings, like she was partly our daughter, and we have never totally gotten over thinking this.

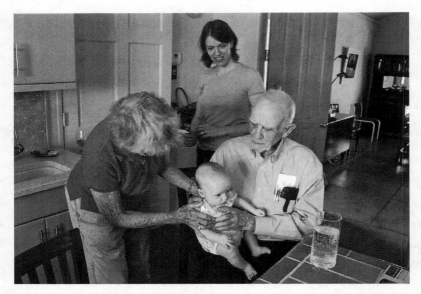

In this photo taken about Christmas 2012, Edith is to the left, Anna Finn in back, David to the right holding Nora in the center. The two apprehensive expressions are on Anna and David.

Anna did well in school and was admitted to Princeton and later to Stanford Law School, where she got a law degree. She met Ed Finn while at Princeton, and eventually they were married. Ed is a really nice guy who grew up partly in Turkey. His father was later ambassador to Afghanistan. Ed got a PhD in English at Stanford while Anna was in law school. He is now a professor at Arizona State University, where he has created a highly regarded program combining English and computer science. Anna had an excellent young-attorney job as a clerk to a federal judge and now works in a law office in Phoenix.

Nora Finn was born to Anna and Ed Finn in Phoenix, Arizona, March 14, 2012. Nora is our first great-grandchild and, as I write, has the distinction of being both the most intelligent and most beautiful baby in the country.

Mary, our second granddaughter, was born in Tucson in 1987. She quickly demonstrated a disinclination to sleep at night that lasted for years. Susie insisted that others needed to sleep, and Mary learned at an early age to use her small CD player for entertainment during the night. She learned to talk, using a large vocabulary as a baby, and also demonstrated mechanical talent, making things and taking an interest in learning how to use all the kitchen appliances as well as her first computers. Mary has a strong personality and a lot of imagination, with her own viewpoint and independent thinking. She became an expert cook and a top student. She graduated from Stanford University with a degree in English in 2009. Since then, she moved to San Francisco, where she held a number of short-term jobs, eventually taking jobs in computer software with a scope for her unusual combination of talents. Mary enjoys running and has competed in races in the San Francisco area.

William David Lowell

Our son Bill was born in Tucson, Arizona, on April 18, 1952. As a youngster he was always interested in mechanical things like motors and trucks and bulldozers and nuts and bolts and welding machines. He was relatively happy and well adjusted. When we were living in the White Canyon, Utah, exploration camp, bulldozers were a common sight. I made Bill, who was one year old at the time, a bulldozer out of a wooden apple crate that he could sit in and make tractor noises.

At White Canyon, we had a Cat skinner named Bill who operated a bulldozer based at the camp. He lived in Blanding, Utah, and had come from the Bronx, New York, during the Great Depression in a CCC program (Civilian Conservation Corps) where he learned to operate a bulldozer. He married a nice Mormon girl, and never left Blanding.

On one visit to our camp, a manager from Grand Junction was taken out to see a road being built, and he said to Leo Miller, camp manager, "I believe that Cat skinner is asleep!" Leo tooted his horn and Bill woke up and waved at them. He was "walking his Cat" along a road to his next construction site, and as he commented to Leo and the manager, "Walking your Cat is like being rocked in your mother's arms." This kind of attitude made Cat skinning look good to one-year-old Bill Lowell.

Bill in his bull-dozer, White Canyon, 1953.

As a young teenager Bill learned to weld and worked on go-cart projects with Reverend Edwards, who was minister of a small church. Reverend Edwards also had a welding business in the middle of a junk-yard on Stone Avenue in Tucson and a small corrugated iron building where he kept his tools, which was guarded by a large dog with a long chain and a "Bad Dog" sign. Our younger son, Doug, was with Bill on one occasion and was told by Reverend Edwards that the dog would bite. But Doug felt that everyone loved him and when he approached closer than the chain length, the dog gave him a painful bite. Doug had big tears running down his face, and the Reverend said something we have quoted many times: "He will do that."

Susie and Bill, camping trip to Morenci, 1955.

In Canyon del Oro High School, Bill was one of the biggest boys, and he went out for football. He broke one of his legs badly and was in a body cast for several months.

As Bill grew older we learned that he had attention deficit disorder. He did well in elementary and high school, but could not concentrate well enough to get through a difficult mechanical engineering course. Bill trained as a welder and a diesel mechanic and later as a commercial fixed-wing and helicopter pilot. He worked as a diesel mechanic in Dallas, Texas, for about twelve years.

In recent years Bill has lived in Nevada and Idaho and has done some work rebuilding cars and building roads with heavy equipment. He has also attended college in Idaho, studying art and history. He enjoys writing short stories with interesting plots and surprise endings. His readers have included a group of inmates in a prison where a friend was serving a sentence for dealing in marijuana. Bill has a kind heart and a lot of friends.

Douglas Glenton Lowell and Roxanne Chernin Lowell

Doug was born June 6, 1956, in Prescott, Arizona, the youngest of our three children. As a baby and toddler he appeared bright and precocious and enjoyed my company. He tried to become involved in anything going on in the family: cooking, carpentry, fixing the plumbing. Susie felt she should have authority over her two younger brothers, but Bill felt a little rivalry, wanting only Doug to participate in a series of make-it-yourself go-carts which sometimes didn't turn out too well. On one occasion Bill had made a go-cart that was hard to start but also, once running, hard to stop. Doug was often the auto mechanic, crouching on the back, adjusting the engine while going at full speed. You might say Bill was the driver and Doug the accelerator, and on one particular Saturday they had successfully arranged a ride with several of Bill's friends to the Canyon Del Oro campus. Also present was the archery team, practicing on the grass with their bows and arrows. With some difficulty, Bill and Doug got their contraption going, with Bill in front steering and Doug trying to get maximum speed out of the one-cylinder motor. Bill steered for the open space and the go-cart went through the middle of the laid out bows and arrows, infuriating the archers, who chased the go-cart. Bill paid no attention to the pursuers running after the go-cart yelling vengeance and retribution. And with his policy to steer toward open areas, Bill made a big circle that routed the go-cart back over the bows and arrows lying on the grass and made it to where his friends were waiting.

As a preteen, Doug raised his horizons to the almost-worn-out-trail-bike level. By this time he had already accumulated one or two concussions in go-cart wrecks, and he was to get more on trail bikes. Early in his career he made a great leap on his trail bike that flattened both wheels. Wheels, not tires. A motorcycle dealer offered to sponsor him for Motocross races when he was twelve. While Edith and I were on our 1970 round-the-world work and vacation trip, Doug rode a friend's motorcycle off a reported twenty-foot-high bluff, which took the paint off the top of his new full-coverage helmet and gave him another concussion. At this point he had been in Tucson Medical Center so often he knew the emergency room staff. This may have been when he decided to become a doctor.

When he graduated from high school he was a National Merit Scholar Finalist. He did a premed course at the University of Arizona and was accepted at both the University of Arizona Medical School and at Harvard Medical School. Doug graduated from Harvard Medical School, took his residency at Chase Presbyterian in Chicago and specialty training as a heart and lung surgeon in Washington, DC, and at Royal Brompton Hospital in London, England. He has had a successful medical career and was voted best doctor in Pima County one year. He is now chief of staff at Tucson Medical Center.

Doug and Roxanne Chernin were married in 1988. In high school in Nogales, Arizona, she was a homecoming princess, and a lifeguard and swim teacher in the summer. She earned an MA in education at the University of Arizona and taught in a junior high school in Nogales. She also helped run family stores in Nogales, Sonora, and Green Valley, Arizona. She is very active in her church and in the children's schools.

Left: Doug and Roxie's children: Marcella, Glenton, Michelle, and Paloma, 2002.
Right: Doug in 1963.

Roxy and Doug have four children, Marcella, Glenton, Michelle, and Paloma. Marcella was born in 1989 in Indianapolis. We were living in Chile and stopped by to meet the new grandchild on a trip home to Arizona. She was a beautiful baby and is a beautiful girl. She is a good big sister and a leader among her friends. A member of the student council and top student in high school, Marcella is a recent graduate of Northwestern University with a degree in Spanish. She is a talented dancer and a nice person.

Glenton Douglas Lowell was born in Tucson, Arizona, in 1993 and is named for his father and great-grandfather Glenton Sykes. He is sociable and athletic and played baseball in high school. He and his grandmother Edith have played golf together since he was twelve. Glen enjoys skiing and snowboarding and swimming in the surf off Mission Beach, San Diego. He is our only grandson. He is a good student, attending the University of Arizona as I write.

Michelle was born in Tucson, Arizona, in 1995. She is small and fair and looks a little like her grandmother Edith. She also is a talented dancer. Michelle has a good voice and takes singing lessons and piano. During summer vacations in San Diego, Michelle spends hours each day swimming in the ocean. She has always been an outstanding student and is thinking of going away to college. She will do well wherever she goes.

Paloma was born in 1998 in Tucson, Arizona. She is also a very good student, plays soccer as a goalie, and belongs to a dance group that wins in statewide competitions. Paloma is a good cook, with specialties in baking bread and cakes. She is also a kitchen helper who knows where everything is and how everything is done. She has dark eyes and curly dark hair like Marcella and her mother.

Epilogue

After my childhood experience working in a silver mine with my father, collecting minerals in Mexico, and other youthful adventures, and then earning an academic degree at the University of Arizona, my career followed a fast-rising trajectory. After graduating, my first job was as engineer, shift boss, and then night foreman in a deep, hot, dangerous underground mine in Mexico. That was followed by an idyllic job living in the field with my growing family looking for uranium for the Atomic Energy Commission (AEC) in the Four Corners area of the Colorado Plateau. Edith and I had two young children, Susie, born in Mexico, and Bill, born in Tucson during our residence at my first field job at Cove School. At that time I already had a foot into the world of scholars. I had published two articles in professional journals; now, I have published fifty more and have received a total of thirty professional awards, including three honorary degrees. Our younger son Doug was born in Prescott, Arizona, in 1956.

I received two AEC promotions and I was in charge of five exploration camps and fifteen exploration geologists when I left to get an MS degree in geology at Stanford University. My grades at Stanford were okay and I finished my course work in nine months, finishing my thesis independently after I left Stanford. After Stanford I worked for two subsidiaries of a large Canadian company and then two years for a large U.S. company. I refused a promotion to manage the U.S. company's Canadian exploration division because I knew Edith wanted to stay in

433

Tucson, and instead struck out on the spur of the moment as an independent consulting geologist with only a two-day-per-month retainer as a listening post in the Southwest for Utah Construction Co. Edith, worrying about feeding our kids, immediately went back to the university to get a teaching certificate, and she also completed an MA in Spanish. She had a very successful three-year teaching career.

Within four years, with the freedom of no company rules or managers, I had found two large porphyry copper deposits, both without any staff assistance. These discoveries resulted largely from the porphyry copper model I had developed. Four years later I identified and optioned a third porphyry copper deposit, also without assistance, and it is now the largest mine in Argentina.

The Lowell-Guilbert Porphyry Copper Model was published in 1970. I had supplied the basic porphyry copper model already used for three discoveries, and John Guilbert supplied the academic descriptions and explanations and phase diagrams. Our paper was translated into four languages and has been widely used in university courses and was the basis for the later discovery of many orebodies by me and by others. It was a turning point for me, and greatly enhanced my reputation and career. I was chosen to be a member of an academic committee that included the best geochemists in the world. I got consulting jobs all over the world, and the things I learned working on all these were at least equivalent to another university degree. I supplied the missing bit of understanding to make two prospects into discoveries in the Philippines and one possible discovery in Canada.

In 1973 I changed my business plan into a unique plan, spending half-time consulting and half-time developing exploration projects to be funded by a mining company, but with me planning and managing the project and receiving an additional finder's fee or percent of discoveries. By 1981 this had produced three large copper discoveries, and two are in production, including the largest copper mine in the world.

From 1981 to 1991 I participated in the discovery of two other medium-sized deposits, both going into production, but in 1991 decided to change my business plan again. I would largely give up consulting and own a part of the equity in new discoveries. I found a new, 8-million-ounce gold deposit in Peru for a junior company of which I was chairman. I later formed another junior company in Peru of which I was chairman to explore a copper prospect called Toromocho. I revised the geological interpretation on the basis of the porphyry copper model and the ore reserves increased ten times. We expect that this deposit, currently under development, will be the largest mine in Peru. The next project was in Ecuador, where I found two porphyry copper deposits, one of which has been sold to a Chinese consortium. The other, which belongs to me, is tied up by Ecuadorian bureaucracy.

Over the past five years, from 2008 to 2013, I have been occupied in small but effective private companies with good friends and business partners. The large titanium iron deposit I identified in Paraguay is moving toward a bankable feasibility study in a joint venture with a large company. It has the largest titanium reserves in the world. Another of the private companies has probably found at least one large bauxite deposit in Brazil. Another company, Lowell Copper Ltd., has become a public exploration company with good prospects of success.

During the past twenty years I have carried out a second career, which is to develop a School of Mines at the Universidad Nacional Mayor de San Marcos, Peru, the oldest university in the new world. We now have about four hundred students enrolled and more than ten new classrooms. It has been a great satisfaction to see most of our graduates rise in socioeconomic status.

In this book, after a brief look at my family history and youth, I have followed my career from a job in a deep, hot, dangerous underground mine in Mexico; a total of thirty professional awards, including three honorary degrees; an MS degree at Stanford and through consulting for more than one hundred public and private companies and governments to ten billion-dollar discoveries worldwide. Each time I have been picked for some honor, especially a scholarly honor, I felt it had been a mistake, and as I wrote this book I felt like I was writing about some person other than me.

To my surprise, and to everyone else's surprise, I was almost immediately successful when I ventured into consulting and was able to capitalize on my largely self-taught expertise in porphyry copper geology, which included development of the framework of a porphyry copper geological model. When the Lowell-Guilbert Porphyry Copper Model was published it became a huge success, with demonstrated practical application across the world. My career was never without challenges, sometimes without success, but often enough with the thrill of discovered treasure in exotic and often difficult terrain.

My life has unfolded in unexpected ways, through an open mind, personal associations, hard work, close attention, and a willingness to take risks and occasionally make mistakes. I have built on my success and my mistakes to achieve unprecedented exploration success across the world. Through it all, my childhood thrill of discovery has never left me.

I have traveled a long road since I was a seven year old allowed to light dynamite fuses and sort ore in a small mine operated by my father. Now I am astonished and can hardly believe it is me who has been given multiple professional awards and honorary degrees and sees my picture on the cover of mining magazines with headlines like "The World's Greatest Explorer." I am sure there is exaggeration and bandwagon effect, but looking back, the whole story is almost unbelievable. To put this into perspective, most of the individual mine discoveries I made were worth ten or a hundred times the value of a Spanish treasure ship, and it has been estimated that my work has altogether provided jobs for 50,000 families. It has been even harder to put a value on the breathtaking satisfaction that goes with the huge discoveries.

I am now eighty-six years old and find it is a lot more difficult to climb 16,000-foot mountains in Peru and ride mules in the jungle in Ecuador, but I am up to at least one or two more discoveries and do not plan to hang up my boots and hammer just yet.

I had planned to put some other stories in this book, but I just got a call from Dutch Goober, who says he has found a really interesting porphyry copper outcrop in French Guinea. I have known Dutch a long time and he is sometimes very truthful. I'm afraid if I don't go right now, one of those big undeserving major companies will get it.

APPENDIXES

J. David Lowell Family Tree

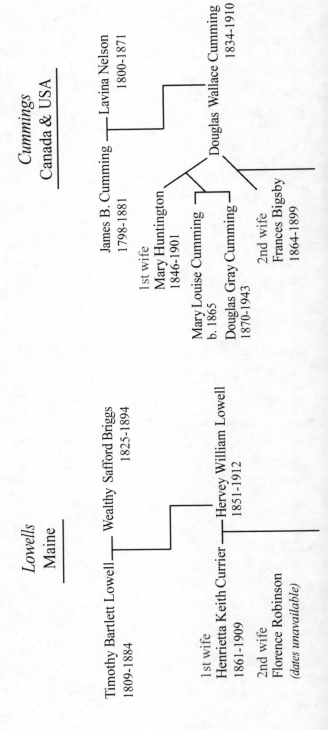

Lowells
Maine

Timothy Bartlett Lowell
1809-1884

Wealthy Safford Briggs
1825-1894

Hervey William Lowell
1851-1912

1st wife
Henrietta Keith Currier
1861-1909

2nd wife
Florence Robinson
(dates unavailable)

Cummings
Canada & USA

James B. Cumming
1798-1881

Lavina Nelson
1800-1871

Douglas Wallace Cumming
1834-1910

1st wife
Mary Huntington
1846-1901

Mary Louise Cumming
b. 1865

Douglas Gray Cumming
1870-1943

2nd wife
Frances Bigsby
1864-1899

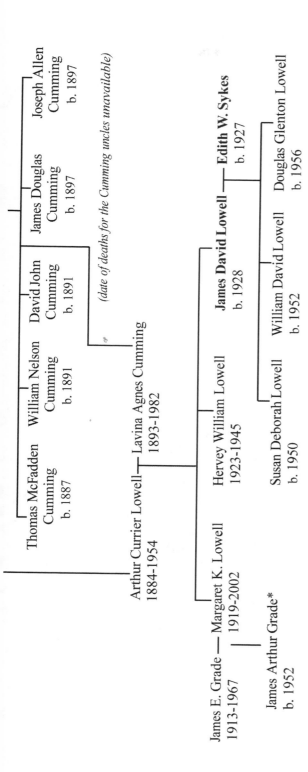

Thomas McFadden Cumming b. 1887

William Nelson Cumming b. 1891

David John Cumming b. 1891

James Douglas Cumming b. 1897

Joseph Allen Cumming b. 1897

(date of deaths for the Cumming uncles unavailable)

Arthur Currier Lowell 1884-1954 — Lavina Agnes Cumming 1893-1982

Hervey William Lowell 1923-1945

James David Lowell b. 1928 — **Edith W. Sykes** b. 1927

James E. Grade 1913-1967 — Margaret K. Lowell 1919-2002

Susan Deborah Lowell b. 1950

William David Lowell b. 1952

Douglas Glenton Lowell b. 1956

James Arthur Grade* b. 1952

This is not a comprehensive family tree; it records only ancestors described in the narrative and David Lowell's immediate family. A * designates an adopted child.

439

Associations with the University of Arizona

Our family has been closely associated with the University of Arizona (UA), and it is truly my Alma Mater. I received three UA degrees, and Edith, two. My daughter Susie taught at the UA for a time, and our son Doug received a degree there before entering Harvard Medical School, and both my brother and sister attended the university. Edith was a good student who was elected to Phi Beta Kappa and Pi Kappa Phi.

More recently, between 1990 and 1995, I was a member of the Geosciences Advisory Board. I also funded one scholarship and an endowed chair in the Geosciences Department. With the current head of the Mining and Geological Engineering Department, Mary Poulton, I participated in organizing the Lowell Institute for Mineral Resources. I contributed only the seed money, but it now ranks as one of the two

David Lowell and Mary Poulton in the entrance to the old UA Mines and Metallurgy building. There is a plan under way, depending on successful financing, to convert the Lowell Institute of Mineral Resources into a new University of Arizona School of Mines.

or three most important mines colleges in the United States. It has borrowed the Australian approach of making it possible for engineers and geologists and metallurgists who have been out of school a number of years to be retreaded with updated technical courses and computer skills. In addition, short courses are offered that can be taken largely as distance learning so the student can keep his or her job while earning a master's degree.

The Institute's stated goals are to "advance scientific, technological, and educational aspects of mineral discovery, extraction, and processing, including the environmental and societal issues that accompany these processes." Its educational and research themes include resources, technology, environmental and social responsibility, health and safety, policy, and economics. Thanks to outstanding management by Mary, and with the addition of the Institute, the University of Arizona now has one of the largest—and in many ways best—college of mines in the country. This has been an enormous satisfaction.

For the past fifteen years Edith and I have found a home in the UA Athletics Department. We have always had a fondness for UA sports. Edith won an athletic "A" sweater. I played varsity football my first year and won a freshman football sweater and a rifle team sweater. We've been honored to contribute to new facilities and programs there, including the construction of the Jefferson Basketball Practice Facility and the North End Football Stadium. We also funded a memorial to the members of the 1942 football team who died in World War II, among them my brother Bill. A bust of Bill and a plaque were dedicated at a ceremony in the fall of 2008, in front of the Bear Down Gym.

We have known and worked with many people in the university and have many friends in the staff and faculty. The following are several we would especially like to thank:

Joaquin Ruiz, Executive Dean of the College of Letters, Arts, and Sciences (as well as Vice President of Innovation and Strategy), combines a number of very unusual talents as an educator and administrator and scientist. Of the many people I have worked with in my career, I have never known anyone who could both conceive and complete major projects with a combination of charm, intelligence, and energy as does Joaquin. He is also a world-class geochemist. I am honored to be his friend. Edith and I were friends and admirers of former university President Richard Shelton and his wife, Adrian, and of Interim President Gene Sanders and his wife, Louise, and have recently become acquainted with President Ann Weaver Hart and her husband, Randy. Arizona has been blessed in recent years with outstanding presidents. Skipping back seventy years or so, Thomas Chapman, Dean of the (then) College of Mines, using both the Weenie and the Stick approach, supported me while I was an immature seventeen year old and found me jobs and made it possible for me to graduate from the College of Mines. Professor Edwin McKee went out of his way to edit a publica-

Scott Shake, Sr. Associate Athletics Director for Development, David, Edith, and Greg Byrne, Vice President for Athletics, at a UA basketball game in 2013. The Lowells made some donations to the Athletics Department and later became acquainted with many people in the Athletics Department and with some Arizona players and coaches. Both Edith and David were University Letter Winners and have enjoyed the later association (UA Athletics Dept. photo).

tion I wrote and also helped me get admitted to Stanford University for graduate study. Professor G. D. Percy of the Classics Department and Melvin T. Solve, head of the English Department, together found a job for Edith as secretary in the English Department, which helped us finance my senior year and finish my degree in Mining Engineering.

We count Senior Athletics Director Scott Shake and Director of Athletics Greg Byrne as good friends, as well as many of the other athletic staff members and coaches. Scott holds a world swimming record and in 2013 placed first in four of eight events (and second in two more) in his age division at a U.S. Masters Swim Meet. Scott is dedicated in his job and has been a real friend. Since Greg was hired as athletic director I have seen him make a series of decisive and correct decisions. He might be the best athletic director in the country. More good luck for the university.

Edith has made contributions to support the study of residues found on pottery and other artifacts conducted by Dr. Nancy Odegaard, director of The Pottery Project at the Arizona State Museum—just one of the University of Arizona's world-class museums, and the oldest and largest anthropology museum in the Southwest. The Pottery Project focuses on the preservation of the world's largest collection of Southwest Indian pottery.

The University of Arizona has been an integral part of our lives, and Edith and I find great satisfaction in supporting its programs.

Discoveries

Kalamazoo	Arizona
Vekol	Arizona
Bajo Alumbrera*	Argentina
Dizon*	Philippines
Lepanto Far Southeast*	Philippines
JA Orebody*	Canada
Casa Grande West	Arizona
Escondida	Chile
Zaldívar	Chile
San Cristobal*	Chile
Leonor*	Chile
Los Calatos	Peru
Pierina	Peru
Toromocho	Peru
Warintza*	Ecuador
Mirador	Ecuador
Alto Paraná	Paraguay

Others also contributed

Honors and Awards

1959 – University of Arizona College of Mines, Professional
     Geological Engineer Degree

1970 – Daniel Cowan Jackling Lecture Award, SME, AIME

1972 – Thayer Lindsley Lecture Tour, SME, AIME

1972 – University of Arizona Distinguished Citizen Award

1974 – Canadian Institute of Mining and Metallurgy Lecture Tour

1983 – Society of Economic Geology Silver Medal

1993 – Keynote Speaker and Chairman, South American Mining, AIC
     Conference, Melbourne, Australia

1994 – American Mining Hall of Fame Medal of Merit

1998 – Universidad Nacional Mayor de San Marcos Peru Doctor
     Honoris Causa Degree

1998 – Keynote Speaker Pathway 98, Vancouver, Canada

1999 – Northern Miner Canadian Mining Man of the Year

1999 – Election to the National Academy of Engineering

2000 – Society of Economic Geology Exchange Lecturer to fourteen
     universities in Australia, Tasmania, and New Zealand

2000 – Sydney SMEDG Distinguished Lecturer

2000 – DREGS, Denver, Colorado, Distinguished Lecturer

2000 – University of Nevada Ralph J. Robert Distinguished Lecturer

2000 – Robert M. Dreyer Award, Society of Mining Engineers, AIME

2000 – Robert Earll McConnell Award, SME, AIME

2000 – University of Arizona Honorary Doctor of Science Degree

2001 – Mining and Metallurgy Society of America Gold Medal

2002 – American Mining Hall of Fame Inductee

2003 – Society of Economic Geology Penrose Gold Medal

2003 – Geología y Exploración de Yacimientos Minerales
     Universidad Nacional Mayor de San Marcos Peru Award

2010 – PDAC Keynote Speaker, Toronto, Ontario

2010 – Tucson High School Hall of Fame

2010 – CESCO Chilean Government Award

2010 – Haddon Forrester King Medal, Australian Academy of Science

2011 – University of Arizona Lacy Lecture

2012 – National Mining Hall of Fame Inductee

2012 – *London Journal* Lifetime Achievement Award

J. David Lowell Publications

1955. "Applications of Cross Stratification Studies to Problems of Uranium Exploration, Chuska Mountains, Arizona." James D. Lowell, *Economic Geology*, vol. 50, no. 2, March.

1956. "Occurrence of Uranium in Seth-la-kai Diatreme, Hopi Buttes, Arizona." J. David Lowell, *The American Journal of Science*.

1961. "Geology and Origin of Mineralized Breccia Pipes in Copper Basin, Arizona." W. P. Johnson and J. David Lowell, *Economic Geology*, vol. 56, no. 5, August.

1967. "Discovery and Exploration of the Kalamazoo Orebody, San Manuel District, Arizona." J. David Lowell, *Mining Engineer Magazine*, 1967.

1968. "Geology of the Kalamazoo Orebody, San Manuel District, Arizona." J. David Lowell, *Economic Geology*, vol. 63, pp. 645–654.

1969. "How the Kalamazoo Was Found." J. David Lowell, *Economic Geology Case Histories of Mineral Discoveries*, vol. 3.

1970. "Lateral and Vertical Alteration: Mineralization Zoning in Porphyry Ore Deposits." J. David Lowell and John M. Guilbert, *Economic Geology*, vol. 5, no. 4.

1970. "Copper Resources in 1970." Daniel Jackling Award Lecture by J. David Lowell, published in *Mining Engineering Magazine*.

1971. "Variations in Zoning Patterns in Porphyry Ore Deposits." John M. Guilbert and J. David Lowell, *Economic Geology*.

1971. "Variaciones en Zonación de Yacimientos Pórfidos." John M. Guilbert y J. David Lowell, Publicado en X Convención Nacional de Asociación de Ingenieros de Minas Metalurgistas y Geólogos de México, October.

1974. "Regional Characteristic of Porphyry Copper Deposits of the Southwest." J. David Lowell, *Economic Geology*, vol. 69, no. 5.

1974. "Three New Porphyry Copper Mines for Chile?" J. David Lowell, *Mining Engineering Magazine*, November.

1975. "Geology and Economics of the Porphyry Copper Deposits of South America." J. David Lowell, *Geology and Economics of World Mining*, June.

1976. "Research Strategy of Mineral Exploration Frontiers for New Renewable Resources." Workshop, J. David Lowell, Pennsylvania State University, October 12.

1978. "Case Histories of Discoveries." J. David Lowell, *Arizona Geological Society Digest*, vol. 40, October.

1978. "The Porphyry Model." J. David Lowell, *International Molybdenum Encyclopedia*, vol. 2, p. 264.

1978. "The Copper and Molybdenum Content of Porphyry Deposits." J. David Lowell, *International Molybdenum Encyclopedia*, vol. 2.

1980. "Metalogenesis and Porphyry Deposits of North America and the Pacific Region." J. David Lowell, International Geological Congress.

1985. "Reseña Técnica del Descubrimiento del Yacimiento de Pórfido Cuprífero Escondida. II Región, Chile." Francisco J. Ortiz, J. David Lowell, Nivaldo D. Rojas, Patrick J. Burns, IV Congreso Geológico Chileno, Augusto.

1986. "Exploration of La Escondida Porphyry Copper Deposit, Chile." J. D. Lowell, J. A. Bratt, F. J. Ortiz, N. D. Rojas, P. J. Burns, AIME paper given at the annual meeting in New Orleans.

1987. "El Mineral de San Cristobal de Minera del Inca." J. David Lowell and Julia Aspillaga, *Mineria Chilena*, November.

1988. "Gold Mineralization in Porphyry Copper Deposits." J. David Lowell. Talk presented AIME Annual Meeting January 27, 1988; later published in *Mining Engineering*.

1988. "The Discovery of the Escondida Orebody." J. David Lowell, *Economic Geology* Monograph: "Historical Perspectives of Genetic Concepts and Case Histories of Famous Discoveries," October 3.

1989. "Gold Mineralization in Porphyry Copper Deposits, Discussed." J. David Lowell. *Mining Engineering*.

1990. "Chilean Ore Deposits and Mineral Belts." Carlos Ruiz and J. David Lowell, Pacific Rim 90 Congress.

1990. "Evolution of Geologic Techniques in Exploration." J. David Lowell, *Mining Engineering Magazine.*

1990. "Base Metal Exploration and Geology." J. David Lowell, *AIME Surface Mining Handbook.*

1995. "The Richards and Courtright Era and Why Some Exploration Programs are Successful." J. David Lowell, keynote article, published by Arizona *Geological Society Digest* 20.

1996. "The La Escondida Exploration Project." J. David Lowell, The Pacific Rim 90 Congress.

1996. "The Exploration and Geology of the Pierina Orebody." *Economic Geology.*

1997. "Why Bigger Isn't Better in Mineral Exploration." Canadian Institute of Mining and Metallurgy.

1997. "How Orebodies are Found" and "The Arequipa Resources-Pierina Project." Two talks published as videotapes to be sold by the Society Exploration Geologists, which were also given as talks during my SEG International Exchange Lectureship.

1998. "Using Applied Geology to Discover Large Copper and Gold Mines in Arizona, Chile, and Peru." Regional Oral History Office, The Bancroft Library, University of California, Berkeley, California.

2000. "Can Big Companies Make Big Discoveries?" J. David Lowell. The Junior Company Perspective, MINExpo International, National Mining Association, October.

2000. "How Orebodies are Found." J. David Lowell. I was the first recipient, in February 2000, of the Robert Dreyer Award, which included a dollar prize and required presentation of a lecture; "How Orebodies Are Found" was later published in *Mining Engineering Magazine* and by the Arizona Geological Society, and as an SEG videotape.

2000. "The Atacama Project and the Escondida Discovery." Published as a videotape and was an alternate SEG Exchange Lecture Talk.

2000. "Where Are We Now in Mineral Exploration?" University of California Berkeley, November 2000. Lecture, J. David Lowell (probably not published).

2001. "Exploración en Companies Grandes y Pequeñas Para el 2002." Asociación de Ingenieros de Minas, Metalurgistas y Geólogos de México, A. C. J. David Lowell, January.

2001. "Junior Exploration Companies, Their Role in Future Mineral Exploration." Published November 2001, J. David Lowell, from a presentation made at ProExplo Lima, Peru.

2001. "Cinturón de Pórfidos de Cobre de Zamora, Ecuador." J. David Lowell and Luis Quevedo, *Engineering and Mining Journal.*

2001. "Oral Biography." J. David Lowell. Una Leyenda y 50 Anos de Exploraciones. *Minera Andina*, May 2002.

2001. Oral Biographical History. J. David Lowell. ProExplo.

2004. "The Toromocho Discovery, Peru Copper Inc. Project. Morococha District, Peru." J. David Lowell. Published as an abstract by Bank of Montreal.

2004. "The Toromocho Porphyry Copper Deposit at Morococha, Peru." PDAC talk with abstract published, J. David Lowell and Angel Alvarez, November.

2005. "David Lowell, World's Greatest Copper Explorer." Oral Biography, *Resource World Magazine*, vol. 3, no. 8.

2007. "How Junior Companies Have Become the Dominant Force in Finding and Financing New Mines." J. David Lowell, Society of Economic Geologists Meeting in Tucson, Arizona, July.

2009. "History of the 1996 Pierina Discovery." J. David Lowell (publication as part of *Economic Geology* Monograph, Special Volume, to be completed).

Acknowledgments

I would like to acknowledge all of the people who assisted in putting this book together. First were David DeWitt and Marcel de Groot, mining associates of many years, who talked me into writing the book. Then there was my wife, Edith, who read the manuscript several times, for which she deserves a medal. She also contributed old letters and did the basic editing. Marcia Racine and Emma Salazar did weeks and months of cheerful work while eight iterations were written and typed and superseded and many photos were considered and few were saved. I would like to thank John Guilbert, my comrade in many ventures—some scientific and some in the field—who kindly wrote the introduction. Dean Joaquin Ruiz is a dear friend of many years who wrote the foreword. UA Press Director Kathryn Conrad has been very helpful and introduced me to Susan Campbell and Linda Brewer who worked to get the text into shape for publication under the Press's new Sentinel Peak imprint. Frank Farias, Associate Vice President for Student Affairs at the UA, helped in getting the book moved along to the publication process. David Brown converted maps and diagrams from our report files into attractive figures for the book. Publishing consultant Harrison Shaffer has been of great assistance contributing to the editing and organizing and countless chores which transform a tall stack of pages and photographs into a beautiful book. I am very grateful to all who made this book possible.

Index